THE VIKING BATTALION

THE VIKING BATTALION

Norwegian American Ski Troopers in
World War II

edited by

OLAF MINGE, KYLE WARD AND ERIK BRUN

CASEMATE

Philadelphia & Oxford

Published in the United States of America and Great Britain in 2023 by
CASEMATE PUBLISHERS
1950 Lawrence Road, Havertown, PA 19083, USA
and
The Old Music Hall, 106–108 Cowley Road, Oxford OX4 1JE, UK

Hardcover Edition: ISBN 978-1-63624-323-8
Digital Edition: ISBN 978-1-63624-324-5

A CIP record for this book is available from the British Library

Printed and bound in the United Kingdom by CPI Group (UK) Ltd, Croydon, CR0 4YY
Typeset in India by DiTech Publishing Services

For a complete list of Casemate titles, please contact:

CASEMATE PUBLISHERS (US)
Telephone (610) 853-9131
Fax (610) 853-9146
Email: casemate@casematepublishers.com
www.casematepublishers.com

CASEMATE PUBLISHERS (UK)
Telephone (0)1226 734350
Email: casemate-uk@casematepublishers.co.uk
www.casematepublishers.co.uk

Contents

Here is 1st Squad, 1st Platoon, C Company, 99th Infantry Battalion (Separate), Camp Hale, CO, in early 1943. TOP ROW: Eivind Guliksen (Browning Automatic Rifle), Erling Abrahamsen (Assistant Squad Leader), John L. Christopherson (Rifle), Kristian Brun (Second Scout). MIDDLE ROW: John Eide (Rifle), T. W. Jacobsen (Rifle), Carl Johnson (Asst. BAR), Bjarne Aanning (First Scout). BOTTOM ROW: Harold Anderson (Rifle), Cpl George Hunsby (Squad Leader), Alden Lecy (Rifle), Sigurd Akselsen (Rifle). Kristian Brun's album. Jacobsen, a Norwegian merchant war sailor, spoke no English when he arrived in the battalion. (Courtesy of the 99th Educational Foundation)

Introduction by Erik Brun

The Saga of the Norwegian American Ski Troopers in World War II

The term "saga" has Old Norse origins and means a story of a journey, comradeship, struggle, sacrifice, and heroic achievement. We feel this is the best description for a compilation of writings by members of the 99th Infantry Battalion (Separate) not only because of their Norwegian heritage but also due to the fact that it is an apt reflection of their service during World War II. This book is a time capsule of wartime histories and veterans' memories, told from their recollections and shaped by their own lived experiences.

This introduction is informed by 10 years of research in classified wartime sources by the members of the 99th Infantry Battalion (Separate) Educational Foundation and provides answers to some of the questions asked by the veterans and their descendants. And, it gives a more complete understanding of the veterans' wartime experiences.

The passing of eight decades gives us a chance to remember what a different time it is now compared with the 1940s. During World War II, the United States Army fielded over 900 infantry battalions, each consisting of 1,000 men, and nearly all of the infantry battalions were one-third of an infantry regiment. These battalions were a sub-division of that regiment, such as the 1st Battalion of the 120th Infantry Regiment, that was supported by a regimental anti-tank, cannon, and service company, and cared for by a detachment of the division's assigned medical battalion. Each battalion was composed of infantry companies that themselves consisted of almost 200 soldiers and two ¼-ton trucks, commonly known as jeeps. The company relied on a quartermaster truck company to move it any distance. Of the 38 jeeps in an infantry battalion (separate); 11 were assigned to support the Headquarters and Service Company to run the communications wire and to courier leaders and messengers; 2 to each of the three rifle companies; 2 to the medics; and 19 for the Heavy Weapons Company to move their observers, 81mm mortars, water-cooled heavy machine guns, and ammunition.

Only a handful of battalions were organized to operate independently. They were given a unique number and augmented with logistical and administrative personnel and equipment that would normally be attached from their higher headquarters. These battalions were designated as "Separate," like the 99th Infantry Battalion (Separate). Of the 18 battalions in existence during World War II, the men of only three of them were credited with combat campaigns, including the Norwegians of the 99th Battalion and the Greeks of the 122nd who served in the Operational Groups of the Office of Strategic Services (OSS) in Greece and Yugoslavia.

But why did the U.S. Army form nationalistic, or ethnic units in World War II? Fortunately, the answer can be found in the records of these units that are filed under "Foreign Legions" in the War Department records at the National Archives.

These units were created through the efforts of the Military Attaché at the American Embassy in London, Brigadier General Raymond E. Lee, during two chaotic years that saw the rise of Nazi Germany, the fall of Poland, Denmark, Norway, Holland, Belgium, and France, the miracle of Dunkirk, and Hitler's invasion of Russia. Lee had witnessed Churchill's creation of the Special Operations Executive, the formation of British Commando units, and the nurturing of Allied expatriate militaries of occupied nations like Poland, Norway, and France. When Lee was recalled to his next assignment at the War Department, in Washington, D.C., his flight landed in New York on December 7, the same day of the Pearl Harbor attack. By the end of that month, he was appointed the senior Military Intelligence officer in the War Department.

As the Acting Assistant Chief of Staff, G2, on January 1, 1942, Lee sent a memorandum to General George C. Marshall, Chief of Staff of the Army, titled, "Creation under the auspices of the War Department of an international combat force recruited from aliens in the United States," where he outlined his proposal:

> By law aliens may not enlist in the United States Army. Yet there are in this country numbers of foreigners who desire to fight under the American flag, and do not wish, or are not eligible, to enroll in other armies at war against the Axis…Such a force would have immense and world-wide propaganda value as giving tangible proof that the Axis was opposed and condemned by all races and nationalities…By organizing it in (units) of homogeneous nationality it could provide most easily and rapidly men for espionage, sabotage, and military intelligence purposes in connection with their native land…These companies would be of great use with the advance guard in landing operations in their homeland.

Lee's efforts led to legislation directing the registration of alien males living in the United States and the creation of the 99th Norwegian, 101st Austrian, and 122nd Greek Battalions. He also supported the creation of the 1st and 2nd Filipino Regiments, the Japanese American 100th Infantry Battalion (Nisei), and the 442nd RCT (Nisei).

Additionally, Lee was behind the thousands of immigrant and refugee soldiers who were selected for the Military Intelligence Services (MIS) Training Centers for Japanese at Camp Savage, Minnesota, and Germans at Camp Ritchie, Maryland. The latter group's graduates are now known as the Ritchie Boys. These graduates provided native language speaking interrogators, translators, and Order of Battle Specialists to the commanders around the world.

Lee had seen the Norwegian government-in-exile begin to form its brigade in Scotland, and their establishment of Independent Company No.1, in March 1941, imbedded into Prime Minister Churchill's Special Operations Executive as Company Linge, provided agents and teams to perform difficult missions in Norway like the heavy water sabotage at the Rjukan hydroelectric plant.

Lee's vision was also vindicated in 1943 when a hundred volunteers from the Norwegian 99th Infantry Battalion and 160 Greeks of the 122nd Battalion were recruited into the Office of Strategic Services (OSS) to form half their new Operational Groups or OG teams, and they deployed to Greece, Yugoslavia, France, Norway, and China by the end of the war. The OG was the predecessor of today's U.S. Army Special Forces A Team.

Looking back today, we know more about the overall vision and motivation that led the U.S. Army to create such a unique unit as the 99th Battalion. Without the revelations from formerly classified materials, many of the events recorded by the veterans of the 99th Battalion may seem improbable. The behind-the-scenes narrative was obscured by both the passing of time as well as the classified nature of the documents.

During World War II a shadow war was waged, consisting of deception plans to create the specter of Allied actions. In the decades that have passed since the end of the war, books have been written, such as *The Man Who Never Was*, about Operation *Mincemeat*, and *Bodyguard of Lies*, which describes Operation *Fortitude* that protected the Allied invasion at Normandy with elaborate operations to distract from the actual invasion plans. Other examples include *Fortitude North* targeting Norway, *Fortitude South* protecting the main landings at Calais, and Operation *Zeppelin* in the Mediterranean.

Allied efforts included whisper campaigns and stories planted in common places and also could involve misdirection as part of a larger plan. In the *Army Ground Forces Study 23: Training in Mountain and Winter Warfare*, Captain Thomas Govan noted that a British officer mentioned to the former G-2 of Iceland Base Command that the mountaineering training team sent to New Hampshire in October 1942 was part of a ruse: "The purpose of the program was not primarily the training of the 36th Division but was part of an elaborate intelligence plan to persuade the Germans that an invasion of Norway was in prospect."

Operation *Solo* was a deception plan where information was presented to the Germans about "planned landings" at Narvik, Norway, in late 1942 as a component of the larger deception, Operation *Overthrow*. It is now understood that this was a ruse to protect the actual preparations for the Operation *Torch* landings in North Africa in November 1942. Similarly, the deception operation in July 1943, named Operation *Tindall*, was focused on Stavanger, Norway, with the goal to pin down

German forces in the far north prior to the invasion of Sicily, Italy, Operation *Husky*. In November 1943, Operation *Tindall* became part of Operation *Fortitude North*, an element of the deception plans for the successful invasion at Normandy, France. These operations contributed to Germany retaining over 350,000 German troops in Norway, preventing them from aiding in the event of an invasion or in fighting on the Eastern Front.

The use of double agents, media reports of training exercises, inflatable tanks and landing craft, whispered troop movements, and phantom units were timed to support the greater goals of deception. One possible example for the 99th Battalion was the publication of photos taken in November 1942 titled, "Norwegian Avengers Prepare for Action." The photos were publicly circulated in the Australia pictorial magazine *PIX* on May 29, 1943. Was this publicity an intentional part of Operation *Tindall* where a Norwegian invasion from Scotland was threatened? Could the publicized review of the Greek and Norwegian battalions by President Roosevelt Easter weekend have been another intentional seed planted in support of deception operations *Fortitude North* and *Zeppelin*?

Concurrent with his role in deception planning, British General Andrew Thorne's Scottish Command was tasked to provide and maintain a series of contingency operational plans for Scandinavia under the Chief of Staff, Supreme Allied Commander (COSSAC), and later the Supreme Headquarters Allied Expeditionary Forces (SHAEF).

The Scottish Command was also responsible for real-world plans such as Project Snow Plow, the development of the M-29 "Weasel," and 1942's Operation *Jupiter* that inspired the creation of the joint U.S./Canadian First Special Service Force. The Operation *Rankin* Norway plans began in the summer of 1943 with three objectives: to intervene in the event of substantial weakening of the strength and morale of the German armed forces, or in the event of German withdrawal from occupied areas, or in the event of the unconditional surrender and cessation of hostilities.

The 99th Battalion was listed in the high-level *Rankin* plans for Norway from 1943, and the later *Apostle* and *Doomsday* plans. These plans led to the creation of the 474th Infantry Regiment (Separate) in January 1945. This new unit was composed of the 99th Battalion, the American veterans of the First Special Service Force, and the 552nd Anti-Tank Company. Additionally, the First Special Service Force itself included over 400 members of Darby's Rangers.

The 474th Infantry Regiment (Separate) was activated in France on January 6, 1945 and given less than three months to produce "a well-trained, hard hitting, fighting team."[1] Until they were needed for the potential mission in Norway according

---

[1] Richard P. Fisk, "1st Endorsement, WD AG 322 (8 Nov 44) CH-I-GROCT-M." *99th In Bn Foundation Archive, Chronological Collection.* December 13, 1944.

to the *Rankin* plan, this new regiment was scheduled for the final campaign for Central Europe in late March.

The first complication facing Colonel Edwin Walker, commander of the new 474th Infantry Regiment, was that the 99th was still fighting in the Battle of the Bulge, but arrived by the end of the month. The 99th joined as the third battalion of the new regiment, and like the famous Nisei 100th Battalion, when it joined the 442nd Regimental Combat Team, the 99th was allowed to keep its name, but lost its "Separate" designation. Since the 99th was the third battalion in the regiment, its companies were redesignated to follow the traditional sequence: Company A became I; B became K; C became L; and D Company became M. The letter J was traditionally omitted at the time to avoid confusion between the script letters I and J.

The second complication facing Colonel Walker's 474th was an order received in late March that tasked the unit with the mission to reorganize as a "Security Organization to Suppress Enemy Agents and Guerrillas." This new mission from General Eisenhower's SHAEF HQ brought a complete reorganization of the regiment for asymmetric warfare, to counter the threat posed by Operation *Werewolf*, a planned Nazis insurgency that could continue the war indefinitely.

Colonel Walker was given direction and transformed the 474th into a motorized regiment, receiving additional jeeps, weapons carriers, and over 30 M8 armored cars to operate independently over large areas. The regiment tripled its 2 ½-ton truck fleet to 109 vehicles, its Anti-Tank Company received M-24 light tanks, and the Cannon Company was issued self-propelled howitzers. The regiment's radio network increased as well, with each battalion receiving 60 additional radio sets, including four capable of transmitting over 1,000 miles.

The 474th arrived at the German border in early April 1945 and was assigned directly to General Patton's U.S. Third Army Headquarters. Each of the battalions was given regional responsibilities within the rapidly increasing area of Germany controlled by Third Army. On the morning of April 15, medics from the unit arrived at Buchenwald Concentration Camp and witnessed the horrors there. In time other soldiers encountered other sub-camps in the area. The regiment also received an order to support the movement of high-priority cargo from its loading points at Merkers, Germany, to its unloading point at Frankfurt am Main, Germany. On April 15 they conducted the first of two Monuments Men missions,[2] moving the Nazi horde of gold and art treasures from the Kaiseroda salt mines before the Soviet occupation of the area. The rest of the operations were primarily cordon and search, looking for indications of *Werewolf* operations and caches, weapons, Nazi sympathizers, and deserters.

---

[2] The Monuments Men were a special unit formed to protect culturally significant items from damage and looting.

On May 6, General Eisenhower directed an alert to "all formations and units this theater required for Apostle including U.S. Task Force Nightlight and auxiliary troops." On May 9 Colonel Walker and his intelligence officer Captain Finn Roll, a Norwegian dual citizen who had joined the force back in Montana in 1942, were ordered to Patton's headquarters for instructions.

The final plan to move Allied troops to Norway was executed by General Thorne as Operation *Doomsday* and *Apostle* in May/June 1945. Force 134 was his command, and the initial troops were the famed British 1st Airborne Division. Plans first proposed in October 1943 also called for an American component of 5,000 soldiers, including the 99th. The Americans under General Summers gathered as Task Force A. Operation *Nightlight* moved the 474th and supporting units via a flotilla of Landing Ship Tanks (LSTs) at Le Havre before sailing for Oslo in June 1945.

The deception plans had been so effective that over 350,000 German soldiers, sailors, Luftwaffe, and civilian personnel still remained in Norway at the end of the war. They in turn became the last mission of the 99th Battalion.

The 474th was the primary muscle behind the three major functions of Task Force A in Norway: to assist the Norwegian government in the smooth transition from the wartime Quisling regime to the expatriate London-based regime of King Haakon VII; to supervise the orderly demobilization and repatriation of German military personnel, contractors, dependents, and camp followers from the country; and lastly and most regrettably in hindsight, to assist in the forced repatriation of 85,000 Soviet prisoners of war that had surrendered to the Germans and had been used for slave labor throughout Norway. Unfortunately, these repatriated prisoners were harshly received back into the Soviet Union.

The Americans in Oslo participated in three major parades: the 4th of July, Allied Forces Day on July 17, and a final parade in October, where the regiment presented its colors to the King of Norway. These were the largest of the very public events the soldiers of Task Force A engaged in, though competitive soccer games and American football games were also well attended. Lastly, over 80 war brides were also reported by October 1945, when the American units sailed for home. Additionally, the OSS men of Operation *Rype* also marched in a May 17 parade in Trondheim with an American flag that had been hidden by a Norwegian family during the war.

The 99th Today

Shortly after the war, small groups of 99th Battalion veterans began gathering regionally, and a national association was formed that produced over 30 biannual newsletters until the 99th Infantry Battalion Education Foundation was formed in 2011. The Foundation supports various events, educational programs, research efforts, book projects, documentaries, museum exhibits, and memorial sites that maintain the memory and the saga of the 99th. Additionally, there are over 2,000 members belonging to the Foundation's active and dynamic social media platforms. This book is an attempt to continue the saga of their activities and memories.

Online Media

99th Educational Foundation website: https://99battalion.org
99th Educational Foundation Facebook group: https://www.facebook.com/groups/99768827050

Museums

Vesterheim: The National Norwegian-American Museum & Folk Art School, Decorah, Iowa
The Minnesota Military and Veterans Museum, Camp Ripley, Little Falls, Minnesota
Vestnorsk Utvandringssenter, Sletta, Radøy, Norway

Documentary

The Viking Battalion by Steinar Hybertsen

Locations of 99th Memorials

Tennessee Pass, Ski Cooper, Colorado
Court of Honor, Camp Ripley, Minnesota
Battle of the Bulge Memorial Wolfe's Pond Park, Staten Island, NY
Avenue de Norvège, Malmedy, Belgium
Vestnorsk Utvandringssenter, Sletta, Radøy, Norway

Introduction
by Magne Roedahl, Colonel,
Royal Norwegian Army (Ret.)

Magne Roedahl began his military service as an infantry soldier in 1980 and served in Norwegian Army Special Operations Command (NORSOCOM) over the next 40 years, and participated in Special Operations deployments to Bosnia, Macedonia, Kosovo, Gaza/ Egypt, and Afghanistan. Colonel Roedahl's last assignment was as Military Attaché and Assistant Defense Attaché at the Norwegian Embassy in Washington, D.C., as a liaison with the U.S. Army, U.S. Marine Corps, National Guard, and U.S. Special Forces.

I cannot fully explain how proud I am to be invited to provide this letter introducing this new book on the 99th Infantry Battalion [the "99. infanteribataljon"]. My involvement with 99th Battalion and their extraordinary history started many years ago when I was Deputy Commander of Norwegian Special Operations Command (NORSOCOM) and I traveled to Belgium and Holland to honor and commemorate the Norwegian participation in the Allied liberation of those European nations during World War II. We started off in the Ardennes where we laid wreaths on the newly erected memorial site at Malmedy, commemorating the 99th Battalion's defense of that town in December 1944. Our Norwegian Special Operations Force honor guard held the unit colors with the blue, red, and white Viking ship flag, the Norwegian and American flags honoring the Norwegian American 99th Battalion's extraordinary sacrifices there. The gratitude of the present Belgian population to 99th Battalion decades later was heartwarming.

My encounters with the 99th Battalion would not end there; it was indeed the first of a string of interactions in my following career in Norwegian Special Forces and as the Military Attaché to the U.S. in Washington, D.C.

While in Washington I was invited by my dear friend Erik Brun to participate at the annual Heritage Ski-In, hosted by the 10th Mountain Division descendants at "Ski Cooper," World War II's Camp Hale ski area, near Leadville, Colorado. I was honored with carrying the 99th Battalion's flag in the Ski-In's "Flagserpent" (Serpentine flag parade on skis) in 2017, followed by reading the names of our 99th Battalion's heroes of World War II at their memorial site, shared with the

10th Mountain Division memorial. I had my family there with me from Norway, and they loved to participate and fully enjoyed the American hospitality. There, we made friends for life with participants from units represented and local Norwegian Americans.

The story of the battalion never seems to fade in either the U.S. or Norway. Today their legacy is very much alive due to the work and efforts of people like Erik and colleagues in the 99th's Educational Foundation, keeping their achievements and memories alive. On several occasions the Defense Attaché's Office and ambassador were involved in presenting World War II participation medals to our 99th Battalion heroes, 474th Infantry Regiment veterans, Office of Strategic Services (OSS) Operational Groups members, and the Carpetbagger aircrews that flew them. All received their well-deserved commemoration. Recognizing these men made us proud to be part of this community and family of warriors.

Further, the half-century-long tradition of cooperation in the Norwegian Exchange (NOREX), the annual exercises with our Norwegian Home Guard and their counterparts in the Minnesota National Guard at Camp Ripley, MN, always recognizes the 99th Battalion. In Norway a group of historians restored the OSS Base Camp at Gjefsjoen farm for Operation *Rype*. This is where Major William Colby's Operation Group men—most were recruited from 99th Battalion in 1943—and Norwegian agents skied almost a hundred kilometers to attack the Northland Railroad in 1945. Today this site is a gem of Norway's World War II sites.

It is key to enhance the population's knowledge of the war, and this new museum is a token of the strong bonds and relationship between our two nations.

Therefore, this book is so important to the broader audience. Freedom is not free, and sacrifices made by 99th Battalion and their families must not be forgotten. One day the next generation might be called to action, and thus the proud legacy of generations before them will motivate them for similar dedication and battlefield heroism—eventually securing freedom and peace.

My final participation at the Ski-In at Ski Cooper was in 2020 where the Special Forces Association's Rocky Mountains chapter honored me with lifetime membership in their distinguished organization. Their plaque and membership card are my most cherished mementos, and they fill a most sacred spot at our house outside Lillehammer, Norway. The 99th Battalion insignia is there as well.

The brother/sisterhood of Americans, Norwegians, 10th Mountain Division/99th Battalion descendants, Rocky Mountain Chapter of the SFA, 10th Special Forces Group (Airborne), the OSS Society, and Sons and Daughters of Norway will forever remain one of my best memories from my professional time as a Special Operations Force operator and officer. Thanks so much for these memories that will forever be with me and my family. The 99th Battalion has always represented such a vessel for fellowship that their saga never seems to fade.

Introduction
by Pete Palmer, Brigadier General,
U.S. Army (Ret.)

Pete Palmer graduated from West Point as an infantry officer in 1977. He served as Chief of Staff of the 1st Infantry Division and commanded its 2nd "Dagger" Brigade's peacekeeping operations in Kosovo as part of Task Force Falcon, with over six battalion-size forces of U.S., Greek, Polish/Ukrainian and Russian battalions. He deployed to Iraq and served as Deputy Chief of Staff for Operations for Multinational Forces Iraq in 2004–2005.

My mother was a first-generation Norwegian immigrant. She had 11 brothers and sisters. I was named after her brother Peter (Per) Hellerud who was born in Norway and immigrated with my grandparents through Ellis Island in 1922 and 1923. Uncle Peter was idolized by all his siblings. He was the first-born male, which holds a special status in Norwegian culture, but more importantly he went off to fight in World War II where he earned a Bronze Star, Purple Heart, and his U.S. Citizenship. Sadly, I never got to meet Uncle Pete. He died of leukemia the year before I was born. I wish I could have known him and heard firsthand from him about his actions and experiences in World War II, both from uncle-to-nephew, and soldier-to-soldier.

As a career Army infantry officer, I became interested in learning more about Uncle Pete and the 99th Infantry Battalion (Separate) in which he served. Pete's youngest sister, Dona Constantine, introduced me to Erik Brun who, with his 99th Infantry Battalion Foundation, provided a wealth of knowledge on the 99th as well as other exploits of American Norwegians during World War II. After reading about the 99th, my wife and I traveled to Leadville, Colorado, and Camp Hale to see where they trained with the 10th Mountain Division before deploying to the war. There is a lot to be said about going to the place where my uncle lived and trained.

While stationed in Germany I toured the Battle of the Bulge area including Malmedy, Belgium and saw the railroad tracks where the 99th held the northern flank of the Bulge. Earlier, as an infantry company commander, I took my company to Alaska to do winter and mountain training where the temperatures sometimes dropped to -50 degrees, helping me to more fully appreciate the extreme conditions the 99th faced while training at Camp Hale. Serving in Iraq from 2004 to 2005,

I witnessed an intensity of urban combat which was similar, in some respects, to the 99th's fight in Aachen, Germany.

This story of the 99th is a classic American immigrant story of young men who came or were born in a new land and took up arms to defend their new country with the hope to also liberate their old country. Like my uncle, many saw it as an opportunity to win their U.S. citizenship as well. It is a human-dimension story about what it means to train for harsh environments, work through the trials, anxiety, and tribulations of combat, and about the joy of returning to liberate their ancestral home—Norway.

Being a second-generation Norwegian immigrant, I am still in touch with many of my Norwegian relatives. As you will learn in the reading of this book, many U.S. Norwegian soldiers who had relatives in Norway were given leave to visit relatives and let them know America was there to help liberate them. During a recent visit to Norway, I met a relative—Randi Hellerud Knold—who proudly brought out a book that was signed by her cousin, my Uncle Pete, when he visited his family during the war. Randi was only a young girl at

A portrait of a proud ski trooper, Private Peter (Per) Hellerud, who sat for this formal portrait showing the iconic ski pins that were very popular among the soldiers at Camp Hale. Officially banned from being worn with the uniform, these unofficial, locally made sweetheart pins are found in many variations using military insignia including cross rifles with unit numbers, Signal Corps semaphores, and artillery cannons representing various units at Camp Hale. His nephew, Brigadier General Pete Palmer, was named after him. (Courtesy of the 99th Educational Foundation)

the time, but the visit left her with a deep and lasting impression of her American cousin who had returned to Norway to help fight their enemies. The impact on the Norwegian people of American relatives fighting for the liberation of Norway cannot be understated.

More importantly, these are personal stories not written by some historian who wasn't there. These men were there. They lived it. Most of us who have served in combat don't often discuss our combat stories with family and friends. But as time goes by the younger generation would like to know what their father, grandfather, great grandfather did in World War II. These stories of the soldiers of the 99th Infantry Battalion capture that history as only someone who has been there can do. They were Americans, and they were Norwegians, but without question they were heroes.

Editors' Note

This book is a collection of stories written by members of the 99th Infantry Battalion (Separate). Many of these stories were put together by veterans, years after the war, when they were often inspired to do so after one of their reunions. Many of these memoirs and letters come from a three-ring binder that Yngvar Stensby (a former 99er himself) and other organizers from the unit started to pull together for a possible book that, sadly, was never published. The rest are letters that family members have shared with us or memoirs that 99ers put together, more than likely for their own families to know what they did during the war.

Reading and editing all of these stories has been something that all three of us have truly enjoyed doing. We all felt we knew the story of the 99th, but reading the words from each veteran added a great deal more information about this special unit that we did not know before. And for that, we are truly thankful that these veterans did take the time to put these memories down in writing.

Although a great project to work on, we also had to wrestle with how to edit their writings, with the overall goal of making sure each soldier got to tell their story the way they wanted to. But there are a number of challenges when doing this.

To begin with, the 99th, although small in comparison to other units, was still a large organization, meaning that often these men were stationed in different locations and witnessed different aspects of the war. For example, while seeing Buchenwald had a huge impact on some of the soldiers, others never mentioned it at all, due to the fact that they themselves did not witness the horrors found there. At Malmedy, arguably their biggest fight during the Battle of the Bulge, Company B was stationed right at the heart of the German attack, whereas other companies were stationed further away. Once they got to Europe, and orders were sent to different companies, platoons, squads, and individuals in various locations, these stories all begin to take on different perspectives, helping to give a much richer and meaningful story about what the 99th was actually tasked with doing throughout the war.

It will be helpful for the reader to know that each soldier's memories of these events sometimes faded over time or they possibly had told/heard a story so many times that they began to believe it themselves. We try to point out some of these discrepancies throughout the book and do so solely to point out that there may be a historical debate happening here as to what actually happened. Therefore, we left these conflicting stories in and did not add our own comments, in order to let each veteran tell their story in their own way.

Another major obstacle was dealing with geographic names that the veterans referred to throughout their stories. Once they left the confines of the United States, the names of British, French, Belgian, German, and Norwegian cities, regions, and various other locations were very difficult to deal with as editors. In some cases they put down names of places that we could not find on a map, while others were proper names, but we questioned if the unit actually was stationed there. But the biggest issue was that in many cases place names were probably heard in their native tongue and then translated through both Norwegian and American English (often by second-generation Norwegian Americans, who had their own way of saying things). Compounded with this is the fact that memories might not have been as crisp as they were when they were younger and you end up with a variety of geographic locations that lead to a lot of debate and discussion between the editors. In the end, we tried to correct the ones we were sure were wrong and tried to comment on others by giving an option as to what the author possibly meant.

It is also important to note that none of these men were professional authors, and although they each tell very compelling stories, their grammar and spelling often got in the way of what they were trying to convey. So, in order to help today's readers better understand what the veterans were trying to say, we often corrected spelling and grammatical issues in many of the stories. We truly hope that this is seen as a benefit to all that read this book and they understand that these changes were made purely to help clarify these stories.

The reader will also find a Glossary with terms that were often used through many of the veterans' stories. This was added to help explain these terms for those not familiar with World War II or military jargon. On top of that we also added some footnotes in individual stories in order to help explain what the author was talking about in that specific instance.

In the end, we truly hope those of you reading this book enjoy these stories told by the men of the 99th Infantry Battalion (Separate) and appreciate, as we did, the fact that a number of them took the time to sit down and put their thoughts on paper.

Acknowledgements

The editors would like to thank the following for their help in getting this book published.

Ruth Sheppard and Casemate Publishers who were willing to give us the chance to share the story of the 99th.

99th Education Board (past and present):
  Bruce Bjorgum, Erik Brun, Harlan Hanson, Bill Hoffland, Erik Kerska, Paula Lindholm, Roger Magnuson, Olaf Minge, Mark Nelson, Irene Sophie Starck, Kyle Ward, Erik Wiborg.

The families of the 99th who contributed information about their veteran:
  Ruth Asleson—Roland Asleson
  Erik Brun—son of Kristian (Christian) Brun
  Carolann Carlson—wife of Lester Carlson
  Dona Constantine—sister of Peter Hellerud
  Darcie Erie—granddaughter of Luverne Ostby
  Olaf Minge—grandson of Raymond K. Minge
  David Minge—son of Raymond K. Minge
  Øystein Nåvik—friend of J. Jarvis Taylor
  Mark Nelson—nephew of Lars L. Larson
  Lisa Nilsen—daughter of Kjell Nilsen
  Betsy Shaughnessy—daughter of Howard Bergen
  Josh Thomassen—grandson of Arne Thomassen
  Jane Voxland—daughter of Owen Voxland

Contributors:
  Magne Roedahl—Colonel, Royal Norwegian Army (Ret.)
  Pete Palmer—Brigadier General, U.S. Army (Ret.)
  Doug Thompson—Curator of the Minnesota Military & Veterans Museum
  Randal Dietrich—Director of the Minnesota Military & Veterans Museum

Joey van Meesen—snafu-docs.com
Gunter Gillot—European Center of Military History
Erick Wand—photo remaster and mapping. Graphics by Erick.

Our families:

To Jodie, Annika, and Grace Ward who endured countless hours of me collecting and transcribing all of these documents, holding numerous meetings, and researching the history of the 99th.

To Amy, Christopher, and Kiran Minge for support for time and attending lectures and reunion events over the years.

To Heidi Brodmarkle-Brun, Maxim Brodmarkle, Alexandr, Christina, and Tatiana Brun for support during years of research and presentations.

Dedication

To those men who served in the 99th Infantry Battalion (Separate). They proudly served to defend two nations, and for some, sacrificed everything in this cause. This book tries to commemorate those men who wrote down their memories as well as the hundreds who kept their memories bottled up throughout their lifetimes.

The editors would like to make a special note to the two 99ers, Donald A. Curtis and Richard A. Lumpp who are the remaining members of this unique unit and our connection to their honorable past.

"We have a date with this (Son of a Bitch)." This sign was posted on B Street at Camp Hale where soldiers passed on the way to the rifle range while training in 1943. The common bond among the Norwegians was anger over the invasion of their homeland. Whether he was born in the United States, arrived in the U.S. as a child, or as a survivor of a torpedo attack, for these soldiers Norway meant family and home. (Courtesy of the 99th Educational Foundation)

THE SQUAREHEAD MARCH

90 pounds of rucksack, and 100 miles to go
Always going up hill, through 50 miles of snow
We're a bunch of square heads, buddies one and all
Fighting is our duty, so freedom will not fall

We do a little drinking, and raise a little hell
And of course we like it, and so we do it well
So look out you dirty Nazis, we're going to cook your goose
For we have a little debt to pay, as soon as they turn us loose.

Maps

Maps prepared for this book are recreations of the tactical situation at key points for the 99th in the action. They use period military maps from 1944, very similar to ones used by the units. Battlefield positions were communicated rapidly, by using tracing paper to draw them by hand, tracing and compiling them onto larger overlays.

The unit positions appear as they were recorded in wartime overlays. Very few of these graphics survived in the 99th unit records but research has found overlays prepared by their higher headquarters.

The maps use standard symbols to identify units and show where units were at that moment. Lower units would provide a tracing of their positions; higher-level units compiled them and shared overviews to all lower units, showing who was on the left, right, and behind a unit.

The full color original maps and map tracings are available on the 99th Infantry Battalion (Separate) educational foundation's website: https://99battalion.org

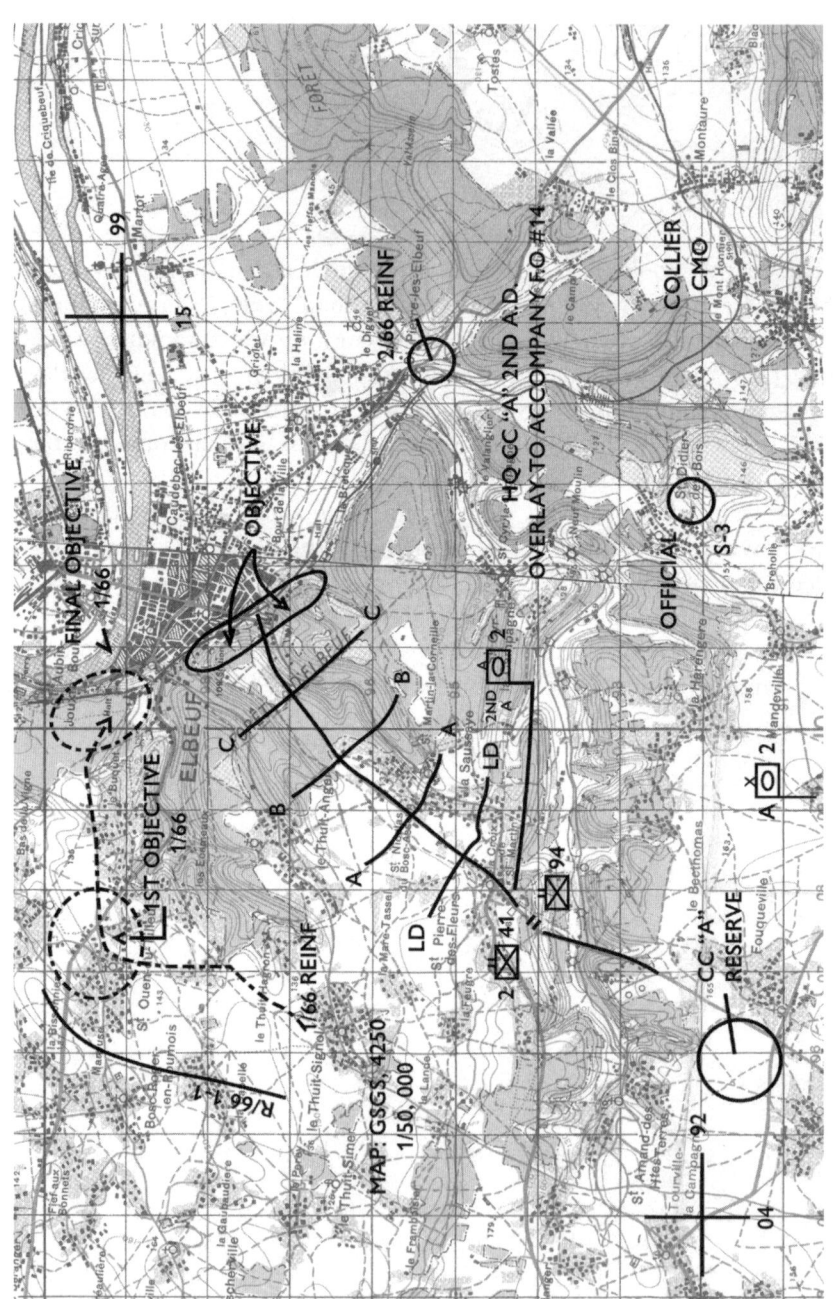

1 Elbeuf, seeing the elephant on August 25, 1944

Elbeuf, the first engagement for the 99th, just south of Rouen. This 2nd Armored Division overlay shows the approach route of the 99th into Elbeuf with 2nd Battalion, 41st Infantry Regiment on their left, from Field Order 14. By August 25, 1944 the U.S. XIX Corps had swept 40 miles northwest of Paris along the west bank of the Seine River, cutting off retreat for the German forces engaging Montgomery's 21st Army Group. (Courtesy of the 99th Educational Foundation/Graphics by Erick)

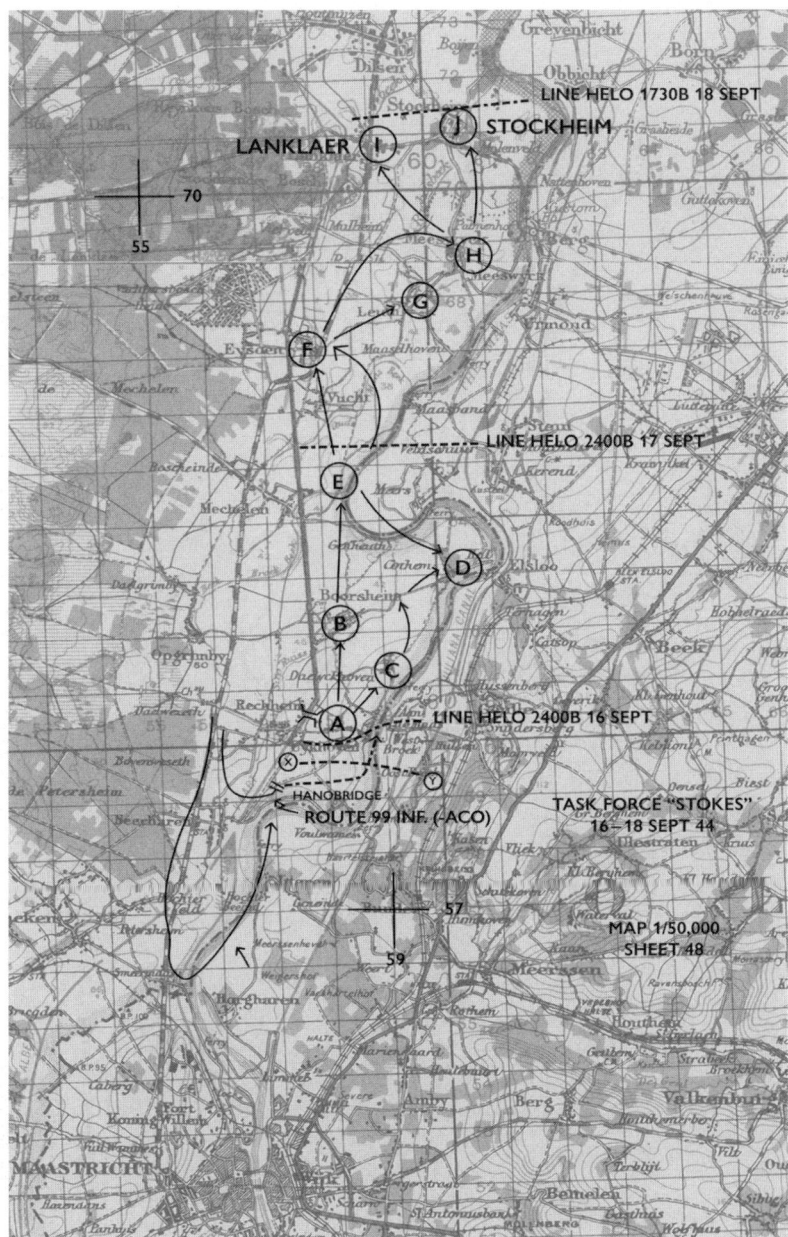

2 Canal Drive, a combined-arms effort on September 16–17, 1944
Task Force Stokes was a combined-arms team with the riflemen of the 99th riding into action on the tanks of the 2nd Armored Division. This overlay shows how the stubborn Norwegian infantrymen paired with the mobile tankers of the "Hell on Wheels" division cleared German resistance north of Maastricht in September 1944. The objective was an area of a corridor of 50 square miles created by the Willems Vaart Canal and the Meuse River on the Belgian–Netherlands border. (Courtesy of the 99th Educational Foundation/Graphics by Erick)

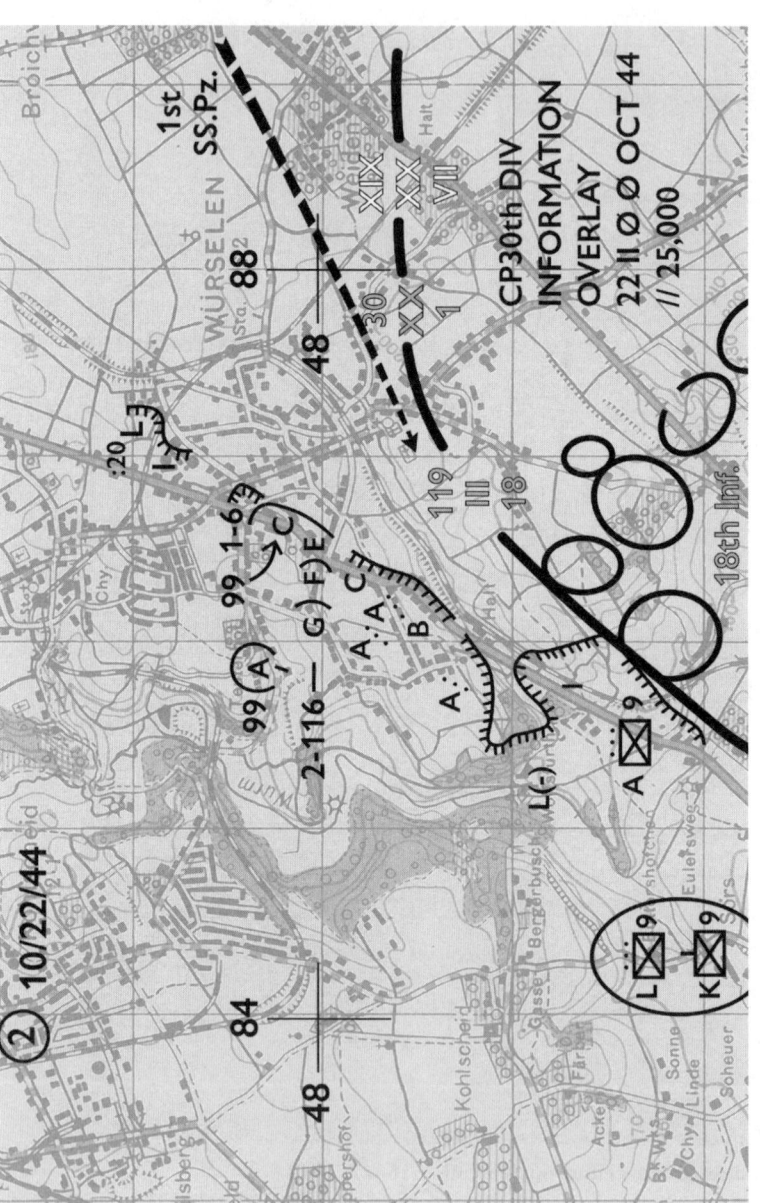

3 Würselen, the 10-day nightmare of encircling Aachen

When the U.S. First Army encircled Aachen, Germany's ancient capital, the neck of the bag closed in the suburb of Würselen, while both sides poured artillery and airstrikes into the area. This overlay is a snapshot of one day, showing units under the 30th Infantry Division in black and 1st Infantry Division in blue from the south. Three kilometers of the 30th's front line was held by five U.S. infantry battalions, of three different regiments, fighting shoulder to shoulder to hold the line. The German 1st SS Panzer Corps tried repeatedly to fight through this corridor to reach their garrison in Aachen, 4 miles away. Units rotated constantly, giving companies brief rests, but all were in artillery range of the enemy at all times. (Courtesy of the 99th Educational Foundation/Graphics by Erick)

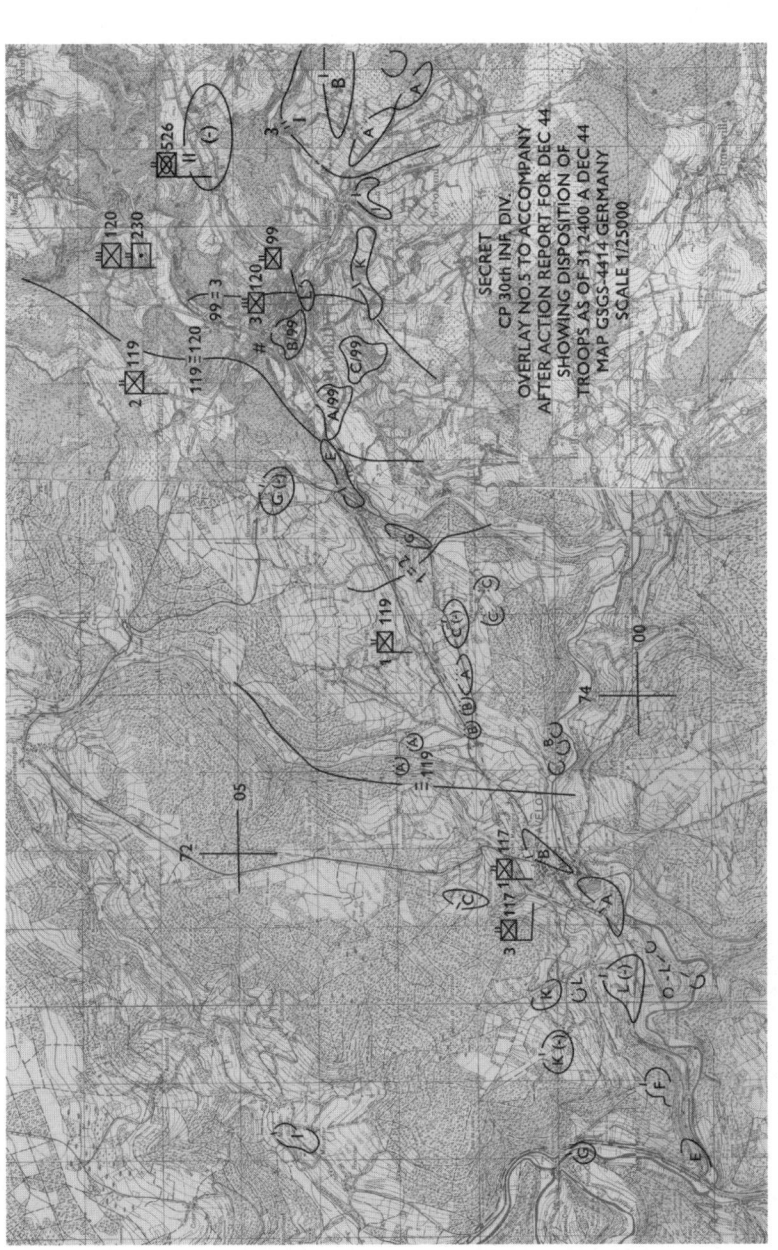

4 Malmedy and the Battle of the Bulge December 17, 1944–January 17, 1945

The German counter-offensive of 1944 broke though the thinly held positions in the Ardennes Forest and forced the evacuation of U.S. First Army Headquarters at Spa. The initial defense of the Malmedy area was affected by Lt. Col. Pergrin's 291st Engineer Battalion, before the arrival of Task Force Hansen on the night of December 17/18, with the 99th, the 526th Armored Infantry Battalion, and the towed 3-inch anti-tank guns of Company A of the 825th Tank Destroyer Battalion. The task force was assigned to defend the town of Malmedy and crossings over the Amblève River at Stavelot and Trois-Ponts, and was reinforced by the 30th Infantry Division that had been trucked down from the Aachen sector. This overlay shows the integration of the task force units into the divisional defense plan of the area. (Courtesy of the 99th Educational Foundation/Graphics by Erick)

Glossary of Terms

Below are a series of terms and abbreviations often used by the men of the 99th while they were training and serving in Europe. Many of these terms became so ingrained in their memories that they were still using them decades after the war was over.

10-in-1 rations: A group ration of canned and dehydrated products that could feed 10 men one meal, developed from the 5-in-1 rations. The 99th was the final field-test unit for this meal in October 1943. Half of the combat rations planned for operations after D-Day were 10-in-1 rations.

AA Batteries: Abbreviation for Anti-Aircraft, or Anti-Aircraft Artillery units.

BAR: Abbreviation for Browning Automatic Rifle, a .30-caliber light automatic rifle that the United States Army used during World War II. Operated by a two-man team of gunner and assistant gunner.

Belgian F.I.: Belgian Forces Interior were Belgian nationals that served in a resistance movement within Belgium.

Bienville, SS: A converted 7,600 ton freighter that served as a troopship in WWII. It brought the 99th home, arriving at Boston.

Billeting: A living quarters, often someone's home, where a soldier was assigned to sleep.

Bivouac: A temporary or semi-permanent military base, for the lodging of an army element.

Buzz bomb or Doodlebug: Nicknames for the German "vengeance weapon," the early flying bomb or V-1. It could fly 160 miles and deliver a onetime warhead. Over a thousand were launched into Liège and Antwerp in 1944–45.

Camp Hale: A U.S. Army training facility, constructed in 1942 as the Mountain and Winter Warfare Center where soldiers trained for skiing and mountain warfare. It was originally home of the 10th Light Division and named for General Irving Hale. It was shuttered in 1945 and officially closed as an Army training facility in 1965.

Camp Ripley: Located north of Little Falls, Minnesota, this military training facility was opened in 1931 and primarily used for training the Minnesota National Guard. Today it is the site of an annual military exchange program between the Minnesota National Guard and the Norwegian Home Guard.

Camp Twenty-Grand: This camp was part of nine other camps in the Le Havre, France region, known to American GIs as "Cigarette Camps." Each camp was named after a popular cigarette of the time (i.e. Camp Lucky Strike, Camp Philip Morris, etc.). They were mostly used as replacement depots during the war.

CCA/CCB: Abbreviation for Combat Command A and B, which were parts of an Armored Division and were comparable to the size of a regiment.

CP: Command Post.

C-Rations: An "Individual Combat Ration"—a box containing canned food formerly used by soldiers up until the 1980s.

Cosmoline: A petroleum-based preservative that was applied to weapons and equipment shipped to units during World War II, used to prevent rust. Many soldiers complained about how difficult it was to get it off of the weapons.

D-Rations: An "Individual Combat Ration"—a box containing concentrated high-energy food bars and other items inspired by traditional foods like pemmican.

EM: Abbreviation for Enlisted Men for soldiers below the rank of non-commissioned officer.

ETO: Abbreviation for the European Theater of Operation.

First Special Service Force: Activated in July 1942, the FSSF was organized as an elite Canadian-American commando force. They trained at Camp William Henry Harrison in Montana. They were also known as the Devil Brigade. The U.S. veterans of the force were formed into the 474th Infantry Regiment in January 1945, with the 99th serving as the new regiment's third battalion.

Fort Snelling: A U.S. Army military installation, which was built in 1819 and is located near Minneapolis, Minnesota, home of the peacetime 3rd Infantry Regiment that was sent to Newfoundland and Iceland in 1941.

Hansen, Lt. Col. Harold D.: Appointed to command the 99th Infantry Battalion (Separate) as a captain in August 1942, he was made executive officer from June 1943 to August 1944, and assumed command again when Lt. Col. Turner was wounded at Elbeuf.

Hedgerows (France): Originally built by the Romans, the hedgerows were linear mounds of dirt and stone raised over six feet high in irregular patterns that served as fences between plots of land in the Normandy region. Most Americans, when hearing the term "hedgerows," incorrectly assumed they would be small shrubbery like that often found in yards in the U.S.

John Henry, SS: A Liberty ship and one of five vessels used to move the 99th to France in June 1944.

Jerries/Huns/Krauts: Various nicknames that American soldiers used when referring to German soldiers.

Jerry Cans: A flat-sided 5-gallon/20-liter container used to transport gasoline and water during World War II. Original German cans were copied and improved by the Allies.

K-Rations: This was a light, ready-to-eat meal with breakfast, dinner, and supper menus. It was an individual daily combat food ration that was introduced during World War II.

KP: Kitchen Police or Patrol. Soldiers are assigned, on a rotating basis, to assist the unit cooks in preparing, serving, and cleaning the kitchen in the field and garrison.

LCI: Landing Craft, Infantry. An LCI could land 200 troops on a beach. Was larger than the Landing Craft Vehicle, Personnel (LCVP), known as the Higgins Boat, that could carry 36 men.

LCT: Landing Craft, Tank. It could carry four tanks and land them on a beach.

LST: Landing Ship, Tank. It could carry 10 tanks, 15 vehicles, and 160 soldiers.

Liberty Ship/Victory Ship: Wartime-built cargo ships of 10,000 tons; 2,700 Liberty and over 500 of the later Victory ships were launched in World War II.

Luftwaffe: Name of the German Air Force.

M1: The M1 Garand or M1 Rifle was a .30-caliber semi-automatic rifle that the United States Army used during World War II.

M4: The main American medium tank, with a 75mm gun and known by its British name, Sherman.

M5: The main American light tank, with a 37mm gun, known by its British name, Stuart.

M8: This Scout Car was a six-wheel light armored car during World War II with a turret and 37mm cannon.

M24: The main American light tank, with a 75mm gun, known by its British name Chaffee.

Malmedy Massacre: A war crime committed against American prisoners of war by German units outside of Malmedy, Belgium on December 17, 1944.

Me-109 (German): This was a light German fighter plane that was commonly used by the Luftwaffe.

Military Time: Based on a 24-hour clock as compared to the traditional American way using two groups of 12 hours; 1300 hrs is 1 p.m.

MP: Abbreviation for Military Police.

NAAFI: Abbreviation for the Navy, Army, and Air Force Institutes, which was an organization created by the British government in the early 1920s. Their main purpose was to run recreational establishments needed by the British Armed Forces and to sell goods to servicemen and their families. Similar to the U.S. Post Exchange system.

NCO: Abbreviation for a non-commissioned officer. A sergeant is a non-commissioned officer, who did not receive an officer's commission. They typically earn their position of authority by promotion through the enlisted ranks.

Nebelwerfer: A six-barreled rocket artillery used by the Germans during World War II.

Nissen huts: This was a British prefabricated steel structure for military use, especially as barracks, like the American Quonset huts.

NORSO: Norwegian Special Operations was a group created in 1945 from the two Norwegian Operational Groups for operations in Norway in 1945 to perform special operations behind enemy lines.

OP: Abbreviation for Observation Post.

Operational Group: An OSS commando unit of 40 specially qualified soldiers who operate in uniform, are organized, trained, and equipped to conduct guerrilla warfare. Two Norwegian Operational Groups were recruited from the 99th in July 1943, and members jumped into France in August–September 1944. Half were selected for NORSO and the others served in China in 1945.

QM: Abbreviation for Quartermaster. This position was in charge of the supplies for various units.

Operation *Werewolf*: Nazi plans for armed resistance to the Allied occupation of Germany in 1944–45.

OSS: Abbreviation for the Office of Strategic Services—the main centralized intelligence service for the War Department during World War II. Divided into Operational Groups, Special Operations, Secret Intelligence, Morale Operations, and other branches.

O.D.: Abbreviation for Olive Drab, a flat green color used by the U.S. Army.

Pando: A settlement at the northern end of the Pando Valley and rail siding, where Camp Hale was built.

Proximity Fuse: An electronic detonator that causes a projectile to explode when it comes within a preset distance of its target using radar.

PX: Abbreviation for Post Exchange. A system of small retail shop for soldiers. Similar to the NAAFI system for UK forces.

Rations: Military food, including fresh food, Class A, Dehydrated, B, and many sub-types of operational or field rations.

R&R: Abbreviation for Rest and Recuperation. This allowed soldiers to be away from their normal duties for a set amount of time.

Red Ball Express: A logistical operation run primarily with African American QM truck units, the Red Ball Express was a truck convoy system that supplied Allied forces in France after breaking out from the D-Day beaches in Normandy in August 1944.

Reveille: A signal, usually from a bugle, to wake soldiers in the morning.

Rype Group/Operation *Rype*: OSS mission in early 1945 with Operational Group men of Norwegian Special Operations (NORSO) element under Lt. Col. Gerhard Bolland. The field element was under Major William Colby.

Separate: A designation added to a unit's title that is not part of a larger organization.

Siegfried Line: The Siegfried Line, known in German as the Westwall, was a German defensive line built during the 1930s opposite the French Maginot Line.

Squarehead: Late-19th-century ethnic slur directed at Scandinavian immigrants.

SHAEF: Supreme Headquarters Allied Expeditionary Force. General Eisenhower's headquarters of all western Allied forces.

Task Force: A military unit organized for a special task composed of different units. Commonly named after the overall commander.

TD: Abbreviation for Tank Destroyer. These lighter armored gun systems were intended to carry larger guns and have more mobility. In contrast, tanks were used to support infantry operations.

Turner, Lt. Col. Robert G.: Commander of the 99th from June 1943 to August 1944 who originally was sent to Camp Hale to take over for Captain Harold D. Hansen. Wounded at Elbeuf and replaced by the same Harold D. Hansen.

USO: United Services Organization, a non-profit organization that provided morale and recreational services to members of the Armed Forces.

CHAPTER ONE

Howard R. Bergen

Howard R. "Bus" Bergen was a private in the 99th Infantry Battalion (Separate) who wrote a historical account of the group's formation and key events titled "History of the 99th Infantry Battalion, U.S. Army." His writing was published in 1945 while the 99th was stationed in Norway at the end of World War II and was the official unit history that was provided as a souvenir for each soldier.

Acting as the editor and lead author to the official battalion history of World War II, Bergen left us with a clear and concise history of the 99th and World War II that remains to this day relevant and seminal. Bergen was on the 99th newspaper staff and it was common among World War II units to write their unit histories soon after the European campaign's completion.

Writing in Norway with access to battalion records and fresh memories, he establishes the war as they knew it. This book is the starting point for historians, descendants, and amateur researchers to understand how the 99th leaders and veterans saw themselves.

He received five Campaign Stars recorded on his honorable discharge and was awarded a Bronze Star by the War Department in a letter dated September 23, 1947 for "exemplary conduct in ground combat against the armed enemy on or about 1 December, 1944 in the European Theatre of Operations."

Bergen was born in Lakewood, Ohio on November 22, 1916. His mother was Bessie Johnson, born in Norway and arriving in Lakewood at the age of two with her family. He was called "Bus" for his entire life due to his large size at birth. He graduated from Lakewood High School and attended Cornell University. He worked for an advertising agency until enlisting in the Army.

Bergen married in September 1945 in the chapel at Smestad in Oslo, Norway. His wife had been working for the U.S. Embassy to the Norwegian government-in-exile in London during the Blitz and returned to Oslo with the embassy staff when the war ended.

Howard returned to Lakewood after the war and immediately went to work as a reporter for the Cleveland Press where he remained for 35 years until he retired. He was inducted into the Cleveland Journalism Hall of Fame in 1998, being recognized as a great writer and investigative reporter. He had three stories selected for a popular radio and television series called "The Big Story"—a crime drama which dramatized the true stories of real-life newspaper reporters.

Howard "Bus" Bergen died October 24, 1991.

Training for Combat[1]

On the tenth day of July 1942, the 99th Infantry Battalion (Separate), a unit composed solely of Norwegians and Americans of direct Norwegian descent, was activated by War Department order at Camp Ripley, Minnesota. Under the command of Captain H. D. Hansen, a small cadre of enlisted men and officers began preparations to receive the incoming men needed to fill the ranks of this

Sivart "Ron" Windh at a dance, while stationed at Fort Snelling, Minnesota. The photo captures the Scandinavian ethnic pride in Minnesota. Windh, a Swede in Company C, was later wounded in Belgium. He was recruited from his hospital by the Office of Strategic Service (OSS) for its Norwegian Operational Groups by some of his old 99th buddies. He jumped with Major William Colby's team into Norway in 1945 in Operation *Rype* under the direction of Lt. Col. Gerhard Bolland. (Courtesy of the 99th Educational Foundation)

---

[1] Howard R. Bergen. *The History of the 99th Infantry Battalion (Separate)*. Oslo: Emil Moestue, 1946.

battalion. They came from far and near, from famous divisions and reception centers, seasoned soldiers and raw recruits, men who had traveled the far reaches of the earth and boys who had scarcely set foot out of the Norwegian settlements in the great Midwest. Day after day they piled out of truck, train, and motor car. Rapidly the companies, platoons, and squads filled with men of every age and description; the War Department order had been circulated in every camp and reception center in the country and eager volunteers flocked to the call.

The roster of the outfit was typically Scandinavian—Hansen, Johnsen, Petersen, Berg, Andersen, Grunseth, Amundsen, and on down the line, but the lives and experiences of these men were as varied as their names were similar. Many were ex-members of the escaped Norwegian Merchant Marine and victims of the ruthless Nazi submarine warfare; many had lived under German tyranny in their native land only to escape and join up to fight with the forces opposing it. All were commonly united in one great resolve: to help to free their country of its oppressor. This feeling was directly transmitted to the American Norwegians and helped to fuse them together into a vicious and capable combat organization.

Near the end of September, the battalion moved to Fort Snelling, Minnesota, where the training in basic subjects was continued and where one of the roughest features of training—constant and grueling speed marches—eliminated all but the physically fit from the ranks of the unit. Various Norwegian officers and dignitaries paid visits to the new, highly publicized organization and found it all that the newspapers said it was and more. The people of the Twin Cities, St. Paul and Minneapolis, opened their hearts to the men and many and constant were the invitations to social events, parties, and dinners.

The toughest training lay ahead. On December 17, 1942, the entire battalion moved from Fort Snelling to the top of the Continental Divide, 9,600 feet above sea level. There at the Mountain Training Center, Camp Hale, Colorado they had the "moon in their laps." As the men of the 99th silently viewed the towering peaks, rocky ravines, and swirling snow, there came to their minds an idea of the things to come.

Warm, new, insulated barracks awaited the men although the camp itself was far from being completed upon arrival of the unit. The two-story barracks were especially constructed to house everyone comfortably in the extreme cold found at this altitude during winter months and the central heating system was highly effective. Showers, indoor latrines, and good beds completed the attractions and it was, as one man was heard to mutter at a later date, "Too damned bad that we couldn't spend more time living in them."

The array and weight of the equipment which was issued within the next few days was staggering to contemplate. Weight of the individual loads to be carried by each ski soldier ran as high as 70 to 97 pounds depending on the mission to be accomplished. Such weights as these necessitated the development of some entirely new techniques in loading, packing, and skiing, because the troops were shortly to embark upon an intensive program of training in the art of winter warfare. To give an indication of loads carried, and definitely needed in this rigorous climate, there is shown the list as given in the *Proposed Manual for Mountain Troops*, Chapter IV, Organizational Equipment:

Load Carried on the Person:	*In the Rucksack:* (pack)
Pistol belt and pouches	PWhite over-pants and over mittens
Gas mask	Tent pegs
Rucksack	Rations **
On the Pack:	Sleeping pad
Rifle	Climbers (pocket) for
Bayonet	skis for steep slopes
Entrenching tool	Extra socks and pocket insoles
First Aid pk.	Tent (green, white, reversible
Emergency snowshoes*	mountain tent) ***
In the Parka:	Sleeping bag ****
Ski wax	Tent poles
Waterproof match box	Underwear and pocket thongs
Spare mittens	Canteen
Ski knife	1 Coleman gas stove *****
Goggles	Cooking Set ******

* *Each man carried three types: Emergency, bear paw, or trail.*
** *Mountain rations: One box carries rations for you for four days or four men for one day.*
*** *This mountain tent is carried by one man in this two-man load. The other man carries the Coleman gas stove.*
**** *Sleeping bag: Two-piece which can be rolled up just as neatly into perhaps an equally small roll as the ordinary two-blanket roll of the regular infantry. It has been used on windswept mountaintops in temperatures of from 30 to 40 degrees below zero, and in blizzards. Men and officers swear by it as the last word in keeping warm and snug.*
***** *Gas stove: Part of two-man load mentioned above.*
****** *Cooking set: Another part of the two-man load.*

In addition to all of this must be added a pair of skis and two ski poles.

The weight carried by the automatic rifleman was some 97 pounds including his ammunition. Yet even with this tremendous load the men managed exceedingly well thanks to a harness-like device, far excelling the harness of the regular infantry, which distributed the weight on the backs and hips instead of on the shoulders alone.

Training, begun in mid-winter, lasted straight through until August 1943. During the entire period the unit was in the field living, eating, sleeping, and training a minimum of three days and nights weekly. The social life of the men reached a new and hitherto unheard of low—it was a constant, grueling round of work, work, work. It was the kind of stuff that many had read about but never experienced. The men made records of speed and endurance, but the publicity raves echoed a bit hollow in their ears. The back-breaking, lung-burning climbs, the bitter, numbing cold, the continual grind of training all served to diminish the glamor associated by newspapers and magazines with the unit. But through the long training, hardship, and work, there flared up within each man a pride of unit; a comradeship which is seldom found in units composed of men with dissimilar backgrounds; a certain intangible something which is the prime requisite of all first-class combat units—the firm and unshakable belief that his unit is the "best damned outfit in the armed forces!"

Much of the training carried out by the unit was experimental in nature, testing various types of equipment thrown in its direction by the War Department. Some innovations were made by members of the battalion, discoveries which met with the enthusiastic approval of the government. First was a mount made for a heavy machine gun from two skis—a mount from which the gun could be placed into immediate action, and second, a three-ski sled for litter bearers.

Among other things during this period the battalion undertook a 50-mile cross-country test march, a march which required four days to complete. All rations and most of the heavier equipment were manhandled with the aid of four-dog teams which helped in pulling the freight sleds. The men wore either snowshoes or skis, depending upon their function in the mission. Many of the mortars were broken down into three-man loads hand-carried while climbing steep, icy trails or skirting deep precipices. For the entire first two days of the trek across desolate, snowclad mountains, the man faced a continual uphill grind to the very top of the Continental Divide and thence on down the other side. In certain places they reached altitudes of over 12,000 feet above sea level.

Frequent "breaks" had to be made to enable the men to catch their breath as heavy loads, the rarified atmosphere, and intense cold made breathing almost impossible. At times it was necessary to stop every 10 minutes. At night, the men found the water in their canteens frozen solid. After cooking a meal on their stoves and hastily eating it before it froze in the pan, they stacked their skis, pitched their tent in a hole dug in the snow, and wearing their clothes, including ski-boots, inside their sleeping bags to keep from freezing solid, they dropped off into sound sleep. The speed and endurance records made on missions of this sort live today in the annals of the Mountain Training Center.

When spring came to Camp Hale, one full month after its arrival in all other parts of the country, skis and snowshoes were put away and straight mountain climbing was put on the schedule. Once more the adaptable members of the battalion proved their mettle and new laurels were added. In June of 1943 many men volunteered for a strategic force of men who were to undergo paratroop and commando training prior to the then considered inevitable invasion of Norway. The battalion was given preference, and many old comrades and officers left to form the nucleus of the new special striking force of warmakers extraordinary.

It was in June, too, that Lt. Colonel R. G. Turner took over the command of the 99th Battalion. Major Harold D. Hansen, having done an excellent job of organizing, training, and initiating the unit, was made executive officer and continued to perform capably in his new position. He had long since endeared himself in the hearts of his men because of his rugged, understanding qualities and because he was a born leader for this type of force.

In preparation for movement overseas, the battalion moved from Camp Hale to Camp Shanks in New York on August 24, 1943. Arriving after a tedious cross-country trip on August 27 the men immediately went into the routine of drawing new equipment, receiving shots for every known disease, and sweating out passes to the big city. For many men who hailed from New York and its environs this was an excellent chance to see their families for perhaps the last time. For those less lucky it was a chance to partake of a social life which would be unknown to them for a long time to come. The men took full advantage of this opportunity before embarking on their great adventure.

The fifth day of September found the battalion aboard the stout ship SS *Mexico* and bound for parts guessed at, but unknown. Outside of being rather rough and very tedious, the passage was comparatively uneventful. A number of "alerts" kept the gun crews on their toes but outside of the warning "Submarines in the direct vicinity," the convoy had no trouble. Time was spent in reading, playing cards, or watching the sleek, swift destroyer escort continually maneuvering about in search of enemy U-boats.

The 99th arrived in Scotland on September 16 and immediately boarded the train which was to take them to their new camp in England. After 16 hours by rail the unit arrived at Perham Downs Camp, Tidworth area, Wiltshire, England. This area is well known as an old and famous training ground for British soldiers. The camp was centrally located between Salisbury and Andover. Both of these ancient and charming English towns offered much in the way of entertainment, study, and relaxation for the training-weary soldier. Accommodations were excellent with permanent barracks of stone, baths, recreation rooms, and NAAFI. The terrain surrounding the camp was highly suitable for the type of training which the unit was now to undergo, and almost immediately upon arrival another strenuous program was begun. Now it was straight infantry training, long hikes, tactical problems, weapons, lectures, classes, week-long bivouacs on the cold, wet ground of England, and of course, numerous inspections. Specialized training was included also, such as the actual firing of the rocket launcher and throwing of fragmentation and assault grenades. One hundred and ten men were sent to St. Agnes, Cornwall, for practical training and firing of the .30- and .50-caliber machine guns. There were actual mortar exercises. Beside this, 26 men attended a combat swimming course in London with all except two qualifying as instructors.

It was here at Perham Downs that 300 members of the 99th underwent one of the roughest phases of their rugged careers. A ration test, as the name implies, is a test by which the War Department determines the actual quality of a new ration by its effect upon men undergoing the conditions which they will undoubtedly meet in combat; it is the final and by far the most important endorsement. The battalion was picked to test the new ration, which is now, by all standards, the most heavily used and popular combat issuance in the American armed forces today.[2] In Dartmoor forest the men marched an average of 20 miles a day, every day for 15 straight days. In continual rain and with full field packs, they marched across some of the roughest and most desolate country in the British Isles. They carried all of their possessions on their backs and at night they slept in an area which resembled an artificial lake more than a bivouac area. Each morning the soldiers were weighed individually, and an accurate check was made daily on their physical condition. The rain failed to dampen their spirits as after a few days it became the normal thing. At last the grind was finished and after a final check-up by doctors, government experts, and SOS officers the men were allowed to return to Tidworth for a well-deserved rest. This contribution was highly commended by the War Department and another notch was cut in the 99th's Hall of Fame.

In the middle of January 1944, the battalion moved from Tidworth by rail to Wales. There, in Nissen huts, the men were to spend the remainder of their time and training in the British Isles. The campsite was beautiful—situated on the spacious park in front of the castle, it lay beside the Glanusk River surrounded on all sides by the Welsh mountains.

Though picturesque and inspiring to the artistic eye, the mountains were a marked source of irritation and discomfort to the men in the training that followed. Day after day, night after night, almost every peak and crest of each mountain was scaled and maneuvered upon by the battalion. It was here that the men first maneuvered with tanks, with live ammunition on field exercises, and entered into competition with forces of the British Home Guard on combat courses. The vigorous training endured prior to the competitive maneuvers really paid off and the record of the 99th was further enhanced in the eyes of the Welsh people by its marked proficiency in these contests.

In the latter part of April, the battalion was accorded the singular honor of furnishing the select group which was to guard invasion plans at First U.S. Army Headquarters then located in Bristol. Fifty-two men were especially picked for this task and they soon gained praise from the highest officers at the headquarters for

---

[2] This statement was made by the author and not verifiable at the time. It is a claim similar to many others that soldiers made to each other about their war experiences.

their smart appearance and their efficiency. They were commonly mis-named "The Swedish Guard."

On the first day of May the remainder of the battalion left Glanusk Park for a camp at Ludlow near Hereford in England. Here for more than a month training continued, but through it all there was the general feeling that "something big was up this time." On June 10, hot on the heels of the invasion in France, the 99th was alerted for immediate movement. The battalion arrived the same afternoon at Uffculme and now they really "sweated it out" for a few days until the movement to Plymouth for embarkation was ordered. After donning their impregnated, gas-proof clothing and eating their last good meal for a long time, the men of the 99th left the shores of England on June 17.

The crossing was rough, and life was anything but pleasant aboard flat-bottomed LCIs. Due to bad weather they were unable to land as scheduled and were forced to lay offshore for a few days until it was considered possible to land. Meanwhile the first taste of real war came with the first boom of artillery in the near distance and the sight of dogfights overhead. Finally, on June 21, the 99th landed on the bleak, shell-torn shores of Omaha Beach in France.

Under Fire

The first night in France was spent in Transit Area number three, approximately 3 miles inland. All about the bivouac area was strewn the wreckage of war and in the distance the sky was constantly aglow with the reflection of a terrific artillery barrage. The men were dispersed tactically and slit-trenches were dug with a gusto never found in the previous "dry-runs." K-rations—the inevitable—were produced. As night fell the men crawled into their holes for the first night on the soil of France.

On the following day the battalion was transported by truck to Colombières and attached to the Provisional Ranger Group, First U.S. Army. The next few days were spent in re-checking equipment and ammunition and in listening to occasional talks on battle experiences by various unit commanders. On June 29, the unit moved to St. Joseph on the Cherbourg Peninsula and the following day entered Cherbourg. Here for the next nine days the unit was attached to the Fourth Port Headquarters and helped secure the city. After Cherbourg had been secured the unit helped guard various military installations against possible sabotage from bypassed German troops or regular saboteurs.

Moving to a new location, Hau de Haut,[3] 8 miles south of Cherbourg, the 99th in conjunction with the Second and Fifth Ranger Battalions and the 759th Light Tank Battalion patrolled the area of Cherbourg Peninsula between Cherbourg and Valognes from the 8th through the 25th of July. In addition, the security patrols

---

[3] The author may have meant Hameau de Haut.

also checked the area for enemy materials, ammunition, casualties, and bypassed enemy personnel.

From July 25 to August 10, the battalion conducted night-firing exercises, field problems and training with the 759th Light Tank Battalion, then on August 11, set up a general defense of the town of Buais. On August 14 the unit became attached to the famous 2nd Armored Division and was assigned to Combat Command "B" of that division for a mission. However, this mission was canceled, and the unit was again thrown into Division Reserve. Until August 19 front-line training was given in the function of armored infantry by the 41st Armored Infantry and included demonstrations in roadblocks, proper use of artillery, and proper use of communications within an armored division.

On August 20 the 99th, still with Division Reserve, moved up to Toureuvre and established roadblocks. Immediately upon completion of these blocks a heavy concentration of enemy artillery started to fall and continued intermittently throughout the entire night. The next day a mine accident killed two enlisted men and wounded one officer and 10 other enlisted men. The 22nd found the battalion once again on the move to Beit where roadblocks were once more set up, but this time the enemy was retreating and reorganizing and no organized resistance was encountered. However, the advance detail of the unit upon entering the town of Le Failly made contact with a fairly large force of Germans and was forced to withdraw for reserves. The town was captured by Division Reserve and over 150 prisoners were taken.

Movement was made to Cesseville on the following day where the inevitable roadblocks were established. Functioning for the time as armored infantry attached to the 2nd Armored Division, the 99th had more than its share of these ticklish assignments. During the night of August 24, 14 prisoners were captured. Despite heavy strafing and bombing attacks by enemy fighters and light bombers on the blocks, no casualties were suffered by the battalion and the men were commended on the increasing efficiency with which they conducted these new assignments. They had now undergone, however slightly, their initial "baptism of fire" and were emerging as seasoned and hardened fighters prepared to meet the vicious infighting yet to come.

Elbeuf

On August 25 the battalion was alerted for an attack on the woods immediately south of the town of Elbeuf with the final objective being the entire south side of the town. Despite heavy artillery fire from the north side of the Seine River and much small arms fire from the front and flanks, the 99th advanced rapidly and entered the town at 1600 hours. In the town itself there followed a furious round of house-to-house fighting. It was discovered that the German defenders had several medium tanks in the town and, because they were considered more than a match for infantry, a request for tank destroyers was immediately relayed back. The unit was informed that they could not arrive for at least two hours, so it pushed forward in the face of mortar, artillery, tank, and small arms fire to take the final objective—the town of Elbeuf—at 1635 hours.

The battalion command post was set up within the town with a rear command post and reserve on the high ground to the south of the town. A determined counterattack was launched by the enemy on the northwest section of the city but was driven off after hard fighting and with the help of the tank destroyers which had arrived to help stem the tank attack in the nick of time. At least four Nazi tanks were personally accounted for by the 99th before the TDs arrived.

On the morning of August 26, the command post was heavily shelled and destroyed, taking a heavy toll of officers. Among the injured was battalion commander Lt. Colonel R. G. Turner. The command of the battalion was then taken over by Major Harold D. Hansen who was at that time executive officer. At 1700 hours of the same day all organized small arms fire ceased; however, the Germans continued to throw in mortar and artillery fire from the north side of the Seine River. Eighty-six prisoners were taken by the 99th against a loss of nine officers wounded, seven enlisted men killed, and 41 wounded. At 1800 hours on the 26th the unit was relieved by the Canadians and went into bivouac at St. Croix de Martin.

Two days later the unit became attached to Combat Command A of the 2nd Armored Division for another attack on the morning of August 30. Six more objectives were taken with only negligible enemy resistance encountered. The final objective was the woods north of the town of Villers in orthies[4] and on the evening of the same day the unit command post was established in that town and the final objective was secured. On the same date the unit was relieved from attachment to the Second Armored Division and attached to the Seventh Armored Group, XIX Corps Reserve. The following day the 99th moved to Drucourt where it bivouacked and established local security.

Here, for a few days, the battalion rested while performing routine duties. Safe from artillery fire, eating warm food, and receiving replacements, many of the men had their first full night's sleep in many weeks. On September 6 the unit was again alerted and moved from La Glanerie to Mons, Belgium, with the mission of securing the city. Immediately upon arrival roadblocks were set up and the city patrolled. The following day the unit relieved the 16th Infantry Regiment of the 1st Division and continued patrolling in the vicinity of Mons.

On September 8 the 99th moved to Valenciennes in France for the purpose of securing the First Army sector against probable attack by an enemy pocket in the British sector to the north and west of Valenciennes. For the next four days the unit conducted motorized and foot patrols in the immediate vicinity of Mons and Valenciennes. Seventeen prisoners of war were taken during this period.

---

[4] The author may have meant Villers-en-Arthies.

Canal Drive

On September 14, A and B Companies were attached to Combat Command "A" of the 2nd Armored Division for another mission. At the same time the remainder of the unit moved to a point 1 ½ miles west of Mechelen, Belgium. The following day C Company was attached to the 2nd Battalion of the 66th Armored Regiment and at 1700 hours moved up to secure Reckheim. Accompanying it in the attack were five light tanks and six medium tanks. In the face of intense mortar and artillery fire, the unit advanced doggedly to its objective. The tanks proved invaluable in neutralizing machine gun emplacements, strong points, and snipers. Meanwhile, A, B, and D Companies moved forward and crossed the Willems Vaart Canal to support the attack. They too met concentrated fire from numerous well-prepared positions and pillboxes but advanced swiftly to secure their objectives despite the stubborn resistance. One officer and one enlisted man were killed during the night's operations and one officer and 14 enlisted men were wounded. Fourteen prisoners of war were taken.

After securing its positions the battalion once again moved into the attack. At 1700 hours, with B and C Companies leading, A Company in reserve, and D Company supporting the leading elements, the 99th kicked off. Light and medium tanks of the 66th Armored Regiment supported the attack and once more were indispensable in clearing up enemy strong points and other fortifications. The resistance encountered was bitter and determined but the attack was of the same caliber. It was here that an officer in the armored force was heard to say, "This is the only damned infantry outfit in the world that tanks have to worry about keeping up with." Again, the objectives were taken, and the battalion reorganized and held strong points to meet the never-failing counterattack. Estimated casualties for this last attack by the 99th numbered 40 enlisted men. One hundred and eleven prisoners were taken.

Simultaneously, units of the 66th Armored Regiment continued to attack and secured their objectives in conjunction with the initial assault plan. With the forming of this line the assigned mission of the operation was completed and the 99th was released from assignment to the 2nd Armored Division. Immediately the 744th Light Tank Battalion was assigned to assist in establishing security of strong points. Casualties for the operations from September 16 through 18 for the 99th were one officer killed, two officers wounded, eight enlisted men killed, 75 enlisted men wounded, and 10 enlisted men missing. A later count located all the missing men. During this period 440 prisoners were taken.

From September 18 to 28 the battalion's front lines were reinforced by over 300 Belgian F.I.[5] These men proved to be invaluable to the unit because of their work behind the enemy lines, sabotage, and information obtained by them through espionage activities. They also served as guards to handle the Nazi sympathizers and prisoners within their districts.

---

[5] It is assumed that the author means the Belgian resistance fighters.

The 99th was attached to 2nd Armored Division's Task Force Stokes in mid-September 1944. The battalion's riflemen rode tanks of the 66th Armored Regiment during the Canal Drive. Members of the Milissen family sit on the medical jeep, while Maria Kuypers and her dog Fikkie look on in the newly liberated village of Boorsheim (Boorsem) around September 17. (Courtesy Karsten Conaert, Mrs. Lisa Jansen collection)

A strong enemy counterattack was reported to be forming to the battalion's direct front the morning of September 20. However, the concentrated and accurate fire of the unit's 81mm mortars, combined with artillery support on the right, and the British artillery on the left, discouraged the attack almost at the beginning and the enemy withdrew to the vicinity of Roermond. For the remainder of the time on the line activity was limited to patrol clashes and artillery fire.

The 99th was relieved by the 7th Armored Division and moved to the vicinity of Eupen in Belgium. On September 30 the unit moved to a bivouac area near Montzen where the men rested, ate hot food, and had entertainment "when it was available." Rain, falling almost incessantly on an area which was a sea of mud and water, made the encampment far from pleasant to the ordinary eye but to the tired men the place was perfect. During the rest period the companies maintained supply, tended and cleaned all equipment, fired new weapons, and adjusted weapons which had malfunctioned in the previous operation.

This life of safety and comparative ease was brought to an abrupt halt on October 12 when the battalion was attached to XIX Corps and moved into Germany near the town of Marienberg. Four days later the unit moved up to Herzogenrath where it was attached to the 30th Infantry Division. On the same day it moved up to Würselen where the mission was to attack and close the gap between the XIX Corps and the VII Corps. The town of Würselen was located just outside Aachen and part of the mission was to close the Aachen–Cologne highway to prevent the Germans from escaping along this important road.

Würselen

The battle of Würselen was, and always will be, a nightmare to the members of the unit who participated in it and were lucky enough to come out of the affair alive. For nine days and nights in the face of a continual and accurate concentration of artillery, mortar, and point-blank tank fire, they attacked daily, were counterattacked and outnumbered, driven from their hard-won positions only to surge back and retake them. The enemy, fighting savagely to keep this last escape route open, threw everything in the book at the Americans during this showdown battle. The men were fighting side by side with other famous fighting units, the 30th Division, the 1st Division, and the 29th Division.

On the first day of the battle, October 16, the 99th moved up to the attack in the face of a murderous crossfire from well-fixed enemy positions. Concrete pillboxes, dug-in-tanks, and many foxholes on the commanding ground gave the enemy a tremendous advantage over the advancing force. In spite of this, the day's mission was accomplished and the objectives secured before nightfall. During the night and in the early morning positions were bombed and strafed by enemy planes. The next day the enemy counterattacked in strength, supported by tanks. Elements of the 99th were temporarily dislodged but succeeded in reorganizing quickly and re-took their original positions. Meanwhile the Germans massed their artillery and zeroed in on all positions, shelling them day and night without pause except when they were attacking. The largest force of enemy artillery in the entire sector attempted to blast open an escape route through the unit, but like their determined counterattacks, they were doomed to failure. Each night enemy fighter planes and light bombers dropping anti-personnel bombs and strafing the 99th's positions added to the din and uproar of bursting shells.

Contact was established with the 116th Infantry and the 18th Infantry Regiment on the following day. Once again, the enemy counterattacked viciously with more men and heavier tanks but this time there was no ground lost. Despite the fact that enemy tanks were firing point-blank into the foxholes they were repulsed with heavy losses. As the Germans withdrew their artillery again opened up, coupling its activity with night visits from the Luftwaffe.

During the entire operation food, water, and ammunition were extremely difficult to deliver to forward areas because of accurate enemy observation. Even during the hours of darkness men bringing up supplies were shelled with amazing accuracy.

To the men lying in the cold, sticky mud of their foxholes under constant attack this was but another grim discomfort with which to cope. Sleep was virtually an impossibility during the nine days, and with the cold rain, incessant shelling, lack of food and water, and perpetual counterattacks, the growing tension was beginning to tell on the hardiest of them.

For the next few days, slight advances were made, and combat patrols were successfully conducted. The original mission had been accomplished and the all-important gap had been closed—it remained closed. For nine full days the 99th had held in the face of the best in determined and desperate German attempts to

Elements of Task Force Hansen arrived in Malmedy on December 17, 1944, relieving Lt. Col. Pergrin's 291st Engineer Battalion. Here markings on the two jeep trailers in the town square that read "1A 991" identify First U.S. Army's 99th Infantry Battalion, and the "D" on the right side confirms Company D, the heavy weapons company, with a M1917 water-cooled heavy machine gun mounted on the dashboard. The half-track to the left could belong to 526th Armored Infantry Battalion, also part of Task Force Hansen. (Courtesy of the Minnesota Military and Veterans Museum)

break out of the Aachen trap. On October 24 at 1730 hours the 99th was formally relieved by elements of the 116th and 119th Infantry of the 30th Division.

After remaining in reserve for a few days the unit moved to the vicinity of Henri-Chapelle, Belgium, for a well-earned rest. The final prisoner count for the period of October 16 to 24 was 105 enemy soldiers. Combat exhaustion constituted the major part of the casualties in this operation; however, there were five officers wounded, two officers killed, 26 enlisted men killed, 40 enlisted men wounded, and four missing.

The 99th Infantry Battalion (Separate) was billeted in the vicinity of Henri-Chapelle, Belgium, from November 1 to 25, 1944. During this period a training program was set up which included firing of weapons, conditioning marches, and training films. This time, due to inclement weather, the men were quartered in farmhouses and barns; steady rain, high winds, and the cold made it far from pleasant. Eating outdoors, most of the time the meal resolved itself into a race to eat the food before it was blown out of the mess kits. Deep mud and manure furnished an interesting mixture for the men to plod through whenever they left the smelly, damp confines in which they were housed. At night the men huddled about the few stoves in the area and vainly tried to dry their shoes or warm themselves in the fire's feeble glow. A few lucky men were allotted passes to Liège or Paris, but the quota was small. All in all, it was definitely "nothing to write home about."

On November 25 the unit was delighted to move to Tilff, Belgium, with a mission to serve as reserve for the Army area against enemy airborne attack, infiltration tactics, and guerrilla warfare. One company was billeted in St. Hubert, Belgium, to guard two enemy ammunition dumps and main supply routes "X," "Y," and "Z." The rest of the battalion conducted foot and mechanized patrols over large areas and guarded vital installations. In many cases separate patrols were stationed and quartered far from the battalion command post and carried their own kitchen, medics, and supplies, each operating as individual units. Work was interesting, quarters usually good, and food plentiful—in short, it was a "good deal."

Ardennes

On the fateful day of December 17, 1944, the Ardennes offensive was launched. The battalion was alerted and proceeded immediately by truck from Tilff to Malmedy to check the advance of the onrushing German hordes in that sector. Task Force Hansen, consisting of the 526th Armored Infantry Battalion, B Company of the 825th Tank Destroyer Battalion, and the 99th Infantry Battalion (Separate), was formed for this mission. Malmedy was completely bereft of Allied forces on Sunday, December 17 except for approximately 60 engineer troops who had chosen to stay and attempt to hold the enemy until combat troops could be moved up.

Into the still, rainy darkness of this almost deserted town moved the 99th, immediately aware of the unfriendly attitude of the inhabitants. From darkened windows and doorways, the pro-Nazi population watched silently, smirking and secure in the knowledge that this mere handful of men could not stop the picked forces of the great von Rundstedt. Had they not been told that this was the turning point of the war? That this was the long-awaited knock-out blow of the disorganized, yet hitherto victorious, rabble that constituted the American armies in the field? Had not the gigantic successes achieved in the previous few hours more than assured them of their ultimate victory? And now a handful of soldiers arrive, uncertain even of the situation, to halt this mighty offensive.

Reconnaissance of all the likely approaches to the city was made at once and the battalion was placed in defense of the city—holding roadblocks and occupying the high ground around the city. The engineers had mined most of the approaches and felled trees across the road to halt the approaching enemy armor, yet these would have proven inconsequential without other support. Needless to say, they welcomed the arrival of the infantry with joy and relief. The first night was spent in digging-in and then crouching wide-eyed in the rain to await the then supposed inevitable attack.

The attack, however, did not immediately materialize and the following day was spent in improving defensive positions and conducting combat and reconnaissance patrols. Because of the congested roads, caused by evacuation of great quantities of materiel and personnel from threatened areas, the arrival of the 117th Infantry Regiment of the 30th Division was held up considerably, but finally came about at 1830 hours on the 18th and the defense of the town was supplemented and coordinated.

Prior to the arrival of reinforcements, minor patrol clashes had occurred. On December 18 at 1645 hours, three Germans with two American prisoners on the front of a jeep approached one of the roadblocks, evidently thinking that the town had already fallen. The jeep had been taken from the 106th Division, one of the units over-run in this vast surprise offensive. As they approached, one of the Americans leaped off the hood and shouted out that the jeep was full of Germans. Before the vehicle could be turned about it was captured and one of the Germans was killed trying to escape. The captured men were members of the 1st SS Division—the enemy had been identified. A few hours later a small enemy patrol was completely wiped out by outposts in a successful ambush. The dead were identified as members of the same SS division.

Later, during the same evening, one battalion of the 120th Infantry Regiment, of the 30th Division, came up to take positions with the 99th in the vicinity of Malmedy. Enemy parachutists were dropped ½ mile west of the town but were never contacted.

On the afternoon of December 19 the rest of the battalion withdrew ½ mile to the northwest of Malmedy while B Company remained in position. The company remaining in position fought off patrols and on the 20th changed positions with B Company of the 120th Regiment. The change was effected during the hours of darkness. B Company of the 99th dug in along the top of a railway embankment about 15 feet in height and covered a front of about 1,000 yards. Directly in front lay a broad field flanked by heavily wooded hills. The field covered an expanse of about 500 yards before it reached the trees and the approaches to it were deep draws in the mountains. The field of fire was excellent, and the entire position was ideal for defense. The riflemen and machine gunners were dug in at the top of the embankment and directly behind them were the light mortars of the weapons platoon protected by the embankment. Back along the edge of the town were heavy machine guns and anti-tank guns trained on the two underpasses which were dynamited, at a later date, to impair passage of enemy tanks attempting to break through. At the time of the initial attack each of the underpasses was covered by an anti-tank gun which was drawn up with its nose practically protruding through this breach in the battalion defenses.

All night the men shivered in their foxholes. An attack was imminent, and the order and information was issued to every man that there would be no retreat as the position could not be lost at any cost. At 0655 hours, on the morning of December 21, the enemy tried its sneak attack; however, the lead columns hit some of the unit's mines and outposts streamed back with the information of the coming attack. The unit did not have long to wait. Across the field streamed enemy tanks and infantrymen firing and shouting as they came. Captured American tanks and enemy tanks poured a heavy fire into unit positions and enemy machine guns opened up from prepared positions in the nearby woods. B Company cut loose with everything it had and the light caused by the flying and ricocheting tracers was enough to light up the surrounding terrain. Several times the enemy tanks and infantry surged to the very base of the embankment to be driven back with grenade and small arms fire. Soon one of the unit's TD guns, with its crew, was knocked out and the enemy tanks, growing bolder, moved back and forth within 20 feet of the embankment pouring point-blank cannon fire into the positions. Enemy machine gunners—paying an awful price—advanced and set up positions directly in front and on the flanks and poured a concentrated fire upon the defenders. The attack was fanatical in its fury. With continual cries of "Surrender or die" the pride of Adolf Hitler died in front of the unit's positions.

Meanwhile, the unit's artillery opened up on the enemy rear with a terrific barrage and the light mortars took a terrible toll in front of the railroad tracks. Reluctantly the enemy withdrew, carrying as many of their dead and wounded as possible from the field and into the protection of the deep woods. During the action three prisoners were taken, two from the famous 11th Parachute Regiment, the other a member of the infamous 1st SS Division. Now the unit knew why the attack had been so fanatical. To take this important town the German High Command had thrown its very best into the gamble—they were good, but not good enough.

In the cold gray dawn the success of the defense of Malmedy by the 99th was counted in the twisted bodies lying in front of the embankment and in the smoking ruins of the tanks knocked out by the two remaining TD guns. The tired men rubbed their red-rimmed eyes, reloaded their guns, and waited for another attack; the German super-troops had many wounds to lick before they came out of the deep woods for another try at the town of Malmedy. The prisoners stated that they had Tiger and Panther tanks as well as much American equipment and that it was their mission to destroy the defending force, destroy the artillery positions, and capture the railroad crossing southeast of Malmedy.

The immediate return attack, however, did not materialize and the remainder of the morning was spent in bringing up ammunition and supplies. Foxholes were improved to resist the coming enemy artillery barrage and probable air attack. The same morning patrols were sent out to determine the damage inflicted upon the enemy and two jeeps and one armored car were retrieved from the field of battle. The flanks of the 99th were secured by patrol action and positions were once more stabilized. More American artillery was moved up plus anti-aircraft, armored units, and tank destroyers. One platoon of the 740th Medium Tank Battalion was attached to Task Force Hansen and remained in the battalion's area. That night 30th Division Headquarters reported the possibility of an airborne attack and another sleepless night was spent on the alert. Meanwhile, enemy artillery incessantly shelled the unit's positions, vainly endeavoring to zero in on the crest of the track and knock out defenses. American artillery answered and the night was alive with shellfire.

The next few days were spent in "sweating out" another enemy attack and dodging the heavy German artillery fire which fell steadily in and around the positions. Enemy air activity was fairly constant, and many dogfights took place overhead. It was during this time that due to poor information large formations of American medium bombers attacked the town of Malmedy on two occasions with devastating results. Many American casualties resulted, and the town was reduced to ruins. Snow had fallen and the cold was severe, adding to the suffering of the tired soldiers on the line.

Christmas Day was spent in frozen foxholes and Christmas dinner consisted of a K-ration. At the time it was impossible to bring up hot food and the report came down that Christmas dinner was being saved until the unit was relieved for a rest period. The strain was beginning to tell on the men. Two weeks had already gone by without sleep, hot food, or being able to wash or shave and still no relief in sight. The Germans were still cutting deep into Belgium far behind unit lines and the information that trickled down to the line was vague and optimistic. Each night furious artillery duels took place over unit positions with American guns hurling as many as 3,000 rounds during the hours of darkness.

At 1600 hours on December 27, Company C kicked off on a commando raid on the enemy-held town of Hedamont.[6] Prior to the surprise attack it was ably supported by an artillery concentration in conjunction with the operation. The attack was successful in as much as the opposing units were positively identified, their positions located, one prisoner taken, and at least 30 Germans killed.

On December 29, Company B raided the town of Otaimont. Supported by artillery and 81mm mortar fire, the men swept into the town with fixed bayonets only to find that the enemy had withdrawn. During the entry of the town a heavy concentration of enemy artillery and machine gun fire harassed the unit. Fortunately, the casualties were extremely light, and the men withdrew in good order, despite heavy Nebelwerfer fire "zeroed in" on the escape route.

From January 1 to 6, the 99th occupied front-line defense positions on the outskirts of Malmedy. Patrol action was common and enemy artillery and rocket fire fairly heavy. Enemy troops who had been wounded in the initial attack or during clashes often came into the lines to surrender because of the intense cold that persisted during this period. During the nights German combat troops dressed in white camouflage suits raided forward positions without success. These nuisance raids together with the cold of the foxholes served to exhaust the men more than did artillery fire or lack of warm food.

On the evening of January 6, the battalion was moved to the vicinity of Stavelot in another sector of the front and its old positions at Malmedy were taken over by elements of the 30th Division. The new positions were in a deep pine woods and the unit's thin line was within shouting distance of German defenses. Combat patrols were continually on the move and clashes with enemy units were frequent. Nights were dark, the woods deep, and heavy snow made action exceedingly difficult on both sides despite the proximity of the positions. The enemy was well supplied with skis and other winter equipment and their sector was heavily fortified. The Jerries had heavy concentrations of Nebelwerfers, mortars, and artillery in direct support of defensive and offensive action. Despite this, the 99th took over offensive action and retained the initiative throughout this phase of the campaign.

The first offensive action in the new positions took place on January 10. Enemy positions were attacked with marked success by the second platoon of A Company and many Germans were killed, wounded, or taken prisoner. Resisting violently with mortar and small arms fire, the enemy was driven from its positions and well-camouflaged foxholes. The attack was in the nature of a raid and after driving the enemy back the unit withdrew.

The second platoon of Company A again attacked the same sector, which the enemy had re-occupied, but with less success, the following day. Hand-to-hand

---

[6] Unclear what location Hedamont corresponds to currently.

fighting followed and the Americans were pinned down by concentrations of enemy mortar, machine gun, and artillery fire. Almost surrounded, the platoon fought back savagely with grenades and bayonets until it had a chance to withdraw with only fairly heavy losses.

The following day elements of the 99th once more attacked in the same sector, Chevofosse, which, according to the prisoners, was strongly outposted and fortified to prevent patrols from infiltrating across the bridge into Thieux. Once again, through a hail of mortar and artillery fire, the Americans attacked and finally knocked out the enemy command post. Again, the Germans resisted fanatically from the comparative security of their well-dug-in positions but to no avail—with grenades and rifle fire they were driven from their holes to be killed or taken prisoner. On the same day, the 119th Infantry Regiment of the 30th Division attacked from the vicinity of Malmedy and across the unit's left front. The battalion supported the attack with heavy machine gun and 81mm mortar fire. During the attack, the enemy heavily shelled unit positions, causing some casualties. The Germans knew the terrain which the unit was occupying, and their artillery was accurate; because the terrain was so heavily wooded enemy mortar and artillery fire was particularly devastating due to tree-bursts.

On January 15 the 517th Parachute Regiment, attacking on the unit's right front, and the 119th Regiment of the 30th Division, attacking on the left front, finally squeezed the 99th out of the front line. Once again, the battalion supported the attack with mortar and heavy machine gun fire, and once again it sweated out the incoming barrage thrown by the desperate enemy. For the next few days, the battalion maintained its positions in this sector and conducted patrols to search out bypassed enemy units or missing men of the unit—both were found.

After 31 days of continuous fighting, living in snowy fox-holes at sub-zero temperatures, and being under unrelenting artillery fire and observation by the enemy, the tired, bearded men of the 99th were formally relieved from their front-line positions on January 18. The danger was over and the forces of von Rundstedt were being hammered back into Germany with appalling losses. Heavy losses had also been suffered by the battalion, but it had not once faltered in its given task; it had fulfilled the mission and had added further praise and glory to its already sterling record.

Then came Tilff and for three days the unit rested, ate hot food, and squeezed out an occasional cognac at the local bar. A bath and a shave were a treat to the men, and they made the most of the opportunity. On the morning of January 22, the battalion boarded a train for the long trip back to the coast of France.

A Regiment is Born

The trip from Tilff, Belgium to Barneville, France meant approximately 74 hours of continuous riding on crowded third-class French carriages. C- and K-rations were eaten, and the men slept on the floor of the car, on the narrow seats, and even in the baggage racks. The fever of speculation ran high. Rumors covered everything from a return trip to the States to an immediate invasion of Norway via Scotland. Regardless of what the future held the men realized that for the present there would be no more of the front line and this fact alone was enough to send their spirits soaring.

Situated on the seashore, the camp at Barneville, France had at one time been an ultra-fashionable summer resort, but little remained of its former splendor. Pretentious homes and hotels were now falling into ruin due to weathering, lack of care, and the ravages of war. The area about the camp was still heavily mined and engineer units repeatedly cleared the surrounding terrain to make way for the training maneuvers which were to follow. For the most part the men were lodged in large tents, but with typical American ingenuity tents were soon equipped with fine floors, wooden doors, windows, and Government Issue stoves. Everyone was comfortable and the food was good. German prisoners were employed each day to improve the living conditions as much as possible.

Just offshore, and easily discernible, was the island of Jersey, one of the two large islands still held by a large and fanatical Nazi garrison. An estimated 20,000 men were holding out there and it was quite possible that an attack on the coastline would be made at any time.

At Barneville, the 99th Infantry Battalion joined another unit, the 474th Infantry Regiment. This regiment was composed of former paratroopers and Rangers of the First Special Service Force, which had distinguished itself at Anzio and in the invasion of southern France. Training here was designed to mold these proven combat units into an aggressive and efficient striking force to carry out the hazardous mission then in the offing. A steady round of tactical problems, firing exercises, use of new assault weapons, and lectures went on week after week. Tanks and other armored vehicles were included in the regiment. The new equipment, training, and added firepower of the unit once again started a wave of rumors among the men as to what was in store for them.

Occasional passes to Cherbourg helped relieve monotony of the training grind; yet after one pass to this ruined city most men felt that they would rather stay in camp. There were no entertainment facilities whatsoever, all bars were off-limits to the American troops, and souvenirs and other articles of no value were exorbitantly priced. Over-crowded with service troops and sailors, the city was nothing but a source of irritation to men of the unit who visited the place.

At approximately 0200 hours, on the morning of March 9, members of the regiment were hauled from their beds and immediately thrown into defensive positions along the beach to repel an attack. The Germans on the islands were raiding the coastline and radar had picked up their approach—but not in time. Crouched in their foxholes, the men listened to the familiar whine of the "incoming mail," silently awaiting the assault. Offshore, German boats shelled the coast. The enemy raiding party struck many miles down the coast at the town of Granville.

They were successful to the extent that they escaped with a small boatload of coal, inflicted a few casualties, and stirred up the coastal defense. Early in the morning, after more than five hours of waiting, the regiment was dismissed and the men filed back to their tents cursing audibly in three different languages. For the next three weeks a state of alert kept the men on their toes with numerous "dry runs" and increased guard. Defensive positions were improved, and had the venturesome Jerries again launched forth from their island retreat they would have met with a warm reception. They had had, however, enough of commando tactics and the alerts were all in vain. Patrol activity was common but there were no more raids. Meanwhile, training continued.

With Patton across the Rhine

On April 2, feeling no regrets, the regiment left Barneville via truck and boxcar for a 500-mile trip to Aachen, Germany, where the final reorganization took place. The battalion made itself comfortable among the ruins, salvaging everything from mattresses to floor lamps, and waited for the next order to move up.

Now temporarily separated from the regiment, the 99th on April 11 traveled 300 miles into southeastern Germany to the town of Hersfeld in the Third Army area. It was the battalion's mission to patrol roads, woods, and towns, cleaning up pockets of SS troops and other German soldiers which had been bypassed by the rapidly advancing American army. Terrain in this section of Germany was ideal for enemy troop concealments and conducive to guerrilla activity. The battalion area was broken down into company areas and the search began. Motorized and foot patrols combed woods, mountains, towns, and roads; the prisoner take was sizeable. In some cases, opposition was encountered but for the most part the superior armament and determination of the searching parties discouraged resistance. The vaunted "Werewolf" and other secret organizations who pledged to die for the fatherland even after Germany was conquered saw the light before they were permanently "blacked out."

The attitude of the German people ranged from arrogance to abject servility. With stoic indifference they watched the searching of their houses, barns, and basements. It was during this period that the men of the battalion saw the horrors of the concentration camps, the slave labor, and the effect of the Nazi machine on the minds of the German people themselves. Due to the thoroughness of the job and the timeliness of occupation, the German people were forcibly reconciled to the fact that they had been completely defeated. Because of the effectiveness of the unit's intelligence section and the excellent performance of the men, many important Nazi Party members, governors, and leaders were captured and dragged from their hiding places. Every system of revolt, sabotage, or other means of tampering with the Allied war effort put into operation by the German High Command at this time of emergency, was effectively stamped out by the completeness of the clean-up in the area allotted the battalion. The roster of prisoners included many big names and without leadership the guerrilla movement failed miserably.

The 99th, which was now bivouacked in a woods about 1 mile from Eiterfeld, left this location on April 21 and arrived at Heroldsbach, Germany, on the same date. Once more each company was allotted sectors and towns to police and the same type of work was carried out. Information was offered by Polish laborers and the German people themselves as to the whereabouts of hidden groups of bypassed Germans. The Germans had a healthy fear of and contempt for the SS organization and now that the danger of retribution had passed, they were happy to inform on it at every opportunity. Heroldsbach lies about 15 miles north of Nuremberg and many prisoners fleeing the fighting in the city were taken. Despite elaborate disguises and excuses, the Nazis were ferreted out of their hideaways by an effective intelligence cross-examination by German-speaking members of the unit.

The German people, victims of the Nazi propaganda machine, now saw through the lies and subterfuges of the past and the desire to resist soon died with their hopes of world conquest. They were a beaten people facing the bitter fact that the cause for which they had sacrificed their sons, brothers, and husbands was irrevocably lost.

Until May 13 the battalion continued doing "clean-up" work. Florsheim, Zeitlarn, Kullmunz, Scheinfeld, and other cities were included in the search. The surrounding country, in the vicinity of the Danube River, the mountains and the forests of Bavaria, all underwent the same search. Vast stores of ammunition, materiel, uniforms, and foodstuffs were uncovered and confiscated. Every trace of military equipment was seized. Nazi personnel were systematically searched out, apprehended, and taken into custody. Thorough de-militarization of these areas was completed by May 11, when units of the Fourth[7] moved in to occupy the territories secured by the 99th Battalion.

Under orders to proceed to Norway the regiment left Germany for the long trip to France via motor convoy on the morning of May 13. The trip required three days of continuous driving through ruined cities and towns, through shell-torn countryside, through crowds of curious people. War was over and the process of rebuilding was already underway. The battalion bivouacked the first night at Aschaffenburg, Germany, the second night at the site of one of the bloodiest battles of World War I, Verdun, France, and the third night they reached Duclair, France, just a few miles north of Rouen. The unit settled temporarily at Camp Twenty Grand in tents previously erected for the purpose of housing troops in transit to the States or elsewhere. The men received good food, occasional passes to Rouen, and relaxed while awaiting further orders.

---

[7] It is assumed that the author means the 4th Infantry Division.

Norway

On May 29 the battalion left Duclair and arrived at Le Havre, France. Here troops immediately boarded LSTs but remained in the harbor until 0800 hours the following day. At this time the convoy, which consisted of 13 LSTs and one cargo ship, got underway for the long trip to Norway via the English Channel and the North Sea. Under ideal weather conditions, the convoy, carrying a powerful task force, made its way slowly through mine-infested waters to the rocky shores of Norway.

To many of the men of the unit the trip to Norway was the successful termination of a hope that had long been in their hearts. The road had been paved in mud and blood yet at long last the dream had materialized. Many others who had wished for this moment now filled hospitals and graves in France, Belgium, and England—it had not been an easy route.

After proceeding up the scenic Oslofjord some elements of the 99th landed at Drammen, Norway at 1200 hours on June 4. The major part of the battalion disembarked at Oslo on June 5, 1945. A large and comfortable camp awaited its arrival. Located at Smestad in the vicinity of Oslo it had formerly been a German anti-aircraft center, complete with air-raid shelters and gun emplacements. Here the 99th settled in comfortable log cabins in an area closely resembling a summer resort in the States, even to an artificial lake on the reservation.

On June 7 the battalion was honored by a request to act as Guard of Honor at the formal return of King Haakon VII to Norway. Despite chilly, drab weather the Guard presented a fine appearance. Resplendent in new battle jackets and bedecked with ribbons and colorful insignia, the men stood rigidly at attention and received the salute and formal inspection of the King and Crown Prince immediately after the King had stepped ashore. For this performance they were personally commended by the Task Force Commander and Lt. Colonel Hansen.

It was the mission of the task force in Norway to remove the major part of 400,000 Germans and to assist the Norwegians in reestablishing themselves again as a free nation. In conjunction with British paratroopers, the unit guarded prisoners, apprehended war criminals who had fled Germany and were attempting to hide out, guarded vital installations, neutralized the extensive military installations which the Germans had painstakingly built, disarmed and shipped out the hundreds of thousands of enemy troops stationed in Norway for the defense of the country, and it assisted the local police in every other conceivable manner. It was a full-time job and the leisure hours were definitely limited. The number of German troops stationed in Norway and the amount of equipment in their possession was astonishing, yet the tremendous task proceeded smoothly. Among the most interesting phases of the mission were the early morning surprise raids which the unit operated on several occasions. Striking unexpectedly in the cold, gray light of early morning, the unit would surround and raid a number of German camps, routing the occupants from

Company A Soldiers Knut Arneson and John Folland, in the foreground, with a Norwegian soldier believed to be Lieutenant Arthur Pevik, of Norway's elite Kompani Linge. The soldiers are near Torggata Bad, the most popular public spa in Oslo, to ensure order as patriotic Norwegians line the sidewalks with flags along the King's motorcade route while the Royal Party is disembarking from landing at the foot of Akershus Fortress at Oslo's harbor on June 7, 1945. (Courtesy of the 99th Educational Foundation)

their beds, and search the entire premises. After extensive questioning by able intelligence officers who were helped by informers, the guilty ones were hustled to prison along with the Norwegian women found in the camps. The raids were conducted with a remarkable degree of efficiency and usually resulted in a successful take of important prisoners.

Many men of the 99th had families and relatives in Norway and furloughs were given to them. For the rest of the men passes, whenever possible, furnished a chance to view this beautiful land and meet its people. A soccer team was organized within the 99th and met some of the top teams of Norway. Parades were held and exhibitions of equipment given for the people of Norway to acquaint them with the American army and the American soldiers. They were invariably received with much enthusiasm, and coupled with the model conduct of the soldiers, Oslo received a favorable and lasting impression of the Americans.

But now the war had ended. Italy, Germany, Japan, and all of the Axis satellite countries had fallen completely and finally before the might of the Allied onslaught. The men of the 99th, tired and sick of war, hate, and destruction, were looking forward to the long trip home. Soon they would leave the Army to take up once more a peaceful pursuit of their regular lives. But regardless of where they went or what they became, they would never forget the 99th and the comrades they had known. For together, these men had gone through fire, death, and hell, and the bonds of friendship and affection forged in that kind of a furnace are never broken or forgotten. They had taken the good with the bad and emerged better men sound in the knowledge that they had always done their part—and well.

CHAPTER TWO

John W. Kelly

Staff Sergeant John W. Kelly wrote a detailed account of the 99th Infantry Battalion (Separate) while the unit was still in Norway. Kelly's book was focused on the specific history of the 99th Battalion's Company D. The 99th was composed of a Headquarters Company as well as four companies (Company A, B, C, and D) that each consisted of men in a tactical-sized unit that was capable of performing battlefield functions independently.

Kelly's work resulted in a bound book, including photographs, that covered the formation of the group, training at Camp Hale, the European campaign, and the time spent in Norway at the end of the war.

Written in a personal and engaging style, Staff Sergeant Kelly's account of Company D provides us tremendous insights into the lives of the soldiers serving in the 99th. The heavy weapons company of an infantry battalion had special missions that gave them mobility that the other 700 members of the battalion could only dream of. For every 81mm mortar, or heavy machine gun section, the company possessed a jeep. Their sections were attached to the other companies in action, and they alone experienced the battlefield from the entire battalion's point of view.

Written for a company of about 150 soldiers, Kelly provides an intimate account of their successes and their tragedies. It provides a perspective from a very different voice on the history of the battalion and its soldiers. The effort and time spent compiling this book is a sign of the cohesiveness and bond that formed within Company D.

The book was printed at Kirste's Print Shop in Oslo, Norway and bound at M. Fredriksen's book binder shop.

John Kelly was born in North Dakota in 1917 and was a Bronze Star recipient.

"Cheering in Norwegian, these soldiers race along an obstacle course at a fort, in the central state of Minnesota, where they are training with the Norwegian avenger unit of the U.S. Army," reads the caption in this photo cleared for release by the Office of War Information. Photos from this series were taken at Fort Snelling October–November 1942. The photos were published as far away as Australia in the Magazine *PIX*, May 29, 1943, perhaps as part of a deception plan to keep up the threat of an Allied invasion through Norway. (Courtesy of the 99th Educational Foundation)

Company D United States Army[1]

Fort Snelling

The 99th Inf. Bn (Sep.) was activated by a War Department Letter on July 10, 1942 at Camp Ripley, Minnesota. Under provisions of that letter, the unit was to consist of personnel who were either native-born Norwegians or who were of Norwegian extraction and had a working knowledge of the Norwegian language.

Organization and training began on August 15, 1942. Emphasis was on physical fitness and on basic infantry training. The battalion was commanded by Captain Harold D. Hansen and the executive officer was Captain David B. Shirley. For

---

[1] John W. Kelly. *Company "D" United States Army*. Oslo, Norway: Kirstes Boktrykkeri, 1945.

the first few days the battalion consisted only of Headquarters Company. As soon as new men and cadres came in, A Company, B Company, C Company, and D Company were formed in that order. The men were new inductees and came from the East Coast, Middle West, and West Coast states, Minnesota and "Brooklyn" predominating.

Training at Camp Ripley consisted mainly of close order drill, manual of arms, and the obstacle course. Many a new recruit sweated out his last civilian hangover going through the obstacle course at Camp Ripley! The course often caused hardened sailors to sweat and swear on a hot summer day.

On October 1, the unit moved to Fort Snelling, Minnesota, where it continued basic training and completed organization. D Company, in which we are here mainly interested, was formed with the following cadre: commanding officer—Captain Erwin L. Anzjon; executive officer—2nd Lt. Howard M. Winholtz; first sergeant—1st Sgt. John J. McGaw; 1st Platoon sergeant—Sgt. Peter J. Elliason; 2nd Platoon sergeant—Cpl. F. Hammerstrom; 3rd Platoon sergeant—Sgt. Raymond O. Enger; supply sergeant— S/Sgt. Arthur Nelson; mess sergeant—S/Sgt. Lars E. Olsen; company clerk—Pfc. Carl E. Nordhagen.

Highlights in training at Fort Snelling were constant and grueling speed and endurance marches. These marches were stepped up and increased in length each day as the men became toughened in and accustomed to the roadwork. It was hard to hit a happy medium, however, because new inductees were coming in every day, and being practically in the Twin Cities didn't help the hardening process to any great extent. However, the old boys in the unit say the speed marches had one good point, and that is, they cleared your system of all excess waste and fixed you up just right for the coming evening downtown at the "Six Twenty Club."

Fort Snelling was the ideal spot to locate a "Squarehead" battalion because half of the Scandinavians in the United States settled in the Twin Cities and the surrounding country. The people were very anxious to entertain their fellow countrymen and invitations to private homes for Sundays and holidays were streaming into the orderly rooms every day.

While at Fort Snelling, the battalion was visited by many officers and notables, chief among whom was Colonel Arne Dahl of the Royal Norwegian Army. Parades were held often, and morale was high. Although the training was stiff, passes were liberal, and the [Twin] Cities offered the best in entertainment.

Camp Hale

On December 17, 1942 the 99th Bn moved from Fort Snelling, Minnesota to the top of the Continental Divide. The station was Camp Hale, Colorado, and it was

Captain Minge, the battalion surgeon, and the battalion dentist, Captain Swenson, at Camp Hale, Colorado, training in early 1943. It was unusual to have a dentist assigned to a 1,000 man battalion, but he was a welcome addition due to his Norwegian heritage and language skills. And, "famously" made the battalion a one-thousand-and-one man unit. Minge and Swenson wear parkas with zippers that replaced earlier parkas with buttons and hoods lined with wolf fur. They also have on bearpaw snowshoes with mukluks, over white camp pants and mitten covers over wool mittens. Both wear the early pattern Polaroid goggles. In the background two reversible mountain tents have their white side out for camouflage. (Courtesy of the 99th Educational Foundation)

located in a valley 9,600 feet above sea level in the Rocky Mountains. Here their most difficult training lay ahead. It is not necessary to state that the men in the battalion were a bit disappointed. You can well imagine the difference in the social and training life of the two camps. However, a new phase of training was entered, new men came in, and soon everything was working smoothly, and training began in earnest. The training at Camp Hale consisted of skiing, snowshoeing, camping, and long treks over frozen terrain. A tremendous amount of clothing and equipment was issued to each man, and most of it had to be carried on a camping trip. This was done by packing it into a mountain rucksack.

When camping out, two men worked together and packed their equipment accordingly. Besides extra socks, mukluks,[2] underwear, sweaters, mittens, and

---

[2] A high, soft boot typically worn in the American Arctic.

shoepacs,[3] one man carried a tent, poles, and one half of the five pounds of winter rations. The other man carried his personal equipment and a small mountain stove, extra gas, the other half of the rations, and a set of aluminum cooking pots. Each man also carried his individual mountain sleeping bag complete with cover. This rucksack weighed approximately 75 pounds when completely packed. Add to this the soldier's rifle, canteen, belt, and ammunition, and then try skiing down one of the rocky, jagged slopes of one of America's most rugged section of mountains, and you will understand what the Winter Warfare Infantryman had to build up to.

The 99th Bn will never forget "Pearl Gulch," "Sugar Loaf Mountain" and the 50-mile endurance [marches] over the mountains that took four days in sub-zero weather and driving snow. Another incident D Company will never forget was the rifle marksmanship course that was fired in January in weather 30 below zero and falling snow. The surprising part of it was the fact that 75 percent of the company made good scores and a very few men failed to make the grade. The marksmanship scores were all generally above average.

While at Camp Hale, weekend passes were plentiful, and some furloughs were issued. The nearest spot of interest was Leadville, and many of the boys will remember the "Silver Dollar Saloon" there. Denver, 130 miles away, and Grand Junction, 100 miles away, were the main spots of attraction. The men worked hard and played hard and only the more rugged could stand the hard training and the high altitude. Many men were screened out for physical reasons and new men took their place.

As spring came on, mountain warfare became the main theme. Rock climbing and mountain climbing as well as physical stamina was stressed. The weapons company of the battalion really received a workout here as the mortars and machine guns were for the most part hand carried and the lightest load for one man was 35lb, plus his individual weapon. Add your lightened rucksack to this and try double-timing in the thin air at that altitude.

One of the highlights of our stay at Camp Hale was the journey to Camp Carson, Colorado. Here the 99th Battalion and another separate battalion received the honor of a personal review by President Roosevelt. Although the review was in April, the uniform for the 99th Battalion was ski boots and mountain jackets. The review parade was a great success and the 99th made a fine appearance.

To Europe

On August 24, 1943, the 99th Battalion moved from Camp Hale to Camp Shanks, New York. Here the battalion was processed, and preparations were made for the trip overseas to an unknown destination. Nearly half of the battalion was from Brooklyn and the evening pass list read something like a page from the phone

---

[3] A warm boot to help prevent frostbite and trench-foot.

directory in one of the phone booths in "Oslo." Besides seeing Brooklyn and New York, the unit found time to have the men outfitted and checked physically for the trip overseas. All too soon the passes to New York ended, and in September 1943, the 99th Battalion left New York Harbor aboard the SS *Mexico*, a 6,000-ton steamer.

The SS *Mexico* was small for the number of men aboard her and no one was too comfortable. The first two days went by happily enough because the sun shone, and the weather was fine. On the third day, the sea became rough, the sky overcast, and we suddenly found that even the veteran sailors missed a meal or two. Those next few days were really rough on some of the men. Almost everyone was a dull green around the gills, and more than half of the meals were not eaten. Even on the roughest days, however, the crap games continued and a fellow would hold on until he either won or lost the dice—dash away and feed the fishes—and come back to take another bet again. Jam sessions were held by the battalion band and everyone tried to make the best of it. About the seventh day, everyone, or nearly everyone, settled down to some extent and the sea didn't cause too much trouble. The main complaint among the men was the food. The food was of good quality, but was poorly or carelessly prepared. However, a good steak could be had for $2.50 any evening below decks, or a bacon sandwich and a cup of coffee could be brought right to your bed for the nominal sum of $1.25 (American money no less). Some of the boys got over their seasickness in a short time if they had any money left after the crap games, but if you were broke, you just let mother nature help you and you sweated it out in the chow line. Many a fellow made it to the steam table and then was forced to hit the nearest port hole and then trudge back to bed.

Taking everything into consideration, the trip was taken pretty well by everyone and on September 15 the SS *Mexico* docked in Scotland and the troops entrained for their permanent station, which was in Wiltshire, England.

On September 16, 1943, the 99th Battalion arrived at Perham Downs Camp near Tidworth, England. Here infantry training was continued and redrawing of infantry equipment to T/E strength[4] was completed.

Orientation

The history as written so far has been very general and has covered the moves and training of the entire battalion. This section will deal mainly with D Company and its men and will contain personal incidents and events that helped to build up and/or tear down our morale while serving with our unit in the United Kingdom.

Several changes had been made in the battalion and in D Company from the time the unit was formed and the time it landed in England. To orient you, the following is listed:

---

[4] T/E refers to a table of equipment. "T/E strength" means re-establishing the equipment of the unit to original status.

Battalion Commander:	Lt. Col. R. G. Turner
	Col. Turner took over command of the battalion in June 1943 at Camp Hale, Colorado.
Bn Executive Officer:	Major Harold D. Hansen
D Company	
Commanding Officer:	Captain Howard M. Winholtz
Executive Officer:	1st Lt. Allen L. Lindholm
1st Platoon Leader:	1st Lt. E. L. Olson
2nd Platoon Leader:	1st Lt. A. K. Stromme
3rd Platoon Leader:	1st Lt. Trygve S. Peterson
1st Sergeant:	1st Sgt. Lars A. Olson
1st Platoon Sgt.:	S/Sgt. Egil Omholt
2nd Platoon Sgt.:	S/Sgt. Maurice R. Hill
3rd Platoon Sgt.:	S/Sgt. Raymond O. Enger
Mess Sergeant:	S/Sgt. Henry E. Emanuelsen
Supply Sergeant:	S/Sgt. Andrew A. Hoiem
Company Clerk:	Cpl. Carl E. Nordhagen

Perham Downs

When D Company arrived at Perham Downs Camp they were assigned two large barracks. The barracks were large two-story brick buildings with a fireplace at one end. The rooms were equipped with lockers, lights, and each floor boasted a shower room and toilets that flushed best if you threw a bucket of water in them. The men had double-tier bunks and the day after we entered the camp everything was in order so that routine inspections could begin immediately. The first week of camp life was spent getting the company equipped to T/E standards of a regular infantry unit. A little training was started, and evening passes were issued. The company was initiated to the English "pub" and mild and bitters at a very respectable place called "The Ram." This pub was a mile away from the barracks, but when "Time Please" was sounded at closing time, and the boys began streaming home, "Roll Me Over in the Clover"[5] could be heard all over the countryside. Many of the men didn't like English beer at first, but they seemed to manage anyway, and since that time many of them have remarked, "I wish I had a mug of mild and bitters right now!"

Soon after reaching camp the 48-hour passes were started and London was the main center of interest to the average G.I. Passes were issued every day of the week to a certain percentage of the company and the monotony of training was greatly relieved in that manner. Training consisted of hikes, tactical problems, weapons

---

[5] "Roll Me Over in the Clover" is thought to refer to a racy song sung after leaving the bar.

familiarization, and general infantry training. An obstacle course was soon built, and everyone ran, crawled, jumped, climbed, and sweated through that several times a week.

Soon after reaching Tidworth, a new T/O[6] for the 99th Infantry Battalion (Sep.) was received and many new ratings came into effect. Platoon sergeants were raised to tech sergeants, section sergeants were made staff, and in the mortars the squad leaders also made staff. The machine-gun squad leaders remained sergeants and feelings ran high between the MG and mortar platoons. The ratings were not automatic, so a few were submitted and approved each week. In conjunction with this change in T/O, 1st Sgt. Lars A. Olson was transferred to HQ Company, promoted to master sergeant, and assumed the duties of sergeant major of the 99th Bn S/Sgt. Maurice R. Hill was acting first sergeant of Company and Sgt. Andrew Hall took over the 2nd platoon. Corporal John Kelly, formerly on SD[7] with HQ Company, took over the first section of the mortar platoon.

In December, seven-day furloughs to any place on the British Isles were begun. A certain percentage [of soldiers] left from the company each week. Most of the men spent their furloughs in Scotland, and some went to London. Scotland was the favorite of most of the company after a few of the men had been there. Edinburgh and Glasgow were the main cities visited. In spite of 48-hour passes and seven-day furloughs, training went on as usual and night problems and compass courses were common events. The compass courses usually ended up with the compass bearer getting lost or the leader of the procession calling back to find out if anyone had seen a tree with a piece of paper on it.

A part of our training area had a large hill which was named "Windmill Hill." There is no accurate record to show how many times that hill was taken or lost, but there isn't a man in the company who will ever forget that hill. One day the company would go into the woods at the top of the hill and dig in a defensive position that just "Could not be taken." Then the next day, they would dig in at the bottom of the hill, wait until the right moment, and then storm and take "Windmill Hill"! The enemy would be another company or just one of the platoons of the company. They would carry flags to indicate automatic weapons or a certain number of men. If they came too fast, someone would call to them to hold it up or signal that they had started too soon. Often it was very hard to visualize the situation as it was intended, but when the company did see action, the training received in England and in the States was brought to good use and greatly appreciated.

On January 13, 1944, D Company entrained and moved to their second and happiest home in the UK.

---

[6] Table of Organization, which is a listing of the organizational structure.

[7] Presumed to mean Special Duty.

Glanusk Park Camp

On January 14, 1944, D Company came to Glanusk Park Camp in Brecknockshire, South Wales. The camp was situated on the grounds of an old picturesque castle belonging to Lord Glanusk. The River Usk ran near the castle and the entire valley was like a picture postcard view. The nearest town was Crickhowell and eight miles away was Abergavenny. The company was assigned 10 Nissen huts in the lower righthand corner of the camp. Officers and office personnel lived in the castle and this was also company and battalion headquarters.

The men were very disappointed when they first saw Glanusk Park Camp. The mud was from 6 inches to a foot or more deep and the huts had recently been used to house sheep. Drainage was the first problem tackled and the huts had to be thoroughly cleaned out and washed. Stoves also had to be located and set up. The first night was a dreary one, but the next few days saw a great change in Glanusk Camp. Everyone set to work with a will, and soon the huts had shelves and small lockers built in, tables and washstands built, and an atmosphere of home could be felt when a radio or two turned up. The sun shone for a short time and soon the mud and water was drained away, and lo and behold—there were roads there all of the time, but they had been flooded with mud and water. Training was started and inspections went on as usual. Class "B"[8] passes were issued, and the battalion furnished transportation to the fair city of Abergavenny.

Abergavenny is a quaint little Welsh town nestled in a beautiful valley. A part of this same valley was used as the setting for the movie *How Green Is My Valley*. The city has a population of better than 4,000, and the main streets had a good number of pubs. The town hall was the social center, and two dances a week and the stage shows and operas were held there. The people were very friendly, and since we were the only large unit stationed near there most of the time, the town was pretty well taken over by the 99th. Two hospitals were near the city and some of the boys from the company found the nurses very interesting. The dances at the town hall were very good and the crowds larger each week. Music was usually furnished by GI bands, but the city boasted a good civilian band and soon they were playing all of the American hit tunes.

Bicycles were the chief means of transportation in England and each evening, after retreat, the road to Abergavenny was filled with 99ers pushing their bikes for all they were worth to get into town to get the first few scotches that were in stock for the evening. Many of the soldiers had girlfriends, but these "dates" were forced to wait until the pubs had all been visited and the scotch finished up. The boys would then pick up their dates and beer would be the stimulant for the balance of the evening. Some of the girlfriends became wise and would wait at one of the

---

[8] A pass that permitted absence between retreat and reveille.

first pubs. This halted the soldier's progress and he was unable to move very fast from one pub to the next and his whiskey ration would be very short that evening.

In the other direction from camp was the little village of Llangynidr. This was only a wide place in the road and the main points of interest were the Red Lion pub, and the dance hall. The Red Lion was very popular for its good beer and the large quantities of it on hand most of the time. The dance hall was small, but D Company was always represented in strong force whenever a party was held there. Each Sunday evening a social gathering was held at the Llangynidr Parsonage. An evening of music and games was highlighted with a lunch of coffee and numerous tarts, cakes, and sweets. D Company had a large group of faithful "social members" whose main interest in the program was the lunch served at 11 o'clock. The people of this small parish were the very spirit of democracy, and the men who visited at their homes and attended social gatherings all agree that these simple village folk did more to establish good relationships between American and British peoples than years of statesmanship could have done. They did their very best to make our stay in England more pleasant, and we owe them a world of tribute.

The training in Glanusk Park Camp was hard and thorough. Platoon, company and battalion problems were carried on almost every day of the week. A part of our training area was a marsh on the top of a ridge of high hills. There was every type of weather in the book on the top of those barren hills. The wind would blow from all four directions in less than 20 minutes and no matter what type of clothing the men would wear, they would be chilled to the bone in a few minutes. Night problems were the common thing and woe be unto the man who showed a lighted match or cigarette on one of these exercises. Forced marches were weekly excursions and tests were given for eligibility for the Expert Infantryman's Badge. Although not a man in D Company fell out of a march and not a man failed to make the necessary points in the tests, Expert Infantryman's badges were not issued while we were stationed in England.

Army life in Glanusk went on smoothly even though the training was monotonous. Passes and furloughs were liberal, and the morale was quite high. Promotions were steadily being made and changes in the company kept everything and everyone on the alert. The third platoon had a shake-up almost every week and the only man who was not moved or affected in some way by the changes was Cpl. Svend (Pop) Lemche. "Pop" remained instrument corporal[9] through it all and proved his ability later when the unit saw combat on the continent.

On January 26 [1944] an accident saddened the spirit of the company. Private Robert Fostvedt and Pfc. Sverre Yri were standing guard at number two gate. An engineer unit had been working on a building in the area and one of the truck drivers

---

[9] Instrument corporal was the person in charge of the aiming and surveying instruments for mortars and machine guns in Company D.

turned in at the gate while traveling too fast. The truck skidded into the gate post and knocked it down. Pfc. Yri managed to leap out of the way, but Pvt. Fostvedt was pinned under the heavy concrete post. One of his legs was badly crushed and the bone was broken in several places. "Bob," as he was called, was in the second platoon and was a great favorite among the men. He was sent to the States and is recovering in a hospital in his native state of New Jersey.[10]

***

One of the necessary, but seldom mentioned groups in any company is the cooking staff. Besides the mess sergeant S/Sgt. Henry Emanuelsen, we have the following men: T/4 Oscar Kleven, T/4 Melvin Bratmoe, T/5 Walter Waller, T/5 Norman Gilbertsen, Pfc. Fritzjof Karlsen, Pfc. Peter Christofferson, and Pfc. Leonard (Tiny) Larson. These cooks and helpers have served us faithfully and long and the food is always well prepared. Good food is necessary to good morale, and the average good morale of Company D can be attributed to a great extent to the meals prepared by this hardworking cooking staff.

On March 17 S/Sgt. Sembrick entered the 279th station hospital with a lung ailment and was later sent to the States. S/Sgt. John Kelly took over company headquarters and managed to hold that position for exactly two weeks. Cpl. Kenneth Gilbertson was then transferred from the mortar platoon, made sergeant, and was reconnaissance sergeant until the company reached Germany. Pfc. Magne Birkeland remained in charge of communications and was promoted to sergeant. The duties of a company HQ man were not very clearly defined while we were in England. Except for the non-coms and office workers, company headquarters was a place to put privates who more or less didn't fit into any of the other platoons. These men were used as enemy detail on problems or for any other detail that might come up. However, when the company eventually saw combat, these same "Odd Lot" men proved to be very good soldiers and in some instances were worth their weight in gold. Two company headquarters men were transferred to the rifle companies. They were Pvts. Trygve Anderson and Mathias Vikse. They were excellent riflemen and good soldiers in combat.

Saturday afternoons were devoted to athletics and sports. D Company had a winning softball team and had several players on the battalion soccer team. The highlight of the softball season was when D Company defeated the officers' team in a fast and heated game. Bob Fostvedt was a very good player and Hilton Lecy pitched a fast curveball. The regular lineup of the softball team was as follows: catcher—Milnor Olson; pitcher—Hilton Lecy; 1st base—Vance Gjelton; 2nd base—Maurice Hill; 3rd base—Donald Anderson; shortstop—Emil Krzykowski; roving fielder—Raymond Enger; left field—Bob Fostvedt; center field—Arthur

---

[10] Robert Fostvedt lived until 2002 when he passed away at the age of 78.

Fredricksen; right field—Merlin Hollen. Maurice Hill doubled in catching and Emil Krzykowski assisted in pitching. Albert Knudsen and Henrik Kathenes also assisted in the outfield. Volleyball was played to some extent, but never became as popular as softball.

While at Glanusk Park, three new officers were added to our company. They were 2nd Lts. John Ottis, Harold Vindal and Walter Thorwald. These officers were all assigned to the third platoon as section leaders of the 81mm mortars. This addition of officer personnel made the third platoon a "little company" within the company.

On April 17, the battalion was alerted for movement, but the move was not made until April 30. On April 30 the following men were transferred to Special Duty as First Army guards: Sgt. Morris C. Koppang, Pfc. Sven H. Rodne, Pfc. Kaare A. Lorentsen, Pfc. Inge A. Foss, Cpl. Arthur S. Fredricksen, Pfc. Roy Seierson, Pfc. Ben Karlsen, Pvt. Finn Gjertsen. These men did not return to the 99th Bn again until after the Ardennes offensive in Belgium.[11]

On April 30, the battalion left via rail from Glanusk Park, the garden spot of the British Isles, and arrived at Ludlow bivouac Area. The trip was uneventful and aside from the usual number of rumors, everything was quiet and peaceful.

Ludlow Bivouac Area

The bivouac area at Ludlow consisted of a number of pyramidal tents. The men were crowded eight to a tent and slept on canvas cots. Training went on as usual and evening passes were issued to the city of Ludlow, ½-mile away, and to Leominster, 10 miles distant. Several pubs were at convenient spots along the way, so everyone managed to find a spot for recreation. Here morale took a slight slump, because Abergavenny was quite a little distance away. Most of the fellows took their 48-hour pass there, and some of the smoother talkers even had their girlfriends come to Ludlow to see them. The stay at Ludlow was rather dull and uneventful. Training continued at a little faster pace and everyone waited for something to break. On May 27, Sgt. Morris Koppang came back to the company and S/Sgt. Hollen took his place with the First Army SD Guard. They were stationed at Bristol, England at this time.

On the morning of June 6, the 99th was out on one of their many tactical problems. The news of the invasion came over the air and everyone was excited. Cpl. Finn Flesche of the 2nd Platoon was stewing around and was heard to remark, "The Greatest Show on Earth and we cannot even buy a ringside seat!!" Was he

---

[11] Estimating that 52 in total from the 99th Battalion, including eight from D Company were used as guards in the First Army. Sometimes referred to as "Swedish Guards." Of all that the 99th provided, some came back to the 99th and some remained.

kidding or ready for a Section VIII?[12] Now everyone knew that something was about to happen, and the men settled down to wait for the move to come.

On June 11 the battalion left Ludlow by train and arrived that afternoon at Uffculme, Devonshire. Here the unit was billeted in a staging area where it remained for only three days. On June 14 a move was made to Plympton, England, and here the final staging and outfitting process was completed. Nerves were a little more tense and everyone had a certain dreamy look in his eye. Was it Norway at last? No one knew, but the rumors were flying as fast as usual. Finally, on June 17, D Company boarded the SS *John Henry*, a Liberty ship, and headed out across the channel. Words will never be able to describe the thoughts and feelings of the men on board that ship. There was very little joking and laughter, and soldiers who before had seemed just punk kids suddenly seemed to have grown up and were willing and eager to take a man's share of the load and responsibility. Although D-Day was 10 days past, everyone knew that danger and hard work lay ahead. Daylight faded to darkness and the mission for which we had trained and worked for so long had begun. On June 19 the shores of France hove into view and the thunder of artillery could be plainly heard. The sea was very rough, and the battalion could not be unloaded until June 22.

On the morning of June 22, all men and vehicles were transferred from the Liberty ship to LCIs. The LCIs went in on the beach as far as possible, but the men were forced to wade ashore in about 2 feet of water. The only bit of excitement occurred when an unfortunate soldier stepped in a hole and went feet over teakettle, duffle bag and all! So wading, sloshing, and sweating under a heavy load and much clothing, the 99th Bn landed in Normandy and began the steep climb up the slope past Omaha Beach where only a few days before many had given their all that others might live. The grim business of war was now at hand and a sober realization of it could be seen in each man's eyes as he gazed row upon row upon row of new white crosses marking the graves of comrades who had fallen on Omaha Beach.

Normandy

After climbing the higher ground from Omaha Beach, the unit marched about 2 miles and bivouacked near Colombières, France. This was only a small village, but the ravages of war and invasion could be plainly seen. Everyone pitched tents, dug slit trenches, camouflaged their work, and prepared supper. Then began the souvenir hunt. Everything German became of interest and of value to the possessor. Later, these articles were thrown away as better and more interesting ones were found. The next few days were spent in minor preparations and physical conditioning while the

[12] A category of discharge in the military, used if a service member is deemed mentally unfit to serve.

unit was awaiting assignment. Some classes were held in familiarization of captured German weapons and equipment. The front was only a few miles away and everyone expected to go there in the near future. On June 29, the 99th Bn was taken by truck to Cherbourg where their first real mission was to begin.

The city of Cherbourg had officially fallen only the day before the arrival of the 99th Battalion. Two forts out on the bay were still holding out, and for two days a continuous artillery and naval bombardment was directed on these positions and the dive-bombers bombed and strafed incessantly. Dead littered the streets and the waterfront positions. American wounded were being evacuated as quickly as possible and the few remaining civilians began crawling out of their basements and air raid shelters. The city was not badly damaged except for the outskirts and the waterfront areas. D Company was billeted in a large school building which had formerly been used by the Germans, and patrol and guard duty was begun at once.

Since the combat troops had pushed on after the retreating enemy, the 99th was the only tactical unit[13] in the city of Cherbourg. Many of the enemy were still in hiding and several positions and warehouses required guarding. Besides motorized patrols, D Company held eight guard positions ranging from big naval installations to U-boat warehouses and underground tunnels. They also had one very important post where several barrels of cognac and wine were stored in a cave. Each post required eight men, including the NCO, and they remained on duty for three or four days before changing to a new post. There was an abundance of German food at the posts and the men enjoyed their work very much. Many souvenirs were collected, and everyone did a good job. The section sergeants of the company were in charge of the motorized patrols and worked out of the company CP. The posts were widely scattered and quite a bit of sniping was done by the Jerry in the early dawn or just before dark. Luckily no one was hurt and the only near hit was a bullet passing through the hood and fender of the jeep driven by Pfc. Odd Lilleheil. Nerves were rather tense the first few days, but everyone became used to it and soon the boys were testing out everything they found just to see how it would act.

One day, Cpl. Lemche tested a German "Egg" grenade in a naval gun position. When he pulled the cord, the thing began to fizz, and he hastily tossed it away. It did not clear the concrete wall and the grenade fell into the 8-foot emplacement with him. As the door was on the opposite side of the enclosure, Lemche merely turned his back to the "Egg," hunched his shoulders against the wall, and waited for things to happen. The grenade exploded and "Pop's" helmet soared several feet into the air, and out he walked with both hands supporting the seat of his pants. He was shaking his head to clear his ears but was otherwise unhurt!

Pfc. Sverre Yri (Two Brew Stew) was the first unofficial casualty in the company. He was trying to detonate a 20mm German AA shell by firing at it with his carbine.

---

[13] An organization of military troops designed to function specifically as a single unit during combat situations.

He was about 15 paces from the shell and behind a concrete wall. The first two shots missed, but the third hit the point of the shell and detonated it. "Two Brew" ducked, but not fast enough to escape the shell fragments. He received a fairly deep gash in his left forearm, but of course never reported the incident to the medics. (No Purple Heart—no points.)[14] Several Renault light tanks were found around the area and were used for post inspection. This tank was low and speedy and was ideal for running around from post to post over hand grenades, helmets, railroad tracks, and sand dunes!

On July 9 the battalion sadly marched out of Cherbourg and headed up the long hill out toward the front lines. The lines had advanced several miles by this time and our next mission was to patrol and guard the areas recently taken. The new bivouac area was established in a field near Hau de Haut,[15] France.

The new area extended from Cherbourg to within a few miles of Saint Lô and covered the entire Cherbourg Peninsula. Vehicular patrols were sent out every four hours on a day and night schedule. About half of the company would be on patrol duty at a time and the other half would train in hedgerow fighting. The stay here was rather uneventful and the long road marches and problems became very tiresome. Quite a few of the men wanted to see action and felt that we were getting nowhere fast. Later they found we were getting places too soon!

On July 24, we packed our duffle bags and marched several miles to our next area which was a German rest camp at Teurthéville-Hague.

The former German rest camp was like a vacation spot to the battalion as we were billeted in barracks and had springs and mattresses to sleep on. Here we joined the 2nd and 5th Ranger Battalions and became a part of the Provisional Ranger Group under Colonel Slappy. Then began a period of intensive training and tactical problems on hedgerow tactics. The Rangers had landed on D-Day and we received many good pointers from them. We learned later, however, that no amount of advice will ever compare with a few hours of actual combat.

While the unit was a part of the Ranger Group, the main training was tank and infantry coordination. This was the first time we had received training on hedgerow busting, and although the work was hard, it was interesting, and everyone buckled down and learned as much as possible. Later the men were to prove the worth of that period of training.

The days at Teurthéville-Hague went swiftly by and on August 7 the 99th was alerted again and moved out by truck on a new mission.

---

[14] During World War II, points were awarded as follows: one point for each month in service in the Army; one additional point for each month in service overseas; five points for each campaign; five points for a medal for merit or valor. With enough points a soldier could be sent home.

[15] The author may have meant Hameau de Haut.

The Race Across France

On the evening of August 7, the new bivouac area was reached, and the company dug in and settled down for the night. The campsite was a wooded hillside ½-mile NW of Le Mensil-Herman. Here we made last-minute preparations and awaited our new assignment, as we had been released from the Ranger Group upon our departure from the German camp area. On August 11 the traveling orders were received, and the battalion departed by truck to join the 2nd Armored Division.

The convoy left in the early evening and proceeded toward the front lines. The road had many sharp curves and long grades making progress fairly slow. About midnight the unit encountered its first air attack. The main part of the convoy was passing through the village of Barcoy, France,[16] when a single plane was heard droning overhead. There was no mistaking the sound of it and soon several AA guns opened up on it. The moon was bright, and vision was good. Soon clusters of flares came floating down and the convoy immediately stopped. The troops were being hauled by a QM unit and the drivers and assistant drivers for the most part bailed out before the trucks stopped rolling. As the heavens burst into light from the flares, trucks rolled into each other, GIs fell or stumbled out, and everything was more or less in confusion. Some hit for the dirt while others stood up to see the sight. Soon several planes could be heard and then the swish, swish of the bombs came whispering through the air. Not a man in the unit will forget that night or the feelings he had for those few minutes. The AA guns sent up red streaks into the air all around, the flares continued to come down, planes droned and strafed overhead, the bombs whispered in the air, and finally the whole earth seemed to rock as they detonated and shrapnel flew in all directions. The bombs were dropped in clusters and hit and exploded at spaced intervals. Each one came nearer to your position and it seemed as if they would never stop. When they did, you took a quick breath and thanked God that there hadn't been one more bomb in that cluster.

A few minutes after the bombers came the AA batteries were almost silenced and it seemed that the end was near. The planes went up and down the roads and strafed and bombed at will. Two men from D Company were stunned by the concussion of a bomb landing close by, and Pfc. Daniel Holm was wounded in the chest from a piece of flying shrapnel.

After what seemed an eternity, the planes departed, and everyone gathered himself together as much as possible and the trucks were again loaded. Everyone was wide awake, but the rest of that trip was the quietest in the history of the 99th. Not a man had a word to say and everyone was thankful that no more damage had been done. In the early morning the new camping area was reached and everyone dug in.

---

[16] Barcoy doesn't show on modern maps, but Barcoy would have been a small town between Teurthéville-Hague and Barenton along the 160 km route they took that night.

The bivouac area chosen was a group of hedged fields near Barenton, France. Here the battalion rested for two days and then made a short move to a wooded hillside ½ mile SW of Barenton. Here we met the 41st Inf. Regt. of the 2nd Armored Division and we became a part of their combat group B. While in this area we received additional equipment and received instructions and training on the setting up and manning of roadblocks. Mobility and mechanized coordination was stressed. The 99th was now attached to one of the best armored divisions in the United States Army.

On August 19 the unit moved to a bivouac area ½ mile south of Essay, France. Here we began patrol work and set up roadblocks on the flanks of the advancing armor. On August 20, a detail from D Company was about to leave the bivouac area on a roadblock mission and one of the saddest accidents in our experience occurred. American M3 anti-tank mines had been placed on the main roads leading into the battalion area. A guard was placed at each of these spots and it was his duty to see that the mines were pulled away to allow vehicles to pass. As the detail approached the mined area, the guard discovered too late that the lane cleared was too narrow. The rear dual[17] of the first truck struck a mine and the truck was blown up. One officer and eight EM were injured. Pfc. Gustav I. Galschodt died on the way to the collecting point. Cpl. Orin P. Semingson died in the hospital. Pfc. Palmer Johnson died a few days later. Pfc. Norwald K. Moksvold, Pfc. Edward K. Iversen, and Pfc. Leonard E. Larson were injured and evacuated. Pfc. Karl K. Kjendal and Pfc. Harold E. Abrahamsen were slightly injured but remained on duty. Captain Howard M. Winholtz received shrapnel wounds and was evacuated. The guard, who was from another company, was killed instantly. T/Sgt. Andrew A. Hall, T/5 Arne Thomassen, and Pfc. Ivan Hennings led the men in the rescue work and were later awarded the Soldier's Medal.[18] All three men were in the truck when it struck the mine but recovered quickly and did a wonderful job in aiding others who were injured or stunned. The truck immediately burst into flames and the heat and smoke of the fire together with the dust and fumes of the explosion made rescue work both difficult and dangerous.

On August 22 another move was made and the 99th Battalion prepared for a combat mission. D Company was now commanded by Lt. Allen L. Lindholm and Lt. Trygve S. Peterson was executive officer and also mortar platoon leader. Roadblocks were set up and nerves became tense. Sgt. Olaf M. Aarseth was evacuated and Pfc. George Skarsvog received a shrapnel wound in the right cheek from an 88 airburst.

---

[17] A vehicle with four tires on the rear axle is sometimes called a rear dual, commonly referred to as a dually.

[18] The Soldier's Medal is awarded to any individual who, while serving in the Armed Forces of the United States, or any citizen of a friendly foreign nation while working with the United States Army, is recognized for heroism not concerning a direct encounter with an enemy.

On the morning of August 25 the battalion moved out in combat formation and the men knew that the moment had at last arrived. Words will never be able to express the thoughts in the minds of the soldiers as they marched warily up the road leading to the city of Elbeuf on the Seine River, which was to be the objective. B and C Companies were in the lead with A Company in reserve. The first platoon of D Company supported B Company and the second platoon supported C Company. The mortar platoon remained in the reserve position to support the battalion front. Everything went smoothly until about 10 o'clock and then the "Screaming Meemies" began coming in. There is no sound in the world that can compare with their eerie, throaty wail as they come through the air, and their blast effect upon detonation is terrific. As the battalion advanced, mortar and artillery began coming in and a few scattered shots from snipers could be heard. Aside from the heavy stuff, very little resistance was encountered until the outskirts of the city itself were reached.

The city of Elbeuf was situated on the west bank of the Seine and nestled in a small valley with a steep hill directly on the west of it and a longer hill on the north. The 99th entered the city from the west coming down over the steep, thinly wooded hill under full view of enemy observation from the north. As soon as the troops reached the first streets and crossed the railroad tracks, weapons positions were taken up and the streets at right angles to the river were covered. Heavy and light mortar began falling, enemy tanks started moving and shooting, and the fun began.

The water-cooled heavy machine guns of D Company set up positions at the main street intersections and gave covering fire to the advancing rifle platoons. After the first street was taken, the enemy tanks began roaming back and forth on the two main streets near the river and they would fire with machine gun and 88s, up each side street. The riflemen would scoot from one doorway to another and would flatten out against the wall or doorjamb, each time a tank would appear at the street corner. Then the three TDs supporting the battalion came upon the scene and began working into position. Soon a Mark IV tank came into view and the heavy machine guns opened up on it. The tank paused for a moment as though the driver was confused and just as it gathered speed again, it received a direct hit from the nearest TD. The Jerry tank skidded a little and burst into flame. The hatches flew open and Jerries began to pile out and run for cover. During this action the machine guns of the second and first platoons kept a steady stream of fire on all side streets and received credit for assisting in destroying two more tanks and three armored vehicles.

While the tank action was taking place in the center of the city, the 81mm mortars had been set up on the south side of the hill overlooking the town and the north hill was zeroed in with white phosphorus shells. This hill seemed to be the Jerry observation point and heavy mortar and Screaming Meemies were raining down into the town and holding up the advancing rifle platoons. After the mortars registered on the crest of the hill, an area target was fired by six mortars and repeated four times, thereby covering an area 400 yards by 400 yards. HE[19] light was fired and as the hill was fairly well wooded, tree bursts covered the area thoroughly. In all, 235 rounds were fired and the enemy action from that point ceased immediately and was not resumed again that day.

After mortar and rocket support had been stilled, it seemed that the Germans became confused and they left vehicles and tanks standing with motors running and scurried for the nearest cover. By midafternoon, almost all resistance had been stilled and prisoners were rounded up and areas searched. The defense of the city was set up and the battalion CP was established in a building near the center of the city. This building had a courtyard with a high wall, and it was used to hold prisoners. The 81mm mortars were brought into town and set up around the railroad station which happened to be the only distinct landmark in the entire area. The courtyard was so small that only four of the mortars could be dug in and they zeroed in on the main approaches of the city.

That evening everyone was lighthearted and felt that the first mission wasn't too bad at that. Although the rifle companies had had a few casualties from mortar fire, D Company had escaped without a scratch. Preparations were made for the night and all seemed to be well.

The following morning the weather was clear and warm and not a sound could be heard from the enemy across the river. An early breakfast was prepared, and the defense of the city was checked. Two OPs were chosen for the 81mm mortars and telephone communication was established. All was well and everyone settled down to sweat out the day. At approximately 10 o'clock, things began happening. [German] 88s began coming in first and then heavy mortar and heavy artillery. It seemed that the enemy had every spot in town covered, and a soldier could not cross a street without drawing down fire. This kept up incessantly all day and the toll was heavy. Early in the day, Cpl. Peder Aadland, an 81mm gunner, received a direct hit from an 88 shell and was killed instantly.

A little later the battalion CP received two direct hits and was blown up badly. The battalion commander, Lt. Colonel Turner, was seriously wounded and many of his staff received shrapnel wounds. The following persons from D Company were wounded at this same time: Lt. Allen L. Lindholm, Lt. Harold M. Vindal, 1st Sgt. Maurice R. Hill, Pfc. Bjarne T. Jorstad and Pfc. Ivan Hennings Jr.—Pfc. Jorstad was instantly killed and Lt. Lindholm later died of wounds.

Battalion command was taken over by Major Harold D. Hansen and company command of D Company was taken over by Lt. Trygve S. Peterson. T/Sgt. Andrew

---

[19] High Explosive.

W. Hall became acting first sergeant and the company was reorganized as much as possible.

While this was going on, the 81mm OPs were having troubles too. Artillery fire had been called for and it was received, right on and around the forward OP. The building stood at the foot of the destroyed bridge about 15 yards from the river. Two heavy artillery barrages came in and landed on the bridge and on the bank between the river and the OP. A call was relayed through the Bn CP for an increase in range of 2,000 yards. A report later came through that the artillery was being fired at extreme range and no assistance could be given.

So, the day wore on and at 1800 hours relief came in the form of Canadian troops who were to take over and hold the town. Shells were coming in as thick as ever and the move out of the city and up the steep hill to the west was one long nightmare. A zig-zag path was followed, and it seemed the enemy knew the exact pattern because shells burst to the front, rear, and on both sides as we scrambled, crawled, and ran up the steep wooded hill. Although many had close calls, D Company escaped without any further casualties. That evening, the company came back to their rear bivouac area where they had left the trucks and kitchen personnel. The men came back weary, tired, and sad. Although they were now seasoned combat troops, they could not quite accustom themselves to the thought that they had seen their comrades fall, never to rise again. The men sat around for a time, smoked, rested, looked at each other, and visualized the places left vacant by their wounded comrades. Very few words were spoken, and dusk settled upon a company of sadder but wiser men.

East of the Seine

About noon on August 27, the battalion made a short move and roadblocks were set up. Three villages were searched, but the enemy had withdrawn, and no action was encountered. On August 30 a short move was made to Willers En Artries[20] and that village was secured. Then followed several days of short moves and bivouacs, but no action was encountered. The 2nd Armored was advancing at a fast pace and the 99th merely followed in reserve. On September 8, the battalion moved into the city of Mons, Belgium and stayed there two days. A short move was then made back to Valenciennes, France, and here a permanent station was established, and the mission was to patrol the area and search for German stragglers and small units hiding out in the wooded hills. Many reports came in from civilians and the battalion was kept busy searching for reported German soldiers who seemed to have vanished just before the arrival of the American troops. However, the quarters were very good, and the rest was very welcome after the long period of moves and outdoor

---

[20] It is not clear what modern location is meant by this reference.

bivouacs. The people of Valenciennes were overjoyed at the German departure and cognac and wine flowed freely.

On September 13, the battalion left Valenciennes and followed the 2nd Armored spearhead once more. On September 15, the unit bivouacked at Mechelen, Belgium and prepared for another mission. Patrols were sent out and the area northwest of the canal was searched for enemy soldiers. Strong enemy positions were reported between the canal and the river in the vicinity of Mechelen and up to Lanclare[21] and Stockheim. On the morning of September 17, the attack was begun by C Company and continued throughout the day. The mortars and machine guns were hand carried and the going was tough. Tanks from the 2nd Armored spearheaded the drive and the riflemen rode the tanks and worked together with them very well.

At the beginning of the drive, the second section of the 3rd platoon and the 1st platoon of D Company were in support of C Company and crossed on the vehicle bridge about 5 miles below Mechelen. The 2nd platoon and the 1st and 3rd section of mortars set up in a little village about midway between the two points on the friendly side of the canal. The heavy machine guns were set up on the bank of the canal and were ready to cover the opposite bank and the open terrain on the other side. As the tanks advanced along the canal, enemy infantry could be seen running back into the woods. The 81mm mortars were controlled from an OP in the tower of the village church. When the Germans left their positions to retreat into the woods, the machine guns on the bank opened up on them and the mortars began zeroing in. This confused the Jerries and a general retreat was begun to a high stone wall at a point about a ½ mile above the village. As mortar fire was being directed to this point, 88s began dropping in. Four rounds burst on the canal bank around the machine guns and although no one was killed, the concussion was terrific, and the guns were momentarily put out of action. Two more rounds came whistling through the air and the OP in the church steeple received two direct hits. The steeple sagged but did not topple. The FOs[22] were stunned but were not injured. Pfc. Berger E. Baardsen sprained his knee retreating from the gun position and Lt. A. K. Stromme was slightly wounded in the ankle from shrapnel. All gun crews were called out of action and ordered to advance across a foot bridge and follow in support of the tanks and rifle companies. D Company followed on foot for the balance of the day and at dusk a defensive line was set up with the tanks forming the forward point. The night was cold, and no one had blankets. Most of the time was spent digging in to keep warm.

The following morning the drive was continued at daybreak and heavy fighting was encountered the entire day. Late in the afternoon C Company reached their objective and defensive positions were set up. The first platoon of D Company remained with

---

[21] Lanclare is not on current maps, but likely refers to the Belgian village of Lanklaar.

[22] Forward Observers.

the forward riflemen, while the balance of D Company set up defensive positions around the battalion CP at the village of Uikhoven. The company and battalion CP were set up in a large brick foundry. Enemy long-range shelling was heavy, but very few casualties were suffered in the CP area. At 2300 hours on September 18, the battalion commander called for mortar support to be furnished to Company C in the forward position. The first and third section of mortars moved out with four vehicles. The night was [pitch] black and was heavy with fog. There were no spare maps, so the route had to be memorized. Progress was slow as two men were forced to walk ahead to feel out the road for the jeeps. After a few hours the slow procession was halted by an American outpost and contact with C Company CP was made. The area to be held was quite long and since the leading company had suffered many casualties the line was thin. Mortar support was very welcome, and plans were made for their use in the early morning. At daylight, an open field was chosen for the mortar positions and the guns were dug in. This was just completed when the artillery began to come in. Heavy mortar shells fell into the city and anti-aircraft guns sprayed the area with airbursts. All enemy positions were plotted on a map and the four mortars began firing in battery. A concentrated barrage would be laid down on a particular area where positions were known, and the Belgian underground men would slip out and observe the damage. They would report where the barrage had fallen and also where the enemy had changed location. Another barrage would be laid down and the same procedure followed. This was done for two days and the enemy was forced to continually change positions.

On the third day, the Germans began closing in and the nearest artillery pieces were only a few hundred yards from the front troops. Everyone expected a counterattack that afternoon and preparations were made for it. Mortar fire continued at a faster pace and each time a mortar would fire, a volley of artillery would come in. Shells burst all around the gun positions as they searched the village for the right spot. The advantage of an open field was clearly demonstrated when tree bursts were observed in a field nearby. Air bursts were frequent, but the enemy did not have direct observation and they were too high to do much damage. Everyone sweated out that day and the night was spent in preparation for the counterattack that was sure to come at dawn. The counterattack did not come that morning, but artillery became heavier and the guns began closing in. White phosphorus was called for by the mortar sergeant and gun positions were shifted frequently all along the front. That day four 81mm mortars poured out more than 1,000 rounds of white phosphorus and high-explosive shells. About an hour after the first barrage, the enemy artillery began to pull back and by nightfall very few rounds came into the town. The mortars fired until 10 that night and everyone settled back to await the almost certain counterattack the following morning. Sgt. Omholt's platoon had been sweating out the forward platoon positions since the day of the drive and had every man at his post bright and early in the morning. At dawn a young Belgian youth came in and reported that the Germans had withdrawn several kilometers during the night. Belgian soldiers immediately set out on patrols and they soon returned with confirmation of the report. Everyone breathed a sigh of relief and motor patrols went out into the area to check the damage that had been done. The remainder of our stay in this area was uneventful except for an occasional happy G.I. who would use his pistol for anti-aircraft fire.

On September 30, the battalion moved to a wooded area 2 miles SE of Eupen, Belgium. Here we stayed overnight and then marched to an area 2 miles south of Montzen, near Aachen. Aachen was partially surrounded by the 1st Division and artillery was pounding the city night and day. While in this bivouac area the following changes in the company were made. Lt. Trygve S. Peterson was evacuated to the hospital. Captain John B. Waltz Jr., who had joined the company shortly before leaving the canal, was company commander. Lt. Paul Testa, Lt. Martin N. Block, Lt. James Q. Parnell, Lt. Asa C. Wilson, and Lt. Milton R. Schultz were assigned to the company. Lt. Parnell took over the 2nd platoon, Lt. Block took over the 1st platoon, and Lt. Olson took over the 3rd. Lts. Testa, Wilson, and Schultz were

Two 99th riflemen of Company C assess a disabled Jagdpanzer IV on Scherberger Straße in Würselen during their engagements October 10–22, 1944. The 1st SS Panzer Corps attempted to reach the nearly surrounded defenders of Aachen along this road. When the First U.S. Army encircled Aachen, it was the suburb of Würselen where the trap was closed. U.S. XIX Corps' 30th Infantry Division reinforced the 116th Infantry Regiment, and the 99th served as the northern jaw of the vise as U.S. VII Corps' 1st Infantry Division moved north to meet them in this suburb. (Courtesy of Volker Dederich)

assigned as section leaders of the 81 mortars. Pfc. Finn Gjertsen and Pfc. Kaare Lorentsen from the First Army Guard Detachment came back to the company and Pfc. Robert Wells and Pvt. Vance J. Gelton replaced them.

Germany

On October 13, the battalion set out again on a new mission. The trucks stopped near a wood ½ mile west of Marienberg and everyone awaited the news of the coming attack. Pfc. Frank R. Hansen of the third platoon was so excited he accidently shot himself through the big toe with his .45 pistol and was evacuated to the hospital. On October 16, the march order was given, and the battalion went into the mission under assignment to the 30th Division. The objective was to close the gap around the city of Aachen in the vicinity of Würselen, Germany. The gap was about 600 yards wide and was held on one side by the 30th Division and on the other by the 1st Division. The terrain was rough and had many buildings. The enemy had heavy concentrations of artillery plotted all around the area. Houses lined all of the roads and streets and enemy tanks had ample cover and concealment and they made the best available use of it. The battalion established a rear CP at a village called Kohlscheid about 3 kilometers from Würselen.

The rifle companies and the heavy weapons company marched forward on foot. A medical aid man from A Company stepped on a Schu mine[23] and had one foot blown off. This was the first casualty from this source in the battalion. Heavy artillery came in periodically and everyone moved forward cautiously. The riflemen advanced into the city of Würselen and defensive positions were set up. The battalion CP was set up in a large building near the center of the village and D Company CP was just across the street. The battalion aid station was in a building near the main road intersection and the first section of mortars set up in the courtyard immediately in back of the aid station. As the company was filing into the village, an artillery barrage came in and Sgt. Morris Koppang was wounded and evacuated. Screaming Meemies and artillery came in constantly and everything seemed to be all mixed up. That evening A Company and the first platoon of D Company set up a roadblock in the valley a short distance from the village. The Germans came through in force and the casualties were heavy. Cpl. Milnor Olson was seriously wounded and later passed away. Pvt. Andrew O. Muri was shot through the leg by a sniper and Adolph O. Kvalvik received a shrapnel wound in the thigh. Arne H. Lee accidently shot himself in the right foot and Pfc. Arthur Petersen was seriously wounded while bringing up a jeep load of ammunition from the ammo dump. The first and second section of mortars kept up a steady siege of fire each day, but the third section could not fire due to the heavy enemy fire that was laid down on their position. On October 21 Cpl. Hans H. Isaksen, Pfc. Royden H. Hawkinson, Pfc.

---

[23] This was an anti-personnel mine developed by Germany in the 1930s.

Harold E. Abrahamsen, and Pvt. Arnold H. Nelson were evacuated to the hospital. S/Sgt. Pervin P. Swenson was wounded by shrapnel and evacuated. The air force[24] kept up a continuous bombing and strafing of the enemy positions and our own artillery screamed overhead night and day. Lt. Olson and S/Sgt. Sorensen were in the forward OP and observed a large force of Jerries coming toward the valley just below Würselen. They called for mortar fire and the counterattack was broken up. The force consisted of about 250 men and five tanks. Two tanks were set on fire by direct hits from mortar shells and the toll on the enemy infantry was terrific. They were coming down a long sloping hill and each mortar shell burst left a large gap in the enemy line. The remaining tanks broke for cover and the infantry ran for a grove of trees. Shelling of our positions continued, but no large-scale counterattack was attempted by the enemy after this. Lt. Martin N. Block and Sgt. Kenneth W. Gilbertson were evacuated to the hospital. On the following day, the battalion left Würselen and bivouacked at Bardenberg, Germany. The city of Aachen had fallen, and the mission had been completed. Casualties had been heavy and the mission had been the hottest yet encountered by the 99th Battalion.

On October 30 the battalion returned again to the area 2 miles south of Montzen and there a complete rest and outfitting was given the men. They sorely needed the rest as nerves were frayed and morale was low. However, the spirits soon came back, and D Company was soon in good shape. A training schedule was established, and conditioning hikes were the order of the day. On November 3 Captain Howard M. Winholtz returned to the company and Captain Waltz was transferred to battalion headquarters. Lt. James J. Bonner was assigned to D Company as first section leader of the 3rd platoon and Lt. Schultz took over the 1st platoon. The days passed swiftly by and on November 23 the battalion moved to the beautiful little Belgian city of Tilff.

Tilff

Tilff was a small city nestled in a valley about 5 miles southwest of Liège. Our main mission here was to patrol the rear areas and to keep on the alert for airborne action. Our secondary mission was to help keep the supply lines rolling to the front. Passes were plentiful and many of the boys found a home in Tilff. The Germans were throwing their buzz bombs at Liège during this period and several of them dropped near Tilff. The explosion was terrific and the very sight and sound of them weighed on one's nerves.

At night, the exhaust light could be seen for miles and the steady drone carried almost as far. It always gave the observer a funny feeling to hear the motor stop and see the bomb nose-dive to the earth and then detonate. Liège had 87 of these monsters land there in one day. The strain was so terrific on the civilians as well as military personnel that traffic was suspended for hours at a time in that city. At this

---

[24] U.S. Army Air Corps.

same time German planes would come over at night and drop flares to see where the buzz bombs were landing and see the damage they had done. The stay in Tilff was appreciated by all, but it was far from a pleasure resort spot at this time.

For almost a month our stay in Tilff consisted of routine patrols and usual garrison duties. On December 9, Pfc. Edmund H. Wyneken of the 3rd platoon was accidently shot in the leg with a .45 pistol and was evacuated to the hospital. He later joined us in France after a nice vacation in England. The buzz bombs paused for a week after the German newscast had stated that Liège was a mass of ruins but resumed at a faster tempo just before the Ardennes breakthrough. Many fell near Tilff and the civilians were nearly frantic. Children, and grownups as well, would scream and hide their faces when they heard the resonant beat of the steady exhaust. Their bodies would be tensed, and they would await the moment when the sound of the motor would stop. When the motor stopped, there would be a pause of about 20 to 30 seconds and the people would shudder and hold their breaths. Then would come the explosion and the concussion, and with haggard, terror-stricken faces, they would return as quickly as possible to their homes and the safety of their air-raid shelters. Many people lived for weeks in a small air-raid shelter in their backyard. The bombs came night and day and there seemed to be no relief for anyone.

Winter Offensive

On December 17, the battalion received a one-hour alert, and everyone began packing his equipment. When the order came to move out, everything was left behind except individual arms, ammunition, and necessary combat equipment. The rear CP personnel and some of the cooks remained in Tilff to man the CP there. The weather was nice in the valley, but when the road wound along the river and came up on higher ground the wind was cold and snow lay on the ground. Our route took us to the city of Malmedy and we arrived there about 0400 in the morning. The city showed every sign of hasty departure of military personnel and civilians peered at us from every nook and cranny. Not a single man will ever forget the look of scorn and hatred that greeted our entrance and the proud knowing look in the eyes of some when they knew that the mighty German Wehrmacht was just over the next ridge of hills and coming to retake the pro-Nazi city of Malmedy.

D Company chose a large concert hall for their temporary home and moved in to eat breakfast and rest. A hospital unit had formerly occupied the building and the supper was still on the serving tables. Evidently the movement orders had come during the meal and they had all moved but quick. Lights were on in most of the rooms and all over town the same signs of hasty departure were evident. A small unit of combat engineers was the only military force in town before the arrival of the 99th. They had worked all night setting out mines to stop the German advance that was sure to come. The attack was expected from the west and B Company was deployed along a high railroad bank that crossed a long valley. C Company dug in along the hill on the left side of the valley. The men had hardly begun to get settled when the first enemy came into view.

The riflemen held their fire for a time because American 2 ½-ton trucks and M3 scout cars led the way. Soon the Jerries opened up with an American .50cal. machine gun mounted on the lead truck and the shooting began. Everyone fired for all he was worth, and the German infantry came on. German tanks began coming down the road to the left of the valley and the lead tank knocked out the right AT gun[25] placed at the left side of the B Company line. The AT gun on the right scored a direct hit on the tank, knocking it out and causing it to skid across the road and block it. One more tank was damaged, and the balance withdrew to take up defensive positions to the rear. Mortar and artillery fire came in our lines and some also fell in [the area of the enemy] due to the rapid advance.

For half an hour the battle raged. Trucks were knocked out and infantry lay strewn across the floor of the valley. Bullets ricocheted off the steel rails and thudded into the bank. Fighting was fierce but the line held, and the nearest German soldier was killed by the fragments of a hand grenade. Finally, the Germans withdrew and then began the battle of nerves.

Before the battle, D Company had moved to the hill on the right of B Company and the battalion CP was established there. The second section of mortars had been dug in behind the B Company line and gave them supporting fire. Artillery thundered all about and German planes roamed about the area almost at will. Visibility was so poor that very little support could be given us by our own air force. When the weather cleared our air force came out and at 10 o'clock one morning the bombers came. Everyone cheered and then the bombs fell—in the city of Malmedy—that the 99th had fought so hard to hold. For three successive days the Allied Air Forces bombed the center of the city and for three successive days the men sweated out those planes and helped evacuate civilians and soldiers. Several units had moved into the city and many casualties were caused by the bombing. The center of the beautiful city was completely gutted. The bombing was terrific and certainly accurate. We will never understand the lack of coordination between land and air forces on that particular instance.

On December 25, the third platoon mortars all moved into the city of Malmedy and set up a defensive position. Targets were plotted and intermittently fired upon night and day. Enemy counterattacks were expected each day but never came. The rifle companies went out on raids each day and a terrific artillery and mortar barrage would be laid down before they came to the objective and just after they departed. The raids were sometimes costly but gained their purpose. The machine-gun platoons of the company dug in behind the riflemen and moved out to give covering fire

---

[25] Anti-Tank gun.

for the raiding parties. Enemy artillery came in steadily and everyone waited and suffered from the cold. The riflemen had it especially rough as they were forced to man their outposts at all times. A dugout was their home for many weary days and the weather became colder each night.

On January 6 the 99th was relieved by the 1st Battalion of the 30th Division and a short move was made to Stavelot. Here we again dug in and the mortars began firing immediately. The area was bleak and cold and only a lucky few had good buildings to sleep in. Artillery and rockets came in much more here and the rifle companies suffered many casualties. The snow made camouflage difficult and raids each night cost the battalion many men. The machine guns were dug in behind the rifle companies for support and the mortars were fired in battery. Several thousand rounds of mortar were fired and the "Nerve Center," as the platoon CP was called, was kept busy most of the time. OPs were in the forward lines and white sheets had to be converted into camouflage suits to keep the enemy from sniping at the soldier in the foxhole. Trench foot took its toll and frostbite was common. The bitter cold, falling snow, continuous dropping of artillery, made the days seem long and endless. Finally, on January 18, after 31 continuous days in the front lines, the 30th Division made a combined drive and the 99th Bn was relieved. The following day they returned to Tilff and planned for a much-needed rest.

France Again

On January 20 the battalion left Tilff and headed out across France once more. Rumors flew thick and fast. Was it to be England this time or would it be Norway? Perhaps it would be England and then the States? So, weary and cold, the 99th Battalion arrived on January 22 at Barneville, France and was attached to the 474th Inf. Regt. awaiting orders of assignment. The quarters were pyramidal tents without stoves and D Company was unloaded in a field and tents were later thrown at them. Morale was not too good, and the weather was miserable. What a letdown for a battalion of soldiers that had just returned from the front lines!

After a few days the men had fixed things up as best they could and stoves were issued. D Company and HQ Company moved into a large concrete building facing the sea. Here things were better as a small resemblance of home could be felt after lights were fixed up and stoves set up. Training was started and routine garrison life began.

On January 25, 1945, D Company of the 99th Battalion (Sep.) was re-designated as Company M, 99th Battalion, 474th Infantry Regiment. We were now the heavy weapons company of the 3rd Battalion of the 474th Regt. The commanding officer of the regiment was Colonel Edwin A. Walker. A new T/O was given the regiment and the 99th was completely outfitted again. M Company was assigned two M8 recon cars and each platoon had a 2 ½-ton truck to carry the platoon personnel. The training was for high mobility and motorized patrol. Night problems and patrol missions were common, and roadblocks were also set up.

The stay at Barneville was long and monotonous. Morale was not too good as there was no place to go. Passes were issued to Cherbourg but everything was off limits there and MPs went around in droves to see that you didn't have a good time. The people in this sector of France were very poor and no effort had been made to repair anything after the land had been fought over eight months before. The men became restless and problems and training became dull and half-hearted. Finally, on April 2, the regiment set out for Germany and for the third time the 99th crossed France.

East of the Rhine

The trip across France was uneventful and the first stop in Germany was Aachen. Here we remained until April 11, and the main duties were patrols and the checking of displaced persons.

Aachen was bombed and shelled very hard before it fell and very little work had been done since the last time we had been at Montzen. The streets had been cleaned up to some extent, but many of the buildings lay in ruin and in some places light and water supply had not been restored. It had been a beautiful city and will take years to rebuild.

After leaving Aachen, M Company moved to a bivouac in the woods near Eiterfeld, on the other side of the Rhine. The Hürtgen Forest was passed through and on every side was evidence of terrific fighting. The Rhine crossing was made near Mainz and that city was pretty well ruined by bombing and shelling. At Eiterfeld, the company began working on motorized and foot patrols in its assigned area. Villages were searched thoroughly, and the woods were patrolled either on foot or by vehicle.

A move was then made to Heroldsbach, Germany. Here we remained for several days and the area was thoroughly searched. Many prisoners were taken and displaced persons directed to the proper channels. M Company was quartered in a large castle near the outskirts of the town and all patrols left from there.

After leaving Heroldsbach the company made a short stay at Markt Bibart and then moved to Regenstauf. This was a small city on the Regen River and the company was assigned the area between the Regen River and Regensburg. This area was thickly wooded and several ammunition dumps were found. Many small villages dotted the countryside and many German soldiers were found hiding out. The stay at Regenstauf was highlighted by the news of the German capitulation and everyone read the story with a deep satisfaction of a job well done.

On May 13, the regiment received movement orders and for the fourth time the 99th Battalion crossed the war-torn countries of Belgium and France. We were headed for the coast of France and everyone was in high spirits.

Our destination was Camp Twenty Grand at Duclair, France. Here we remained for several days resting and receiving a complete issue of new equipment. We were told that Norway was the next stop and the 99th Bn was eager and ready to go. On May 29, the regiment boarded LSTs at the port in Le Havre and the long-looked-for trip to Norway began.

Norway

The convoy formed in the harbor early in the morning of May 30 and set out for the straits of Dover. The coastline of France was in view all day and the next morning the convoy followed the coast of England. Finally, the course was changed and the trip across the North Sea was under way. The weather was ideal and the ships were not too crowded. Meals were prepared by the ship's crew and the food was good. The days were spent in lolling around the decks and taking sunbaths. Many of the boys were at last going back to the land where they were born and raised, and they talked of the folks back home with a dreamy look in their eyes and a smile on their face. The thoughts uppermost in their minds concerned their folks and they wondered if Norway had changed much in the past five years. Would she ever be the same again?

So, the days passed and the convoy moved on. On the morning of June 3 there was an unusual stir up on the deck. The coastline of Norway had been sighted and every "Squarehead" on the ship was crowding and pushing against the rail to get a look at the shores of this rugged little country. As the land became more distinct and buildings became visible, the excitement rose to a new pitch and some of the men hardly took time to eat. The first point of land sighted was Lista, the southwestern point of Norway. The course of the convoy was altered and followed the coast up toward Oslofjord. All day the men lined the rail of the deck, and from time to time one of the "Old Salts" would point to a village nestled near a rocky fjord that had formerly been his home. Everywhere could be seen happy smiles and dreamy eyes. The boys were at last coming to the land for which the battalion had originally been intended. Although the war in Europe was over and the mission had been changed, they were happy to go there and morale was at an all-time high. Norway looked bleak and rugged from the sea and some of the fellows suggested that she may be only a breakwater for Sweden. However, as the convoy rounded the southern part of Norway and larger cities were passed, the coastline took on a softer hue and a more livable atmosphere.

The entire trip had been one of soft breezes and bright sunshine. However, the morning of June 4 brought overcast skies and drizzling rain. The rain continued all through the day and visibility was very limited. The men were disappointed as the trip up Oslofjord had been looked forward to by former Norwegians as well as men who had never been in Norway before. About noon the LSTs pulled up to the docks and the boats were tied up. Vehicles were unloaded and the men were all ready to file off the ramp. After everything was in order, the men were informed that their quarters had not been vacated in Oslo and one more night would be spent on board ship. Four-hour passes were arranged, and half of the men trouped joyfully ashore and caught the "Trikk" [street car] for town. When they returned, the balance of the company went out and most of that night was spent talking about Norway and the changes seen.

The following morning M Company was loaded on trucks and with the balance of the battalion rode through Oslo to their new home in Norway. The camp was located in Smestad and consisted of a number of two-story barracks formerly used by the Germans. Quarters were assigned and soon everyone was busy making the best possible use of all materials on hand. Evening passes were issued to those who

99th armored cars in one of many parades on Karl Johans Gate in 1945. This formal avenue leads from Oslo's central train station past the parliament, formal parks and the National Theater to the Royal Palace. The photo captures the festive nature of the event, with flowers decorating the vehicles. You can decipher from the photo that the vehicles have the small pentagon markings painted on their hulls that were the 474th Infantry Regiment's distinctive marking. The pentagon design is also mirrored in the large white stars, that have been modified to create solid pentagons in their centers. (Courtesy of the 99th Educational Foundation)

had relatives and friends in Oslo and Smestad Camp quickly settled down to routine garrison life.

One of the first missions of the 99th Bn was the Honor Guard Parade on June 7. On this day thousands of Norwegians stood for hours in the rain to catch a glimpse of their king who was coming home after five years of exile in England. The Honor Guard was composed of British soldiers, Norwegian soldiers, and picked men from the 99th Battalion and were drawn up three deep on three sides facing the pavilion from which the King was to speak. The balance of the 99th Battalion acted as security guards along the route which the King would pass on his way to the Royal Palace. The arrival of the King was a great day in Norway and the happy people paraded and danced in the streets of Oslo far into the night.

The mission of the 99th in Norway seemed to consist mainly of guard details and checking of German camps. Raids were made and high German officials taken into custody. The days passed swiftly by and on July 4 the American soldier had his day. Every man that could be spared took part in the parade and every vehicle that the unit had brought to Norway was displayed. The streets were thronged with people and the air force thundered impressively overhead. Although the day was very hot, the parade progressed at a fast tempo and the Americans made a fine appearance. The Norwegian papers lauded the Fourth of July demonstration as one of the best ever held in Norway. The citizens of Oslo were very much impressed, and the American soldier came into his own here just as he has in every land he has visited.

M Company pulled guard details in turn with other companies of the battalion. Some trips were made to the surrounding countryside in quest of displaced persons or to check a German camp. German soldiers were processed and loaded in Drammen for the trip back to Germany. Passes to Oslo were liberal and furloughs were given to the men who had relatives here in Norway. Although the long periods of guard duty became monotonous, spirits were high and morale was good. Invitations for soldiers to visit local homes became more numerous than they could be filled and as the American soldier became better known, his popularity increased.

The days passed swiftly by and one day the news flashed over the radio of the end of the war with Japan. A great Victory Day parade was held by the Allies in Oslo and everyone rejoiced. Happily, no casualties were suffered, and everyone settled down to await the day when the 99th would sail for America and home!

CHAPTER THREE

Yngvar Stensby

This chapter consists of an unpublished manuscript created by the veterans of the 99th Infantry Battalion (Separate). It was spearheaded by Yngvar Stensby and comes from a collection of materials that he had curated. What follows is what he had already written, but throughout this book there are numerous references to other letters and materials that veterans had sent him that he preserved in his collection. Unfortunately, the 99th's unit historian was never able to complete the entire manuscript and get it published.

The brave men of the 99th were involved in, and captured, many experiences during their time together. Their writings range from letters home, to accounts of specific aspects of their experiences, to more ambitious efforts that attempt to capture the full breadth and spirit of the 99th. The first selection of Chapter 3 starts with an accounting of the 99th's formation and training written by Yngvar Stensby.

Stensby was a dedicated member of the 99th who after the war became the battalion's unit historian. It was in this role that he gathered up and interviewed many fellow soldiers. Unfortunately, time and the years took their toll and the effort was not seen to completion. However, we are left with a solid accounting of the formation and training of the 99th.

Stensby's writing style conveys the gung-ho attitude of many in the 99th. The members of the 99th celebrated their heritage and enthusiasm for the mission. As the 99th got closer to the actual war and associated battle scenes, the writing shifted to a more somber tone.

Stensby was the 99th's informal poet laureate, having written dozens of poems. While this section doesn't fit the typical definition of a poem, it is representative of the vignettes that he wrote to capture the sentiment of the troops particularly due to the tragic death of such a well-liked individual that many in the 99th had written about.

He captures the sentiment of the Norwegian American soldiers' resolute approach to the task at hand…defeating the Nazis and achieving liberation for their fellow Norwegians.

Norway's bravest sons

A wave of resentment flooded over me. Hatred of the Nazis bored into every organ of my body. Why Sergeant Skarning? Why not me? I was sitting right beside him!

It seemed he had so much more to live for than I. In a seething rage I checked my rifle and headed for the canal again. I was joined by every rifleman in the area.

Stensby was born April 28, 1914 and died June 22, 1986 at the age of 72. Married to Myrtle Stensby, they spent most of their lives together in Minneapolis where they raised three children. In addition to his role with the 99th, he wrote a book called Poems and Memories *and also* Imperfections of a Preacher's Kid.

The book that Stensby had planned had a title of The Saga of the Yankee Commanders and Their Norwegian GIs: A Revised History of The 99th Inf. Bn (Sep.), The Rype Group, and the 474th Inf. Regt. *In addition to the text, there were plans for sketches by Ray Helle, an artist and soldier in the 99th, that had been created for the book. The effort was sponsored by the 99th Infantry Battalion (Separate) Historical Committee.*

Foreword

From the day of its activation at Camp Ripley to the day of its deactivation at Camp Myles Standish, the combat unit featured in this book was officially identified as the 99th Inf. Bn (Sep.). It had also been called the Norwegian American Battalion, the Norwegian Ski Troopers, the Ski and Mountain Battalion and, in a lighter vein, The Brooklyn Brigade.

Physically rugged, mentally alert, and morally dedicated though they were, the men of the 99th would not have attained the reputation of tenacity and dependability on the field of battle had it not been for the inspirational leadership of the unit's two battalion commanders.

I have chosen the title *The Saga of the Yankee Commanders and Their Norwegian GIs* for this book. It is a fitting tribute to the two colonels of the U.S. Army whose leadership and guidance made the 99th a closely knit combat team that successfully fulfilled every task to which it was assigned.

Capt. Harold D. Hansen was appointed battalion commander when the 99th was activated at Camp Ripley in August, 1942. Promoted to the rank of major, then lieutenant colonel, he was with the 99th until its deactivation in November 1945.

Lt. Col. Robert G. Turner was appointed battalion commander in June 1943, while the 99th was in training at Camp Hale, Colorado. Col. Turner was seriously wounded in the battle of Elbeuf, France. Unable to return to the 99th, he was replaced by Col. Hansen.

It is with pride and gratitude that we salute our two Yankee commanders!
Although the writers of this book cannot identify with commanders of the NORSO (Rype Group) and the 474th Inf. Regt. on the same personal basis as we do the commanders of the 99th, we respectfully attribute to the commanders of Rype Group and the 474th the credit due them for their outstanding leadership.

Birth of a Battalion

They came by ones…by twos…by multiples of either;
They came by train…by bus…by truck.

"They" were the men in the U.S. Army who had been transferred to Camp Ripley, Minnesota as the cadre for the newly activated 99th Inf. Bn (Sep.). In accordance with orders issued by the War Department in July of 1942, the battalion was to be composed of Norwegian nationals and Americans of Norwegian descent. The prerequisite for joining the 99th was the ability to speak the Norwegian language.

In addition to Americans of Norsk descent, the ranks of the battalion were subsequently to include Norwegian seamen, survivors of Nazi submarine warfare, as well as Norwegian patriots who had escaped their native land after it was invaded by the Nazis. Not until the vanguards of servicemen arrived at battalion headquarters at Camp Ripley did they learn the true nature of the unit. The 99th was an ethnic group of battalion strength. Its purpose was to invade Norway and help drive the hated Nazis from their homeland.

Initially, the battalion staff at Camp Ripley included:

Capt. Harold D. Hansen, CO
Capt. Lear, Exec. Off.
Capt. Adler Holland, Adj.
2nd Lt. Conrad Sorvik, S2
Capt. David B. Shirley, S3[1]

Servicemen stationed elsewhere were undoubtedly content to exchange duty in army camps in such faraway places as Newfoundland, or the torrid sands of the south for the comparatively beautiful state of Minnesota. Arriving at Camp Ripley, they found it to be a National Guard summer training camp. The facilities were not adequate to allow expansion of an entire battalion.

During its formative days at Camp Ripley, training included the familiarization with equipment, and physical conditioning. One can jovially assume "swimming" in Minnesota's high summer humidity or swatting at the always hungry mosquitoes were "extracurricular activities" and not orders for the day!

The steady arrival of men into the ranks of the 99th soon made it apparent that facilities at Camp Ripley were "bustin' at the seams." The end result was that the 99th was moved to Fort Snelling, Minnesota, there to occupy a series of old Army barracks.

A paragraph in the original order from the War Department that activated the 99th stated: "Norwegian-speaking soldiers who are United States citizens may, with their consent, be transferred to the Battalion…"

---

[1] S1 is personnel, S2 is Intelligence, S3 is Operations and Training, and S4 is Logistics.

With their consent! There wasn't a red-blooded American Norskie who wouldn't have given his most prized possession to be transferred to the 99th!

Twenty-five men from the regular Army who were stationed in Newfoundland were automatically transferred to the 99th. The group boarded a Norwegian freighter, envisioning a relatively short trip to an East Coast port. Due to mechanical trouble, as well as roving Nazi U-boats, the normal passage of three days turned into a 12-day journey!

There were obviously two methods to implement transfer: either by the U.S. Army (as in the case of the Newfoundlanders), or individual requests by GIs for transfer.

Many a GI stood awkwardly tongue-tied at the desk of a commanding officer, trying to justify a request for transfer "through channels." The latter was always the slowest way to gain entry into the ranks of the 99th!

Fort Snelling

Compared with most Army camps, Ft. Snelling wag a veritable Garden of Eden. Situated at the southern vortex of the Minneapolis-St. Paul Metro area, it provided 99ers with a larger range of activities during off-duty hours than had been available at Camp Ripley.

Long-established Scandinavian cultural centers welcomed the 99ers with open arms. There was never a shortage of invitations for the new contingent of Vikings to attend social functions. Nor was there a dearth of invitations from other residents in the Metro area. The 99ers were royally treated wherever they went. Minneapolis and St. Paul, as well as suburban localities' reputations for hospitality, soon became legend among battalion members,

On occasion it also provided personnel for involuntary KP duty! At times a 99er on pass for the evening failed to watch the time and reported to the orderly room a bit later than the pass dictated.

Following a special "partying" evening, 99ers failed to return on schedule to their company barracks. In true military fashion, a list of offenders had been compiled by the officer of the day.

The next morning after reveille, the officer announced: "Fourteen of you men reported in late last night. Would the 14 please step forward?"

No one moved a muscle.

The officer repeated his demand. Again, no response.

"Very well," the officer snorted. "I have a list inside…you will stand at attention until I return!"

In a matter of minutes, the officer returned. His mumbled apology inferred that he had "misplaced" the list. The company was dismissed.

What the officer hadn't counted on was 99er No. 15, who happened along at precisely the moment when the OD had gone to answer the call of nature. No. 15, known for his addiction for "one more for the road," briefed the rest of the company before reveille: "I saw dat list yust before I sneezed, an' de ting yust vent sailing. I tink it vent under de raddiator, an' maybe I pick et opp to putt on de desk, but, by yingo, hven I vent to bed dis morning, dere it vass in my pocket!"

As service records of incoming men began filling the filing cabinets in respective companies, so did the battalion ranks. Each newcomer checked in with gusto and pride. He wasn't just another Army serial number. He was a 99er. He had an avowed purpose for being there. That attitude solidified the unit into what would be a closely knit combat group recognized for its dedication, determination, tenacity, and ferocity!

No one questioned the necessity of grueling day and night marches, or field maneuvers. Companies "attacked" up and down the Minnesota riverbanks so often one wondered if there remained a single square foot of ground where the determined boot of a 99er had not trod! Similarly, white armbands charged through the reeds and brush of the river bottoms, bent on dislodging fanatical green-banded "foes."

Nor did it matter how many hundreds of lunging bayonet thrusts decimated the straw-filled gunny sacks. Extreme physical exhaustion seemed a balm for the soul that had been goaded into harboring a seething hatred for Nazis.

***

To a certain extent the arrival of the new rifles was something to write home about. Compared with the Enfield rifle of World War I fame, this was a beauty to behold!

Except for one irritating feature! The inside and outside of the barrel, the stock, and every moving part was all but submerged in a thick, unyielding coating of a sticky concoction called Cosmoline! It was nothing short of horrible. The gooey mess stuck to hands, clothes, and cleaning rags alike. Unprintable expletives of both Yankee and Norsk origin desecrated the air as one after another discovered that the nap of the cleaning cloth stuck to the Cosmoline rather than the goop adhering to the rag!

One exasperated 99er, trying to wash his hands in hot water while holding the "gooped-up" rifle barrel, discovered that as hot water sprayed onto the barrel, the Cosmoline slithered into the sink! Thus, in a baptism of hot water, the rifles came out clean and sparkling like a brand-new silver dollar!

The posted guard rosters of the 99th often read like the Who's Who at a Scandinavian Syttende Mai celebration.[2] On many an occasion the entire roster—from the officer of the day through to the bugler—had names ending in the suffix "-son." There were Abrahamsons, Bensons, Carlsons, Danielsons, and so on down that alphabet. An O'Malley or a Smith may have been a welcome change of pace for the typist!

---

[2] Literally translated meaning the 17th of May, this is an annual celebration in Norway and often referred to as "National Day."

Military dignitaries from Norway occasionally reviewed the 99th, as did the Norwegian ambassador from Washington. Civic leaders from the Twin Cities area, as well as representatives from the Minnesota National Guard, were pleased to see 99ers with heads held high and a definite snap in their steps pass in review.

As inviting as prospects of spending Christmas at Ft. Snelling were to the 99th, such a treat was not in the cards. On December 17, the battalion was alerted for its move to Camp Hale, Colorado. Major Harold D. Hansen, battalion commander, posted this notice:

"Men of the 99th:

"A Message from Major Hansen:

"I hope each one of you will enjoy this trip. We will arrive shortly at Camp Hale, our new training center. You will like the campsite and the landscape, as it will remind you of Norway. To those of you who have not been to Norway, it will create a lasting impression. It will be typical of Norway as the climate, weather, and terrain are the same. In this camp our training will really begin, and you will participate in the most interesting and elaborately designed training in the U.S. Army."

The message was signed "Your Battalion Commander, Major H. D. Hansen."

"Mail Call, Camp Hale Mail Call at the first ski bivouac Capt. Larsen doing the calling." Kristian Brun's comment on a soldier's most important formation. At reunions names like "H. K. Hanson," and "John L. Christopherson" were easily remembered, as they were necessary in a unit with over 25 Olsen/Olsons. Short summers and unpredictable snowfall extended winter training into mid-1943, then focus shifted to mountain operations. (Courtesy of the 99th Educational Foundation)

Camp Hale

Major Hansen's message to the 99th by Headquarters was prompted by Special Order No. 300. It was issued by Headquarters, Fort Snelling, Minnesota, and dated December 14, 1942. It read, in part:

> 1. Pursuant to authority contained In Ltr, Hq AGF, Army War Colleges, Wash, DC, dated 25 Nov 42…Subject: "Transfer of 99th Infantry Battalion (Separate) to Camp Hale, Colorado," and instructions contained in Ltr, Hq, Second Army, Memphis, Tenn, dated 2 Dec 42, Subject: "Transfer of 99th Infantry Battalion (Separate) to Camp Hale, Colorado," the 99th Inf. Bn (Sep.), consisting of the following named Officers and enlisted men (*less* 1 Officer and 23 Enlisted Men who acted as an advance detail and departed from this station in compliance with Par 12 SO 297, this Hq, dated 10 Dec 42 and 5 enlisted men who departed from this station as guards for the rail movement of organizational equipment in compliance with Par 5 SO 297, this Hq, dated 10 Dec 42) will proceed by rail (except as noted) to Camp Hale, Colo, at such time as will enable them to arrive there at on or about 16 Dec 42, for permanent change of station…

The order then listed the names of 30 officers. Omitted was the name of the officer on advance detail. Of the 792 enlisted men named, 120 were NCOs. As the battalion's authorized strength was 931 enlisted men, the unit was 139 men short of full strength.

Maj. H. D. Hansen and Maj. Sofus E. Urberg were appointed train commander and medical officer on Train No. 1.

Capt. Adler Haaland and Capt. Thomas G. Herrick held the same positions on Train No. 2.

The monotony of the first day and a half of travel across the winter-bleak plains states were tolerable because of the growing sense of excitement as the trains neared Colorado. The 99ers were also aware that the training that lay ahead was one step closer to the long-awaited participation in an invasion of Norway!

As the first slivers of dawn pierced the darkness of the second night, 99ers beheld a glorious sight! Silhouetted against the early-morning sky were rugged, snow-covered mountains. Huge locomotives, belching smoke and steam, began climbing a long, rather steep grade.

The train eventually ceased its creaking and lurching, and its motion was perceptibly down-grade. A frigid sun broke through the clouds, moments before the south end of the camp came into view.

Expletives salted normal conversation as the panorama of the camp became apparent. When the train began its descent toward Pando, row after row of barracks appeared to the right. They nuzzled the snow-covered streets that criss-crossed the camp area. As uniformly aligned as ribs on a lefse rolling pin,[3] the buildings snuggled in contemptuous disregard of the steep, rocky slopes to the east, and the distant towering mountains.

Crisp, cold air greeted the 99ers as they detrained. At an altitude of 9,600 feet they found their lungs suddenly inadequate. The least physical exertion brought a chorus of rasping breaths as lungs struggled for oxygen.

Maj. Hansen addressed hie 99ers:

"OK, Men! "We've got a little hike ahead of us. We established a reputation for spirited marching at Snelling, and we'll do the same here! Hold your heads high, put spring in your step! Let's show the rest of them here what a tough infantry outfit is like! In case you feel you can't make it, don't be the first to fall out...always let the other guy be first!"

Wheezing his words, a 99er chortled:

"I hear they spent 40 million bucks on this camp. There wuz still some credit on the books, and they wuz gonna put in streetcar tracks, but it's so damn cold up here the rails split!"

A stream of tobacco juice bored a brown hole in the snow, punctuating the caustic comment.

***

Soon after arriving at Camp Hale the ranks of the 99th began to fill with an influx of Norwegian nationals—Norwegian seamen who had survived Nazi U-boat torpedoes; Norwegian patriots who had escaped Nazi tyranny in their homeland.

Their welcome presence created a temporary inconvenience with the spoken word. Many of the new 99ers spoke little or no English; others belabored the listeners with various dialects from the Old Country. Midwestern 99ers who had felt secure in their mastery of Norwegian were soon to find that North Dakota or Wisconsin or Minnesota Norsk was a far cry from Norge-Norsk! Service club personnel and clerks may well have been baffled by the sudden deluge of strange jabbering that ensued when members of the 99th entered either facility.

Consider also the dilemma of a company commander not too sharp on his Norwegian. His runner lurched up to the CP and wheezed: "Hr. Kap-TEIN, e har opplysning fra han Mah-JOOR Hansen." The captain eyed him with a quizzical look. "Han Mah-JOOR Hansen sa at du skulde flytte OPA-en din ne til di grønne buskana ve elva." Nailing the nearest 99er, the captain asked: "What the hell is he talkin' about?" "Sir," began the translator, "he said, 'Major Hansen wants you to move from OPA to the cluster of green bushes down by the creek. But confidentially, Cap'n, I think the Major referred to your *CP*, not your *OPA*!"

***

---

[3] A baker's rolling pin made specifically for the Norwegian potato pancake, with uniform, equally spaced grooves carved into the surface.

Had the men had any inkling of the strenuous training that lay ahead, they may have been more appreciative of the barracks. They were brand spankin' new, and luxurious by any standard. As a result, pre-inspection chores were light.

Officers who made one Saturday inspection were amazed to note the ceiling of one barracks that appeared to be "sweating." That eye-catcher, though, rated nothing more thorough than a passing glance.

Carpenters who had rushed the barracks to completion had left a small aperture in the ceiling. And resident 99ers who came in from a strenuous field exercise found the opening a handy place to store their empty beer bottles until such time as they could muster the strength to throw them where they should be. Each empty bottle had evidently dribbled enough drops to create a pool which, for some strange reason, began leaking through the ceiling on inspection day!

Needless to say, the next inspection revealed a dry ceiling. Flecks of brownish stain were second-guessed as "sweated" Compo-board.

That the errant 99ers "sweated" a lot more than the ceiling was a foregone conclusion!

***

As days stumbled into weeks, and weeks cascaded into months, the endurance and physical stamina of 99ers became evident. Pride in their unit, and a growing hatred for Nazi tyrants in Norway, were the catalysts. Each man also bore in mind the slogan on a sign near the battalion parade ground. A caricature of Hitler prompted the reminder: "WE'VE GOT A DATE WITH THIS SON OF A BITCH…"

The list of equipment issued to each man was staggering, as was the weight. A fully packed rucksack weighed from 70 to 90 pounds and contained provisions in food and clothing to sustain a man for days. Added to that were the two-men split loads—cooking sets and rations.

Properly adjusted, the rucksack could be carried hour after hour on rigorous marches and field exercises.

***

Numerous "attacks on" or "defenses of" the many gullies or mountain slopes surrounding the camp were deemed penny-ante stuff compared to the grueling 50-mile cross-country marches for four days every able-bodied 99er participated in. Under the strenuous weight of rucksacks, the men in the battalion proved their mettle and determination as they doggedly scaled the snow-covered mountains that soared to an altitude of 12,000 feet.

The rarified air made frequent breaks a necessity, as both altitude and the cold made breathing difficult. Men plodded along on either skis or snowshoes. In an instance or two, 99ers made the entire march on emergency snowshoes, "just to see if it could be done." More round than oval, they required the wearer to adapt an awkward A-legged gait so as not to step on one snowshoe with the other.

To make for easier going, 99ers were free to improvise equipment-moving techniques. Included was a two-ski sled mount for heavy machine guns. A three-ski sled would have been a boon for litter bearers. Four-dog teams helped haul rations and equipment.

On the battalion's way toward the top of the Continental Divide, the extreme physical exertion began to tell on the men but not a one of them called it quits. To a man the attitude seemed to be, "I've just about had it, but I'll be damned if I'll be the first one to drop out!"

The comparative warmth of the afternoon dissipated rapidly as soon as the sun disappeared behind the mountains. The sudden chill grew in intensity and numbing cold soon crept in. Although night-time temperatures were usually in the 30–40-below range, the men slept comfortably in down-filled sleeping bags inside tents pitched on the snow. It was also a common occurrence on day-night marches for 99ers to dig shallow trenches in the snow and, using the sleeping bags, snore the night through in cocoon-like fashion.

At the end of a day's march men found food preparation an exercise in patience. Snow that appeared spotlessly white when scooped up in pans, melted down and revealed a surprising array of foreign materials in the water. The evening's cook usually fished out pine needles, small parts of branches, rabbit droppings, and tree bark. When the cooking utensils were at long last full of relatively clean water, it was brought to a boil and correct quantities of dehydrated food added. Such tent meals were nourishing and palatable. Growling stomachs of tentmates appeased, there followed a semblance of snowbound KP and a restoring of utensils to make room for the sleeping bags. Leftover water was *never* thrown out. Although it would turn into a chunk of ice before midnight, it would be thawed out for breakfast rations.

As the leading elements of the 99th ascended to the western boundaries of Cooper Hill on the forenoon of the fourth day, the rest of the battalion stretched out in a long peninsula of humanity, all of them as determined as ever to complete the march. The speed with which the march had been completed underscored the do-or-die physical stamina of the 99th.

Its accomplishments were recognized as worthy of mention in later *Mountain Training* manuals.

The endurance and speed march of the 99th was a "first" for any GIs assigned to training in winter mountain warfare. Any or all innovations the 99ers created were forwarded to the War Department and were enthusiastically accepted!

***

Whoever planned the layout of the rifle range at Camp Hale ignored the slogan, "Woodsman, spare that tree!" As the Vikings blazed away at the targets a hundred yards distant, the slugs chipped away at tree trunks behind the targets. With hundreds of thousands of 30-caliber slugs from the rifles of 99ers, and 10th Mountaineers before them decimating the girth of tree trunks, it was not an uncommon sight to see a tree shudder, its branches emitting a swirl of snow before it crashed to the ground.

Nothing was as miserable throughout the winter months as a stint on the rifle range. There wasn't a glove made that could keep the trigger finger from feeling like a piece of wood after an hour on the range. And no amount of clothing could keep the cold from seeping into a man's body when firing in a prone position. Nor was it a picnic at kneeling or standing. Then the prevailing winds created swimming pools for the eyeballs. At times just *seeing* the target was hard enough, let alone drawing a bead on the bull's-eye.

Complaints brought the reminder: "Remember, the Finns on the Russian front! They not only froze their tails off—they had the Russians shootin' at 'em too! And they didn't have any warm barracks or hot food awaiting them at the end of the day!"

"Nothing is so bad but what it couldn't be worse…"

Amen!

***

No one knows for sure just where or when the 99th's orchestra came into being. That it became an element for the entertainment of 99ers was a certainty soon after the battalion arrived at Camp Hale.

There was Rose on the trumpet, _____ [4] on the sax or clarinet, Skarning and Tollefson on accordions, and Johanson on the drums. Many was the time when the battalion, exhausted after a grueling bout with altitude, cold, and snow, returned to camp to be refurbished mentally and morally by the orchestra. It soon became apparent that even the battalion's "brass" considered the orchestra a therapeutic influence on the men.

***

When first sergeants "volunteered" 99ers to attend Bugle School, they should have explained the eventual metamorphosis of the bugler. Stretching the truth, a bit, they could have added:

"In this man's Army, bugling is mostly ceremonial, except for reveille each morning when the bugler acts like an alarm clock, and like an alarm clock is cussed from hell to breakfast…!

"Retreat is definitely in the ceremonial category. It's sort of like patting a tired horse on the rump after ya take the harness off. And being ceremonial, retreat should not be sounded in unison with two beat-up brass bugles, two brand-new plastic bugles, and a bass bugle that sounds like a love-sick coon hound a-brayln at the moon…!

---

[4] Stensby left this blank in his original document.

"Church call is S.O.P.[5] Those who want to go to church know what time to be there, and the ones who never attend ain't gonna have their souls realigned by the pleading notes of a bugle…!

"There are a lot of other calls too, but nobody pays any attention to 'em. Like chow call. I'd hate to be in an army where the guys have to be reminded when to eat…!

"As company bugler you will be assigned rotational stints at guard duty, as well as other in-between jobs like: messenger…orderly…pack-mule…rifleman…machine gunner…scout…and any other crappy detail that needs attention…!

"If your lips freeze to the mouthpiece some 40-below morning, it may be 'TS' for you but at least you won't wake anybody up with your racket…!

"In due time, you'll chuck the bugle for a radio. You will be much more popular as a radioman than you were as a bugler. In combat you'll be singled out as a 'prime target' by enemy snipers. They'll go to any length to put you and your radio out of commission. Think of the eventual transformation as your road to glory…!"

***

As stated before. Norwegian nationals, or seamen who had been in the Norwegian Merchant Marine, had language problems when they came to the U.S.—and later to the 99th. For one 99er in particular, the hindrance turned out to be a blessing in disguise. As he related it:

> I was on a Norwegian freighter when the Nazis invaded Norway. As there was nothing to go back to, I made up my mind I would jump ship when we got to New York. That I did, but found it awfully hard to express myself, as I knew very little English. When I asked a man in Brooklyn about becoming a citizen he answered, "Join the Army." I didn't waste any time volunteering.
>
> They took me right away. At the first camp they sent me to [take] one of those IQ tests. I didn't understand the questions, and I couldn't write English. But then we came to a test where you either circle a letter or X a box. There was an Indian sitting ahead of me, and he kind of let me see his answers, so I just copied them.
>
> It wasn't long after the test that they sent me to Camp Hale. The word "Hale" in Norwegian means "tail" but I hoped in this case it wasn't the tail-end for me.
>
> I was happy when they said there would be lots of Norwegians there. When I got there, it seemed like everybody was talking Norwegian! Anyway, when I checked in I gave them the brown envelope with my records.
>
> A sergeant said, "We'll put you in the Communications Platoon." I said I'd rather be a rifleman as I didn't know anything about the word [he] used. The sergeant snorted, "You don't know anything about communications? Who are you trying to kid! Your record states you scored very high in that part of the test!"

---

[5] Standard Operating Procedure.

All I really knew then about communications was that it was an awfully long word. But as time went on the other fellows in the platoon showed me the ropes, and I got by.

So when I got my PFC stripes, I said, "Just remember that it was the Indian [who] I copied from and the men in the platoon that earned [these] stripes for me. I just wear them to keep the sergeant happy!"

***

A typical mountain maneuver was the planned "assault" on Camelback Mountain. Its summit was etched against the eastern sky at an altitude of 13,200 feet.

Weapons Platoon of A Company, with attachments from medics and communications, left at 9 a.m. The rest of the battalion would depart for the overnight snow-safari at 1 p.m. In columns of two the lead-off platoon made a smart right at the mule barns, then down the road toward the rifle range. At the precise moment an unspoken "left oblique"[6] took the men into a shallow ravine that grew in girth as the altitude increased.

As the timberline came near, breaks were more frequent.

"Hey, Lootenant..."

"Yeah?"

"D'ya know there's bears up here?"

"I doubt it." As hard as it was to breathe, the lieutenant said he felt the conversation unnecessary.

The lieutenant's suggestion fell on deaf ears.

"Yes, Sir, Lootenant, there shore are bears up here, but ya don't spell 'em like the four-legged critters. Ya spell 'em like B-A-R-E-S and we take us a right—obleek about here we'd end up near the Cat Houses over yonder. There's a-plenty 'bares' over there...and 'twould be a sight mor sporty than a-kicking' through the snow here...!"

Facing the summit that loomed above them, the men noticed a curtain of white swirling beneath the Dome of Camelback.

"We hafta climb up into *that*?"

"Yeah, Soldier, we have to climb up into that. It's only snow, you know. It isn't the first time you've done it, and it won't be the last!"

"I heard tell once that 'Camp Hale' is Cherokee for 'Wind—Driven Snow and Assorted Kinds of Crappy Weather'!"

Thousands of feet below the platoon and several miles distant, the rest of the battalion looked like a congregation of ants zeroing in on a saucer full of honey. An ever-graying mass of clouds to the west looked ominous.

Shards of gale-driven snow laced the faces of the men as they plunged into the sea of white. Pants legs chattered in the unrelenting wind. Hooded parkas suddenly seemed sizes larger than they had been an hour earlier.

---

[6] Ordered to move at an angle.

The lieutenant turned to his radioman and yelled: "Send a message that we've reached the summit!"

The radioman tried everything in the book. No response.

"Any luck?"

"No Sir...can barely hear *myself* talk!"

Squads were broken down into five-man units to serve as windbreaks until tents were pitched. Tent pegs seemed to hold firmly in the snow.

"Take it easy on your rations, men!" the sergeant bellowed. "No telling when this storm will let up!"

"And secure your tent flaps! If the wind flips it open it might either rip the tent to shreds or take you and it on a one-way flight to Denver! If the wind direction changes, maybe you'd wind up being attacked by those 'bares' we've heard so much about!" The words were nearly swallowed up in the screeching wind.

As the tent fabric crackled and gnarled, the fury of the gale hurled sheets of powder-dry snow against it. Amidst worries that the tent pegs would pull out of the snow, or that the fabric itself would be torn to shreds, harried 99ers voiced concern as they tried to rest. The crackling and billowing tent and the retching of snow, as it clawed at the fabric, became a lullaby of sorts, and tentmates on the summit of Camelback eventually drifted off into fitful slumber.

A blindingly bright morning sun revealed a colony of drifts where none had been before. Tents were half-buried in snow. Opening tent flaps, early-risers had to kick down drifts before they could spot the tent of a neighbor.

"Hey, guys! We've got a Chinook this morning. It's only 38 below!"

Another attempt at radio contact with battalion headquarters was futile.

"Maybe they're holding a memorial service for its Lost Platoon," commented the radioman.

"We can't contact Headquarters," explained the lieutenant, "so we'll proceed as originally planned."

"We'll go due north 'til we hit the next deep valley. That will eventually take us down to the north camp road. It's a bit chilly today, men, but it's all downhill. And when we hit that camp road, let's pick 'em up and lay 'em down as though we're off on a weekend pass!"

Returning to camp the men in Weapons Platoon found out that the exercise the previous day had been canceled at about noon because of the impending storm.

"Storm? What storm! All we had was a little snow a-flittin' around!"

After making a detailed report of the night on the summit of Camelback, the lieutenant returned to the barracks.

"Here's another order from battalion headquarters: Major Hansen sends his compliments for a job well done. He also said, take the rest of the day off...YOU'VE EARNED IT!"

***

More or less marooned by the intense cold and seemingly endless snowfalls, the Viking Battalion anxiously awaited spring. It *did* arrive, but at Camp Hale spring showed up weeks later than in the rest of Colorado.

Throughout the winter the news media had gorged itself on the exploits and record-breaking accomplishments of the 99th. Its members were, for the most part, entirely ignorant of the fuss the press and radio made over them. Occasional clippings from back home hadn't meant that much.

Rumors ran rife as spring approached. The 99th was being transferred…to Alaska! …to Mt. Rainier in the state of Washington…to Camp McCoy, Wisconsin…to Hell's Canyon, Idaho. Those who survived the roaring rapids would be sent to Sun Valley, Idaho, for a week's rest and recreation.

One rumor seemed more far-fetched than the rest: the battalion was to be shunted via truck convoy to Camp Carson, Colorado, there to parade in the presence of the President of the United States, Franklin Delano Roosevelt and his Chief of Staff, General George Marshall!

The latter was definitely a rumor!

Toward the end of April, 99ers proudly watched as Major Hansen, in his ramrod-straight posture, and with his distinctive military bearing, approached the white car that whisked the President of the United States and his aide across the parade grounds to Camp Carson. To a man, the 99ers stood tall, tough, and proud throughout the entire Presidential Review. It was a special honor accorded the 99th. On no other occasion had the President of the United States and his Chief of Staff ever inspected a unit as small as the 99th Inf. Bn (Sep.)!

After the Presidential Review, the 99th returned to Camp Hale, there to renew its endless attacks on our defenses of mountain slopes or valleys. Days-long maneuvers saw men resolving every kind of a pre-arranged "predicament."

Using entrenching tools to hack holes in a snowdrift was one thing; trying to carve shallow trenches in the rock-studded mountain slopes was something else! Barrages of multilingual profanity usually shattered the mountain solitude long before acceptably deep holes were dug.

As the summer wore on and daily training hours lengthened, the unit was visited by Col. Munthe-Kaas and Col. A. D. Dahl, Norwegian military men. The purpose of their visit was to interview 99ers and ask for volunteers to be trained as paratrooper commandos. The end result was that about 80 enlisted men and 12 officers were transferred to the OSS unit.[7]

In June 1943 the battalion was surprised and temporarily incensed when Lt. Col. Robert G. Turner was assigned commander of the battalion. Major Hansen became Col. Turner's executive officer.

---

[7] Stensby has a note here that the reader could "go to Ch. ____, p. _____ to learn more about this." Unfortunately, since this book was never published, this story does not seem to have been saved by this particular group of 99ers.

Visibly rankled over Col. Turner's arrival, 99ers soon began to realize that the West Point graduate was to "fine-tune" the 99ers in military tactics of mountain warfare heretofore not available to Major Hansen. Col. Turner readily admitted he felt ill at ease as commander of the ethnic unit.

It was not long, however, before respect for his military rank turned to respect for the knowledge and fairness of the individual, Col. Turner. Nor was it long before the men realized that Col. Turner and Maj. Hansen would add to the hardiness and prestige of the battalion.

Although Col. Turner was not able to boast of Norwegian ancestry, no one judged him on such a flimsy technicality. Every 99er soon "adopted" the colonel as a bona-fide Norwegian American and accorded him the respect and the cooperation he deserved!

***

As summer breezed into the Colorado Rockies, so did storms. On maneuvers that saw 99ers at altitudes at or above the timberline, summer storms often rattled below them. It was undoubtedly a first experience for many to climb through the clouds, then stand in brilliant sunshine and watch the lightning ripping across the clouds below them.

Although [while out on maneuvers no soldier wanted to be bothered with a toothache, especially if] it needed instant care. That possibility was considered by the battalion dentist, Captain Gustav Svendsen, [who] "set up shop" on many summer maneuvers. A foot-operated treadle furnished the power for his grinding tool. Whatever shortcomings "Doc" Svendsen experienced in the mountains were corrected long before similar dental services were offered in actual combat zones in France, Belgium, Holland, and Germany, many months later.

Toward the end of July, the entire battalion was marched down to the camp's dental clinic. Three days later the unit had inherited the identity of "The Toothless Battalion." Camp dentists who conducted the examinations said they had never found so many "store teeth" in one specific group. It was assumed that consumption of foods rich in sugar had decimated the God-given "choppers" of the Scandinavians!

Something was definitely in the air! The men could feel it during training periods as well as during off-hours.

A move seemed imminent.

On the Move Again

A scant two weeks after dental exams, the battalion was alerted for another move. Having become acclimated to Camp Hale and its surroundings, many Vikings felt a reluctance to leave. Yet they knew each progressive move would take them one step closer to the goal they had trained to achieve: invasion of Norway!

As the Viking Battalion marched north on the camp's so-called "main drag" toward the troop trains at a Pando, they felt the glow of pride. They had survived months of the most rugged training the Army had to offer! Greater things lay ahead, and whatever the challenges, they were anxiously awaiting them.[8]

Personnel from the 10th Light Mountain Division appeared along the 99th's line of March, saluting, waving, or shouting their best to the Norwegians who had shared so much in giving camp Hale a glowing reputation:

"So long, fellas…"

"Good luck…"

"See ya in Berlin…"

"Wherever you go, give 'em hell…!"

Not all 99ers who had trained with the battalion were able to accompany the unit. No one can forget the unfortunates who watched the loading of the troop trains. They stood transfixed, many with tears coursing down their cheeks.

As departing 99ers mounted the steps to the railroad coaches they also felt a sense of loss at having to leave some of their comrades behind. More than ever before, that moment revealed the deep feeling of kinship and brotherhood that had developed among them since the unit had been activated a year earlier.

Their destination was rumored to be Camp Shanks.

"Where's Camp Shanks? Parked on a mountainside, half-way up to the summit of Mt. Everest?"

The picture was clear, yet it was disturbingly unclear. After Camp Shanks… *then* what?

Giant locomotives, belching steam and smoke, thundered up the incline toward Tennessee pass as the 99ers watched camp slipping away below them. And as Cooper Hill faded from view many a 99er felt a deep longing for the camp as well as friends they left behind.

"When we came here," said one, "we were kinda soft and maybe a little scared. But now we're as tough as they come, and we're proud of the fact that there wasn't one single mountain around here that stopped us! We don't have to take a back seat to anyone!"

Another chirped: "If Camp Shanks is near New York, I'll bet we'll be going through Chicago!"

"You ought to know by now that troop trains don't go as the crow flies! Years from now you'll look at a map and retrace our route and wonder why the Army made such a long drag out of a relatively direct route!"

---

[8] Stensby wrote a note in the margins, which gave the date as August 24, 1943 for this event.

A long drag it was! From Pando the troop trains went South to Colorado Springs, then east across Kansas, Missouri, Illinois, Indiana, clipped the northwestern tip of Ohio, and entered Port Huron. From there the route swung into Canada before dropping south again, to their destination, Camp Shanks.

At various places along the route, the trains stopped. Hundreds of travel-weary 99ers jumped off. They were given a few minutes to limber up before strenuous calisthenics. At a stop in Kansas, an oval track around a football field beckoned. Vaulting the fence, 99ers barreled around the track at full speed. Witnesses were amazed.

"How come all you guys can run lickety split around the track and end up breathing as normally as when you started?"

"Simple, friend! When you charge up mountains to 12,000 feet altitude carrying a load equal to ¾ of your own weight, you develop more endurance than you can imagine! Lungs expand to make even the puniest runt barrel chested!" GIs the world over had a reputation for smearing it on a bit thick now and then, and 99ers were no exception.

The days at Camp Shanks were hectic. New equipment was issued, orientations were scheduled, and inoculations were plentiful. At the end there wasn't a 99er who hadn't had a shot of everything available, except whiskey and aquavit![9]

It was only a matter of a few days before the battalion, re-outfitted and inoculated, mounted trucks and a few hours later unloaded in the New York harbor area, there to board the SS *Mexico*. As the coastal banana boat glided out past the Statue of Liberty, tear-rimmed eyes beheld America's symbol of freedom…many of them for the last time![10]

The SS *Mexico*

"We gonna cross the Atlantic in *this* tub?"

"Whaddaya expect…first-class accommodations on the *Queen Mary*?"

Silence.

"Ya think we'll be going over alone or in a convoy?"

"Either way, we're safe…"

"How d'ya figure that?"

"The Krauts ain't gonna waste a torpedo on this overgrown tugboat!"

"Even if they don't, ya think this boat is safe?"

"This ain't a boat…it's a SHIP! Don't let a crewman hear you call it a boat, or he'll probably throw you overboard!"

Idle chatter designed to take the edge off the gnawing feeling in the pit of the stomach that comes from the apprehension and uncertainty of what lies ahead.

---

[9] Stensby wrote a note in the margins, which gave the date, August 27, 1943 for this event.

[10] Stensby wrote a note in the margins, which gave the date, September 4, 1943 for this event.

Nosing its way through the Narrows, the SS *Mexico* steamed around the Brooklyn "horn." Brooklynites crowded the deck to peer fondly at the landmarks they knew so well. The haze of the late September afternoon soon obliterated the New York skyline as the seagoing vessel wallowed into the waves.

***

As the sun broke above a watery horizon, the following morning guards manning post on the top deck were amazed to see the SS *Mexico* in the middle of a huge convoy. The entire flotilla seemed to sit motionless on the Atlantic. There were ships of all sizes in front and back, to the left and right. Sleek Navy destroyers and a cruiser patrolled the outer fringes of the convoy.

A penetrating chill borne on the winds of the North Atlantic broke the monotony of a complacent sea. The ship transporting the 99ers rode the waves as gamely as any, though many a Midwesterner succumbed to the annoyance of seasickness. Adding to their physical discomfort was the mental anguish of sweating out frequent alerts which, often as not, were punctuated by the hollow boom of distant depth charges.

On the 11th day after leaving New York, the convoy dissipated as it approached the coastline of Scotland, [and the men were thrilled at] the sight of approaching fighter planes. Excitement rose as the sleek British Spitfires roared overhead. In a matter of a few hours, the ship eased its way toward the harbor.[11]

Upon leaving the ship, men of the Viking Battalion were treated to Scottish hospitality as they gratefully partook of "TAY and KROMP-its" (tea and cookies) offered by ladies manning food carts outside of the nearby railroad station. After a hasty repast the men boarded quaint troop trains which, 16 hours later, arrived near Perham Downs Camp, Tidworth, Wiltshire, England.

***

Officers in charge of orientation classes jovially laid it on the line: "The first thing we have to do, men, is to learn to talk English!" To illustrate that the language *was* a bit different in England, an example was given:

Two Englishmen were admitted to the hospital. To alleviate the starchiness and boredom, they spoke to each other.

"Did you come in here to-DIE?" ask the one.

"No," the other answered. "I came here yester-DIE."

In addition to the little booklet explaining the differences between terms used stateside and in England, there were a host of "Don'ts":

"Don't refer to an Englishman as a 'Limey'...

"Don't be a know-it-all...

"Don't guzzle your beer...sip it like the natives do...

"Don't reveal the identity or purpose of our unit to anyone—especially the British military...

---

[11] Stensby wrote a note in the margins, which gave the date September 15, 1943 for this event.

"Above all, DON'T TALK NORWEGIAN! It sounds too much like German!"

In spite of the latter, it occasionally happened that 99ers on a pass "forgot" and were arrested by British MPs who suspected them of being German spies! On such occasions, getting back to the 99th usually proved to be a hassle and a half!

England

Except for the mattress covers that enlisted men had to fill with straw, the barracks of Perham Downs exceeded expectations. The buildings were of brick and had baths and recreational facilities. The camp had previously been occupied by British soldiers and the surrounding terrain was ideally suited to infantry training. Equidistant from the cities of Andover and Salisbury (pronounced AHN-dau-VAH and SELLS-bri by the English) the camp gave 99ers an opportunity to visit either city frequently.

It seemed a foregone conclusion that training in England would be different than "the same old thing" of charging up and down the steepest, highest hills in the vicinity as the battalion had done near Fort Snelling and at Camp Hale. The men assumed England was the last step before engaging in actual combat either in Norway or France.

Training began shortly after arriving at Perham Downs. Long hikes that wound through the quaint English countryside were interspersed with classes, lectures, orientations, tactical problems, weapons familiarization, firing rocket launchers, and mortar exercises using live ammunition. Days-long marches honed physical stamina, and simulated combat often left the individual to his own resources.

Over 100 men were sent to St. Agnes in Cornwall to fire .30- and .50-caliber machine guns. Others were taught to make flotation devices by shaping tree branches into a circular frame to which shelter halves were attached. Two dozen 99ers also completed combat swimming courses in London.

In a test of endurance instigated by the War Department, 300 99ers conducted a rations test in the dreary Dartmoor Forest. Each day for 15 days the contingent marched an average of 20 miles a day under full field pack, all the while slashing across swampy land and through the marshes of the moors with rain pelting them day after day.

Each participant was weighed in the morning and evening. Accurate records were kept of rations eaten, palatability of rations, and each man's physical condition.

All possessions were carried in field packs. Tents and bedding were continuously damp due to the waterlogged ground on which they slept. Unrelenting rain during the day didn't help matters any.

On the rare days when the sun would appear for a few hours, it was common to see a country squire starchily dressed in a shirt and vest, knickers, argyle socks, and brown oxfords waiting at the roadside until the men had marched by. The contemptuous stare of the nattily attired Englishman translated into the two words most commonly heard by GIs and 99ers alike: "Bloody Yanks!"

After the rations test was completed, the results were evaluated by representatives from the War Department and the SOS.[12] The test won laurels from the War Department. It was definitely another star in the 99th crown!

Back at camp participants noticed their feet had turned brown from the dye in their perpetually wet boots.

"Look at that!" blurted one of them. "My muscles must have turned into bands of steel … How else could my feet get so rusty?"

***

It is safe to say the 99ers greeted the new year, 1944, with elation. Months and months of rugged training had had a definite purpose, and the men felt 1944 would be the year in which they could settle a few scores with the Nazis. There seemed to be a growing consensus, though, that their cherished goal of invading Norway would not come to pass.

This is not to say there were not feelings of foreboding. They had seen firsthand the widespread devastation in England brought by the Nazis' saturation bombing raids. Targets did not appear to have been selected. Civilian populations had suffered as badly as so-called military targets. Occasional meetings with English soldiers who had survived the hell of Dunkirk revealed the bestiality of the Nazi war machine.

Assuming the same conditions existed in Norway, especially, as well as other occupied European countries, the 99ers' hatred for the Nazis rose to a fever pitch!

Glanusk Park

Around the middle of January an announcement was made:

"We are moving to Glanusk Park Camp near Abergavenny in Brecknockshire, South Wales. The nearest town is known as Crickhowell...!"

A beautiful countryside greeted the 99ers as they entered South Wales. Glanusk Park Camp was a picturesque, inviting area. A stately looking building, Glanusk Castle, would house the battalion headquarters staff, while the rest of the men were in Nissen huts. Adding to the pleasantness of the camp were the Welsh people, all of whom were very friendly and outgoing.

Surrounding the camp were high, steep, rugged hills. In Wales they were referred to as mountains, though 99ers who compared them to the Colorado Himalayas, downgraded the terrain features to that of "just plain hills."

Whether small mountains or just plain hills, they were to prove formidable barriers to the men who were at once thrown against them in a new, vigorous

---

[12] Services of Supply, a logistical organization of the Army.

training program. Bone-chilling winds tore at the men on long day-night marches, and woe to the nicotine fiend who tried to light a match at night for a quick drag or two. The physical aspects of training grew more strenuous in an atmosphere of "simulated combat conditions."

Maneuvers with tanks, using live ammo on field exercises, as well as boning up for physical dexterity that was needed to compete against British home guards on combat courses, honed the 99th to a razor-sharp edge. In the latter, Viking competitors performed so fantastically that Welsh observers praised the 99th's proficiency.

***

On a cold, rainy night at Glanusk the lilting notes of an accordion beckoned. Upon hearing the music one of the men waded through the rain and mud toward the source of the music.

After the outside Nissen door slammed shut, the blackout curtain parted to reveal a dismal-looking fan. Water dripped off his helmet onto his rivulet-infested raincoat. A crescent-shaped puddle of water gathered round his muddy boots and soaked pants cuffs. Wiping the water from his face and eyes he cast a glance at the musician, then threw up his hands in dismay.

"Nei, Fah'n skjaere mig, da! Her kommer e sørpande vaat a me møkk te knee-arna mine for aa høre knosert fra'n Tollefson, men saa er de bare han Arneson som sitter der aa klonker paa trek-spill!"
(Translation: "Well I'll be damned! Here I am, soaking wet and with mud up to my knees just to hear a concert by Tollefson, and all I find is Arneson sitting there horsing around on the accordion!")

***

Physically exhausting though the training would be, men were rewarded for their diligence to duty with many passes. Dances were held twice a week in nearby Abergavenny, a city of about 4,000. There [were no] pubs, nor the watered [down] brew the natives called "ile" (ale). Though the brew bore little resemblance to beer in the States, it was good enough for an evening out, either with fellow 99ers or whoever of the local citizenry accepted the invitation to join the Scandinavians.

As April drew to a close 52 men from the battalion were handpicked to serve as guards for the U.S. First Army Headquarters in Bristol. They were soon to win the praise of high-ranking officers for their efficiency and precise military bearing.

***

The approximately 100 men who were selected at Camp Hale by the Office of Strategic Services were stationed in Swansea, Wales.

A prerequisite for selection was their agreement to take parachute training. That inferred they would learn commando tactics, later to be dropped behind German lines in Norway, as the name "Norwegian Operational Groups" implied. After landing in Norway they would engage in sabotage and guerrilla warfare against the Nazis. Having been handpicked from a Norwegian American battalion also lent credence to the fact that Norway was to be their eventual destination.

Although the British commando training center was near Swansea, the 99ers in the NORSO group were sent to Manchester, England, headquarters for the British parachute school. Five jumps had to be completed to qualify as a paratrooper by British standards. They were later sent to Inverness near Loch Ness in Scotland.

***

The first of May, the 99th left Glanusk Camp for what many felt was a staging area of sorts at Ludlow, near Hereford, England. The entire area was swarming with GIs, and an unbelievable, miles-long array of military equipment stunned the newcomers. As tents housed the men, they somehow felt it was not just another training site.

Something BIG was in the air!

D-Day

No one will ever forget the tersely worded announcement over the BBC radio network on June 6, 1944:

"Allied forces under the command of General Dwight D. Eisenhower have landed on the north coast of France..."

Throughout the day news bulletins inferred that all was not well with the invasion. In spite of the thousands of Allied bombers that rained destruction on coastal defenses, and intense shelling of the French coast by Canadian, British, and United States naval units, a severe channel storm made the outcome of the invasion questionable. In spite of the obstacles, however, there were military analysts who predicted eventual success.

Huge steel underwater obstacles hampered landing crafts carrying GIs from transports to the beaches. Intense shelling of coastal areas by German long-range artillery and fierce encounters with the enemy added to the uncertainty. By nightfall, however, 130,000 Allied troops had a tenable foothold on French soil. In addition, 17,000 Allied paratroopers were fighting inland.

Mindful of the thousands of gallant young men from the United States, Canada, and England who had been killed or wounded in the Battle for the Beachhead, 99ers chafed under the verbal tirades of the English who insisted that the "Bloody Yanks" were staging only a Dieppe-type raid while the English were doing all the fighting and dying. Hence the long-awaited order to "move out" was welcome. Its primary destination, Uffculme (England), was reached the evening of June 10. After five days of "chompin' at the bit" the battalion was moved to Plymouth where, two days later, it received its orders to board ship.

The 99th left England on June 17 aboard the Liberty ship SS *John Henry*. A warning that the channel crossing "might" be rough was the understatement of the year! Battalion rifle marksmen on the top deck were ordered to keep their eyes peeled for floating mines and U-boat periscopes and to pepper away at either. A lucky hit could detonate a mine, and at least shatter a periscope.

Marksmen found it utterly impossible to maintain the required stands on a deck that heaved as the ship lurched through the waves. Tin cans tossed overboard as "targets" were swallowed up in the waves before anyone could draw a bead on them.

Anti-aircraft guns bristled aboard the SS *John Henry* and all nearby ships. The assortment of ships that steamed out from Plymouth and nearby ports had formed into a large convoy. Navy ships patrolled the outer fringes of the convoy, and planes zoomed overhead.

The morning of the third day of the crossing revealed a sight to behold! Troop transports, supply ships, Navy ships as far as the eye could reach! The low-lying mass of brownish gray in the distance was France! Hundreds of barrage balloons tethered to ships near the coast hung motionless in the haze.

Riflemen crowded the deck, anxious to lend their firepower to the event of a strafing attack by Nazi planes. Whatever the odds, the 99th was ready for a fight with the hated foe, though not in Norway as they had hoped.

The SS *John Henry* nosed its way into an assigned niche off the French coast. A breakwater of sunken ships lay between it and Omaha Beach. As darkness settled over the ships at anchor, the distant sky was aflame with the flashes of artillery bombardments. German observation planes, flying high overhead, invited an inverted cone of anti-aircraft tracers from the dozens of ships in the harbor. A diffused flash and a trailing tail of flame periodically marked the sudden end for the Nazi plane.

Helmeted 99ers on deck beheld the spectacles as an omen of success. Amid the "thunk" of shell fragments that rained down on the deck, they raised a Bronx cheer each time a German plane met its fate.

A raging storm prevented the 99th from unloading as scheduled. For nearly three days the Liberty ship creaked and groaned as it pitched about on the waves. In the early afternoon of the third day the 99ers were ordered to don impregnated gas-proof clothing and prepare for landing. Ex-seamen and land lovers alike crowded the railing, there to await the signal to clamber down the cargo nets to the flat-bottom boat below them.

As the hatches of the LCIs were lowered 99ers expected to wade hip deep to shore. Instead they found themselves struggling in water up to their necks or over their heads, depending on their stature.[13]

Making their way onto the debris-littered beach, they caught a glimpse of the temporarily erected white wooden crosses marking the graves of invasion casualties.

The crosses appeared to be blood red in the rays of the setting sun!

---

[13] Stensby wrote a note in the margins, which gave the date June 21, 1944 for this event.

"Zigarett Pour Pa-Pah…?"

The 3-mile hike inland to Transit Area 3 was a welcome diversion. Days aboard a troop transport that had wallowed at anchor and the channel gale made muscles beg for relief!

Along the line of march the men were soon to see the frightful carnage of war. Huge bomb craters and lesser gouges in the earth from heavy artillery had desecrated what had once been a beautiful countryside. Squatting menacingly, knocked-out German pillboxes bore the scars of direct hits from naval bombardments. Large trees had been uprooted as though yanked out of the ground by a giant hand. Wrecked farm buildings and burned-out military vehicles littered the area. Here and there lay discarded signs bearing the warning "Achtung! Minen."

Reaching the bivouac area, 99ers wasted no time digging in. Existing slit trenches were dug deeper, while the majority of men tackled the hard earth crust with pickaxes and entrenching tools. Whatever semblance of protective trenches they were able to complete offered at least a degree of safety in the event of a Kraut artillery barrage.

Clawing at many a conscience was the hollow intonation of a combat MP: "If you get a direct hit, don't worry about it!" Grinning at his own callousness, he added: "There are many bypassed Germans in this area…BE ALERT!"

As darkness closed in on the bivouac area, the men were conscious of a lone plane droning overhead. "That's a Kraut observation plane," explained the MP. "We call him 'Bedcheck Charlie.' While he's snoopin' around, don't light a match or we'll all be dead ducks afore mornin'!"

Physical exertion beckoned sleep, though nervous tension aborted it. The constant, undulating flashes of artillery glowed in the distance, and the rolling thunder of the big guns were, in a way, reminiscent of an approaching thunderstorm.

When at long last fitful sleep began to overtake the men, many of them felt the tense, gnawing illusion of being entirely alone. A light breeze that skittishly scampered across the low-lying hills brought with it wisps of a sweet, sickening stench. The stomach-churning smell was later to be identified as that of decaying human flesh!

***

The following day a truck convoy transported the 99th to the vicinity of Colombières, several miles inland—there to be attached to the Provisional Ranger Group of the First U.S. Army. The move brought the 99ers into close proximity to the Germans. An embankment below its front line revealed a swampy terrain. From it came the unmistakable crack of a rifle!

"Hey, Sarge!" yelled a startled 99er. "Some sonnafabitch is shootin' at us!"

"Wuffacripsake, shoot back! What tha hell ya think we're here for!"

M1s up and down the line barked their protest and defiant challenge of the unseen target. The labored "thunk-thunk" of a BAR added its vengeance. Then, like an exhausted pianist running the scale, the firing subsided and stopped.

"Damn snipers! I hate 'em! They ain't got no guts!"

"They don't need guts. They're just robots doing what Der Fuehrer's lackeys tell them to do!"

The first Sunday on French soil dawned clear and warm. Because Germans were said to have crept ever closer during the night, there were constant reminders to be very quiet. The demands for no unnecessary noises cast an almost zombie-like spell over the otherwise aggressively inclined 99ers. That trance was shattered in a volley of snorts and guffaws when it became known that the chaplain had dispatched an order:

"Have the bugler sound church call at 10:00 am."

***

Contrary to the GIs' *Guidebook to France*, the French people were not friendly. They created the impression of being afraid to talk to Americans. Dominated and browbeaten by Nazi occupation troops for five years prior to D-Day, they may have been warned of dire consequences if they befriended the Yanks.

Armor-clad indifference among 99ers toward the unfriendly French melted only when seemingly shy boys or girls sought favors. Tense and wide-eyed boys frequently approached a 99er and asked: "Zigarett pour Pa-Pah?" Scampering behind the nearest trees, they would light up and smoke it themselves. A girl's plea for "Sjokolat pour Ma-Mah" met the same fate of self-indulgence.

Thus, mamas or papas, who probably hadn't seen either chocolate or good cigarettes for years, never benefited from the 99ers' consistent generosity!

Up the Normandy Peninsula

After the first encounter with a sniper, stray shots from suspected enemy positions were usually ignored. Keeping a low profile rankled the Vikings as all of them were eager to tangle with the Krauts. The logic behind abstaining was: you can't win a war by shooting holes in the air!

"By-the-book" tactics came to life as 99ers intently listened to lectures by officers and enlisted men who had been attacking the Germans after D-Day. The personal experiences of combat veterans carried much more weight than the printed word.

The 99th's association with Colombières was relatively short-lived. Checking and rechecking equipment seemed to be a prelude to an order that would change the scenery.

"Be ready to move out at 8:00 a.m."

"Where to?"

"Carentan, St. Joseph, and Cherbourg."

A couple of miles east of Carentan the truck convoy was halted by combat MPs. They said there had been skirmishes in Carentan only hours before.

Rifles and machine guns bristled from every truck as the convoy entered Carentan. Feelings of apprehension mounted as the trucks wound through the narrow streets.

The entire town lay in ruins. Most of the buildings had been leveled by bombs or artillery. Others—roofless shells—had been gutted by fire. Wisps of smoke curled up from buildings apparently destroyed in the fighting earlier in the day.

As the convoy proceeded north the men witnessed unbelievable destruction. Ste. Mère Église, a prime target of paratroopers in the early morning of D-Day, also bore grim evidence of a terrific shellacking. Without further incident the convoy proceeded to St. Joseph and into the port city of Cherbourg. Nowhere along the road did 99ers detect an iota of friendliness. The children would scamper into the street to pick up whatever tidbits the 99ers offered; there were never any "Mercis." Never a greeting of any kind in return. Whenever adults ventured out to see the Yanks pass [by, they would] glare "daggers" at them.

"They must have liked being slaves of the Nazis...They sure as hell have a cold welcome for us guys!"

**

Cherbourg

"The 99th entered Cherbourg and secured the city..."[14]

"Just like that?"

"Hardly!"

No sooner had the battalion been billeted than patrols were on the streets. It soon became apparent that the city was well populated by fifth columnists and bypassed German troops, intent on "preserving" the city until the Nazi slave masters returned. That belief seemed to have been hammered into the French before the Germans were driven out.

Each company was assigned a segment of the city, ever on the alert against the sabotaging of military installations, fuel depots, harbor, and rail facilities. An isolated contingent of German diehard troops manned positions that guarded Nazi U-boat pens. Constantly bombarded from air and sea, the Krauts eventually surrendered. As the inner and outer harbor areas had been heavily mined, 99ers found it a ticklish assignment to cross the harbor waters, especially since many of the mines could be detonated by sound waves! When no motorboat could be gotten from the French, 99ers crossed to the U-boat pens, and [picked up] surrendering Germans, in a sailboat!

**

A squad on patrol soon experienced a "baited booby trap." Momentarily distracted by shouts of "Viva la Yank!" the men spotted three mademoiselles at a window, waving and throwing kisses. As the sudden outburst of friendliness was inconsistent with the coolness of the French, the 99ers became suspicious. Roving eyes spotted two

---

[14] Stensby wrote a note in the margins, which gave the date June 29, 1944 for this event.

gun barrels being eased out onto the ledge of a nearby upstairs window. A chorus of M1s brought yelps of pain from above, and the subsequent clatter of two German rifles as they fell onto the cobblestones below.

Sent to retrieve a jeep, a 99er barely got around the corner before a sniper's bullet chipped masonry above his head. Ducking into a doorway, he tried to spot the sniper's location. Facing back the way he came, he saw the belltower of an old church. Firing a clip at the tower, he darted back to his safety zone, drawing enemy fire as he ran. He repeated his advance-fire-retreat tactics until half of his ammo was gone.

Drawn to the scene of the duel, several other 99ers joined the fight. Concentrated rifle fire poured into the belfry until the sniper bolted upright and lurched backwards.

The sniper had been silenced. He had earned his just reward!

Blasted out of the solid rock on the southern fringes of Cherbourg was Fort du Roule. The massive fort had four levels, each level having several tunnels arranged like the spokes of a wheel, all of them accessible from a central hub—a perpendicular shaft extending from the first floor to the deepest level of tunnels. Each tunnel was stocked with ammunition, food, clothing, cigarettes, cognac by the barrels, soft drinks, water, and whatever miscellaneous products the Germans deemed necessary for indefinite survival.

Dominating the harbor area and the English Channel beyond, were the big German coastal guns, useless to them in defense as U.S. First Army's VII Corps had attacked the Krauts in Cherbourg from the rear. The big coastal guns were kept in the tunnels that were open at the north ends.

Tunnels cradling coastal guns were stocked with thousands of shells fused and ready to go. The projectiles may have been equal to 105mm, or so. Guns of larger caliber were also seen, though none of them came even close to the caliber of German railroad guns.

It became a daily ritual for guards stationed at the fort to gather up arms full of canned meats, fish, butter, bread, and cigarettes to the west wall of the fort. At night, the "confiscated" staples were thrown over the wall to eager French people waiting below. Such occasions did bring expressions of gratitude from people fortunate to be on the receiving end of the 99ers' thoughtfulness.

Many cases of canned fish bore the labels of Norwegian canneries. That made guards' blood boil! That people in Norway were starving was common knowledge amongst the 99ers. It added to the seething rage and hatred they had for the thieving Nazis.

Manning a guard post on the upper outside tier of the fort was downright spooky! Beyond the southern perimeter were many hydraulically operated one-man encapsulated foxholes, many of which contained the body of a dead German soldier. Huge police dogs, evidently shellshocked, appeared to snarlingly attack the guard, only to charge past until they either collided with a wall or plunged off a ledge and onto a street far below.

German planes flew high overhead, triggering a lusty response from anti-aircraft guns. In the unbelievably quiet early morning hours, many a guard heard wailing that turned into heart-rending screams, often as not terminated by a shot. Whether pantomimed for the benefit of unnerving the Yanks, as well as the populace, it grated against the heart and soul of the beholder. Occasionally there came sounds of a German "Burp" gun that fractured the stillness. At times it would be followed by another short burst of gunfire from another location within the confines of the city that sprawled beneath the fort.

It was on the south road leading to the fort that a 99er on guard halted a jeep carrying Gen. Eisenhower. Not having permission to proceed, the jeep had no recourse but to turn around and leave. The following day Gen. Eisenhower contacted Battalion with the praiseworthy message: "Your guard was the best I have ever encountered in the American Armed Forces!" The end result was that the general asked for 50 99ers to serve as guards for Army headquarters.

"E viste han var sint," remarked the guard, "men naar ingen ska gaa forbi, saa meiner de jo INGEN!" ("I knew he was mad, but when no one is allowed to proceed, that means just that—NO ONE!")

Upon completing its assignment to the Fourth Port Headquarters at Cherbourg, the 99th was moved to a new location 8 miles south of the port city. From Haut de Haut[15] the 99th, in conjunction with the 2nd and 5th Ranger Battalions and the 759th Light Tank Battalion, patrolled an area between Cherbourg and Valognes. Intermittent activities included night-firing exercises, and field training with the tank battalion. Security patrols also conducted sniper hunts and sought out bypassed enemy troops, their materials, and ammunition.

When the situation around Haut de Haut became well stabilized, Col. Turner issued the welcome order that a dance would be held in the area. A truckload of females was promised from Cherbourg. The considerate colonel had assumed all instruments for the orchestra were available.

They were...almost!

There was one exception: the drums! The drummer's explanation, though understandable, was nevertheless a bit irritating:

"The only place I could haul 'em was on Nick's[16] kitchen truck. Nick arranged his load so he had room for my stuff just inside the tailgate.

"That went OK 'til we had the 'fluid front' crap. Nick would unload his truck, then in a short time we'd get orders to move out again. A few times like that and Nick got his dander up.

So he told me, 'If you're gonna use my truck to haul your stuff all over France, you better be here to load and unload 'em yourself! I've got enough to do without taking care of *your* junk!'

---

[15] The author may have meant Hameau de Haut.

[16] Stensby's original footnote says, "Nickolai Nickolaison, A Co. Mess Sergeant."

"I couldn't do that, as I was in another platoon. So, I told Nick he didn't have to tote my drums anymore. He gave me a kinda funny look. So, I said, 'Don't worry about 'em Nick,' and let it go at that. That's the day I buried 'em in a field next to a hedgerow."

As hedgerows were a dime a dozen in Normandy, and as one hedgerow looked pretty much like any other, it was small wonder that the exasperated drummer had a bit of difficulty locating his buried treasure in time for the dance!

***

A grisly reminder of Nazi brutality was witnessed by three 99ers on patrol. Having read about such horrors was bad enough; *seeing* evidence that the Nazis subjected human beings to torture was something else!

An older man limped toward the jeep. He was wild eyed, and his hair looked like a little gray bush. His shirt was open, and his tattered trousers were held in place by a length of dirty string.

"Gestapo! Gestapo!" he screamed, pointing to a low mustard-colored building near the road.

Rifles ready, the four went toward the building. Blasting the lock with rifle fire, they wearily entered the short hallway. The air was unbelievably putrid!

At the end of the hallway a door led to a relatively small room. The patrol retched at the sight and the indescribable smell!

Jabbering in French, the man pointed to the meat hooks hanging on the walls, then indicated that victims were hung upside down after the hooks were thrust into the tendons above the ankle. Taking off his shoes, he showed a jagged scar behind the ankle bone of each foot.

He called attention to two walls that were blotched and stained a reddish brown, then revealed the contents of a cabinet in the corner. It contained an assortment of whips —the worst one having been made out of strands of barbed wire! A short length of steel cable had barbed wire tightly wrapped around it.

A couple feet off the floor was a concrete slab with shackles at both ends and small gutters on the sides, which the Frenchman indicated was to drain away the blood of the victim. He also found a collection of knives. Ripping off his shirt he showed his back that was laced with long scars and clusters of welted flesh.

"Le Bosh!" he screamed. "Le Bosh! Le Bosh!" He drew his finger across his throat, emitting a long, wailing scream of hatred for the Germans!

The Breakthrough[17]

With men and materials pouring into France at an ever-increasing pace, scuttle-butt prompted opinions as to when and where the First Army would attempt a

---

[17] Stensby wrote a note in the margins, which gave the date July 25, 1944 for this event.

breakthrough. Although the 99th was in reality "just a pebble on the beach," it would shortly be sent to one of the hot spots the breakthrough created.

Pressured by British and Canadian armies on its retreating northern flanks, and by the U.S. First Army from the Normandy Peninsula, the Germans had but two choices: either attempt to break through to the west or continue to retreat still further into the Falaise Pocket.

After a saturation bombing raid on St. Lô, the stunned and demoralized German resistance cracked to the extent that the First Army surged forward. At approximately the same time, the Germans massed men and materials northeast of Mortain, Barenton, and Domfront. The Krauts' goal was to halt the First Army advance and push through to Avranches on the west coast.

**

A truck convoy with the Viking Battalion aboard entered St. Lô well after dark. The entire area was smothered under a blanket of intimidating odors—burnt cordite, smoke, dust, and the horrible stench of decomposing human flesh.

There was no warning of the presence of German aircraft until the first bombs exploded in fields to either side of the road. Men were in the ditches before the trucks had stopped. Fighter planes followed the bombers and strafed one side next to the convoy. Swinging into a high arc, exhaust stacks telegraphed a run on the other side of the road. Sounding feeble against the exploding bombs was the racket from anti-aircraft guns. Men who had sought safety in the fields away from the trucks found their exits blocked by high, thorny hedgerows. As none of the trucks were bombed or strafed, the blocking hedgerows proved to be their salvation.

**

Reaching their objective by early morning, the 99th was deployed along the Mortain–Barenton line of defense. The entire area was in a "fluid-front" situation. Defensive positions were changed repeatedly during the battalion's first couple of days.[18]

The 99th braced for an attack that never came. News trickled in and revealed that the Germans had suffered terrible losses in men and materials at the hands of rocket-equipped English fighter planes. Its breakout attack blunted, the Germans retreated into what became known as the Falaise Pocket. As the Germans began a headlong retreat of its armies eastward, it became identifiable as the Falaise–Argentan Pocket.

To aid in keeping pressure on the Germans in its area, the 99th was assigned to Combat Command B of the Second Armored Division. No sooner had the assignment been made than the mission was canceled and the 99th put in reserve status.

---

[18] Stensby wrote a note in the margins, which gave the date August 14–20, 1944 for this event.

Strung out later along the Mortain–Barenton–Domfront line were C, B, and A Companies with attachments from D and, of course, the incomparable medics! Long gaps existed between the companies. As a result, C Company could not know the exact locations of B or A, and vice versa.

In order to assemble the battalion in the A Company area, two messengers known for their exceptional memories for details were given a jeep and told to guide C and B to the assembly area.

Leaving the A Company area in late afternoon, the guides knew well enough they could not make it back to the assembly area until long after dark. With Krauts roaming the nearby hills, it was anything but a pleasant job.

"The hackles on my neck tingled when I thought of what could have happened if we picked the wrong road. These snake trails the French have the gall to call roads, all look alike in the daytime, say nothing of at night," said one of the guides. "But we paid special attention to every terrain feature going out, and even if it was blacker'n the ace of spades coming back, we *did* recognize the same features and got the whole battalion back together again!"

"Amen!" wheezed the other guide. Turning to his partner he said, "Ya know, it's funny they'd send us on a detail like that. Buck-ass privates aren't supposed to be that intelligent!"

"Maybe after this tour guide service we won't be holding our BA degrees for long...!"

"Ya wanna bet?"

"Nope...I know the Army works in wondrous ways at times, but never *that* wondrous!"

***

The cat-eyed headlights of yet another truck convoy ferried the 99ers into another pitch-black night. Their new assignment was that of armored infantry for CCB of the Second Armored.

A brilliant flash of light followed by a thunderous BLAM! to one side of the road brought the convoy to a screeching halt. Men wasted no time piling out of the trucks.

It was, undoubtedly, another air attack by the Krauts. Minutes later the 99ers remounted the trucks, perhaps feeling a bit sheepish that the big guns were their own firing at distant German military targets.

The new bivouac area was reached at about 3:00 a.m. Serenaded by the muffled boom of distant artillery, the 99ers were able to judge the area as that of long, low-lying hills. Entrenching tools soon grated against rocky soil. Efforts to dig a decent slit trench were further stymied by tree roots that laced the area.

Exasperated over lack of progress, some of the men resorted to verbal tirades to vent their ire. Momentarily forgetting where they were, they salted their commentaries with Norwegian profanity. That led to the natural desire to talk Norwegian amongst themselves.

Noting unusual activity in its midst, the 2nd Armored Division sent a recon patrol to investigate. As the area between Domfront and Alençon to the east was still in danger of German attack, the strained jabbering on the hill was suspected to be that of Krauts who had wandered into the division's "front yard." They lost no time in relaying the information to Division Headquarters.

Within minutes every artillery piece within range had zeroed in on the terrain manned by the 99th. Then at a most opportune time the recons heard someone rip into a tirade of profanity such as only a Yank could master.

After the 99th had been identified an officer asked: "Where the hell did you guys come from! You sounded just like a bunch of damn Krauts!"

The incident of near annihilation of the 99th throttled the habit of talking Norwegian in a combat zone!

With the 2nd Armored Division[19]

Reattachment to CCB of the 2nd Armored Division east of Domfront gave the 99th a renewed feeling of pride. Except for very short periods when it was attached to the Rangers, the Viking Battalion had been a separate unit. True to the spirit of the 99ers though there were those who felt the 2nd Armored should rather be attached to the 99th!

Their new associate immediately launched into an instructional crash course. The 99ers were briefed on tactics that personnel of the famed "Hell on Wheels" armored division had learned in many fierce encounters with the enemy. CCB's 41st Armored Infantry demonstrated how to establish effective roadblocks, proper use of division artillery, and the right way to use communications within the division.

After the Germans aborted their attacks in the Mortain Barenton Domfront areas, the 2nd Armored and the 99th made a headlong dash some 60 miles east, to the vicinity of Toureuvre. There the 99th immediately set up roadblocks to stop any German troops still trying to escape the Falaise–Argentan Pocket.

No sooner had the roadblocks been set up before the 99th drew heavy concentrations of enemy artillery that continued sporadically through the night. Throughout the intense shelling the Vikings suffered no casualties.

When a defensive unit is subjected to intense small arms fire, or when it is the target of artillery bombardments, or encounters air attacks, casualties are expected. It seemed a strange twist of fate, however, when lives are lost due to an accident in an area not drawing enemy fire.[20]

Landmines had been planted on a road that led to an assembly area for the 99th. A guard was posted at each spot where a mine was located. The guard's responsibility was to remove a mine if it endangered passage of a battalion vehicle. A guard at one

---

[19] Stensby wrote a note in the margins, which gave the date August 14–20, 1944 for this event.

[20] Stensby wrote a note in the margins, which gave the date August 21, 1944 for this event.

of the mines noticed too late that an approaching vehicle would not have enough clearance. The resulting mine explosion killed two enlisted men and wounded an officer and 10 enlisted men. Long before the dust had settled the incomparable battalion medics were at the scene, caring for the wounded.

The following day the 99th advanced to Beit where roadblocks were set up. The Germans had bypassed that town but were found in strength at Le Failly. Forces from division reserve captured the city and took approximately 150 prisoners.

***

Squeezed out of the Falaise–Argentan Pocket by the continuous pressure from the British and Canadian armies on the north, and U.S. First Army on the west and south, the badly decimated German forces found escape routes diminishing. In an effort to slam shut the gates on escape routes, the 2nd Armored, with the 99th, swung north of Toureuvre to Verneuil.

In the vicinity of Verneuil the Germans launched a night attack, first with artillery, then air attacks. Bombers and fighter planes repeatedly swept over the armored columns that were illuminated by parachute flares. Men who dove under the tanks felt relatively secure as the area was strafed. Had the planes attacked the armored column broadside, casualties could have resulted. [As] intense though [as the] enemy shelling, bombing, and strafing would be, neither the 2nd nor the 99th suffered any casualties.

With artillery concentrations known as either "stonks" or "serenades," the [2nd Armored Division] silenced enemy guns, and its anti-aircraft batteries persuaded German planes to depart. The assault ceased as suddenly as it had begun.

The 99th continued north with the 2nd until rumors had it that the Seine River was just a short distance away. En route the 99ers traversed a British Army sector, and found it amazing that its soldiers seemed more concerned about brewing a "spot of tea" than they were about German troops in the area.

There was no evidence of apprehension when 99ers were briefed on their next assignment: "Tomorrow we attack the city of Elbeuf…!"

Elbeuf

On August 25, the entire battalion launched an attack on the city of Elbeuf, which straddled the Seine River. By 1600 they entered the town in the face of heavy artillery, mortar, tank, and small arms fire and pushed all the way to the river by 1635, knocking out four German tanks before the tank destroyers could catch up. Artillery fire from the other side of the river continued all that night, and the next morning the battalion command post was hit, injuring several officers and enlisted men, including the battalion commander, Lt. Col. Turner, who was evacuated. Major Hansen then took over command of the battalion.

At 1800, on the 26th, the battalion was relieved by Canadian forces, and left town under heavy artillery fire from the north side of the Seine, after losing nine officers, seven enlisted men killed and 41 wounded.[21]

August 28, the battalion was attached to Combat Command A of the 2nd Armored and took several enemy positions on the way to Belgium.

August 31, the battalion moved to Drucourt, where they rested and received replacements, while establishing local security.

September 6, they moved to Mons, Belgium to secure the city. Then on September 8 they were moved back to Valenciennes, France to guard the First Army sector against probable attack by an enemy pocket in the British sector to the north and west of town. Motorized and foot patrols were conducted between Mons and Valenciennes for four days, and 17 Krauts were taken prisoner.

The Battle for Elbeuf…

It was a weird entourage to meet in a combat zone!

At first glance it was but a funeral procession of sorts. Building the group was an erect man dressed in clergy garb. (A mere 100-foot distance lay between the "grievance train" and the left flankers of the advancing units of the 99th, making it easy to detect details that otherwise might have been ignored.)

The clergyman, black book in hand, appeared more interested in the GIs to his left than the somber procession he was leading. His hat was a three-cornered monstrosity reminiscent of male headgear in colonial days.

Behind the clergyman came a two-man "span," leading an old black horse, as swaybacked a nag as ever was. Its large hooves beat a slow "clop-clop" cadence over the roadway. In the brilliant sunshine of that August 25 morning, only one attachment was strikingly reflective.

A long, thin rail ran the length of the black horse-drawn hearse. Though its windows were heavily draped, there was a certain something that did not ring true. Did someone detect movement inside the hearse?

Of course not! The poor soul was dead!

…or was it?…

Hardly had the reserve elements of the 99th cleared its line of departure before the Germans opened up on it with uncanny accuracy. "Screaming Meemies" by the dozens left their pods to come screaming like all the banshees in hell were on parade. Crashing to earth, they effectively "boxed" the 99ers in reserve. Several rounds of long-range artillery punctuated the serenade, though the entire barrage did little to ruffle the nerves or the determination of the attacking 99th!

***

---

[21] Stensby had a note in the margins here stating that there were 86 German prisoners taken.

Located on the Seine River, Elbeuf was a scant 10 miles due south of Rouen, France. As one of the last remaining escape routes to the east, Elbeuf was well supplied with bridges and watercraft to ferry defeated German troops to safer temporary areas. It would soon become evident to the 99th that Elbeuf was heavily defended by the Germans.

CHAPTER FOUR

Stensby Collection

In addition to the manuscript that Yngvar Stensby created of the 99th Battalion's actions throughout the early training and to the battle of Elbeuf, there are additional materials that had been collected by him but not formally included in the manuscript. This chapter includes two such items of note.

The first is a typed document that was found in the materials collected by Stensby. It was written by Stensby himself, but he wrote on it "Recollections," which were memories from individual soldiers and not put in the actual manuscript. It tells the heartfelt story of the death of the beloved Sgt. Skarning in the battle at Canal Drive in Belgium.

The second inclusion is a letter in which Stensby is responding to the book titled The Damn Engineers, *by Janice Holt Giles, originally published in 1970. Reading this book, and what it said about the 99th, seemed to get Yngvar to reminisce about the war. He wrote this on November 14, 1984. The letter is assumed to be a copy of a letter that Yngvar Stensby sent to someone named "Gus."*

Canal Drive—Sergeant Skarning

In early fall the 99th, again with the Second Armored, found itself in the vicinity of Mechelen, Belgium, poised for the Canal Drive. A Company's advance halted abruptly one afternoon when we found the bridge over the canal had been destroyed by retreating Nazi forces.

We were greeted by occasional bursts from Nazi Burp guns,[1] as well as harassed by snipers hidden in trees on the other side of the canal. "Volunteers" from various squads in the 99th soon lined the canal bank intent on locating the snipers and putting them out of action.

Among the riflemen was Sgt. Skarning. He had a pleasant, reassuring air of confidence about him, and his ever-present smile was balm for the harried soul. At his urging, we sprang out along the bank so as not to provide a group target to

---

[1] American nickname for a German submachine gun.

the snipers. His eyes narrowed to slits as he surveyed the trees on the east side of the canal; then, without a word, he emptied several clips of ammunition at what he surmised was a suspicious-looking treetop. Riflemen to his left and right joined in until it was obvious at least one of the snipers had been dispatched.

The following morning several tanks arrived in our area. Riflemen climbed onto the rear decks of the tanks before they churned south along the Willems Vaart Canal on combat patrol.

Of the half-dozen men on our tank, the only one I distinctly remember was Sgt. Skarning. He was sitting on my left and slightly behind me. One moment he was there; the next moment he was missing.

Returning to the bivouac area someone asked what happened to Sgt. Skarning. The commanding officer assumed he had been pitched off the tank when it lurched across a small ravine. He also said that none of the tanks had drawn enemy fire, hence the possibility of being hit was ruled out.

We knew a tank would not stop for one dislodged rifleman. To do so would have made the tank vulnerable to enemy anti-tank guns. As it was hard enough to maintain one's balance on a tank without anything to hang on to, we hopefully assumed that our amiable sergeant had, indeed, been bounced off the tank when it crossed the ravine.

A grim-face lieutenant approached. We sensed the gravity of his announcement before it was made. Call it a sixth sense; call it intuition.

"Sergeant Skarning is dead!"

A wave of resentment flooded over me. Hatred of the Nazis bored into every organ of my body. Why Sgt. Skarning? Why not me? I was sitting right beside him! It seemed he had so much more to live for than I. In a seething rage I checked my rifle and headed for the canal again. I was joined by every rifleman in the area.

"Some damn sniper got him!" cursed a 99er.

"Some damn sniper is going to get his just reward!" screamed another, as volley after volley of rifle fire poured across the canal.

The 99ers had suffered many deaths before, but none struck me as numbingly as the knowledge that our highly regarded, respected, talented, beloved Sgt. Skarning had been killed.

***

Sgt. Skarning's smile still lingers in my memory. And never do I listen to the plaintive notes of a bugler's "Taps" but what I feel his presence and hear again his reassuring assessment in a tense situation.

Yngvar Stensby
Co. A
99th Inf. Bn (Sep.)

Response to the Damn Engineers

Hi Gus…

Thanks so much for the report reproducing excerpts from the book *The Damned Engineers*. From personal experience I knew the situation at Malmedy was pretty much touch and go, but I hadn't realized the situation was as precarious as the book described!

And your question, "Where was A Company?" set the ol' noggin too grinding away. Seems strange that a war episode of such caliber as our defense of Malmedy leaves so many gaps in my memory!

Before the Nazis blitzed Allied lines in what came to be known as the Battle of the Bulge, the night headquarters were at Tilff, but A Company was assigned to patrolling highways in a half-moon that extended west-northwest of Bastogne up to where it turned northeast-east to La Roche. Part of A Company was at St. Hubert, about 15 miles west of Bastogne. Part of A Co. was stationed at a town called Libin, 9 or so miles west of St. Hubert.[2]

Night patrols, via jeep, were frequent on the Bastogne–La Roche route, and we were instructed to keep an eye peeled for "unusual activity" in the area.

The Libin detachment left Libin on Monday, the 18th, and joined the rest of "A" at St. Hubert for the advance to Malmedy. The most direct route would have been to Vielsalm and up to Stavelot, but due to an advancing German armored column, the "A" entourage had to detour west of Vielsalm and head north.

I remember so clearly the relatively narrow road was crowded with Belgians who were fleeing the German invasion. It was pathetic to see the scarce belongings they carried, and to see the fear etched on their faces and in their eyes. I guess that was the first time a lot of us really grasped the importance of our move.

We got into Spa after dark. It was a hell of a mess, what with military vehicles, uncertainty, buzz bombs roaring overhead. Spa was about 14 miles northwest of Malmedy.

Once in Malmedy, Capt. Svarstad and I had to hoof it to find Col. Hansen's HQ. I clearly remember Svarstad telling me, "Keep an eye peeled—there's going to be a German attack." Keep your eyes peeled. Thanks. In the middle of the night, blacker than the ace of spades, not knowing if the Krauts were in town, and wondering what good one lousy M1 would do if the situation arose!

Where "A" was positioned after that I can't recall. I do remember being at "A" CP which was a paper warehouse, which undoubtedly would have been close to the paper mill mentioned in the excerpt you sent. How long we were there is uncertain.[3]

---

[2] In the margins, Stensby wrote that this was "2nd Platoon," and that "1st PLT. MARCHE AND 3RD PLT AT ARLON."

[3] In a handwritten note, Stensby wrote, "1st PLT. OF A CO. WAS AT RIGHT FLANK OF B CO. ON R.R.R ALL THE TIME IN MALMEDY."

In the period right before Christmas, though, "A" was defending a line on the crest of some hills between Malmedy and Stavelot. Shivering in a poor excuse for a foxhole, I remember it was Christmas Eve, and thoughts and emotions went to the comforts of home, in the hundreds or thousands of voices they're singing "Silent Night" while in our corner of the world buzz bombs were growling their messages of death and destruction as they roared overhead. "Peace on earth" seemed a farce for me—and thousands of other GIs that Christmas Eve!

I also remember one of our officers getting the message that "B Company kicked the holy-hell out of the Krauts outside of Malmedy!" That sticks in my memory because that was about the only thing we had heard of a positive nature since we got into the mess.

While in that sector I also remember a guard relaying the information that "there's a whole big mess of German tanks down there on the road!" Though artillery shells were in short supply, they dropped several rounds where they supposedly did the most good.

There was also a platoon on the south slope of a series of hills east of us. They had an artillery spotter with them. We were in contact with them until the Germans dropped five rounds of artillery right behind their position, cutting the phone line between us. A GI by the name of Forde in "A" [Company] and I, both of us having had a smattering of communications at Camp Hale, were given the assignment to go out and splice the break.

Forde "palmed" our end of the wire until his hands got cold, then I'd take over. Thus we leapfrogged our way until the break in the line was found. Then the parachute flares. Jeez, how I hated those things! I swore I was as noticeable as the rock of Gibraltar would have been squatting out there under the glare. Then the zing of a bullet which we knew damn well wasn't "just a stray." The line crew from the other end met us at last, and the break finally repaired, it was just as hair-raising returning to our position, what with understandably trigger-happy guards ready to blast anything that moved!

We must have relieved "B" at the railroad tracks sometime before New Year's Day. On that day I was on guard, and a Kraut Me-109 [Messerschmitt] came barely in at treetop level. I could see the pilot in the cockpit, and I suppose he saw me. The plane climbed, then banked and returned, but a battery of anti-aircraft [guns] opened up on him and it was as though the Kraut had run into an invisible wall. BLAM! No more Kraut plane.

[Company] "A" returned to the Stavelot sector soon after that and began attacking the German lines. The Allies were pretty well consolidated by that time and were attacking the north and northwest flank of the Germans. I also remember Capt. Svarstad saying that the Second Armored had stopped the Krauts' advance in a hell of a battle just north of La Roche. Daily advances of the 2nd Armored [were made] between Jan. 2 and Jan. 10 [where] they had advanced only about 6 miles. It took them until Jan. 16 to capture Houffalize, about 10 miles further on. (Houffalize was about 10–12 miles north-northeast of Bastogne.)

I got clobbered on the Stavelot front on Jan. 10, and didn't get back to the 99th, as the war appeared to be "winding down" (ain't that a hell of a way to describe it?) as the field hospital staff put it.

When "A" attacked on the 10th, I remember the aid station being filled with our wounded, as well as a couple of Belgian civilians. Outside were several dead, one of which I recognized as a rifleman named Nataas.

At about the same time, as I recall, "B" made several jabs at the Krauts in a town south of Malmedy—Hedamont and Otaimont, and that "C" was preparing to attack another town called Bellevaux, or something like that.

I've always been proud of being in the 99th, but after reading the excerpt you sent, I'm REALLY proud to have been a member of such a fighting unit!!! And material that [Morton] Tuftedal read at the business meeting in Colorado Springs bore that out also. Being regarded as one of the toughest fighting units in combat against the Krauts is really something, isn't it!!!

Sincerely,
Yngvar Stensby

P.S. Enclosed is a rough map slash sketch taken from the 2nd's book.[4] The solid red line is A Company's approximate patrol route. (I was in Bastogne at least three times on those patrols.) The broken red line indicates the route A Company probably took between St. Hubert and Malmedy via Spa. We spotted the German tank column in a valley south of the road between Vielsalm and La Roche. Obviously, not too far from the point where "A" left the Vielsalm road to cut cross-country up to Spa. I imagine there was reason to assume that the Germans were west of Vielsalm; they were also into Stavelot, which might explain the "detour" through Spa.

I also now recall that when we got into Malmedy, the church bells began playing "Yankee Doodle" supposedly to welcome us but I'm sure they were doing it to let the Germans know we were there.

---

[4] No map was available in the archived materials.

CHAPTER FIVE

J. Jarvis Taylor

This next entry comes from a former board member of the 99th's Education Foundation, James Jarvis Taylor, who was born June 26, 1922 in Raleigh, North Carolina. Taylor joined the 99th as a replacement in November 1944 after having served in the 106th Division. In the 99th, Taylor was a heavy weapons .30-caliber machine gunner in Company D.

In his writing, Taylor covers the time period from just before the Battle of the Bulge through to the end of the 99th's time in Norway. With a sense of curiosity and adventure, Taylor captures many stories of the people he met and the places he saw. This includes quite a few interactions with the locals and relationships established at each leg of his journey.

Taylor had a personable nature and a knack for quickly getting to know people. The people he met had unique stories, including an interesting brush with infamy when, at the beginning of May 1945, Taylor's company was billeted at a German estate. In this instance, Taylor made the acquaintance of the lady of the house. This woman was the widow of the German officer executed by Hitler for the failed assassination of July 1944, whom Tom Cruise played in the 2008 movie Valkyrie.

As is evidenced by Taylor's writings, every soldier's experiences were unique. Luck and chance determined each individual's fortune, and on occasion a matter of moments or feet were the difference between life and death. For Taylor, this includes several experiences during the Battle of the Bulge in which he was spared as a buzz bomb passed 100 feet above his head, a night-time Nazi bombing that struck 25 yards from where he slept, and a patrol mission that fortunately just missed the Nazis' round-up and shooting of soldiers known as the Malmedy Massacre.

One of many touching moments shared by Taylor came on Christmas Eve 1944, which was in the middle of their month-long Battle of the Bulge experience. He and some other soldiers of the 99th were gathered in the cellar of a farmhouse for an impromptu Christmas program. Taylor read from the second chapter of the Gospel of Luke and undoubtedly there were no dry eyes amongst the men.

There are no indications from Taylor of any resentment or challenges by not having a Norwegian background. His summary of the months that the 99th spent in Norway

Company D, Headquarters Section, from John Kelly's *Company D* book. The photo includes many names mentioned in Jarvis Taylor's account of his time with the company, including John Kelly standing at left, Arne Thomassen, Kenneth Raby, Andrew Hall, Ordean Halla, Karl Kjendal, unidentified, Andrew Hoiem, and Jarvis Taylor at right. Kneeling, the second soldier is Antony "Tony" Sciacca next to Clarence Becker, with Art Holm at right. (Courtesy of the 99th Educational Foundation)

include stories of the warm reception and embrace that the Norwegians had for the 99th, for their heroic role in the war, and their visible presence during the Norwegian liberation. If there were challenges he faced being a non-Norwegian member of the 99th, he didn't write about them.

Taylor's extensive writing on his experiences as a private first class in the 99th are a living testament to the bravery that he and others exhibited throughout their experiences.

In recognition of his actions, he was awarded the Bronze Star; the Combat Infantry Badge; the Good Conduct Medal; the American Campaign Medal; the Europe, Africa, Middle East Medal; the World War II Victory Medal, and the World War II Occupation Medal. J. Jarvis Taylor passed away at the age of 94 on June 19, 2017 in Arlington, Virginia.

99th Infantry Battalion (Sep.)

It was the first day of November 1944. Our convoy had been on the road for three hours when the trucks came to a halt near the railway warehouse at Henri-Chapelle, Belgium, a small village 14 miles southwest of Aachen, Germany. We were met by a small contingent of soldiers who told us we were to wait here for the battalion commander. In the meantime, they gave us something to eat. About an hour later the battalion commander, Lt. Col. Harold Hansen, appeared. He gathered us around and gave us an official welcome to the 99th Infantry Battalion (Sep.), Norwegian American and gave a little of the history of the unit. The 99th Infantry Battalion (Sep.) Norwegian American was made up of mostly Norwegian nationals and men of Norwegian descent. It was activated in July 1942 at Camp Ripley, and trained at Fort Snelling, Minnesota and Camp Hale, Colorado. Their initial mission was a possible invasion of Norway. That invasion never took place. The 99th had landed on the French coast on 22 June 1944 and being attached to various other units from time, fought bravely and aggressively from Omaha Beach, France, Holland and into Germany. When I joined them, they had just returned from heavy fighting in Germany to close the Aachen Gap.

Col. Hansen said most of us would be assigned to rifle companies but would like to have 10 volunteers for D Company, heavy weapons. I thought for a minute and decided this would probably be better than a straight-line infantry so I stepped forward. After the assignments were finished, we were escorted down the road to join our new companies.

D Company headquarters was located in a large red brick barn beside the road that led to Aachen. It appeared to be a fairly new barn and more modern than most you see in Belgium or other European countries. We were greeted by the first sergeant, Andrew Hall. He didn't appear to be very friendly at first but after you got to know him, he was a real nice guy. He told us the rest of the company was out on a hike and would return soon. Just before the Red Cross mobile unit pulled up with coffee and doughnuts.

We weren't assigned to our squad or platoon until the next day. We were issued sleeping bags and bedded down in the barn with the mortar squad. At breakfast the next morning Sgt. Pedersen came to me and told me one of his men had slid down from the hayloft above where I had been sleeping and landed on my pipe, breaking the stem. He said he had reprimanded the guy and offered to give me the stem from one of his pipes. I told him not to worry, I wasn't much of a smoker anyway. After breakfast we met our platoon sergeant, Palmer Olsen. He gave us a very warm welcome and introduced us to the other men in the platoon. Each man greeted us with a hardy handshake and made us feel as part of the team and not as new replacements. I was assigned to the second platoon, fourth squad. I would be an ammo bearer and assistant driver. Second platoon was quartered in a barn about a quarter mile down the road from headquarters. The farmhouse and out buildings were situated in a "U" shape, providing a courtyard between the house and the barn. We were able to use the living room of the farmhouse as a dayroom. In the evenings the guys would gather there to read, write letters, and listen to the radio. It was here I met two really nice guys who would become my very good friends. They were Kenneth Raby and Lee Gardner. Ken was from Detroit, Michigan and had been a telephone man. Lee was a devout southerner from Memphis, Tennessee and was still fighting the Civil War. He was in the first squad. Ken was attached to the fourth. Though he was just a PFC, he was more or less an instrument corporal for the platoon, whatever that is.

The next morning after breakfast the company formed to go for showers. We hiked about 3 ½ miles along the railroad tracks to the twin cities of Welkenraedt and Herbesthal. On the way there I saw my first buzz bomb. It flew right over us a few hundred feet in the air. The shower house was an arrangement of two pyramidal tents placed together with a network of pipes running from a large water tank. There were a number of shower heads attached to facilitate several people showering at the same time. The water had been heated and provided the most comfortable shower I had had since leaving England. (I had missed the one in Heerlen.) As an extra treat we were given a new suit of much-needed underwear which added to our comfort.

On Sunday morning, church services were held in the barn where company headquarters was located. Just as the services ended, we heard a terrific explosion. A buzz bomb had come down near the town of Eupen a few miles away. A few months later, I read an article in *Reader's Digest*, "The Diary of a German Girl," in which this same explosion was mentioned. The girl in the article was writing to her SS boyfriend in the German army telling him how badly she had been treated and her contempt for the Americans and the Belgians. She told him, "Today a buzz bomb exploded near Eupen and [I] hoped it found its mark."

In the afternoon Ken Raby and I took a walk up the road to the village of Henri-Chapelle. We wandered through the ancient church cemetery and the edifice itself. Services were being conducted [at] that time so we waited in the back of the church until it was over before having a look around. In the evening I was on guard duty just outside the old farmhouse. It was a very dark night indeed, interrupted only by the low rumbling of artillery shells exploding in the distance. We were only a few miles from the German border and the front lines.

As I stood guard duty that night my right foot began to hurt again. It was the same one I had trouble with just before leaving England. On Monday morning I reported to sick call and was sent to the battalion aid station to see what could be done for it. The only thing they did was to apply a heat pad to my foot. It didn't seem to help very much. They had me return again the following two days for the same treatment. In the evenings I would sit around in the living room of the farmhouse and write letters or perhaps Ken and I would go back to the kitchen and keep with the Schein family who owned or worked the farm. Each evening Madam Schein would make hot chocolate for us with cocoa that Sergeant Olsen managed to get for us. They were very nice and friendly people indeed. They were Flemish and spoke French and German. It was interesting to try to talk with them and Ken was rather good at it. In fact, after the war, Ken continued to correspond with them for quite a while.

On Thursday I reported to the aid station as usual. My foot was no better. By evening it was decided that should be evacuated to an evacuation hospital. I didn't like this idea at all. I didn't know what to expect. I had only been with the 99th for a week and now would be leaving it. I was taken back to my company in a jeep to get my gas mask and shaving kit. This is all I took with me. I had hoped to return in a day or two. An ambulance took me to a hospital in Eupen where I was examined and assigned a cot in the corridor. The place was crowded and a lot of activity was going on. I was given something to eat then settled in for a little sleep.

A little sleep is just what I got. A corpsman awakened me, pinned a tag on me, and said I was moving out. Along with others I was herded into an ambulance and off into the night. A short time later we arrived at the Eighth Field Hospital in Verviers about 15 miles from Eupen. The front door of the hospital had been draped with a large canvas put up for blackout. We entered into the large hall of what must have been a school building. The room was dimly lit. On the floor was row upon row of wounded soldiers lying on stretchers. Up to this time I had not seen any wounded soldiers but now, seeing so many, it really strikes home. Perhaps many of these had just been wounded in the past day or two and brought here. I was placed in a room with about seven or eight other soldiers.

The next day, I thought something may be done for my foot, but nothing was. I kept asking the nurse about it and she always answered, "In a little while, we are too busy right now." Looking back on it now, I wonder just how dumb could I be, how thoughtless. Here all around me were men in really bad shape, seriously wounded and some about to die and I was worried about a little sore toe. Damn. Right now, as I think about it, I feel like an idiot. I finally got the nurse to give me one of those chemical heating pads that are activated by water.

Shortly after noon, it was rumored that some of us would be leaving on a hospital train for Paris. As much as I would like to see Paris, this was not news for me. I wanted to get fixed up and back to the 99th as soon as I could. When an officer told me I would be leaving, I protested, telling him I didn't want to go back any further. My foot wasn't too bad off and with a day or two of care I would be ready for duty again. The captain had the last word and said I was to go. About three o'clock in the afternoon those of us who were going were loaded into an ambulance and taken to the train. The rail cars were designed inside with racks three deep on both sides for litters to be placed. My litter or bunk was on the bottom.

The trip from Verviers to Paris wasn't too bad. I don't remember how many days it took but the train moved very slowly, perhaps in consideration for its passengers. All the soldiers in my car had been wounded in combat, some in very serious condition. The one in [the] bunk above me was in very bad shape. He had a bad time of it on the trip. I did my best to comfort him. Occasionally his pain would ease a bit and he managed to smile and talk a little. I had with me the carton of chewing gum one of George's[1] friends gave me back in Holland. I had stuck [them] in my gas mask before leaving for the hospital. I took it out and passed it around to all the men in my car. Perhaps it would help them to relax a bit. They all appreciated it and it made me feel good. It was the least I could do. After all, they were in worse shape than I.

When we arrived in Paris, those of us who could walk were taken to the Red Cross for coffee and doughnuts. When we left, I forgot my helmet. I didn't discover the loss until we were at the hospital. Our hospital was the Hospital Beaujon, the best hospital in Paris, now known as the U.S. Army's 108th General. It had also been used by the Germans during their occupation. I was placed in a semi-private room on the eighth floor which was known as the skin disease floor. Across the hall from me was the V.D. ward and there were a lot of patients there. From the balcony of that ward you could see the Eiffel Tower, the Basilique du Sacré Coeur de Montmartre (Basilique of the Sacred Heart of Montmartre) and the top of the Arc de Triomphe. Perhaps others could be seen also but these were the only ones I was familiar with.

Service in the hospital was the very best. They immediately began treatment on my foot. For several days I was not allowed out of bed except when necessary. All my meals were brought to me. All of the hospital staff with whom I came in contact treated me the very best. Experiencing this myself, I was confident that all the soldiers coming here would get the best possible care.

It is a small world indeed. Shortly before leaving the hospital I came across a soldier whom I had trained with in the 13th Armored Division at Camp Beale, California. I don't remember his name, but I knew him just the same. At this particular time he was with the OSS attached to the American Embassy in Paris. We spoke only briefly and went our separate ways.

It was a chilly morning on November 20, 1944 as a group of patients boarded the train for the short ride to the 7th Convalescent Hospital in Étampes about 25 miles west of Paris. Upon arrival we were assigned quarters and given a physical examination. I told the officer, a major, that I was perfectly well and had no reason to remain here and wanted to return to my outfit as soon as possible. He said he would arrange it as soon as possible. Nevertheless, I expected to be here for several days more or perhaps a week at least.

Directly across the road from the convalescent hospital were the ruins of a castle. I have always been interested in history, [so] I thought I would have a look. No one seemed to know anything about the history of the castle except it was erected in 1140. Now, only one of its towers remain. There would be a lot of history in Paris, so knowing I would be in Étampes for a few days I decided to try for a pass. The commanding officer asked when I would like to go. I thought now would be a good time, realizing it was Wednesday and tomorrow was Thanksgiving, [so]

---

[1] George was Jarvis' brother who also served in Europe during the war.

I decided to wait until Friday. I wouldn't want to miss the Thanksgiving turkey with all the trimmings.

Friday morning I was driven to Paris in a jeep. I was let off at Rainbow Corners, a service center for GIs on leave to the city. The first place I decided to go was the American Embassy. It is on the Avenue des Champs Élysées near the Place de la Concorde. It was on the Place de la Concorde where stood the guillotine upon which Louis XVI and Marie Antoinette were beheaded during the French Revolution. The site is now occupied by the Luxor Obelisk, a 75ft granite monument set up by Rameses II in a temple at Thebes in upper Egypt. Next, I visited the Church of the Madeleine, a block away. After a visit to the church I walked the length of the Champs Élysées to the Arc de Triomphe. Inaugurated July 29, 1836, to the victories of Napoleon, the Arc de Triomphe stands as one of the landmarks of Paris. In a vault under the Arc lies the body of the Soldier of France. Upon the vault burns the Remembrance Flame. Soldiers, as they pass the tomb, are required to salute.

From the Arc, I made my way down the Avenue to the Palais de Chaillot and the Eiffel Tower. The Tower at this time was used by the U.S. Military as a signal station and was not open to the public. Next on my list was the Invalides and the Tomb of Napoleon. Upon leaving the Invalides I met a soldier coming in. He was alone and I was alone. I thought perhaps he may know his way around Paris a lot better than I so I spoke to him. As it happened, he was stationed in Paris with an ordnance outfit[2] and was on pass visiting the city again. He told me his name but unfortunately, I have forgotten it. I told him I was interested in seeing Notre Dame Cathedral and the Place de la Bastille. He knew where Notre Dame was but not the Bastille. He also showed me how to use the bus and subway so we hopped on the subway to see the ancient cathedral. It was raining slightly when we arrived.

There was very little light inside the cathedral. We visited the main chapel and a small room that was open to the public. What we were able to see I enjoyed very much. In the center of the triangle across the street from the cathedral is a bronze disc. It is from this disc that all mileage from the city is determined.

By this time it was getting a bit too late to go looking for the Place de la Bastille and I thought I should find how I was going to get back to Étampes. My friend was not familiar with the trains and couldn't help there. Also, it was time for him to go. Now I was left without a guide or a clue. I stopped several people and asked the way to a station that would take me to Étampes. I had no luck at all; no one seemed to understand English to know what I wanted. I crossed the Seine River back and forth several times before I finally found someone who spoke a little English. He told me I should take the Gare de Orleans (train to Orleans) and directed me to the station. When I got there, I was in trouble again. The ticket agent didn't know

---

[2] This unit made sure that weapons systems, vehicles, and equipment were ready and available, and in perfect condition at all times.

what I wanted. Finally, I was able to get my ticket to Étampes but found out later I didn't need one. The military rode free.

The next day I was transferred to a replacement depot a few blocks down the street. I thought to myself, "déjà vu, here we go again, back through the replacement depots." I was there for one week and did absolutely nothing. Why couldn't they send me directly back to my outfit? However, at this depot, once again I came across someone I knew back in the States. This time it was two. I had trained with both of them in the 13th Armored Division at Camp Beale, California. One of them was named Bettinger. I forget the name of the other. Bettinger had been wounded three times and was going back to his outfit now for the fourth time. They were no longer in the 13th Armored Division. They had left it months before. The 13th Armored did not go to Europe until January 1945. After I had been at this depot for a week, I made a visit back to the convalescent hospital to see a sergeant friend of mine and ended up staying the night. He was going to Paris the next day and knew where he could get some combat boots. I needed a pair and thought he may be able to get them for me. I gave him 400 francs—all the money I had (about $8 U.S.). He would get them if he could.

When I returned to the depot the next day, everyone had been looking for me. I was on orders to move out. I quickly packed my things and made roll call on time. Now I began to worry about my money or my boots. I had no idea where I would be going or if I would ever get back this way again. We boarded the trucks and in about an hour we were dismounting inside a French garrison at Fontainebleau, 45 km from Étampes. During the few days here, we were re-outfitted and issued our weapons. I was issued an M1 rifle. To keep us busy, we took a few hikes and fired our weapons on the firing range. Otherwise there was little else to do.

One afternoon, sometime around December 6 or 7, we had just returned from a hike or some exercise, when I noticed a convoy of trucks entering the garrison bringing other replacements in from Étampes. I was told these trucks would be making another trip to and from Étampes that day and thought it may be possible to go back with them to see if I could get my combat boots or my money. I asked the officer in charge of us if I could go. He gave his permission and I was on the next truck to Étampes. When we arrived there, the driver told me to meet them back here at the same place they let me off in about two hours, which would be about five o'clock, for the trip back to Fontainebleau.

At the convalescent hospital I learned that my friend had gone over to the replacement depot to see me, not knowing I had already left there. It seems our paths had crossed and consequently we never met up. It was getting too late to be looking for him now so I headed back to the meeting place for the convoy back to Fontainebleau. I arrived a few minutes before five and waited. When the trucks hadn't come by 5:30, I thought maybe I had missed them or they wouldn't be coming at all. It was about 27 miles back to Fontainebleau, so I had better start walking.

It was getting dark now and there would be no moon. Although I had observed all the landmarks along the way to Étampes, they would be difficult to follow in the dark. There were only a few cars and trucks on the road. I tried to thumb a ride but no one would pick me up. Finally a jeep with three air force men in it stopped and gave me a ride. They took me to the crossroads at Milly where they turned off to their base. I had no idea how far I had to go until I came to the small village of Arbonne. I saw a sign here that said 8 km to Fontainebleau. I was very tired and thirsty. I saw a light beneath the door of a dwelling beside the road and thought I could get some water there. I tried the door, but it was locked. I knocked several times. Someone inside answered in French, but I couldn't understand them, so I knocked again. Suddenly the door opened and a heavy-set Frenchman of medium height stood there. Recognizing that I was an American soldier, he gave a great smile and invited me in.

Once inside I noticed it was not just a house, but also a tavern or bar. The owner and his family lived upstairs. The only light was coming from the kitchen, a room in the back of the bar. Since I didn't speak or understand French it was difficult to communicate with the man and his family. I tried as best I could to indicate I wanted a drink of water. I made gestures of turning on a faucet, moving a pump handle and drinking a glass of water but they didn't understand. The man took down a bottle of wine thinking that was what I wanted. I shook my head, no. The young girl, probably the man's daughter, was observing all this display and seemed to understand. She motioned me into the kitchen to the faucet at the sink and on the water. "Oui oui," I said, and all gave a big smile. She got a glass for me and I had a big drink of water. We all said something in our own language trying to have the other understand. I indicated that I had walked all the way from Étampes on my way to Fontainebleau. They seemed amazed. They offered me more water but I refused. The old man offered me some wine or a glass of cider. I took the cider. They were very friendly indeed and I thoroughly enjoyed my brief rest and refreshments. I said goodbye to them and was on my way. I had 5 more miles to go.

On my way out of town I came to a fork in the road. There were no signs to indicate where either may go so I decided to take the left. It was the wrong road. Fortunately, I hadn't gone far before realizing my mistake. I backtracked to the other road and proceeded on my way. It was exactly 11:45 p.m. when I entered the gate to the garrison and on to my quarters. I was really tired. The next morning 1 could hardly move. I ached all over and could hardly walk. Unfortunately, after all the trouble I didn't even get my combat boots or my money back.

Periodically, the troops are entitled a distribution of PX rations such as cigarettes, tobacco, candy, gum, etc. These items are usually given free except when you are in a replacement depot. Then you have to buy them, but they don't cost very much. When the distribution came for us at Fontainebleau, I was flat broke: didn't have a dime. I borrowed enough money to get my ration of cigarettes, some candy, and a few odds and ends. I figured since I didn't smoke I could probably sell the cigarettes to pay back the money I owed and have a little left for myself. I had no idea when I would get paid again.

That evening I went into town. With the carton of cigarettes tucked under my arm plus a few extra packs in my pockets, I walked slowly up and down the street hoping to get an offer. American cigarettes were a prized commodity in Europe and they should fetch a pretty good price. I was approached several times but ignored them since I couldn't understand what they were offering. Finally a tall man dressed in a black overcoat, black hat. and a dark brown briefcase approached me and asked in English if I had any cigarettes to sell. When I told him I did, he suggested we go somewhere else to negotiate the deal. We walked about a block then down a dark narrow street. The man offered me 60 francs a pack and without hesitation I accepted. He pulled out his wallet and gave me 600 francs (about $12 U.S.). I probably could have bargained for more, and got it, but I was a bit uneasy about the deal in the first place and was in a hurry to get back to the barracks. Anyway, the carton of cigarettes only cost me about a buck or two. This was the only time I ever sold anything on the "black market" and would not have done so this time if I hadn't needed the money.

On December 8 we moved again. We traveled all day and all night with only short breaks once in a while. Shortly before daybreak the trucks pulled into the city of Verviers, Belgium. We were billeted in an empty champagne warehouse located in town but just out of the shopping district. We were there only a few days and had absolutely nothing to do. We were left pretty much on our own and could go and come as we pleased, so long as we let the commanding officer know.

On Tuesday morning, December 12, I ventured into town to have a look around. As I passed a book shop, I noticed a card in the window with the Belgium Boy Scout insignia on it. I went inside and inquired about the organization. The clerk was not quite sure about what I was asking about but gave me an address and pointed me in the direction of it. When I got there, it was a shop which sold Scouting equipment. A man there gave me another address and pointed me in that direction. After passing the book shop again I knew I had taken the wrong turn somewhere. I stopped two Belgian boys on the street, showed them the address I had been given. They couldn't understand me either. About that time a well-dressed gentleman approached and in very good English asked if he could be of any help. I showed him the address I was looking for and without hesitation, he asked me to follow him. We went about two blocks down the street where we entered a tailor shop. A tall, well-dressed gentleman named Monsieur Moekel greeted us. My guy told me I was interested in the Boy Scouts. Monsieur Moekel was secretary of the Boy Scouts in the District of Verviers and gave me the name and address of a Dr. Felix Brasseur, the Commissioner of the Fédération des Scouts Catholiques, District de Verviers. I was assured Dr. Brasseur spoke English.

I arrived at Dr. Brasseur's home about noon. His wife met me at the door and asked me in. I told her I was a District Scout Commissioner in an area in California and was directed to Dr. Brasseur by Monsieur Moekel. Madam Brasseur told me the doctor was busy with a patient at the moment but would be glad to see me as soon as he was finished. [It was] only a few minutes before the doctor appeared. He greeted me very warmly. We spoke of the Boy Scouts in Belgium and in the United States for a few minutes then insisted I stay for lunch. He said they didn't have much but would like to share what they had with me. We had a small steak, brussels sprouts, bread, and a light wine. I enjoyed it very much. During lunch Dr. Brasseur telephoned his chief scout whom he called George. He wanted George to come over and talk with us. George arrived just as we were finishing our meal. The three of us spoke together for quite some time, after which George was to take me to the office. Dr. Brasseur expressed his appreciation for my coming to see him. I thanked his wife for the very nice lunch and we departed.

The Boy Scout office was a back room in Monsieur Moekel's tailor shop. It had its own entrance in the rear of the shop through which we entered. We were greeted by the Secretary. We were at the Scout office for only a short time during which I was given a letter for Honorary Membership in the FÉDÉRATION DES SCOUTS CATHOLIQUES, District of Verviers. It was December 12, 1944.

The next day, a group of us were moved from this replacement depot, a few miles away to another location where we would be picked up and delivered back to our outfits. About four o'clock in the afternoon we arrived in front of a huge gray stone chateau on the top of a hill overlooking the valley between Verviers and Liège. I don't remember the name of it, but I believe it was the Chateau de Colonheid. As it happened, on this particular day, Major General Ben Lear, ground force commander, was coming to inspect the chateau. Those of us who had just arrived were not aware of it and were not prepared for the inspection. We were hustled off into the attic until the general had left.

The chateau was a very beautiful place indeed. The rooms were quite large with a fireplace in each. There were no light switches in any of the upstairs rooms. There was a panel of switches in the hall with the names of each person whose room it was. No doubt when the chateau was occupied by the owners, the servants or parents would control the lights for the children when it was bedtime. On the staircase there was a large carving of the family crest. I had hoped to be here for a few days to have a look around but that was not to be. The next day a jeep came for me and another soldier returning to the 99th. I did not know this soldier; he must have been from another company in the battalion.

While I was away, the battalion had moved from Henri-Chapelle to the town of Tilff, 5 miles from Liège. The driver stopped the jeep in front of the town hall where my company was billeted. The first person I spotted was Ken Raby. He was on guard duty. Ken seemed glad to see me and I was glad to see him. Moreover, I was happy to be back with the 99th Infantry Battalion and my company. Ken helped me in with my gear and showed me where I would sleep. There were many things I wanted to tell him and Ken had a lot to tell me. While I was cleaning up and shaving, Ken told me about a family he had met here in Tilff and was anxious for me to meet them. He had met this nice lady at the battalion dance one evening and they had become friends. Her name was Jeanne Damas (Madame Joseph Damas). Her husband, a Belgian officer, was a prisoner of war. She had two teenage sons, Pierre and Jean-Marie, who were away at school and a daughter Annette [who] was at home.

After chow, Ken took me over to meet Madame Damas and Annette. He had told them about me while I was away. Madame Damas was particularly interested in knowing I was with the Boy Scouts back in the United States and very pleased to learn I had made contact with the Belgian Scouts and had been given an Honorary Membership. Her sons were also Boy Scouts. Scouting is a big thing in Belgium and is even included in part of their activities in school. She was sorry her sons were not at home at this time. Madame Damas served us tea and cake and enjoyed talking about her family. She was also interested in hearing about ours. At one point she pulled out a big drawer of photographs of her family and placed it in my lap. There must have been hundreds of them. Perhaps because the war had caused so much hardship on her family, her husband being a prisoner of war and her children away to school most of the time, she enjoyed the company. When it came time to go, Madame Damas left her house also. There was still danger of air raids so she and some of her neighbors would spend the night in a nearby air raid shelter.

On Saturday, December 16, I was scheduled on KP duty. All the cooking, serving, and cleaning up is done outside since there was no suitable place in the town hall to accommodate such activity. I didn't mind the washing up of all the pots and pans and cleaning up in general. The part I didn't like was, after each meal, many of the town folk came up the hill to the town hall to get the leftovers. It was up to me to ration it out. I hated to see these old men, women, and little children holding out their pots and pans for the little bits they might get. I did the best I could.

Early in the afternoon, as I scrubbed away on the pots and pans, I noticed a young girl and boy approaching, half walking and half running up the hill toward me. I also recognized the girl right away as Madame Damas's daughter. I also recognized the boy from the many photographs I had seen, as her son Jean-Marie. Jean-Marie had returned home early in the morning saying he was not feeling well. His mother had told him of our meeting the night before and of my Scout activities. She told me later Jean-Marie couldn't get all his chores done fast enough so he could go to the town hall to meet me. He discovered the pipe I had forgotten the night before and used that as an excuse to come to meet me instead of waiting until evening when Ken and I had expected to visit them.

As soon as we arrived at the Damas house that evening, Madame Damas immediately began to make tea. Ken and I had put together a small box of candy, gum, and other rations we had saved to take to the family for their kind hospitality to us. Jean-Marie had heard I had had a bad foot and thought perhaps it may still be bothering me. He immediately brought in a leg and footrest and insisted I prop my leg on it. In fact, he went so far as to lift my leg and place it there. All of the Damas family spoke very good English, so we never had difficulty in communicating. We had a most delightful evening indeed. We didn't know it at the time, but this would be our last evening with the Damas [family] for quite some time.

The Ardennes: The Battle of the Bulge

On Sunday, December 17, 1944, we were awakened by the C.Q.[3] around seven o'clock in the morning. The first thing he said was, we were on a momentary alert and to be prepared to move out in an hour's notice. I was scheduled on a jeep patrol that day beginning at noon. The patrol would go as scheduled unless other orders were received before then. In the meantime, church services would be held at 10 o'clock as scheduled in the local movie theater. Ken and I were in attendance. On the way back to our quarters, Jean-Marie came riding up on his bike. He wanted to know if we could come for a visit in the afternoon. I told him we couldn't today because we had duty. We said nothing about the alert.

We started on patrol right after noon chow. We were to drive from Tilff to the German border of Aachen and return. There were four of us on the mission. I was driving the jeep with Lt. Milton Schultz beside me. On the back seat was the mess sergeant and a PFC whose name I forget. As we drove through Liège we passed many houses and buildings that had recently been destroyed by buzz bombs. There were people still digging through the ruins probably looking for missing persons. As we exited the city we were on a hill overlooking it when we heard the ominous sound of a buzz bomb overhead. As it approached the center of the town the motor cut off and the bomb nose-dived straight down. We saw a flash of fire and seconds later the sounds of the explosion as fire and black smoke rose from the devastation it had caused. Our hearts went out to those unfortunate and unsuspecting innocent victims of this Nazi atrocity.

Upon reaching the crossroads at Battice just beyond Herve, Lt. Schutz suggested we stop for a short rest and refreshments. The lieutenant treated us to a glass of beer and cognac. I accepted the beer but not the cognac. As we were enjoying our rest and refreshments, we noticed what seemed to be an unusual flow of tanks and trucks passing through the crossroads. The PFC with us remarked he thought he saw what seemed to be dead bodies in the back of one of the trucks. We wondered

---

[3] Means Charge of Quarters in the Army, and it is an around-the-clock shift made up of two members.

for a minute if perhaps it had anything to do with the alert we were on. Finishing our drinks we continued on the patrol. By the time we got to Henri-Chapelle it was getting late and we still had about 20 miles to go. Lt. Schultz decided we should turn back. We turned around and headed back to Tilff.

As we approached the town hall there were a lot of trucks lining the streets and the driveway. Men were hustling around getting them loaded. We were told to grab whatever we could find to eat and pack up as quickly as we could. To make things worse, buzz bombs began falling near the town. One felt a little too close for comfort for me. The building shook and glass went flying everywhere. Glass fell out of the window and on the desk where I was packing my gear. Fortunately, I was not injured. By six o'clock the trucks were all loaded and we were on our way. We still had not been told the reason for the alert or where we were going. The townspeople lined the streets waving and wishing us good luck and safe return.

The convoy of trucks carrying the soldiers of the 99th Infantry Battalion (Sep.) rolled on through the darkness of night. A cold drizzle of rain began to fall in the early morning of December 18, as the trucks carrying the men of D Company came to a halt in front of a deserted concert hall in the town of Malmedy, Belgium. The hall had been occupied by an outfit of medics, who from the evidence of things, had left in a hurry. Clothing and equipment still hung on the walls and yesterday's supper was already cooked and ready to be served. The town too seemed to be deserted except for a handful of engineers who chose to remain in an attempt to hold back the enemy until combat troops could arrive. We learned the Germans had launched their winter offensive and had broken through the American lines and the Ardennes Forest. Their objective was to overrun the Allies and make a drive for the port of Antwerp. The 99th had been moved in to help halt the advance of the Germans in this sector. We would be facing the heavily armored battlegroup of the 1st SS Panzer Division, Kampfgruppe Piper. Just the day before at the time I was driving patrol, a contingent of SS Obersturmbannführer Jochen Piper's [Joachim Peiper's] men had herded a group of American soldiers into a field at the crossroads at the village of Baugnez, a short distance southeast of Malmedy, and massacred them.

A reconnaissance was made of all roads and approaches to the city and roadblocks were set up. B and C Companies occupied the high ground in the vicinity to secure the city. D Company established their headquarters in the concert hall, occupied the city, and maintained patrols within. I was on one of the first patrols sent out that cold night. It was a three-man team composed of Sgt. Knutsen,[4] Hilton Lecy, and myself. We patrolled the town for several hours. Sgt. Knutsen walked the center of the street. Lecy took the right side and I took the left. As we walked the dark

---

[4] In the 99th Battalion, there were at least 12 men with a similar last name spelled various ways (three spelled Knudsen, three spelled Knutsen and six spelled Knutson). Consequently, it is difficult to verify which soldier is represented here and if the spelling is correct.

streets of this pro-Nazi town, the attitude of the local populace was immediately apparent. As they peered through the windows and dark doorways, they seemed confident this handful of American soldiers would not be able to halt the great German Wehrmacht they knew to be just over the next ridge. Fortunately, the night was quiet and uneventful.

Late in the afternoon an American jeep with markings of the American 106th Infantry Division approached a roadblock at one end of the town. It was occupied by three German soldiers and two American prisoners riding on the hood. Evidently thinking the town had already fallen, they expected to ride right on through. One of the American soldiers jumped from the hood and shouted the jeep was full of Germans. Before the startled Germans could turn the jeep around it was captured. One of the German soldiers was killed trying to escape. Using captured American vehicles and dressed in American uniforms, some of the German soldiers, on orders from SS Obersturmbannführer Otto Skorzeny, infiltrated American lines and caused considerable confusion among some American troops. Some of the Germans captured in American uniforms were subsequently placed before a firing squad and executed.

The 106th Division was the division I had transferred from in late August, as replacement for overseas [duty]. The division left for overseas about a month later, arriving in England on October 20. After additional training they were eventually sent to Belgium and placed on the front line on the Schnee Eifel east of the Our River. It was supposed to be a good location for these green and untried troops. The fighting had calmed a bit and it seemed as though things were settling down for the winter. But, unknown to the Allies, the Germans were secretly building up a massive force in the Ardennes Forest in front of the 106th Division and emplacements. They started their move on December 16 and on the early morning of the next day, broke through the 106th lines, overrunning the 422nd and 423rd Regiments. Both units were virtually wiped out, most of their troops being killed or captured. My former regiment, the 424th, hadn't been hit quite as hard. When learning about it, I felt very fortunate to have left the unit when I did.

D Company was in Malmedy for only a couple of days before being relieved by a unit of the 30th Division. We moved back from the city about 2 miles near the village of Bévercé and held up at a small farmhouse. D Company was being held in reserve. However, there was a rumor that we may be going back to Tilff as soon as trucks were available. In the meantime, one of our men, Jack Wilkinson, got into a little trouble with a girl. He was placed under house arrest pending a court martial when we returned to Tilff. As it happened, we did not return to Tilff. A couple of days later we received orders to move back to the front. Wilkinson was told that pending his satisfactory performance of duty during this engagement, the charges against him would be dropped.

Orders were received to move and everything began to happen. Tanks, jeeps, and trucks began to move toward Malmedy again. We gathered our equipment, uncovered our weapons, and began to march. Lopez, the machine gunner in my squad, was on leave in Paris so the job was given to Hilton Lecy and I was second gunner. As we marched back down the road toward Malmedy, a single column on both sides of the road, a jeep passed slowly by with a German prisoner sitting on the front. About ½ mile down the road from where we started the engineers were mining the bridge that crossed the Warche River. Signs printed in big red letters had been posted on the trees saying "Caution, this road under enemy fire." We marched through Malmedy, passing the concert hall where we had first stayed, and continued through to the edge of town. We crossed another bridge and made our way up a steep winding road to the top of the hill northeast of the city. There had [been] a report of Germans in the area so we set up our guns and waited for a report from the reconnaissance team sent out to investigate. The report came in about an hour [later] that the Germans had moved out of the area. D Company moved back down the hill a bit to a little road on the left. A short distance down the road was a small farmhouse where we established the battalion CP. My platoon was also quartered there.

The next afternoon several men were picked for patrol duty. They were to move into a nearby town which was occupied by the Germans and try to take prisoners for questioning. The plan was for the patrol to move to a point of departure and wait. At a given time the artillery would bombard the town for five minutes. At the signal, the patrol would rush in and take as many prisoners as they could in the time allowed then move out. They would be covered by another barrage of artillery. Everything went off as planned except the taking of prisoners. The Germans had already vacated the town. The few stragglers left behind were killed by the first artillery barrage.

I had not seen much of my friend Ken since we left Tilff on the evening of December 17. He was the company clerk and always stayed close to headquarters. Nevertheless, he pulled his tour of guard duty as well. My platoon being quartered with the command post, I was able to see him a little more often. One morning, Ken told me of an incident which occurred while on guard duty the night before. It was a cold night and all was quite still when suddenly out of the darkness of the night, a terrified voice cried out, "No, no, no," each "no" becoming more horrifying; then a shot rang out echoing through the hills and all was quiet again. There is no telling what it may have been about. In any case it sounded as if someone was begging for his life.

While on this hilltop outpost, buzz bombs were flying over regularly day and night. Usually they were quite high up but late one afternoon I heard an especially loud roar coming in my direction. I looked up and saw a buzz bomb flying less than 100 feet above me. I thought to myself, "That won't go far," and seconds later as it cleared the next hill there was a terrific explosion. The area it hit was mostly fields and woodlands so I doubt if much damage was done. The closest we came to being hit and probably killed while on this outpost was one night just before Christmas. Strangely enough I didn't even know what had happened until morning. During the night, the Germans laid in 12 rounds of artillery on our hill. The range was perfect; the direction was only less than 25 yards to the left of the farmhouse we occupied. Probably the reason I didn't hear the noise was because of where I slept; it was a room underground. Access to it was through a hole in the floor from the room above. Though no one was injured, virtually all of our vehicles had sustained damage to some degree; shrapnel had flattened several tires, put holes in the sides of our trucks and jeeps, and destroyed the water jacket on the water-cooled .30-caliber machine guns mounted on the jeep. All things considered, we were quite lucky.

The food situation during this time was not too bad. Once in a while the kitchen or mess crew would be able to get through to us with a hot meal, but most of the time we had to rely on our C- or K-rations which we always had plenty of. While on the outpost, we were introduced to a new kind of ration called "10 in 1." One unit would supply 10 men for one day. It contained such things as cereal, canned milk, butter, crackers, cheese, dehydrated corned beef hash, canned ham and scrambled eggs, coffee, chocolate, and a few other things I can't remember. As I recall, it all tasted pretty good.

The weather closed in for a few days and all aircraft was grounded. It wasn't too bad up on the hill, however, but fog hovered over the valley until about noon when it cleared. With binoculars, we could see Germans in their new positions below. When the weather finally cleared and planes could fly again, giant armadas of American bombers took to the sky headed for the Third Reich.

Unfortunately, the first fleet to fly over mistakenly dropped their bombs on Malmedy, destroying parts of the city. As other missions made their way toward Germany, anti-aircraft guns began to blaze away at them as shells burst all around. I saw one bomber get hit. It began to smoke and pulled away from the formation. Another was hit and a blaze of fire came streaming from it, then an explosion, and [the] plane shattered into a million pieces. I saw other planes lose a wing or an engine and come spiraling down to the ground. I searched the sky with my binoculars and counted the number of parachutes of the men who were able to bail out. In one case I counted six parachutes, another four, and some, none at all. Where they landed is anyone's guess.

One day I witnessed a dogfight between the American fighter planes and the German Luftwaffe. They were all over the sky blazing away at each other. I didn't see one of either side get shot down. While watching this spectacular event, it never occurred to me those planes were diving and strafing in all directions. I could have been hit by a stray bullet and probably killed. It's a bit scary now that I think about it.

On December 24, 1944, it was Christmas Eve and all was quiet on this cold hilltop outpost overlooking the city of Malmedy. In the evening, a group of us decided to hold a brief service to celebrate Christmas. We assembled in the cellar of the old farmhouse about eight o'clock. Sitting there upon the straw, I had the privilege of reading to our group the Christmas story as recorded in the second chapter of the Gospel of Luke. After we sang "Silent Night" and said a prayer. We sat there quietly, reflecting upon the season and thinking of home and our loved ones.

The next morning was Christmas. The kitchen crew managed to get up to us with a hot breakfast. It consisted of pancakes only. I had two or three and that was all I had the whole day. After the "good meal," the whole company, except those on detail, gathered in the hayloft of a nearby barn where the chaplain was holding Christmas services. He was accompanied by his assistant who played the portable organ. We sang many of the familiar hymns and Christmas songs and listened to the chaplain's message.

About mid-afternoon the company was assembled and made ready for another move. We abandoned the outpost and marched back down the hill toward Malmedy. In the meantime Lopez had returned from Paris and assumed his position as machine gunner. As we approached the city, the effect of the accidental bombing by the U.S. Air Force[5] was clearly evident. We crossed a small bridge and entered the city. Everywhere, the streets were littered with rubble and ruin. Once again we passed the concert hall where we had stayed our first night in Malmedy. The place was completely destroyed. Only the foundation and chimney remained. Many were heard to say they were glad we moved out of that place when we did. We halted at an abandoned house on the edge of town and waited for further orders. Around six in the evening they came, and we were on the move again.

South of the city and across the railroad track, Second Platoon of D Company established their command post in the kitchen of an abandoned house. About 100 yards down the tracks from the CP, 4th squad began digging a foxhole and machine gun emplacement. Sgt. Knudsen, Lopez, and I started the dig. The ground was frozen solid. It was all we could do just to dent the earth. It was about 10 o'clock at night before the "L"-shaped emplacement began to take shape. According to the original orders we were supposed to have placed our machine guns further up the hill from our present location but our platoon leader, Lt. James Parnell, told the CO and executive officer he had rather not do that because we would have no cover in case we had to retreat. In case of a counterattack the Krauts could quickly overrun our position and massacre the whole platoon before they could get down the hill and across the railroad tracks behind the embankment. Here, where we dug the emplacement, we would at least have a chance for a quick move to a second line of defense.

Sgt. Olsen, our platoon sergeant, suggested we split our six-man gun crew. Three of us would work on the machine-gun emplacement and the others could go back to the CP and get some rest. Sgt. Knudsen, Karl Kjendal, and I would

---

[5] This would have been the U.S. Army Air Corps.

go first. I tried to sleep on the cold marble floor underneath the kitchen table but even being fully clothed and wearing my big heavy Army overcoat and two additional blankets over me, I still just about froze. Bright and early the next morning we were out to finish the job on the gun emplacement. Lopez, Lecy, and Petersen went back for a rest. They would not have to return until the next morning. We constructed the emplacement a bit larger than usual to make it a little more comfortable and to have space to store some of our gear. We lined the hole with Army blankets we had taken from some of the stuff left by the medics when they evacuated the concert hall. We found some boards which we put over the left side of the hole and piled some dirt and rocks on top for a little extra protection against artillery [attacks]. On December 27, we had a pretty big snow. Although it was miserably cold, the snow provided excellent camouflage for our gun position.

About seven o'clock one morning when I was back at the house on my break, I was awakened by the roar of aircraft flying back and forth over the houses on our road. I got up and went to the window just in time to see a German Messerschmitt fly directly over the house. The plane was so low I could see the pilot. Looking over to my left I saw our company commander, Captain Winholtz, in the backyard of a nearby house taking shots at one of the planes with his .45-caliber pistol. I doubt if he hit anything. However, one plane was shot down in the wooded area not far from us. The pilot bailed out but some of them who went over to the scene reported that he had died. He was still in his parachute hanging from a tree with a bullet through his head and one in his stomach. It wasn't known if the wounds were inflicted before he landed or afterwards.

The kitchen crew was only a mile or two away and was able to keep us pretty well fed. They would not, however, bring the chow to our gun position; we had to go to the CP to get it. One evening as I crawled out of our foxhole to go get some chow the Germans opened up with a couple of bursts of machine-gun fire. I dove behind the railroad embankment and made my way to the CP. No one got hurt. When I returned to the gun, I took a phone with me and strung combat wire to our position. I thought we may have a use for it. We ushered in New Year's Day 1945 listening to the chaplain service over the phone.

Little or nothing was happening here at our location and since I was also the assistant driver for the second platoon, I was moved right after the new year to another house down the road where the drivers stayed. This was only a temporary assignment. I was there for four or five days, with practically nothing to do. It snowed one morning and I shoveled off our small front porch. In the afternoon I threw snowballs with some of the kids in the neighborhood.

On my way to the CP one morning I saw someone waving a white flag from a nearby hillside. As the person came closer, a rifleman from one of our companies went forward to investigate. It happened to be a family of refugees who had evacuated their home when the Germans occupied their town. They were considered harmless and allowed to proceed on their way.

After a couple of days being housed with the other drivers, I heard the battalion was planning an advance or another move but knew none of the details. I decided to go down to the platoon CP to see what I could find out. Just as I stepped out of the front door, a German artillery shell whizzed overhead and exploded on the railroad tracks across the street from me. My next step was backward into the house and [I] slammed the door. I got down on the floor expecting more artillery but fortunately none came.

On January 6, 1945 the 99th was relieved by the first battalion of the 30th Division. The tripod of our machine gun had frozen to the ground and we couldn't move it. We just lifted the gun off, let the 30th have it, and took their tripod with us. This same day, I was transferred from the fourth squad to the first. The section sergeant was Staff Sergeant Don Anderson. It was late in the afternoon and I had only been there for about an hour when we got orders to move out. We moved to the edge of Malmedy and into a schoolhouse that had been used as a hospital. Evidence indicated it had been used by the Army medics and had been quickly evacuated, probably on December 17. X-rays and other equipment had been strewn about in a hasty retreat.

Our stay at the schoolhouse was only about 24 hours. We waited until dark before making our next move. Around nine or 10 o'clock we disembarked near the village of Masta, about halfway between Malmedy and Stavelot. We hiked about another hundred yards to where we would establish our new gun position. On the way we encountered a group of engineers trying to remove some anti-tank mines off the road. They must have been new recruits because they didn't know how to make a mine safe to move. We showed them how it was done then moved on down the road. Ice and snow made walking very difficult especially when you have a heavy machine gun on your shoulder. Just as we were getting set up, orders came that we were in the wrong place. We shouldered our weapons again and made for the trucks. Before we got to the road, I lost my footing and fell with the machine gun on top of me. I managed to survive without injury. We moved only about a mile down the road and crossed under a railroad bridge. We came to a halt next to an old water turbine mill. My squad set up our gun on the forward side of the railroad embankment overlooking a small wooded area.

The old stone mill was a rather quaint structure. The inside mechanism was all made of wood except the grinding stones. It was operated by a large water turbine wheel turned by a stream of water flowing over it from a creek running alongside the mill. The mill had a small room attached to the far end of it. The first section of the second platoon occupied it as a place to stay and sleep when not standing watch on the gun. The owner of the mill was Monsieur Charpentier who lived on the second floor of the mill with his wife and her sister. He told us we could use the upstairs room anytime we like to rest, read or write letters. The room was quite large and used as their living room and dining room. Monsieur Charpentier still operated the mill and seemed quite busy during the time we were there. Farmers would bring their grain to the mill on horses, on small wagons or sleds to be ground into flour. Monsieur Charpentier would keep a portion as payment.

We kept watch on the gun in shifts but only two would be on watch at a time. The rest of us were free to do as we pleased but always were nearby and on alert. No one was to leave the area. My watch was shared with our hardnose, dyed-in-the-wool rebel, Lee Gardner from Memphis, Tennessee. Lee was a good-natured sort of guy but was still fighting the American Civil War. It might be wise not to say anything bad about the South, and never sing the Yankee song "Marching Through Georgia"; he might turn the machine gun in your direction.

One evening around eight o'clock, Don Anderson and Sgt. Knudsen, my old squad leader, came to our little room at the mill escorting a young man and a young lady. The young man was Rene Charpentier, son of the mill owner, and the young lady was his fiancée, named Kathy. They were to have been married on Christmas Day but on the eve of that day, they and several older people were held prisoner by the Germans in the basement of Rene's house in Stavelot, the city just west of the mill. They were held there for several days. Rene was allowed out from time to time only to get food and water for the others but was watched very carefully. When our troops pushed the Germans out of Stavelot they were released. Rene and Kathy were on their way to the mill when intercepted by Anderson and Knudsen and brought in. Both spoke very good English and we enjoyed their company the few days they spent at the mill. Rene told us he and Kathy would be going to Verviers as soon as he could get back to Stavelot to get his papers and motorcycle. I mentioned to them I had been in Verviers and had met a Dr. Brasseur there. Kathy told me she was the doctor's assistant and would be seeing him. I asked her to give Dr. Brasseur a message for me when she saw him. She said she would.

Rene went to Stavelot and retrieved his papers and motorcycle and returned to the mill to pick up Kathy. They stayed in Verviers for only a day then returned to the mill. They had seen Dr. Brasseur and he told them he was very pleased to hear from me. He sent me the shoulder ribbons of the Rover Scouts.[6]

We encountered very little resistance at our position at Masta. However, some of the patrols that were sent out each night did run into some opposition and a few men were lost. As Lee and I were going on watch one afternoon we were cautioned to be on the lookout for a German patrol reportedly headed our way. Though we would be on the machine gun we took along our M1 rifles as well. The patrol never showed. Later that night a German reconnaissance plane flew over our position but I doubt they saw anything.

---

[6] A Scouting organization usually associated with adults.

About the middle of the afternoon one day my friend Rolf Nicholaysen and I were upstairs in the old mill preparing to write letters when suddenly there was this terrible screaming noise, similar to an elephant trumping, then a terrific explosion. The building shook violently but held up. We were stunned and dazed for a moment and the two old ladies were quite shaken. We knew the explosion was from a so-called "Screaming Meemie," a German concussion shell. They usually fire off one and a few seconds later the other five in rapid succession. After the first explosion, Rolf and I recovered quickly, and threw open the windows to keep them from shattering. Almost before we could get the two ladies to the floor for protection, the other five shells roared in and exploded. I thought the old mill would be tumbling down but it held like some medieval fortress. Fortunately, no one was hurt. The two old ladies were shaken a bit but otherwise OK.

The two comedians of our outfit were Robert Taylor (no kin to me) and Fred Larsen, better known as "Scrink." Robert was from Bel Aire, Maryland and had come to the 99th the same time as I and volunteered for the heavy weapons platoon when I did. Fred or "Scrink" was a small Norwegian fellow from Brooklyn, New York. The two were inseparable, always together and seemed as though they were always eating a can of C-ration beans. One morning several of us were in the little room at the end of the mill just lying around. The peace and quiet was broken when suddenly an explosion shook the building. Everybody hit the dirt. We thought someone had set off a grenade. As it happened, Fred had placed a can of beans in the stove to heat without puncturing a hole in the top first. The can got hot and exploded, blowing the door off the stove. When Fred pulled the can out of the stove, there wasn't a bean left in it.

Chow was pretty regular at the mill. It was brought up to us twice a day; eight in the morning and four in the afternoon. We were the last ones on their stop and there was always plenty. Most of the time there was quite a bit left over which we gave to the family at the mill. One morning we had more pancakes than we could eat and gave them to the Charpentiers. That afternoon we had some very delicious chicken a la king. Again, there was more than we could eat so we gave that to the family. Later in the evening Rolf and I were upstairs writing letters when it came meal time for the Belgian family. We offered to leave but they insisted we were not in the way and should stay. We noticed they had the chicken a la king for dinner which they seem to enjoy. For dessert, they had the pancakes with a little sugar sprinkled on top.

It was mid-January 1945 and the weather for this time of the year was not too bad. The Allied forces had pushed the German lines back, leaving D Company of the 99th at the mill. We had been at this position for about two weeks. None of us had been able to get a good bath since leaving Tilff. Our commander decided to send us all, a few men at a time, for a shower in the town of Spa, about 20 miles away. I was in the first group to go. The baths were located in a large building built specifically for baths and nothing else. The city of Spa has been famous for these baths for 100 years. When we arrived at Spa we were given a new suit of underwear. We had to pay for the bath, but it was only about 20 francs. There were showers and tubs; you had a choice. To get a tub, you had to wait a long time, so I settled for a shower. It was just good to be clean again.

***

On January 18, two days after our visit to Spa, orders came for us to return to Tilff. We had been at the front for a whole month. A unit of the 30th Division moved into the area we were evacuating. We packed our gear and loaded it in a jeep trailer. We hurried to the assembly area only to find we were playing the old waiting game again, "hurry up and wait." There weren't enough trucks to take us all back at once so some of us had to wait for the second trip. It occurred to me they had had enough trucks to bring us up here, what happened? The trucks returned about mid-afternoon and we were back in Tilff before dark. Those who returned first were already in the process of cleaning their weapons, clothing, and other equipment. I decided to wait until the next day to start in on mine.

Mail had piled up for us in Tilff and was being distributed. Most of it was Christmas packages. In this lot I don't recall getting anything. However, we did get a few letters delivered to us at the front. In the second lot of mail, I got my share. The folks back home had not forgotten me.

The first thoughts of Ken and I were to visit the Damas family. We were quite anxious to see them again. As soon as we had cleaned up a bit and were free, we took off for their home. Both Ken and I took a bag of goodies with us such as chocolate, candy, cans of meat, and cheese which we had saved from some of our different rations. We knew they were things Madame Damas could use. As soon as we knocked on the door we heard the sound of footsteps racing down the stairs inside. When the door swung open, Jean-Marie, Annette, and Madame Damas threw their arms around us and jumping up and down shouted our names. This continued for what seemed like minutes as they expressed such a joy to see us again. Ken and I were just as happy as they were.

We were taken upstairs where the family had been living since we left. It had been difficult to get enough coal to heat all of their large house so they moved to a large room upstairs to conserve fuel. Upstairs we met a Dr. Hanet, a staff member of the school which Jean-Marie and Pierre attended. The German breakthrough had made it possible for Jean-Marie to return to school since it had moved to Brussels. Now that the school had moved back, Dr. Hanet had come to take him with him. Jean-Marie wanted to wait until I had returned to Tilff. Dr. Hanet was also a Scout leader of the troop in the school. His home was in Verviers and he knew Dr. Brasseur quite well. He was very interested in my Scout activities in the States and told me he would like to plan a reception for me at his school if I could come there for a visit. Unfortunately, we were to leave Tilff soon; therefore such arrangements were impossible. Nevertheless, we spent a very nice evening with the Damas family. We had tea and cookies and enjoyed looking at the family photographs. Annette told us that each morning at 7:30 they would go to church and pray for us. It gave us such a good feeling to know they thought so much of us. Later in the evening, a lady friend of Madame Damas, whom we had met before, joined us for a short while. She had with her a soldier friend whom we had not met. He was a sergeant from battalion headquarters who had been sent to ask if Madame Damas would consent to let her house be used to give a party for the officers. Madame Damas refused, saying she was sorry but she was entertaining her friends here. It was very gratifying indeed to know we had such good friends while we were so far from our own homes.

Friday morning I learned we would be leaving the next day for France but didn't know the destination. I was badly in need of a haircut so I went down to the local barber shop. When I came out I was met by Jean-Marie and Dr. Hanet. They were preparing to return to the school at Marche. They would be going to Verviers so I asked Dr. Hanet if he would convey my good wishes to Dr. Brasseur. He said he would. I said my goodbyes to my friends and returned to my quarters. After noon chow I decided I had better get some of my clothes washed. My field jacket was in worse condition so I thought I would do that first. Everyone else had the same idea. I couldn't find a spare tub or bucket anywhere. I thought perhaps Madame Damas would let me wash it at her house. When I went over to ask, she took the jacket from me and said "washing clothes is no job for a man, I will do it." I insisted on doing it myself but she insisted otherwise. I had no choice but to leave the jacket with her.

This would be the last evening Ken I would have with the Damas family. I was looking forward to the visit but was scheduled for a meeting at battalion headquarters with the other drivers so I told Ken to go on and I would meet him there later. I arrived at headquarters about 7:30 p.m. The room was dimly lit and was further dimmed by the thick cigarette smoke which filled the room. Seemed everyone was a smoker but me. The transportation officer oriented us on the conditions and route to travel we would take back to France. Each of us were issued a slip of paper stamped "Secret," listing highway numbers and the major towns and cities along the route. There were few questions and the meeting was soon over. I left and went straight to Madame Damas's house.

When I arrived, I noticed my jacket hanging on the back of a chair near the stove. It had not yet completely dried. We had tea and cookies and had general conversation, but it seemed no one had much to say. Ken and I had enjoyed our visits with the Damas family, and we were all saddened by the fact this would be our last night. It was a bit like leaving home. Ken and I did not leave together; he left first, and I followed about a half hour later.

Back to France

Saturday morning, January 20, was a very busy one. Everyone was up early hustling about getting their gear packed and loaded onto the trucks. A train was provided to transport the troops. The only personnel going by vehicles would be the drivers and assistant drivers. I was the assistant driver for Art Holm who drove the company headquarters jeep. By nine o'clock the troops were on board the train and the vehicles were lined up ready to go. Our jeep was in line directly in front of the Damas house. I looked to see if I could see anyone but in vain. The signal was given and wheels began to roll. As we crossed the railroad tracks, I saw Madame Damas and Annette standing by the side of the train. They saw me and called after me until I was out of sight. The convoy of trucks and jeeps moved slowly down the narrow street, out of Tilff and onto the highway leading to Liège. Just south of the city, the highway takes a sharp turn to the left on route 43 and follows the Meuse River through Huy then picks up route E41 through Namur, Charleroi, Mons and Valenciennes. We stopped about every two hours for a break and to change drivers. It was very cold, but we managed. We spent our first night in an old chateau near Cambrai. The next day was much colder. The icy winds blew right through our jeep; we had no protection at all. On one of our breaks I got out a large piece of canvas I had picked up near Malmedy and pinned it to the side the wind was coming through. It made a lot of difference and a lot more comfortable too. Our convoy continued on through Amiens and on to Rouen.

In Rouen we stopped at a transit depot maintained by the British. They fed us and provided us with a place to sleep. That night I pulled a tour of guard duty at the motor pool. We were off again bright and early the next morning. By mid-afternoon we had passed through Caen. Caen had been in the British sector during the invasion on the Normandy coast and was hit pretty hard. The highway approaching Caen from Lisieux was once a modern paved road. Now it resembled only a country road filled with craters and shell holes; we had to detour around many of them. A small village which once existed along that road had all but disappeared. On the left we could see what was once a beautiful big house hidden behind a grove of trees. Now only the charred ruins can be seen through the broken naked trunks of those trees trimmed bare by flying shrapnel from bombs and artillery.

About six o'clock in the evening we passed signs pointing the way to Isigny and Omaha Beach. A bit later we passed through Carentan. I am sure we spent one more night on the road but I just can't remember where. I am sure it was in the morning of Tuesday, January 23 we arrived at our destination, Barneville on the coast of France. The troops that had traveled by train had arrived the day before and were getting settled. D Company and Battalion Headquarters Company were billeted in a large building overlooking the English Channel. The building was being constructed as a resort motel but was never completed before the war.

Barneville

The unfinished motel where D Company and battalion headquarters were located was not in the town of Barneville but on the coast road of an isolated community on a small peninsula surrounded by tidal flats called Plage de Barneville. We had a beautiful view of the English Channel. At low tide, the beach would extend for almost ½ mile. About 20 miles out in the channel and a bit south was the island of Jersey, one of the two Channel Islands owned by the British and still occupied by the Germans. The other was the island of Guernsey. The British did not want the small islands destroyed by the war and since the German troops there were not considered a serious threat to the Allies, they let them be for the time being. Standing on the top floor of our motel on a bright and clear morning, and with the use of a pair of binoculars, I could see the rooftops of houses on the island of Jersey gleaming in the sun and smoke rising from the chimneys.

The first few days were spent fixing up the place to make it livable. My room was shared with two other guys. There were no frames or glass in the windows and there was no door but we made ourselves fairly comfortable nevertheless. I had been transferred back to my original squad with Sgt. Knudsen as squad leader and with this change I was able to see more of my friend Ken Raby.

There was considerable speculation as to why we had moved this far from the activities of war except just as a rest area. Rumors ran rampant. There was one suggesting we would be going to Iceland to set up an outpost. Another, we would prepare for an invasion of Norway. And still another, we would be going back to the United States; not likely. The rumor that was true was a change in the organization. The 99th Infantry would be joined by two other battalions to form a new regiment to be known as the 474th Infantry Regiment. We were joined by a battalion of Rangers of the First Special Service Forces who had distinguished themselves in the invasion of Anzio in Italy and southern France and a battalion of US Army and Canadian commandos. The 99th Infantry Battalion would constitute the third battalion and D Company's designation would be changed to M Company. We also received several new replacements. Two of them were assigned to my squad. One of them was a short young kid who called himself "Bim." The other one's name I don't recall. "Bim" told us he had trained as a paratrooper in the States and claimed to have seen action already. He told us he had jumped in Normandy during D-Day. We later found that most of the stuff he told us was untrue.

A training program was scheduled soon after we were settled. Most of the training was in the morning, sometimes lasting until two o'clock in the afternoon. We had field problems both day and night. Some took us miles away from Barneville and would last for two or three days. There was one night problem we encountered which was totally unscheduled. About two o'clock in the morning of March 9, we were routed out of our beds to man our defense positions along the coast. Intelligence had been received that the Germans from one of the Channel Islands were planning an attack on the mainland of France. They did in fact come ashore and attacked the town of Granville about 75 miles down the coast. A few civilians were killed and some supplies were taken. We waited at our positions for hours and nothing came our way, so we left and returned to quarters. About three weeks later as Ken and I were returning from picking up our laundry from a French woman's house, we spotted L Company dug in just behind our quarters. One of their officers yelled for us to "get down, don't you know there is a war going on?" It turned out that a small fishing boat had been spotted off the coast and it hadn't been determined if it was friend or foe. It was French. For a while I guess they thought it might be a repeat of March 9. But there again, you can't be too careful.

Dotted around the countryside, where we conducted some of our field exercises, were a number of ancient stone and brick towers. Most of them were in excellent condition. Upon inspection I noticed a Latin inscription carved into the stone above the door. I assume they may have been lookout towers dating back to Roman times.

Early one morning we were taken on an exercise south of La Haye-du-Puits. There seemed to be nothing to do here but scout around the area. From the evidence around us it seemed this was an area where an airborne unit jumped in the early days of the invasion and had assembled after landing. From the looks of things, it may not have been a happy landing. There was discarded clothing and equipment strewn all around. Some of the clothing was full of bullet holes, indicating perhaps the paratroopers had been ambushed and some killed during landing. Nearby the site was one lonely unmarked grave. In a way, the grave was offset by the profusion of wild daffodils growing around it. Also, a few paces from the grave site was a fenced-in minefield. I picked a handful of the daffodils and took them back with me.

One of our night problems found us several miles north of Barneville in an area where Germans had built a concrete pillbox for use as a radio or radar station. The steel tower had been knocked down and water filled the room in the pillbox. Over the doorway was carved the inscription, "Gebaut bei Adolph Hitler in Seinem Kampf gegen England" (Built by Adolph Hitler in his fight against England). It stands now as one of many landmarks of Hitler's defeat.

One afternoon in February, the company was called to assemble in the courtyard of the motel; our company commander read the following:

> Under the provision of War Department Circular No. 408, dated 17 October, 1944, and upon recommendation of their organizational commanders as individuals who have demonstrated satisfactory performance of duty and ground combat against the enemy, the following named enlisted men are awarded the COMBAT INFANTRYMAN BADGE retroactive two dates showing opposite their respective names.

I was one of only three men from M Company to receive the award that day. About a month later there was another assembly in which a similar citation was read.

Twenty-four men from M Company were awarded the Good Conduct Medal. I was one of the 24.

We had plenty of free time while at Barneville, especially on weekends. Ken and I would go exploring the area. One Sunday we decided to visit Carteret, the town across the inlet from Barneville. There are rocky cliffs around the point at Carteret and we thought it might be fun to brave the hazards of the narrow rocky ledges of the cliff. The tide was in and water splashing against the cliffs which made it more of a challenge. We climbed along the ledge for about 100 yards encountering several narrow escapes and finally came to a dead end. The only way past it would be to climb up the cliff and over the top. It was an arduous climb. Ken went first and I followed. As Ken reached the top and peeked over, he ducked down so quickly it almost knocked me off the cliff. "Let's get down from here quick," he said. I asked him what was wrong. He told me there was a big sign right on the edge of the cliff with a skull and crossbones on it. The sign said "Achtung Minen."[7] We made our way down the cliff OK and decided to try the climb again another day.

That other day came about two weeks later when a friend of ours, Arnie Hendricksen, decided to accompany us. We took with us a variety of foodstuffs from packages from home and some of our rations for a picnic. The tide was in so we would still have to risk our necks along the jagged rocks and slippery ledges to find a convenient spot for a noonday snack. In a package Arnie had received from home was a can of rattlesnake steak, as it was called. He shared it with us but it was not much to my liking. As we sat enjoying our little snack the tide went out and soon the townspeople were seen walking along the beach.

There was a lighthouse on the top of the hill that interested me so I strayed away from Ken and Arnie and made my way up to it. As I approached the top I found a path leading to the lighthouse. I followed it a short distance then stopped. I wanted to go further but didn't really like the looks of the area. I thought of the mine area we had encountered earlier and decided not to risk it. I knew the Germans had used the place as an observation post during their occupation and no telling what they may have left behind. There was an empty machine-gun tripod left in front of the lighthouse and another one had been thrown over the cliff. I was tempted to have a further look around but decided not to.

Passes to Cherbourg were issued while we were in Barneville. I was way down the list and one of the last to go. Actually, I didn't find the visit very interesting. I visited some of the shops but didn't buy anything except a few lightbulbs for our squad rooms then visited the Red Cross canteen for a short time. As I left the canteen and crossed the plaza in the center of town, I saw a small convoy of Army staff cars turn the corner. I noticed that one of the cars had a five-star insignia on the front. I followed the cars back to the canteen. I arrived there just in time to see General Eisenhower come out of the building. A huge crowd of French people had

---

[7] In German this means "Attention Mine."

gathered. They clapped and cheered loudly as the general made his way to his car. Looking for something else to do after Ike's convoy left, I decided to take in a movie. Playing at the theater nearby was *Wee Willie Winkie* starring Shirley Temple. I had seen it before, years ago, but it was something to do to take up time. I thought it might be in English with French subtitles; instead, it was dubbed in French. I didn't know Shirley could speak French—just kidding. I sat through the whole picture and didn't understand a word they said.

During the last few weeks at Barneville considerable changes were made. M Company was issued an M8 armored car. Staff Sergeant Andrew Hoiem was assigned as car commander, Ordean Halla driver, Elias "Bob" Popejoy gunner, and I was assigned as radio operator and assistant driver. The M8 armored car is similar to a small tank but has six wheels instead of treads. It is equipped with a 37mm anti-tank gun, a .50-caliber machine gun and a .30-caliber light machine gun, all mounted on the turret. The car commander was issued a Tommy gun, the driver a .45-caliber pistol, the gunner a carbine, and I was issued a .45-caliber pistol, but also managed to acquire a carbine.

Now, with the reorganization completed, it was time to move again and get on with this business of the war.

Jarvis Taylor in a German tank crewman's helmet with his M8 Scout Car and crew. The 99th Battalion received the equipment when they took on a Counter-*Werewolf* mission in March 1945. The scout car carries the unit's new M Company, 474th Infantry Regimental markings, including their pentagon on the vehicle's sloped glacis plate. Each of the three battalions received 11 M8s, and three M24 light tanks were attached. The Cannon Company was equipped with six 105mm self-propelled howitzers as part of their special mission organization. (Courtesy of the 99th Educational Foundation)

Across France to Germany

Early on the morning of April 2, 1945, the day after Easter, we packed our gear on trucks and jeeps and made ready for our departure. Ken had been out most of the night with Arnie Hendricksen and was still a little happy drunk. I helped him to get his gear together and packed on the truck. This time, the company would not be riding the train; they would be on the trucks. I would be in the M8. We said goodbye to Barneville and the trucks rolled out of the town and into the open country.

The convoy headed south through Coutances, Avranches, and Laval, then east to Le Mans and Chartres. We would stop about every two hours for a break. Each time I would go to Ken's truck to check on him. Our M8 was situated about the middle of the convoy and used as a relay station to transmit orders throughout the column.

Our first bivouac was near Chartres. It was also a fuel dump where we would refuel our vehicles. During refueling, an M8 from another battalion caught fire and burned beyond repair. The radio operator had failed to turn off his radio and a spark ignited the gas. From there on we were extra careful.

About two or three o'clock in the afternoon of the second day we were in Paris. We stopped to refuel at a fuel depot on the street that ran alongside the hospital where I had spent a couple of weeks not many months before. It took us a long time to get through the city. Because of the traffic it was difficult for the convoy to keep closed up. It was especially difficult when crossing through large intersections. Other cars would get between us and slow us down and create big gaps in the column. At times we had to speed to catch up. In one incident Halla was speeding through an intersection to catch up and almost struck an old lady who had started crossing the street in front of us. When she saw the vehicle coming at her she was frightened and didn't know whether to go on or go back to the curb. She just stood frozen. Halla jammed on the brakes and managed to stop a few feet from her. We managed to get out of Paris without further incidents and drove on to Soissons where we bivouacked the second night. There was no mess crew to prepare meals for us during the whole trip so we had to [fend for] ourselves with C- and K-rations.

We were up early the next morning, Wednesday April 4. This would be the last day of our journey. As usual, Halla and I would take turns driving. Today's route took us first through Laon then to Montcornet, Rocroi, and across the Belgian border to Philippeville and on through Dinant. We continued on Route 36 through Ciney to Liège. On our approach to Liège we came within a few miles of Tilff. I'm sure we all wished we could have had another night there. Leaving the city of Liège we took the same route I had taken on patrol on December 17, 1944. We passed the crossroads at Herve and were soon approaching Henri-Chappelle. Passing through the village the convoy slowed and with horns blowing we drove by the places we had stayed six months ago. Many of our friends rushed out and waved as we passed by. We crossed the German border sometime between 8:30 and nine o'clock and a few minutes later we were in Aachen. The convoy halted on a dark street between rows of apartment buildings. We made out as best we could the rest of the night and in the morning were assigned rooms and some of the damaged buildings. M Company was located on Steubenstrasse. The M8 crew, Halla, Popejoy, and I had a room together, while Hoiem shared the room with the mess sergeant. Our apartment was located on 12 Steubenstrasse Apt. 21.

We had no assignments or duties while in Aachen except to make ourselves as comfortable as possible. Each day Halle and I would go down to the motor pool and just piddle around with our M8 for a while. The only duty we had was a few hours one morning when the M8 crews were ordered out for firing practice with the guns mounted on the vehicles. Since our room had no furniture, Popejoy and I were scrounging around for something we could use. We found a good bed spring and innerspring mattress which we propped up on our four boxes to make an excellent bed. It was the first real bed we had slept on in months. Hella was content to spread out his bedroll in the corner. We also found a small table which made up the only other piece of furniture in our modest little apartment. Ken was in the building next to me and we saw each other often. When he came over to my apartment in the evenings, we would light up the old Coleman burner and brew a cup of tea. Sometimes we would go exploring through some of the buildings which had been destroyed. During the search, we had acquired some china cups, a china teapot, and a small copper pan for boiling water.

One of the things we enjoyed most while in Aachen was the chance to take a shower. It was a treat seldom available to us. However, the shower facility was not in Aachen. The whole company was loaded on trucks one morning and taken to the town of Herzogenrath about 6 miles away. En route the trucks passed through Würselen and Bardenberg, places familiar to the then D Company during the campaign to close the Aachen Gap in October 1944. It was here the company underwent about 14 days of continuous bombardment and suffered a number of casualties. I was not in the 99th at that time but in a replacement depot in Heerlen, Holland, less than 10 miles away. I would join them about a week later. Herzogenrath is also about 6 miles as the crow flies from Heerlen. We took our shower in a large modern factory shower room. There were no lockers to place your clothes in. You secured your clothing by hanging them on a hook at the end of a chain suspended through a pulley on the ceiling and pulled them up as high as you wanted, then secured the chain on a hook on the wall. It was possible to lock the chain for better security if desired. Showers were always refreshing and did wonders for the morale.

Back in Aachen the company decided to issue passes for a visit back to Tilff. Only a few men at a time would be permitted to go. Names [would] be drawn for each trip. My name was drawn for the first group to go. I was quite excited about seeing our friends again. Unfortunately, Ken was not in the first group but sent his regards to the Damas family. Suddenly, our dream fell through. The company changed its mind, and no one was able to go. Tough break.

Crossing the Rhine and Beyond

On Wednesday, April 11, we were packed and ready to move again. The convoy of trucks, jeeps, and armored cars lined up and off we went. We took the main highway, 258, out of Aachen and headed southeast. The route took us through the Siegfried Line, the "Dragon's Teeth," and the Hürtgen Forest, the site of one of the most fierce battles of World War II in Germany's struggle to defend their Fatherland. Their fortifications extended from Wesel in the north to the Swiss border in the south. All along our route through this area pillboxes, which once guarded the frontier, were upended and demolished. The Hürtgen Forest had been devastated. Not one tree survived the intense firepower that rained down upon the area. There was also grave after grave of German soldiers buried where they fell and marked with only a crude wooden cross topped with the soldier's helmet.

The original plan was to go to Koblenz, travel along the Rhine, and cross the river at Bingen. This would have been the most interesting and scenic route, seeing many of the ancient castles atop the cliffs on both sides of the river, and perhaps the shortest. However, this was not to be. A few miles before reaching Koblenz, it was reported the bridge to the city was down and we would have to detour. We backtracked on 258 to Mayen and took a secondary road south to Düngenheim and Cochem. At Cochem we turned east on Hwy 49 and followed the Mosel, enjoying the beauty of the river on the right and the terraced fields and vineyards on the left. We crossed the Mosel River at Treis and traveled south up a winding road from which you had a commanding view of the whole countryside and the valley below. Ordean Halla was driving so I stood up through the hatch to enjoy the view.

About six o'clock in the evening the convoy made its way down the steep hills overlooking the Rhine and on into Bingen. We refueled in Bingen and took time out for chow. The 99th Infantry Battalion started their crossing of the Rhine on the narrow pontoon bridge about nine o'clock. It was slow going and took quite some time for the whole convoy to cross. The vehicles were started across at intervals to reduce weight on the bridge. We drove along the Rhine through Wiesbaden and to the autobahn, Germany's superhighway. By this time, I had fallen asleep.

About two hours later I was awakened by a lot of commotion going on outside our vehicle. We had stopped and I heard someone ask for a fire extinguisher. I looked out the hatch and saw an Army flatbed semi-truck loaded with Jerry cans of gasoline. It appeared the brakes had caught fire. The driver of the truck was frantic. He didn't seem to know what to do. Sergeant Hoiem had taken our fire extinguisher and was helping to extinguish the fire. After a few minutes it seemed the emergency was over. The driver started on his way and we followed closely behind in the left lane. The semi sped up and was soon out of sight. As we continued our convoy pace up the autobahn, we began to see bits of fire on the road. It appeared the truck was again on fire. On each revolution of the wheel it left bits of burning rubber on the road.

We finally approached the burning truck again. The driver had climbed on top of the gas cans stacked about four or five deep and was throwing them off in an effort to save some of them from exploding. Someone yelled, "Get that crazy fool off that truck." Sergeant Hoiem ran over, climbed up, and pulled the driver off just in time to see the first can explode and go sailing through the air. Hoiem urged the driver to unhitch the cab and pull it away from the burning trailer. He could at least save the cab. After the first explosion, it was like the Fourth of July. Can after can went flying through the air. We had parked a safe distance from the burning truck so there was no danger to us. When the fire was finally out, we continued on our way.

We had been on the road for almost 24 hours including the time lost at the burning truck. About five o'clock, on Thursday morning, April 12, we turned off the autobahn and onto a secondary road leading to our bivouac area in the Eiterfeld Forest near the village of Wolf. Ken and I fastened our shelter halves together, pitched our tent. Making conditions as comfortable as we possibly could, we were soon fast to sleep. The next morning, we received word that President Roosevelt had died. We were all quite shocked and saddened by the news. It was difficult to believe until we had word over the radio and in the *Stars and Stripes*.[8] We were very sorry indeed that the President had not lived to see the victory he had fought as hard as anyone to achieve.

***

From the time we left Barneville, we were a part of Patton's Third Army. Our duties would be with Military Intelligence. These duties consisted of complete searches of all houses, buildings of all kinds, and wooded areas and sectors assigned to us. We were to confiscate all weapons, knives, cameras, binoculars, and other military equipment which could be used by the enemy against our forces and apprehend all stragglers and suspicious persons. This duty began while here in our present bivouac. Squads were sent out to nearby towns and villages each day to see what they could find.

Early on we had been issued a card from Headquarters, Twelfth Army Group, Europe with instructions as to how we are to conduct ourselves in Germany and with the German People. It read:

> We are now fighting on German soil, and we are in contact not only with the soldiers of our enemy, but also civilians of Germany. As conquerors, we must now consider our relations with the people of Germany
>
> It is imperative that you do not allow yourself to become friendly with the Germans, but at the same time you must not persecute them.
>
> American soldiers can and have beaten German soldiers on the field of battle. It is equally important that you complete the victory over Nazi ideas.
>
> To guide you I have issued these special "battle" orders. They may appear to lead along a narrow path, but they are NECESSARY. You personally must prove to the German people that their acceptance of Nazi-ism is responsible for their defeat, and that it has earned them the distrust of the world.

---

[8] A magazine published in World War II by the U.S. military providing news for soldiers.

It was signed, O.N. Bradley, Lieutenant General, U.S. Army Commanding.

The "battle" orders were under the following headings:

1. To remember always that Germany, though conquered, is still a dangerous enemy nation.
2. Never to trust Germans collectively or individually.
3. To defeat German efforts to poison my thoughts or influence my attitude.
4. To avoid acts of violence, except when required by military necessity.
5. To conduct myself at all times so as to command the respect of the German people for myself, for the United States, and for the Allied cause.
6. Never to associate with Germans.
7. To be fair but firm with Germans.

I doubt if all these orders were carried out to the letter though we did the best we could and conducted ourselves according to the circumstances we encountered.

Though there may have been an element of danger in our duty, I found it interesting to see how the people lived and how the war had affected their lives. Because most all the able-bodied men had been forced into Hitler's army, the women and children had to do all the work. I saw one old lady on a farm pushing a hay wagon to the barn. In the fields, cows were pulling the plows. All the horses had been requisitioned or confiscated for Army service. There was little or no war damage in these farm communities, but you could see the people had suffered in so many other ways. In some ways you couldn't help but feel a bit sorry for some of them but you could not show your feelings.

Most places I went, I found the homes very neat and clean and the people very friendly and cooperative. You could usually tell when anyone had something to hide. They would follow you all around the place and watch you like a hawk. Usually in these places you may find something such as a gun, knives or a sword or perhaps a complete Nazi uniform. In homes where the people paid no attention to you, you usually found nothing. In one house I searched, the lady followed me everywhere I went saying, "Nix for Militair, nix for militair." In the bottom drawer of a chest upstairs, I found a German dress bayonet. In another incident I found a complete German uniform, boots and all. When I was taking it away the lady, probably the soldier's wife, kept protesting. It could be that her husband had been killed and she wanted to keep his uniform. She asked that I at least leave the boots for her son. I saw the child; he looked only about five years old. It would take him a long time to grow into those boots. I took the whole outfit.

Most afternoons when we returned from our duties Ken and I would sit around outside our tent and have a cup of tea and have a nice chat about what we did that day. Frequently we would invite some of the officers to join us. They seemed to enjoy the chat as well as the tea.

One night about 10 o'clock, as Ken and I were chatting away, we heard what we thought was a German aircraft coming in our direction. We quickly blew out the candle and hoped the others did as well. It was an anxious few minutes until the plane flew over. Shortly after, we heard bombing and strafing of the town of Bad Hersfeld a short distance away. On another time, about midnight, the whole company was routed out by the sound of a Tommy gun. Sergeant Knudsen was on guard. He had seen two men crossing the field at the edge of the woods of our bivouac area. When he challenged them, they ran. Knudsen opened fire on them but apparently missed. The next morning a German soldier's cap was found in the field.

Early in the morning of April 17, our M8 and crew along with other trucks and elements of the 99th were detailed to the town of Merkers only a few miles away. Our mission was to provide armored escort for a convoy transporting priceless treasures the Germans had looted from museums and wealthy homes all over Europe. Much of it too was Germany's own art treasures in cold reserve which had been stored in several salt mines around Merkers. There was such an overwhelming amount of the treasure that it took several days to move it. Colonel Walker, commander of the 474th Infantry Regiment, was in charge of security and assumed command of the convoys transporting the treasure to Frankfurt. The first convoy left Merkers on the 15th.[9]

On April 17, at 8:30 a.m. the 99th Infantry Battalion contingent of the treasure convoy, named Task Force Hansen, moved out from Merkers, entered the autobahn, and headed for Frankfurt. It consisted of 26, 10-ton trucks loaded with art, two loaded with POWs to do the loading and unloading, and two empty trucks for use in the event [that transferring some of the loads] became necessary. In front of and behind every cargo truck was an armored vehicle. My M8 was in the center of the column. Fighter planes flew at a low altitude up and down the column for air cover and Military Police patrolled up and down the convoy allowing no other vehicles to pass. Along the way we passed the burned-out trailer we had encountered a few days earlier. Our convoy arrived in Frankfurt at 2:45 p.m. The Reich Bank, where the art treasure would be stored, was on Adolf Hitler Ave, a street one block long between Landesstrasse and Kaiser Wilhelmstrasse. Machine guns had been set up behind a mound of sandbags on each side of the entrance to the bank. Both ends of the street were blocked off. Our M8 was positioned at the corner of Adolf Hitler Avenue and Kaiser Wilhelmstrasse. With our weapons uncovered we stood guard while the treasure was being unloaded. The unloading and storing of the treasure began about an hour after we arrived and was completed by 10:30 p.m. Our convoy assembled a half-hour later and we were on our way back. Since Halla did the driving to Frankfurt, I did the driving back to our bivouac area. We arrived about five o'clock in the morning.

---

[9] The presumption is that another convoy had left on April 15, a few days before the 99th arrived.

The next morning we were sent on a mission to search a wooded area reported to have German soldiers in it. When we arrived at the area a couple of squads formed a skirmish line through the woods while we drove the M8 around to the other side to catch anyone who came out. We parked on top of a hill overlooking a small village, uncovered our guns, and waited. When we first arrived on the hill we noticed three houses had white flags hanging out the windows. The longer we stayed, the more flags came out. By the time we left, virtually every house in the village was flying a white flag. In about two hours we spotted the squads at the edge of the woods. Only one person was found and he was a civilian.

Our last mission while at Eiterfeld Forest took us a few miles south near the town of Fulda. It had been reported a small band of German soldiers had been gathering near there for possible resistance behind our lines. We made a quick search of the villages near Fulda but found nothing. The only things we found were a few guns, knives, and uniforms.

We Move Again, and Again

We packed our gear and left Eiterfeld Forest early on the morning of April 21 and headed south. We drove through Fulda, Brückenau, and Schweinfurt. In Bamberg we encountered a massive traffic jam. Military vehicles were bumper to bumper on both sides of the highway. Traffic was almost at a standstill. When we reached the town of Forchheim, we turned left onto a secondary road leading to the village of Heroldsbach. Here we made another left turn onto a narrow road which came to a dead end at the gate of a large castle estate called Schloss Thurn. M Company would establish their headquarters in the castle and the troops would be billeted here for the next few days. As I recall, I had a small room all to myself with a small window which looked out over the moat. Many of the upstairs rooms were "off limits." Also off limits was the family's private chapel on the ground floor, on the left as you cross the bridge over the moat into the courtyard.

The castle had been occupied by a German colonel and his staff and used as his headquarters sometime prior to our arrival. As Ken and I were walking around the castle garden one afternoon, we came upon a small area at the far end of it which, from the evidence, seemed to have been used as an incinerator. There were fragments of burned documents strewn all around. It could be the colonel may have burned some of his papers here as he prepared to evacuate the castle when Allied forces began to close in on the area. From the ashes we discovered one piece of paper bearing the name of Granville and dated, as near as we could make out, with the date the Germans had made their raid on that town in March. We speculated, the activities of the German troops left on the islands of Jersey and Guernsey may have been controlled from here.

We continued our search operations from Thurn. On one outing we were on a narrow country road to a village where German soldiers had been reported. As we approached, we came upon a muddy area of very deep ruts in the road. Halla turned off into the field to go around them to avoid getting stuck. The field was wet and soft and the heavy M8 sank to the axle. The two jeeps accompanying us sped on to the village, leaving us stranded. We uncovered our .50-caliber machine gun and I radioed for a truck to come and pull us out. Before the truck arrived, the jeeps returned, having found no one. The German soldiers apparently had fled. The jeep drivers chained their vehicles together and succeeded in pulling us back on the road.

The M8 crews didn't go out as much at Thurn as we had other places. We had some guard duty from time to time but that was about all. The rest of the time we were pretty much on our own. Ordean, Popejoy, and I spent a lot of time fooling around with our vehicle and exploring the estate. Late one afternoon I approached the guard talking with a young German boy at the castle gate. The boy had two eggs and was trying to negotiate with the guard for something he had. When I made the casual remark to the guard about the boy who may have been in the Hitler Youth, the boy responded by saying that all German boys had to belong to the Hitler Youth. This began a conversation between the boy and myself. We spoke of the Hitler Youth and the American Boy Scouts. I learned his name was Hans Muller. He was 15 years old and lived in Bamberg. For the time being he was staying with his grandmother in her house just outside the castle gate. I knew it was against regulations to fraternize with the Germans; nevertheless, Hans and I became friends of sorts, and met several times during our stay at the castle. Incidentally, Hans gave me the two eggs and asked nothing in return.

I met Hans at the gate one afternoon to give him some tea, candy, and a few odds and ends I had salvaged from my rations. He invited me to his house. I felt a bit uneasy about going even though it was only a few yards from the gate, but went with him anyway. We had been in the kitchen for only a few minutes when I decided to leave. Hans exited the room ahead of me. As we started down the hall Hans suddenly pushed me into another room and quickly closed the door, saying in a loud whisper, "Hauptmann, Hauptmann" (Captain, Captain). My company commander, Captain Winholtz, had just come in the front door to pick up his laundry that he had left for Hans' grandmother to do. Hans kept peeking out the door to see when the coast was clear. I believe he also knew we were not supposed to fraternize with the German people.

I believe it was on Saturday, April 28 when we left Thurn. The weather was overcast and a bit chilly. After approximately two hours on the road, we pulled into the railway station at Markt Bibart. It was rumored we were to pick up an SS officer here but during our three days' stay no one seemed to know or hear any more about it. In the meantime, we were billeted in the living quarters of the stationmaster above the station. I don't know of anyone being assigned to any details while we were here. The men seem to content themselves with playing cards and drinking the wine someone had found. The several bottles they found didn't last very long. When the wine finally ran out, a rather stout fellow in one of the squads called "Tiny"—I don't remember his real name—boasted of having once been a bartender. He concocted some weird solution made with alcohol mixed with sugar and hot water. After it was heated again and ready to drink, a flame was set to the liquid so that it burned on top. "Tiny" said this was to purify it. Nevertheless, it seemed to satisfy the men's thirst. It's a wonder that no one died or went blind from the stuff. Drinking is not one of my diversions, so it didn't bother me at all.

A few feet away from the station, next to the railroad tracks, there was a German light tank which had been knocked out. I decided to have a look and crawled inside. I found some earphones and a throat mic I thought may be useful in the M8 and yanked them out. They were under some live rounds—some were bent and scattered around the interior. I felt a little uneasy pulling on the wires and cables for fear something might explode. It really was a dumb thing to do in the first place but I succeeded in getting them out. I found the earphones to be too weak but the throat mic worked perfectly. I used it with the M8 radio from then on.

On Tuesday morning a detail was sent to the town of Scheinfeld about 2 miles away to clean some barracks of a former German camp. It was thought we may be there for at least a week. In the evening the rest of the company moved into the camp and settled down for a comfortable stay. Those of us in my barracks selected a bunk, arranged our belongings neatly, and did additional cleaning to make the place more livable. We were all going to sleep late the next morning. Wrong! We were routed out of our beds and on the road again by six o'clock. The convoy backtracked to Markt Bibart then turned southeast to Neustadt, Furth, and Nuremberg. We continued southeast to Regensburg and turned north for about 8 miles to the town of Regenstauf. Most of M Company was billeted in two or three houses while company headquarters was in the town hall. The M8 crew had a room upstairs that we shared with three medics who were attached to our unit; they were Arnie Thomassen, Clarence Becker, and Anthony "Tony" Sciacca.

Early the next morning M Company resumed their operations of search and seizure. We had searched the neighboring village and farms and were headed back to Regensburg when we encountered a farmer, a Polish slave laborer, with horse and wagon. Halla stopped the M8 and the farmer stopped the wagon. The road was too narrow for the two to pass. On our right was an embankment 5 or 6 feet down. We motioned for the farmer to pull over or pass. Apparently, he did not understand too well but did move over a slight bit. Thinking he had enough room, Halla started to pass. He had less room than he thought. As he moved forward, the weight of the vehicle caused the edge of the embankment to give way and the M8 slid downward. The vehicle would probably have turned over had it not come to rest against a fence post. The left wheels were still on the top edge of the road. We were alone on this mission and without jeeps for assistance. I doubt if they could have pulled us out of this one anyway. I radioed for help.

In the meantime, all we could do was to wait. Sergeant Hoiem suggested we make some coffee. We had the water but somehow we forgot to bring our Coleman burner. There was a farmhouse nearby and we thought perhaps we could get some water heated there. Hoiem asked for a volunteer. I picked up the copper pan and dashed off to the house. The people there were nice and friendly and anxious to help. The water was heated and I dashed back to enjoy a cup of coffee with the crew.

While still waiting for help, I returned to the farmhouse a second time to heat some water. While waiting for the water to boil, a young German boy, about 16 years old, came in expressing some excitement. His English wasn't too good but I was able to understand what he was saying. He told me his father had just returned from Regensburg where the newspapers there said the Americans and the Russian soldiers were fighting against each other. I told Hoiem about it when I returned to the M8. He said it was crazy. The Germans were very much afraid of the Russians and wanted to stir up trouble between the Americans and the Russians if they could. The front lines were just a few miles away and the Germans knew the war was almost over. They certainly did not want the Russians around. Back at Thurn, when Hans and I were talking one day, he knew Germany had lost the war and asked me who would occupy it. I told him all the Allies would take part but felt sure the Americans would occupy this sector. "God be thanked," he said.

It seems the maintenance truck was taking quite a long time to get to us. I suggested to Sergeant Hoiem we might be able to move our vehicle by using some logs offered by the farmer whose fence we rested against. Hoiem refused. I told him we should at least try something, not knowing when help would arrive. The sergeant still refused. His stubbornness somewhat angered me and I went on to say, "I'll be. If this guy was strong enough to pick this thing up, and set it on the road all by himself, you wouldn't let him, would you?" Hoiem shouted back, "Hell no!" He claimed he didn't like the Germans and didn't want to have anything to do with them or anything they had. I noticed [though that] he didn't hesitate to drink the coffee made from water heated in a German's house or eat some of the eggs we were able to get from the Germans from time to time. Aside from this little incident, Hoiem and I got along quite well. The maintenance truck finally arrived and pulled us back on the road.

Sundays were no different than any other day as we headed out to search another nearby town. As we crossed the bridge just out of Regenstauf I noticed a soldier who seemed familiar. He was still in place when we returned and I recognized him as being one of the MPs I served with back at Camp Beale, California. I could not think of his name then, nor do I remember it now. When we pulled up in front of our company headquarters, I jumped from the M8 and went back to the bridge to talk with him. I learned he was now in an engineering outfit. I never saw him again.

On Tuesday, May 7, we went out on our last police detail. We went north to Schwandorf, a city which had sustained considerable damage. We started our search in the abandoned factory area. Any doors that were locked, we broke open. When we tried the first building, we couldn't get in. Lopez, using the side railing of a hay wagon as a ladder, climbed to the second floor and, breaking the window with the butt of his pistol, climbed in. Finding nothing, he knocked some tiles off the roof from inside and climbed out. I broke a few windows myself but not for the fun of it.

When I entered one house that morning, I found two of my sergeants busy talking to a couple of girls that lived there. Seems they were too distracted to do the searching, so I proceeded to do it myself. The old man of the house followed me everywhere I went. Upstairs in the attic I found a large cabinet which was locked. I asked the man for the key. I couldn't understand what he was saying but he indicated he had none. I continued to ask, and he continued to put me off. I was determined to look into that cabinet one way or another. I pulled out my .45 and pointed it at the door ready to shoot the lock off. The old man threw up his hands shouting, "Nein, nein, nein," and ran down the stairs. He returned in a minute with the key. He opened the cabinet, but it was empty. He knew it but I didn't. I could not take that chance.

As we worked our way further into the city, we saw more and more damage. Many of the houses we went through had been damaged. The second floor of one house I checked out was being supported only by the rubble of the destroyed first floor. An old man, a veteran of the Kaiser's army, lived there alone. His family, or other people that were in the house, may have all died and [been] buried under the rubble of the house for the stench of the dead filled the air all around. Being so close to the front, the damage to Schwandorf had been caused only recently. The city had not had any chance to recover in any measure from the advancing Allied troops. Now and then you could see a body or two still lying beside the road. At our assembly point, the body of a German soldier laid decaying in the sun on an abandoned stretcher.

On our way back to Regenstauf we covered a couple of other small villages. In one of them we came across several men who had been internees in a concentration camp. They looked weak and frail and some had ugly sores on their legs. They could hardly stand. They were still wearing their dirty and tattered striped prison clothing. They were standing by the gate of a small schoolhouse they had been using as a shelter. As we approached them, all but one retreated back into the schoolhouse. The one remaining looked as if he may be in worse condition than the others. We tried to question him, but he could hardly speak. Lee Gardner, one of the guys on the mission, went straight to a nearby house, yanked a nice suit of clothes right out of a closet, and brought it to the man. We gave the poor fellow every eatable [sic] thing we had and told him we would return with more, later. Back at the company, we put together a big food package and dispatched a jeep to take it to those unfortunate victims.[10]

Upon returning to Regenstauf we heard rumors of the war being over. We couldn't believe it. So far there hadn't been confirmation of it but we surely hoped it was true. That evening we heard the news on the radio and the company command car. The Germans had signed the surrender document in a schoolhouse in Reims, France at 2:41 a.m. that morning. It was to take effect at midnight, May 8. There was no shouting, yelling or celebrating—seems like no one had anything to say except, "Thank God it's over." The few who had gathered around, slowly and quietly drifted away. I returned to my room and wrote a letter to my mother.

Patton was at his headquarters in Regensburg when the news of the surrender came. Although hostilities had ceased, he wasn't about to let his troops sit by and savor the moment. He ordered that all the troops would have close order drill every morning beginning immediately. We had most of the time in the afternoon to ourselves. Many of the guys went fishing in the Regens River. I spent some time exploring around town. There was a path going up a hill and into the woods behind the houses and town hall facing the main road. The path led to a wooden tower that had been shot all to hell. The stairway had been shot away with what looked like .50-caliber bullets. Opposite the tower was a small shrine to the Virgin Mary. It had not been touched.

One morning, while standing on the steps of the mayor's office, I turned around facing the street just in time to see the back of the head of "old blood and guts" as he drove by in his jeep. In the afternoon I was standing beside the road when an unguarded convoy of German trucks of all sizes and descriptions passed by. They were loaded with soldiers packed in like sardines. It looked as if most of them had been wounded and many wore bandages. Though the townspeople lined the route waving, shouting, and cheering and some crying as the trucks bounced down the cobble street road, the German soldiers had only a look of despair. It was a sorry sight to see and, in a way, a sad one too.

**

On Saturday evening, May 12, I was standing on the banks of the Regens River talking to a German boy who had been a member of the Hitler Youth. A messenger came and told me everyone was to report back to the company. We were to pack our gear and be ready to move out the next morning.

We left Regenstauf early Sunday morning, drove through Regensburg and north to Nurnberg.[11] We continued northwest to Aschaffenburg where we bivouacked the first night. We camped near the river. It had been a hot day and it wasn't too

---

[10] There was a concentration camp at Regensburg, just 20 miles south of where he says they were located at this time.

[11] Nuremberg, Germany.

late so several of the men decided to take a swim. Unfortunately, the swim ended in tragedy. One of the men from another company drowned. Such is the irony of fate. A man endures all the hardships and hazards of war and survives only to die a few days later in the pursuit of a little recreation.[12]

We left Aschaffenburg the next morning and traveled west. We crossed the Rhine at Oppenheim near Mainz and proceeded on into France, stopping at Metz only to refuel. We then drove onto Verdun where we spent the night. Verdun was the site of one of the fiercest battles of World War I. After settling in we were given leave to go into town if we wanted. I decided to go in and have a look. On the way, I came across a sergeant whom I had seen before, back in the States. He was a medic at Camp Beale, California when I knew him. He was assigned to the hospital there and issued me my first pair of glasses. Though I didn't remember his name, he remembered me, or so he said and we enjoyed a few minutes of conversation.

Tuesday night we bivouacked at Soissons again. This was the second time we had stayed here. The first was the night of April 3. That too was a Tuesday night about a month and a half ago when we passed through here on our way back to Germany.

Wednesday would be our last day on the road. We passed through the ancient city of Rouen in the afternoon and continued on for a few more miles to Camp Twenty Grand. Here we spent 13 days of rest and relaxation with practically no duties at all. We were issued new clothing and equipment and had our money exchanged. Now that the war was over, one of the prime concerns was when will we be going home. Eligibility for going home would be determined by the point system. The number of points would be determined by such factors as length of service, time overseas, etc. However, this was not the concern of the men of the 99th. Many of these [soldiers] WOULD be going home, but not to their home in the United States but to their ancestral home of Norway. The men of the Norwegian American Battalion could not have been happier, including those other Americans who joined as replacements.

Camp Twenty Grand was visited almost every day by swarms of airmen anxious to buy or trade for any German souvenir they could get their hands on. Anything with a swastika on it was worth at least a bottle of scotch to them. No telling what stories (lies) they may have told their family and friends as to how they came by their trophies of the war.

Liberal leave was granted while at Camp Twenty Grand. One afternoon, I obtained a pass to visit the ancient city of Rouen. After visiting several points of interest including the magnificent Gothic cathedral and the market square where Joan of Arc was burned at the stake (May 30, 1431), I decided to look up the Boy Scout Office. I was given an address of Rue l'École and told to ask for Monsieur Gilbert. On the way there, I passed under the famous clock built more than 400 years ago

---

[12] The individual who drowned was Peter L. Vergnetti from the 2nd Battalion of the 474th Regiment.

in the arch spanning the street, Grosse Horloge. This clock, built in 1511, has only one hand which shows the hour. Beyond that, you have to approximate the minutes. Monsieur Gilbert was not at the address given but workmen there referred me to another. At this address I met a tall slender man who looked more like a mortician than the rug merchant he was. This gentleman escorted me to another address which was a small shop just under the ancient clock. The gentleman there gave us directions which led us to a French military garrison in the city. There I met a French sergeant who was connected with the Scouts. After the introductions, my guide left. The French soldier and I spoke for a while then he gave me another address and asked me to meet him there at six o'clock in the evening.

I arrived at the new address at the appointed time period. The sergeant had already arrived and with him was another gentleman. This gentleman was Monsieur Gilbert whom I had been looking for. He was the Commissioner of Scouts of France and the Province of Normandy. We were introduced. After some discussions, I was given several Scout insignias, a Scout pin, and a card designating me as a member of the Friends of the Scouts of France. Later, I was invited to a glass of wine at a nearby sidewalk cafe. The soldier had to leave shortly thereafter. To further entertain me, Monsieur invited me to a theater to see a variety show in which friends of his were playing. I had to leave about nine to meet the trucks for the trip back to camp.

Norway

Early in the afternoon of May 29, 1945, the 474th Infantry Regiment left Camp Twenty Grand and traveled in convoy to the port of Le Havre. Pulled up on the shore, with their big double-bow doors open wide and their ramps down ready to receive us were several LSTs. It was late in the afternoon by the time all vehicles and personnel were loaded on board. The next morning the convoy of ships formed in the harbor ready to sail. The weather was good as the ships began to move slowly northward up the English Channel and through the Straits of Dover. As we sailed into the mine-infested waters of the North Sea a couple of days later, armed lookouts were posted on the ship's bow to keep watch for floating mines. A few were spotted but they were too far away to be a threat to the convoy.

The voyage to Norway took about four days and was relatively uneventful. On board the ship I met two sailors with whom I became friends. One was Carl O'Gara the radioman, the other, Jack Dowd, a signalman. The three of us spent [as much] company with each other in as much as their duties would allow. One evening I took Carl below where the vehicles were parked to show him the armored car. When I slipped into my position next to the radio, I noticed the beautiful chrome German dress bayonet I had kept as a souvenir was missing. I had wanted to show it to Carl. No doubt, the sailors, much like the airmen back at Twenty Grand, were hunting for souvenirs also. I suggest they may have plundered all the vehicles they could for whatever they could find.

June 5 would be our last day at sea. About three o'clock in the morning as our convoy steamed its way up the Oslofjord, I was on my way to the ship's radio room to keep Carl company. As I did so, I saw several German submarines pass by going out to sea. I could also see a number of German seaplanes moored in coves along the fjord.

It was early afternoon when we drove our M8 off the LST and onto the dock at Oslo. Carl and I had planned to keep in touch by radio and I would describe everything I saw as we drove through the city and onto our camp area. Carl's call sign would be "Sailor" and mine was "Soldier." As we drove away, I could hear Carl loud and clear but for some reason he could not receive me. We discovered later I had failed to align my radio frequency to his. We never made contact.

Driving through Oslo seemed like any other American city—the houses, the shops, the parks, and even the Gulf and Esso gasoline stations. It was almost like being at home. There were very few civilian cars on the streets because there was no gasoline to run them. We continued through the city and on for about 2 miles into a suburban area called Smestad. There was a former German Luftwaffe camp here which would be our home for the next five months. As soon as we had settled in, several of us decided to go into town and have a look around. I wanted to return to the ship to see Carl and find out what had happened to our radio communication.

Hans Larson, and another fellow whose name I can't recall, and myself, caught the Trikk (street car) into town. Hans had been born and raised in Oslo and pointed out various places to us as we made our way to the ship. My companions were not particularly interested in going on board again so they went on their own way. When I boarded the LST, I learned the crew had been given shore leave and Carl had gone into town. I went ashore and waited, hoping to see Carl as he returned to the ship.

After waiting for quite some time and he didn't show, I decided to return to camp. My friends had left me and I was on my own to get back as best I could. I found the station, but thinking all the trains went the same way, I took the first one that came along. As the train rolled on into the suburbs I didn't recognize any familiar scenery and I had also forgotten the name of my station. Finally, I decided I had gone far enough and got off at a stop called Holmenkollen and took the next train back to Oslo. I found someone who spoke English and was put on the right car and told the name of my stop: embarrassing ain't it?

The next day Nordby[13] and I went into town again. We arrived at the ship about chow time. A deck officer asked if we had eaten. We told him no. He ushered us to the ship's kitchen and told us to help ourselves. When we had finished, Carl had shore leave again so the three of us went back into town. We spent most of the time

[13] Presumably a 99th soldier.

watching a parade, honoring Denmark. About mid-afternoon Carl returned to his ship and Nordby and I returned to our camp at Smestad. This was the last time I saw Carl until I returned home. In the meantime, we kept in touch.

When Nordby and I returned to camp, we found the company had moved to more permanent quarters. Company headquarters occupied [buildings that resembled] barracks [and were] somewhat set off all by [themselves]. My M8 crew, Sergeant Hoiem, Ordean Halla, Elias Popjoy, and I were located on the second-floor front. The medics, Arnie Thomassen, Tony Sciacca, and Clarence Becker, who were attached to company headquarters, had a room on the second floor.

The King Returns to Norway

When the Germans invaded Norway in 1940, King Haakon VII, his family, and cabinet fled to England to avoid capture. The war was over now and after five years living in exile the King of Norway was returning to his native land. The Norwegian people were excited and feverishly preparing for the celebration. The 99th Infantry Battalion, the Norwegian Americans, would also take part in this momentous occasion. Select members of the 99th were picked to serve as the Honor Guard for the King upon his arrival. The rest of the battalion would serve as security guards along the parade route from the ship to the Royal Palace. Hundreds of thousands of people jammed the streets to see their king. This was a great day for the King and his people. This was a great day for Norway. The Norwegian people, in the spirit of celebrations, paraded through the streets far into the night. Every lodge, club, and organization marched in the greatest parade in Oslo's history.

After the King arrived at the palace and all the other dignitaries had passed by, the security guard was dismissed and given the afternoon off to witness the rest of the parade. While standing on the steps of the National Theater watching the parade, a gentleman spoke to me in clear English commenting on the parade. He told me he was waiting for his wife who was marching with the American Woman's Club. He told me he was a Norwegian and had lived in Galveston, Texas for many years. He married an American girl there. They had been visiting in Norway when the country was invaded and were forced to remain. The man told me his name was Harold Hansen. He introduced me to his wife, when she had finished with the parade. They asked me to visit them sometime. I was able to do so on several occasions.

My first visit to the Hansen home was on a very warm Sunday afternoon. I took the Trikk to the Hellerud stop, a small community in the suburbs of Oslo. Mr. Hansen met me at the stop and escorted me the few blocks to his house. Mrs. Hansen had dinner waiting for us so we sat down almost immediately to a big feast prepared especially for my visit. There was so much food on the table there wasn't room for another thing. It was, indeed, a feast to behold. Everything was most enjoyable, especially the mackerel. I think it was as much a treat for them as it was for me.

Mrs. Hansen had been able to get some white flour to make rolls. That was a rare treat for the Norwegians too, since all they were able to get for the past five years was black or brown bread.

After dinner we sat around, had pleasant conversation and a few drinks. About six o'clock I thought it was time I should leave. The Hansens suggested we should first have a little snack. The table was set and we had, not just a snack but another complete meal. I couldn't get up and just leave after that so I stayed another couple of hours. At about nine o'clock I suggested again I must leave. Again, they suggested we should have a cup of tea and a sandwich. Out came the dishes again and more food. When this was over, I told them I just simply had to leave. This time they allowed me to leave without too much protest but on the promise I would visit again, and soon. Such hospitality I had never experienced before.

The Hansens were the first family I met during our tour of duty in Norway but by no means the last. We were welcomed everywhere and the people were anxious to have us. However, our tour was not all fun and games and socializing. We had our many duties also.

Our Duties in Norway

Our main duty in Norway, aside from being good guests in the country, was guard duty. The Germans had established many installations in and around Oslo, such as radar and radio stations, motor pools, warehouses, etc. to prevent further damage and looting. We were also there to help repatriate the German soldiers who had occupied this country. When the war was over the soldiers had been disarmed and confined into several camps around Oslo. They were allowed to keep 10 percent of their weapons and provide guards for their own camps. Three camps that I knew of were at Roa, Sognsveien, and Holmenkollen. In time, with few exceptions, these soldiers would be returned to their homeland.

During the five years of occupation there were crimes committed by some German soldiers against the Norwegian people. In order to locate and weed out those responsible and bring them to justice, early morning raids were made on some camps. The soldiers were routed out of their beds and lined up in front of their barracks. Hooded informers would be escorted down the formations to point out any suspects. Those found would be taken to prison camps to await trial. The prison camps were compounds surrounded by two wire fences, separated by about 10 feet with two watchtowers overlooking the compound. A .30-caliber machine gun was mounted in each tower. Two guards watched from the towers with Tommy guns while other guards patrolled the perimeter. When I was on guard detail, my watch was in one of the towers. Guard duty at the prison camps would be for a week at a time.

Some of the prisoners were used for special details outside the compound. One morning, as several of them were working around our barracks, I spotted a young prisoner about 18 or 19 years old standing on the porch by himself. Thinking to test my limited knowledge of the German language, I went up to him and said, "Achtung." The German lad immediately snapped to attention. Very good, I thought. Now what do I do? I walked away for a minute or two then came back. The young soldier was still standing there. Gad, How do I tell this guy, "At ease." Stupid me, I ain't so smart, is I? I quietly walked away thinking, "What a lousy thing to do to that guy." I think that poor kid must have stood there for half an hour or more before someone gave him an, "At ease."

For the more serious crimes and notorious prisoners, such as Vidkun Quisling, the Norwegian traitor and Nazi collaborator known as the Benedict Arnold of Norway, German SS and Gestapo agents, [they] were imprisoned in the Fortress of Akershus in Oslo. There were also other prison camps located within a few miles from Oslo.

Late one afternoon a shipload of prisoners arrived in Oslo from the north of Norway. I was part of a guard detail dispatched to meet them. The authorities determined it was too late to unload them at this time and sent the ship to anchor offshore. Early the next morning we were on hand when the ship tied up at the pier. As the prisoners were unloaded, we ushered them to an awaiting train and loaded them into boxcars. As each car was filled, the doors were closed and locked. The guard detail rode in another boxcar. The train took us to the town of Josheim some 30 or 40 miles south of Oslo. There we unloaded our prisoners and marched them in groups of about 50 to a camp a half-mile down the road. The route from the train yard to the prison camp was lined on both sides of the road with security guards spaced about 10 yards apart. Only one other guard and I, with Tommy guns and pistols, escorted one of the groups of prisoners to the camp. My partner walked in front of the group and I was in the rear. At one point a fat little German colonel in full uniform bedecked with medals was huffing and puffing trying to keep up. Somehow, some of his precious metals came loose and fell off his uniform. As he stooped down to retrieve them, he was also holding up the line. One of these security guards came over and gave him a swift kick in the butt sending him on his way. He didn't recover his medals.

It was said that these were some of the more ruthless offenders among the German prisoners. It [was] suggested [that] some of these were involved in the tragic story told to me by a Norwegian friend as we walked around Oslo one day. My friend pointed to a man and a woman walking through the park by the National Theatre. He told me that sometime after the Germans had invaded the north of Norway, they went about moving some families from their homes. This particular family lived in a section which was more accessible by boat than by road. One day a German patrol came to their house to take them away. They put the man and his wife into a small boat and started out from the landing. The wife begged and pleaded with the Germans to wait for her six-year-old son who had been playing some distance from their house. The child showed up just as the boat left the dock. He ran to the pier and called to them, but the Germans would not turn back. One of the soldiers who remained at the house aimed his pistol and shot the little boy. He then walked down to the pier and rolled the body of the young child into the water. It was such men as these that were kept under heavy guard in what used to be the concentration camps which they built for their Norwegian prisoners.

Not all German soldiers were criminals. For the most part they were just the average soldier much like ourselves, glad the war was over and glad to be going home. On several occasions I was on the detail sent to various camps to escort convoys of vehicles loaded with soldiers to ports of embarkation, either at Drammen or Kongsberg for transport back to Germany. The trucks the Germans used looked old and were of different makes and sizes. They used anything they could find. There was no gasoline available. The trucks had been converted into wood burners. Frequent stops were necessary for the drivers to clean out the clogged burners and stoke them up again to make them go.

Early one morning I was detailed with a group to meet with a British officer at the German Air Force camp at Roa. After rounding up a group of soldiers for shipment, the officers and men of our detail returned to Smestad. I was instructed to remain with the British officer until all arrangements were finished. He had agreed to drive me back to my camp. The major had for his use a super Mercedes convertible German staff car, much like the one Hitler used. The top was down. His driver was a British sergeant. On the trip to Smestad, the major rode in the front seat next to the driver while I had the whole back seat to myself. I directed "my chauffeur" to Smestad and rode in style. When we arrived, the car pulled up on the parade ground and stopped where my squad was waiting and another doing close-order drill. I stood on the floor of the back seat and gave the Nazi salute and stepped from the car. I was greeted with nothing but howls and heckles.

On some guard details [we] would be some distance from the city and would be there for a week at a time. My favorite was a former German radar station at Nordstraum on a hill outside of Oslo. We took over the detail from British troops which had been sent home. When we first arrived the place was absolutely filthy, unbearable. Whether the Germans made the mess or the British is anyone's guess. Perhaps the British could live with it but we couldn't. Not used to living under these conditions and realizing we would have to be here for a week, Sergeant Hoiem and I began cleaning up the place. When we had finished, it was clean enough for the King to move in.

One of my guard posts was a German motor pool at Ullevaal Station. Most of the vehicles were jeeps, light trucks, and ambulances which looked as if they may have been used in Rommel's desert campaign in North Africa. They were painted a tan color with the insignia of a palm tree on the side. When I finished my tour of duty one morning I decided to go into town. I took the trek in what I thought was the direction of Oslo. In a few minutes I found myself, not in Oslo but at the end of the line at Sognsveien. I had to get off the train and cross the tracks to the other platform for the trip back. As I crossed the tracks at the rear of the train I heard a sharp click. I looked up to find a German soldier about 20 feet away standing at attention rendering a salute. It startled me for a moment but I returned his salute and proceeded on my way to the platform. The soldier was standing guard at the entrance to one of their camps.

The favorite guard post was a former German warehouse at Kampen just outside Oslo. The warehouse was filled with wine, cognac, champagne, and a variety of tobacco products but none were American or British brands. Every guard detail that worked that post managed to take away something. I was neither a drinker nor a smoker so none of this interested me. However, I did get a few packs of cigarettes for a friend. Next to the warehouse there was another building where the British stored their food supplies. From here they would issue certain supplies to the Norwegian Army. As I stood guard there one day, I noticed the British loading food on a truck for the Norwegians. It was mostly damaged crates of British rations and barrels of cheese from Denmark which had been broken and the cheese oozing out the sides. Stacks of American rations sent to the British were not touched. The British kept those rations for themselves.

I was on duty at an ammo dump inside a Norwegian garrison one evening about chow time. The soldiers had to pass me on their way to their mess hall. I noticed only a few stayed there to eat. The others returned to their barracks with their cup of coffee and two or three slices of bread with a small square of butter or cheese, I couldn't tell which. This was their evening meal. I was at the same post the next morning when they passed by with their mess kits to get breakfast. Again, most of them returned to their barracks with their meager rations. I noticed this time they had a cup of hot chocolate, two or three slices of dark brown bread, a square of butter or cheese, and a slice or two of cold cuts which look like bologna. I feel quite sure some of the American rations sent to the British were intended for the Norwegians as well but they didn't seem to get any.

The British were the first of the Allied troops to arrive in Norway after the war had ended and considered themselves to be more or less the saviors of the country. The Norwegians were grateful of course and glad to be free again. They gave the British more blind respect and were willing to tolerate them perhaps a bit more than they should. From my observation, and what I heard, the British gave very little consideration to the Norwegian people. When the Germans surrendered they left behind tons of usable material and equipment. Instead of leaving it for Norwegians to help in their reconstruction, the British took or destroyed everything that wasn't nailed down. I learned from one of my friends that in the northern part of the country, the Germans left quite a lot of heavy equipment such as tractors and bulldozers. Since the British couldn't take everything back with them, they pushed them off a pier into deep water so no one could use them.

Not all of our guard duty was outside the camp at Smestad. We had some interior guard duty as well. I had interior guard duty only two or three times during our five months there. Once I was reprimanded for not "walking my post in a military manner" (General Order No. 2) on any detail. It happened early one morning as I was standing guard on the back gate of our camp. We were supposed to wear our steel helmets at all times when on guard duty but on that morning I had taken mine off because it was heavy and uncomfortable and hung it on the fence. I still had on my helmet liner. I leaned against the gate and proceeded to read a magazine I had brought with me. I had just gotten comfortable when I saw Major Anzjon, the battalion executive officer, crossing the road several yards away on his way to breakfast. When he turned in my direction, I quickly shoved the magazine in my jacket. As he approached, I rendered a snappy salute which he returned, then began to bless me out for reading on duty and not having my steel helmet on. When he turned to leave he added that I should stand on my two feet. This was the only such experience I ever had with any officer. From all I had heard, Major Anzjon was supposed to be a rough and hard-to-get-along-with officer. It seems no one in the battalion liked him. Actually, I was a bit disappointed with him. As he stood blessing me out, he seemed quite nervous, so much so he sort of stammered and could hardly get out what he wanted to say. Perhaps he lacked confidence in himself. I thought later, if I suddenly said "BOO" to him he would have jumped over the fence. Perhaps not. Anyway, no one ever saw him on the front line at any time. Some say he had heard too many rumors throughout the battalion.

We didn't have a jail or stockade at Smestad; it wasn't felt it was needed. Jack Wilkinson of our company had been in trouble before. Just before he went up to the front in the Battle of the Bulge he was arrested because of some trouble with a young girl but charges were dropped because of his satisfactory performance in that campaign. Now he was in trouble again. This time he was arrested for stealing German vehicles from a motor pool and selling them on the black market. Since Jack was one of our friends and not considered to be particularly dangerous, he was confined in a small wire enclosure near the mess hall with only a pup tent for shelter. Nevertheless, he was guarded 24 hours a day.

During noon chow one day several of us were discussing Jack's situation. It was mentioned it would be the duty of any guard to shoot a prisoner trying to escape if he did not halt when he was told to. Jack, though a friend, would be no exception. One of his close friends overheard our conversation and reported it to him. It seems that report was directed toward me since I had been his guard that day. He sent a message back to me saying if, and when, he got out, he would be looking me up. About two days later he did escape. That night was the only time I ever slept with my .45 under my pillow and did so for only a couple of nights. Jack never showed. I guess he was more concerned about making his getaway than getting even. It wasn't long before he was apprehended again and confined in a more secure compound.

It was one built by the Germans for Russian prisoners and slave laborers. A real Houdini this Jack, he escaped again and [was] later picked up trying to board a Polish ship disguised as a Polish seaman. This time he was confined in a jail inside the garrison used by other units of the regiment, but as the poet Richard Lovelace (1618–58) said, "stone walls do not a prison make nor iron bars a cage." Apparently, Jack was a believer in poetry, for subsequently, he was on the run again. This time he really made good his escape. He was still missing in October when the 99th Battalion boarded the ship and sailed for home. Someone said they had seen him in the crowd of people on the dock seeing us off, dressed as a girl. He was crying. Jack had the same opportunity as we all did to have fun and enjoy the visit to Norway. Unfortunately, he realized his mistake a little too late.

The People

It wasn't all work and no play for the members of Task Force A on their mission in Norway. General Summers, Task Force Commander, stated in his directive, "We are not conquerors in Norway. There is no non-fraternization policy with the Norwegian people. You will have the opportunities to have a good time. But remember the people will judge us all by your individual actions. Always act in a manner that will make the Norwegian people glad that we are stationed here."

The Norwegians were indeed glad to see us and very gracious as well. Aside from the Hansens, my first acquaintances, I met so many people it was difficult to get around to visit them all very often. One thing that made it easy was the fact that everyone I met spoke English and during the summer months, it didn't really get dark at night. It was not at all uncommon to be visiting friends at 11 and 12 o'clock and even later. They were always glad to have company.

Soon after moving into Smestad, a young boy was running around the place anxious to meet as many American soldiers as he could. He was a very friendly kid, always smiling and wore parts of his Boy Scout uniform. Our conversation went to Scouting, as we both had something in common. His name was Rune Malterud. He lived about 2 miles down the road, a place called Lilleaker. He came to Smestad frequently and I was a guest in his home many times. The only place we went together was the famous ski jump at Holmenkollen. Eventually, Rune came to the United States and worked for the Norwegian Embassy in Washington, D.C. for several years and married an airline hostess.

Another frequent visitor was a young fellow about the same age as Rune, [whose name was] Rolf Bebo. Rolf lived in the house right next to the camp. He had been born in Chicago, Illinois. His family returned to Norway when he was about two years old. One of Rolf's [hobbies] was playing the game of tennis. I too enjoyed tennis and had been on the team in high school. Fortunately, there was a small tennis club near the camp and Rolf provided the rackets. We were able to enjoy many afternoons of play before leaving Norway. One afternoon, as Rolf and I returned from tennis, Captain Winholtz, my company commander, saw me with the racket and said he too enjoyed the game and we should play sometime. We met on a date convenient for both of us and had a very nice time. I forget who won.

Early in the evening one day, I was in the barracks alone. I was looking out the window and the back room which was occupied by the medics. I noticed a boy riding a motorcycle with another boy seated on the back. By the way they were riding, I thought to myself, no good will come of that. A few minutes later, Rolf came running in with the boy who had been on the rear seat. His face was all bloody and skinned up. "Take a look at this boy," he said. Rolf was not one of the riders but had seen the accident as the motorcycle flipped on the wooden bridge sending the boy on the rear sprawling. The injured boy had a large wooden splinter and several smaller ones lodged in his face just below his left eye. No medic was around, and something had to be done so I had to play the doctor. I sat the boy in a chair, cleaned the area around the wounds with antiseptic, and carefully extracted the splinters from the lad's cheek. I cleaned the area again and dressed it with a small bandage. The next afternoon the boy returned, and to show his gratitude, brought a few eggs and a liter of milk. Clarence Becker was in and re-dressed the wounds.

I was standing guard one evening when an elderly gentleman came by walking his dog. He stopped and asked if it was permissible for him to speak with me while I was on duty. I told him it was alright. He introduced himself as Tor Andresen and told me he was an officer in the Christiana Bank in Oslo. We spoke for quite some time, mostly about the war. When I was relieved from duty at midnight, he invited me to his apartment. Even at midnight it was still light, but a little too late, I thought, to be visiting, so I declined, suggesting perhaps some other time and returned to camp. I did visit Mr. Andresen several times during the next few months. Though he was not a young man, he liked to hike and suggested we go hiking sometime. We took our hike on September 16, 1945. It was a Sunday and I was scheduled for KP but I managed to get a friend to work the detail for me.

We started out very early in the morning, accompanied by a young boy, Jonas Collett, whom I had met earlier. It was a very nice day as the three of us boarded the Trikk for Roa. There we began our hike along the road and through the fields, finally reaching Skutehogda in Nordmarker about noon. We settled ourselves on a ridge overlooking a small lake. As we began to unpack the many things we had brought along for our picnic we were interrupted by a brief shower. Jonas saved the day by quickly spreading his raincoat over the limb of a small tree for protection. The rain was soon over and we were able to enjoy a delightful afternoon. We returned to Roa by six o'clock and took the Trikk back to Oslo.

I met many of my Norwegian friends while on guard duty. As was the case with Mr. Andresen, so it was with Jonas Collett. He was a boy about 16 who had come by my guard post one day and stopped to talk. This meeting with Jonas developed into a very nice friendship. He liked the Americans and wanted to know more about America and hoped to go there someday. Right now, he wanted to spend as much time with me as he could. I was invited to his home many times. On one occasion I was invited to his birthday party. On another [occasion], I was invited there to a diplomatic reception for his uncle who was preparing to leave for his post as attaché in the Norwegian Embassy in Manila in the Philippines. Jonas and I attended a couple of concerts together and several movies. He also came to visit me at Smestad. When it came time for us to leave Norway, Jonas came to see me off. We had become quite good friends and he was a bit upset over my leaving, but knew it had to come sooner or later. The morning we were leaving he was on the dock. He told me he would write. I threw my fountain pen down to him. In a letter from him shortly after returning home, he wrote this: "Wednesday morning, the day you was going to U.S.A., you saw that I went away from the boat very fast, and dared not to look at you. I felt that some thing swelled in my throat." He was too emotional and didn't want it to show.

Another young fellow I met while standing guard was Finn Lysheim. We met early one morning to go to the Norsk Folkemuseum in the area of Oslo called Bygdoy. Here they have an interesting display of very old houses which were disassembled from various parts in Norway and reassembled in this park. They represent the types of houses found in various parts of the country. Also at the Folkemuseum house [are] the remnants of three ancient Viking ships: the Tune Ship, the Gokstad Ship, and the Oseberg Ship built in the ninth century. They had been burial ships for great Viking chieftains. The Gokstad Ship was excavated in 1880 and the Oseberg Ship in 1904. We spent the whole day at Bygdoy and I found it extremely interesting. I did not see as much of Finn as I did others I met but we did make a return trip to Bygdoy to visit the Fram House to see the polar ship *Fram* built for the Norwegian explorers Fridtjof Nansen and Hjalmer Johansen for their second Arctic voyage in 1893–96. They failed to reach the North Pole but had penetrated further north than any private expedition had up to that time. In June 1910 Roald Amundsen set out on an expedition to the South Pole. By February 15, 1911 the *Fram* had penetrated farther south than any vessel had before, and on December 14, 1911 Amundsen and his four companions reached the South Pole. I was able to visit Amundsen's home at Svartskog on one of our few bivouac outings. Though I did not see Finn as much as the others, I did enjoy his company.

In a letter from my mother, she told me the minister of the Baptist Church she attends, in Lynchburg, was from Norway. I knew Dr. Nordenhoug also but had not considered his nationality when I went to his church. She told me he had a brother in Oslo named George and I should go to visit him. She enclosed his address and phone number and suggested I give him a call. I called George and was invited to visit. I did so on two or three occasions.

Except for Jonas Collett, the family I spent the most time with was the Bergersen family. Both Mr. and Mrs. Bergersen were teachers. They had two sons. I had met the younger son, Berger, in town one day while looking for a small souvenir Viking ship. I was having no luck until this young boy agreed to direct me to a specialty shop. I found the items I wanted and expressed my gratitude to the young chap. It seemed as if every Norwegian you met wanted you to come home with them. This occasion was no different. I accompanied the boy to his home in V. Aker, a suburb of Oslo, and met his parents and older brother, Hans. I could not have been treated better on this or any of the other many visits I made to their home. Both parents were educators and we enjoyed many stimulating conversations about our two countries and the war. The two boys, Berger and Hans, were in their middle teens. They loved hiking and invited me along on one of their outings. We took the Trikk up the mountain to the end of the line to a place called Frognerseteren. From there we continued on foot up the mountain, down through a small village to the top of another hill where we settled down for a picnic. While we were enjoying the outing, we were caught in a brief thundershower. It was a most enjoyable day nevertheless.

A week later, the Bergersen family went to visit relatives at Harstag in Nordland in the north of Norway, the land of the midnight sun. They had not seen their relatives for five years during the German occupation because travel was practically impossible. Berger wrote to me frequently while he was there telling of all the things he was doing and how much he enjoyed seeing his grandparents again. They returned in late August, and on the 31st, Berger and I attended a concert by the Oslo Philharmonic Orchestra, conducted by Odd Gruner Hegge. Berger was a little late arriving; consequently, we missed getting our [assigned] seats. We noticed they were occupied by two fat British service women. Not to worry though; right after the first selection, the usher rushed us down to two seats in a much better location. We were just in time for the performance of Edvard Grieg's "Piano Concerto in A Minor," Eva Knardahl as soloist. It was an excellent performance. A couple of weeks later, on September 10, Berger and I attended a performance of Henrik Ibsen's *Peer Gynt* at the National Theater. The play of course was in Norwegian. I couldn't understand a word of it but could follow the plot pretty well. Berger translated for me. There were several movie theaters in Oslo, most of which were playing old American films. Berger and I spent some time in these also.

While standing guard at a Norwegian garrison one day, a young Norwegian officer stopped by to chat. During our brief conversation he invited me to visit him at his barracks in the evening. I accepted his invitation and arrived at his quarters about eight o'clock. He had a private room at one end of the barracks in which his men were quartered. As we talked, the young officer offered me a drink. Not being a drinker, I accepted somewhat reluctantly. I took one sip of the stuff and it was like fire. It burned all the way down. I tried not to show my dislike of this potent liquid and took only the smallest sips. At one point, the young officer excused himself saying he had heard a noise in the barracks and must go to investigate. When he left, I attempted to pour the fire water back into the bottle. In doing so, some of it ran down the side of the bottle and onto the table. This stuff was like acid. Where it ran on the table, it took the paint right off it. I was embarrassed. There was a newspaper lying on the table, so I put it over the spot and placed the bottle on top of it. When the officer returned, I made some excuse to leave.

Another family I enjoyed visiting was the Thorstensens. They also had two sons. Odd was the older, about 23, and Shjalg, about 17. Mr. Thorstensen was also a schoolteacher. He took me on a return trip to Bygdoy and the Folkemuseum and gave me a lesson in the history of Norway. Odd had been in the Norwegian underground during the war and told me of some of his experiences. He came to visit me at Smestad several times and one evening we attended a concert. I didn't see much of the younger boy but one evening I was visiting the family and he gave me a German SS knife he had picked up at the Gestapo headquarters after the war had ended.

Captain Winholtz's driver was a rather shy young fellow. He was a nice guy and I knew him well, at the time, but unfortunately I have forgotten his name. He was not the outgoing type and didn't seem to have many friends, if any at all. It was not because he didn't want friends perhaps, but he just wasn't the kind to draw people to him and stayed pretty much to himself. I don't believe he had ever been out of camp on a pass before. Actually, I felt a bit sorry for him and thought to do something about it. So one day I asked him if he would like to go into town with me. He said he would. It was such a surprise to everyone, the office couldn't write out his pass fast enough. The first place I took him was to visit the Thorstensens. They were delighted to have us and were most hospitable indeed. I thought this family would be the one that would impress him the most. I was not mistaken. The young fellow enjoyed himself more than at any other time in the service. I was glad for him to have the opportunity.

Perhaps the most noted park in Oslo is the Frogner Park located in the northwest part of the city. One area of the park, known as the Vigeland Gardens, is most unique in that it contains the collected works of the Norwegian sculptor Gustav Vigeland. The statues themselves are rather unique as they portray the human figure, both the male and female unnaturally too buxom. Nevertheless, it is an interesting display of Vigeland's works.

Near the Frogner Park I met a young man about 18 or 19 years old, who gave his name as Iorg Berg-Hansen. I later learned his name was Iorg Beumelburg and was the son of German Major Georg Beumelburg who had been attached to the intelligence services in Norway under Admiral Wilhelm Canaris. Canaris was Chief of the Armed Forces Supreme Command Foreign Countries/Counterintelligence. Before coming to Norway Iorg lived in Berlin. His family apparently was among the privileged class and had some social standing, especially in military and Nazi circles.

He showed me a photo taken at a Nazi rally in Berlin that pictures him sitting only a few rows behind Hitler. During the occupation of Norway, Iorg served as one of the leaders of the Hitler Youth.

After the failed attempt on Hitler's life on July 20, 1944, Canaris and many officers who worked for him were implicated in the plot and were arrested. Canaris was eventually executed. Iorg's father was arrested and taken to Berlin and was never heard from again. He told me his father had been executed along with some of the other conspirators. Iorg and his mother remained in Oslo and changed his name from Beumelburg to Berg-Hansen. I don't recall seeing his mother or a photo of her on any of my visits to his home. There was, however, a framed portrait of Major Beumelburg in full uniform on a table in the living room.

Although I visited Iorg at his home on several occasions, I can't recall if we ever went any place together. Nevertheless, we enjoyed each other's company and I considered him a very good friend. On some occasions, when I visited Iorg, there would be an old gentleman standing in the yard next door that would [frown at me] and say under his breath, "Nazi, Nazi," and try to wave me off. I paid no attention to him.

After returning to the States, Iorg and I did exchange letters for a while. In one letter, he told me he had finally gotten his citizenship papers and was now a Norwegian citizen.

Time to Go Home

As summer faded and the hours of daylight and nighttime became more normal, the 99th was preparing for the return to the States. Even now, six months after the war was over, going home was determined by a point system. Unfortunately, there were a few at our battalion that did not have the required number. My friend Ken Raby was one of them. The sad day came one afternoon when those unfortunate friends of ours were assembled for our last goodbyes. The whole company gathered around our departing comrades to reminisce a bit, shake hands, and wish them well. They would be returning to Germany with the occupation forces for a short time before being able to go home.

Now it was time for the rest of the 99th Infantry Battalion (Sep.), the Norwegian Americans to leave Norway. We packed our gear and on October 15, boarded the so-called Victory Ship, *Bienville*. Crowds of people had gathered on the dock to bid us farewell. The next morning the ship left Oslo harbor, sailed down the Oslofjord and into the North Sea. We docked at the port of Southampton a day or two later to let off some British troops.

We left Southampton after nightfall and sailed out into the Atlantic. The sea began to get a bit rough. I went to the galley for some chow. This was almost an exercise in futility as it was hard to know whose mess kit you were eating from as they slid up and down the long table bolted to the bulkhead. I tried to get some sleep but sleep was impossible. By morning about half the troops were sick as a dog, me included. A drill for abandon ship was called and everyone scrambled on deck and headed for the rail. The captain didn't think we moved fast enough so the drill was repeated.

For several days the sea played games with our ship, tossing it from one huge wave to another; up one wave and down another. When the ship went down the wave, the stern was completely out of the water and you could hear and feel the propellers spin. Finally, one day the ship stopped going up and down, and it began to roll. It rolled over so far on the starboard side, the water was almost coming on deck. For me it was really scary. A soldier standing next to me, realizing my concern told me there was nothing to worry about. "When I get to worry," he said, "it's time for you to worry." I still worried.

About two days out of Boston the seas calmed, but a thick fog rolled in. You couldn't see your hand in front of you. The ship sounded its foghorn. We had survived the worst storm to hit England and the Atlantic in 25 years. It was learned later that other Victory Ships such as ours had broken in two during the storm. We were lucky.

On November 1, 1945 the *Bienville* steamed into Boston Harbor. We met the aircraft carrier *Enterprise* on its way out.

After leaving the ship, we boarded an awaiting train that took us to Camp Myles Standish about two hours from Boston. Once there, we settled into our barracks and waited to see what comes next. We had nothing to do except relax. It was good to be comfortable again after the hectic 14-day voyage across the Atlantic.

The next morning after chow, our platoon leader Lieutenant Parnell called us to assemble at a large boulder near our barracks. There was nothing formal about it; we just sat around or leaned against the huge boulder waiting for our leader to speak. It has been a long time since that day and I can't quote him exactly but he said something like this:

"Men, we have all been through a great deal together and have made a lot of good friends. We have memories enough to last a lifetime, some good and some bad. We have served together in a great battalion." Parnell hesitated a moment, looked up, and said, "I regret to tell you that as of this moment, the 99th Infantry Battalion (Sep.) is decommissioned; it no longer exists." There was complete silence. In a way, we had all expected something like this, but it still came as a big shock. This was not the way to end the life of a great battalion, platoon by platoon or company by company. The entire battalion should have been assembled on a parade ground with the commanding officer and perhaps other dignitaries addressing the troops expressing praise and appreciation for a job well done. This way, it tends to make one feel we were somewhat insignificant as if we had never done anything and we're just being thrown away like so much rubbish. Surely, a great battalion deserved better than this.

What happens now? We were told we would be sent individually to a separation center near to where we lived and would there be formally discharged from the

Army. I was sent to Fort Meade, Maryland. I turned in all my equipment except the uniform I was wearing. I was given the opportunity to re-enlist on the spot with an upgrade in rank, but I said no thanks. They checked the records to make sure I had all the medals to which I was entitled. I received copies of my service records, $300 in cash, and was sent on my way. It was almost as if the past three years didn't happen.

Anyway, it was good to be back home.

CHAPTER SIX

Donald Curtis

Private First Class Donald Curtis joined the 99th in March 1943 as the men were training in Camp Hale. Curtis brings an honest perspective of life as a private and eventual lead scout for his company. He is keenly aware of being seen as expendable due to rank, his position, and his lack of Norwegian ethnicity. Through his honest portrayal, he draws insight into the unspoken rules of war that protect the men in scout roles on both sides of the battle lines. He compares this mutual respect to the unwritten rules that respect the generals at their command headquarters.

He also provides insights into the life of a non-Norwegian private in the 99th where he believed that respect was hard, if not impossible, to obtain despite his solid and heroic contributions. He was called upon for his clear English-speaking skills, when radio communications were critical, as well as for his rudimentary knowledge of French to interview the locals. With some practice, his French grew and the conversations with the locals are interesting to read.

In his writings, Curtis shares several compelling and detailed accounts of pivotal battles in Europe. As lead scout for his company, he was the first to enter Cherbourg, France, which was one of the first cities in northern Europe to be liberated after D-Day. He also points out that the 99th was a key part of the force that conquered Aachen, the first major German city to fall to the Allies.

Curtis met Gerd, a Norwegian woman whom he later married, in the five months that the 99th was stationed in Norway at the close of the war. This was not the only romance spurred during that time period, as there were several marriages that emerged between the 99th and Norwegian women. Curtis lives in New York state. His wife, Gerd, passed away in 2021.

My View

There were about 4 million privates [in the] U.S. Army [during] World War II. We all had a narrow view. Narrow, because no one ever told us anything. We had no radios. Once in a while, a copy of the Army newspaper, *Stars and Stripes*, would arrive a week or so late. The GI's "patron saint," Ernie Pyle, wrote articles of sympathy and support. Our favorite was Bill Mauldin, who did satire with his great cartoons of Willie and Joe, [which] were always right on target. These two journalists told of war the way we saw it.

I was lead scout for the 3rd squad, third platoon of the third line company—C Company—of the Viking Battalion, XIX Corps, U.S. First Army, Northern Europe. In military lingo ETO (European Theater of Operations). Wow!! Lead scout was out front of his squad about 20 yards and 10 beyond the second scout. Far more used than providing a route of movement, was the importance of information. His view! Most of my time in the forward foxhole was trying to observe what I might determine from the enemy out there somewhere. My view and study of the terrain was limited to 75–100 yards and to the sides to where another squad scout was doing the

Lars L. Larson and other 99th soldiers in parade uniform with a group of women in Norwegian Bunda national costume, in the Hardanger style. Possibly taken on June 7th, 1945 when the 99th Battalion stood as honor guard for King Håkon VII at the Honnørbrygga (Oslo's inner harbor), when the royal family returned from five years of exile. The U.S. flag was sewn on their uniforms to counteract public suspicion that they were Soviet troops. (Mark Nelson, Lars Larson collection)

same. I sent signals to No. 2, who would get messages to our squad leader. Usually, a buck sergeant, three stripes. This was my view and duty for 168 days. There were another 150 that I was under fire, but not out front. We rotated the squads and the platoons. Even the line companies, battalions, regiments, and divisions were on a two-up, plus one-back rotation when order could be in place. Lead scout would be a private forever. That is what this vital position was ranked. I was a private for the war (PFC). To the command, privates were nobodies, the expendables, along with the other line soldiers. We were the expected casualty cost of front-line fighting. I didn't have much knowledge or sight beyond that immediate few yards, but I sure had a view of the cost, waste, and tragedy.

War, in a sense, was the real game of chess and played by the generals. Those up front were living pawns. We were called "grunts." Sacrificial pieces for some officer's ego. In the board game, the king is blocked, checkmate. He is not captured or killed. Game over and the players shake hands and drink to a good game. The generals have the same rules. We won't bomb or shell your headquarters and you don't pound mine. The unwritten understanding from all previous wars. Immunity for the leaders. I called this "the Generals Club of Immunity."

Altogether, the 99th Battalion was under fire, short-range[1] [for approximately] 320 days. From landing on Omaha Beach to the Austrian border on the Danube, we saw our share of changes. We had many assignments, because a naked military force of 1,000 infantry was a diamond for the taking. Even divisions wanted us. With the XIX Corps (three divisions to a corps) there was the 29th and 30th Infantry Divisions and 2nd Armored Division. We were first with what was left of four shattered units. The 82nd and 101st Airborne and the 2nd and 5th Rangers. We worked with a light tank battalion clearing the Cotentin, then with the 30th Division, and after August 1 we were part of the 2nd Armored Division. Also, the 99th had furnished expert personnel for the heavy water raid on Norway (very successful and vital), as well as the 60-man guard for General Bradley, U.S. First Army. We [were also attached] to Ninth Army, 29th and 30th Divisions at Aachen. Under Montgomery in the Bulge, the 474th Ranger Assault Regiment, Third U.S. Army (Patton), from the Rhine to the Danube. Quite an exquisite array! I'm told three recommendations for Presidential Citation. We got one. There were 600 deserving battalions. Winning was a game of roulette. In all this committed action and exposure, this excellent fighting bunch of Norwegians never gave one inch back.

Smart View

Often, I was asked, "How were you so lucky?" Lead scout is reputed to be "the worst." This was what the ignorant at West Point believed. What they don't know is that we are generally smart and astute young guys. Athletic and alert; or dead. We have the same as the Generals Club of Immunity. If I don't shoot at your front people, they won't shoot at ours. Our values are information and observation. Dead lead people don't tell anyone anything. Besides, once the shooting starts, everyone joins in a fire fight that, at best, kills or maims a few expendables. The front-line squads don't want the shooting to start. If it is "all quiet on the Western Front," these guys may live through the day. If we were to advance, I chose the best route I could. I could send a hand signal to No. 2 and tried to do this unobserved. I allowed five seconds to get to whatever protection I could attain. Dead soldiers are less of a deterrent than wounded. Sometimes it takes four or five squad members to get a wounded soldier to the rear. This disrupts an organized procedure. I was pretty good at my job as a

---

[1] As opposed to being "long-range," which refers to artillery, mortars, etc.

fixture. From my forward position, I never fired a single shot, and I survived. Yes, lucky, but also smart. Few uniformed know that 70 percent of front-line casualties are by mortars and not direct fire. Even with mortars, if neither front orders them, returning fire will be rare, and again, both sides survive. Our officers never ordered fire on guess work. They insisted, from observation, as a reasonable target. We had fine leadership in the 99th. Many of us are alive because they didn't play live chess. When doing war, we do as little as we can, while completing the mission.

Audie Murphy[2] may have believed he could make a difference by his astounding heroism; the facts are that the result of the day was exactly the same, with or without all that he did. Our line was several hundred miles and was as strong as the weakest squad. The line all moves forward or it stays put, even may realign, but it is one front and rarely a hero's game. Audie was truly a war machine. The most decorated soldier in our history. He was great news and a morale builder and had a great after-war career. We all salute this incredibly able and lucky "grunt."

If I were asked what makes a hero, I would say the drive, adrenalin, temporary insanity, instinct, and above all, necessity by opportunity. Audie had to be inspired by urgency to just do the things he did without hesitation. I'm just glad I was never so pressed. My advice to any new recruit [would be to just] be smart, be patient, do your job at as little risk as possible. The front line is Russian roulette: don't play it, if there are other honorable choices.

A View of War

There never will be 16 million in service again. No country will [have the need] to mass anything [that large again]. Some technician in a bunker with fingers on a red button will send some form of missile halfway around the world to a target that all the tech knew about was a bunch of numbers. The accuracy will be read from a satellite and will send it "up a camel's rear." Future technology will make manned warfare obsolete. We won't need West Point generals, admirals, or bombers' flights. War will be with atomic explosions, chemicals, fiber electronic and verbal interference. Hands off, no-boots-on-the-ground conflicts. Wars will be devastating and brief; complete evaporation of cities the size of New York. Intolerable loss of life and value. It would be 10 times what happened at Hiroshima. Consider that amount of damage by one bomb. The major nations, with their own hardware, know how terrible the results of a third World War would be. We have witnessed 70 years of restraint. What will the have-not nations of undisciplined sects do when they possess uncontrolled power?

The future leaders of this earth will face dilemmas that we today can hardly imagine. I shudder at [what] the world's present generations are handing down to their heirs and grand-heirs.

---

[2] Murphy was one of the most decorated combat soldiers during World War II. He would later go on to become a Hollywood star.

A View of Hate

Did I hate the Army? We all hated the dirty jobs that were ours to do. We did them in distaste! I hated the generals who lived like kings and played the war like chess. They lived in their world, removed, with no empathy for the thousands praying for their toy. They did not share our mirage.[3]

When I was sent in a 6×6 for supplies with others, we walked by a sign on a fine building: "Officers Club. Enlisted Not Allowed." Myself and a million like me were volunteer patriots, there for democratic and Christian principles. Freedom, equality, fraternity and liberty. In my view, this was un-American and fascist. I had not joined to fight for two classes of Americans. I was young, politically stupid, and hating those who had made ordinary soldiers low-class expendables.

Just think about this. General Eisenhower decided he and his staff should live and rule from Versailles Palace, the most brilliant building in Europe, fit for King Louis XIV. Fit for our king and 2,500 serving him. General [Mark] Clark in Italy, the same, the great Italian palace north of Naples, his forever, if the war didn't end. Montgomery, no different. No one had more pomp and ego to display.

These were all piss-poor generals. Why in the hell would we select a lousy general to be a useless President? My view.

I was a poor soul in a foxhole, not knowing how or why. My enemy—a poor soldier in his hole out there on the other side. He didn't know how he got there or why he was supposed to kill or be killed. I didn't know him, he didn't know me, and we were inspired to hate. I'm sure his hate was directed at those who were directing his fate too. Those immune generals!

One of the idiotic missions we did was test five different rations. The test was—hike 18 miles per day for two weeks. This would require the energy of 14 days of combat. This general had no idea of how much energy it took to crouch in a foxhole. The mission did decide that our K-ration was the only answer.

The Army had a host of these ego-centered generals. I hated them all, once I learned of their incompetence and refusal to weigh alternatives. I did not get along with any supervision. Because I was not a Norwegian, I was treated like a black boy in an all-white prep school. This meant more KP and latrine duty than anyone else. In some ways this was fine. Our mountain training was rugged. I missed some of the worst. Like the Rangers and Airborne we were on a ration and a half.

While we were hiking the moors there was a call for volunteers who could swim. Six of us thought this was for a Dieppe-type raid, but it was to become instructors for the battalion. Water safety program at the Marshall St. Baths in London for eight days. A great time. The worst was a robbery while I slept—all eight pounds.[4]

---

[3] It is unclear what the "toy" and "mirage" allusion is regarding.

[4] It is assumed that he is talking about having his British pounds (currency) stolen from him at this time.

I was in England for six months and Wales for about four. In between, I was able to see and truly like Britain. I had two weekend passes. Went north to Bradford and south to Southampton. [I saw] much of London and Cardiff on a day pass. Our last camp in England was on the Welsh border of Ludlow. The castle there is 17 acres, fully the same as when the Normans built it about 1080, except there were no roofs or floors. They had rotted away over 900 years, but everything else was intact. Two of my friends in 2nd platoon and I went to the castle whenever we could and climbed all over the battlements. Of all 3,000 castles in Britain, not one is a better example of the Middle Ages. I have been a castle freak ever since Ludlow.

[Company B] was alerted for Normandy as soon as D-Day, June 6, 1944. We were moved to Plymouth and delayed for a very severe storm that nearly ruined the invasion. The Americans landed on the Cotentin Peninsula, Utah Beach, and at Omaha Beach, along with the British landings, Juno, Sword, and Gold, all west of the Seine River exit. We were considered third wave and reserved for the 2nd and 5th Rangers at Pointe du Hoc. This was all U.S. First Army, under General Bradley, who took 60 of our tall Vikings for his elite guard!

During the storm, only absolutely essentials were landed. Some of us on LCIs landed D+11 (June 17). Our headquarters listed the arrival as June 21. My letter to my father stated that I waded ashore on Omaha June 17, and from there walked past Pointe du Hoc to a hedgerow quadrangle northeast of Insigne. We assembled, piecemeal, and were joined by stranded survivors of the air drop on June 6. A soldier, dazed and hungry, joined the third squad and was with us all the way. Gerald Plank[5] became a close friend [of mine, as did] second scout, Gordon Vogelson.

The three of us were the youth among 12 grunts. As lead scout, I also had skills that the Norwegians never learned. Norway is a very cold country; most could not swim. That is why so few volunteered for London. French was not taught to working-class students, so I was the only interpreter in C Company. Also, I spoke clear American and could be understood over the static on our crude radios. I was a very unpopular private, but whenever the American tongue was needed, I was sent for. I was the worst French student, but used it often, whenever there was a civilian to interview. Essential information for our command, and how they hated to send for me. I took French for three years in high school.

When all our five companies were assembled, we were joined by what was left of the two Ranger battalions and those of the two Airborne [units], the 82nd an 101st, and transported by 6×6 past Utah Beach and unloaded at the approach to the city of Cherbourg. We went out in full attack formation, B Company on the left, C in the middle, and A on the right. The fourth company of an infantry battalion is weapons, so follows the line companies. The fifth company is headquarters and is responsible for administration, transportation, communication, and supply. They were somewhere

---

[5] George Plank's story is included in this book in its own chapter.

with D Company. We had no idea of what we were doing—50 yards in front! When I, as lead scout, "conquered" the Normandy pier I had no knowledge that our 9th Division had fought for the city, the first city of northern Europe to be liberated, and that we were there to protect the CBs[6] and Army engineers to open the essential harbor.

From the pier, we could see all the equipment and debris the Germans dumped in the harbor before they gave up Cherbourg. We were there for about a week, until paratroopers relieved us and were everywhere. Prosperity returned to this distressed city, which quickly became the port of eloquence for American supply. I had guard duty two hours on, plus four hours off, for seven days at the north-side exit of the Cherbourg hospital, which was loaded with wounded German soldiers and the normal ill people. It was feared that healed Germans would try to leave, so the gates had to be covered. Private dwellings were across the street from my guard post. The house opposite the gate was the home of a city baker and his family, the Bouchards. They were very friendly and conversive, especially their 16-year-old daughter, Evette. She was trying to learn English, and I, French. We got on very well, and [I enjoyed the] French pastries. The Army furnished a small conversion booklet, so, between these hours, [with] her help and the convenient translator, my French became far more fluent in one week than after three years of [being in the] classroom. I left Cherbourg and Evette, sadly. This had been a great duty with the worst yet to come.

We left on foot, heading northwest to the western coast of this totally occupied peninsula. Still ignorant, we marched on rural roads and through the hedgerows, poverty-stricken ancient farms, and clusters of dwellings. [It was] 3rd Squad, 3rd Platoon [that] was leading C Company along a very rural dirt road. I was [out front as the] point soldier. For those who have heard of hedgerows...they were high-ridged quadrangle farm fields, several to each farm, all about 100 yards, with solid windbreaks surrounding each field or pasture. The hedgerow was 5 or 6 feet of solid earth, 8 to 10 feet wide, with a forest of growth on top. These were necessary because of the severe west wind and weather from the ocean. On one quad there would be the essential buildings and several fruit trees. The animals and chickens had open access to the barn and domestic area. It had been this way for much of Normandy for 1,000 years; many of the house/barn buildings were centuries old. These farms sustained ancient families but provided little else. It was an absolute priority for the rural people, but no different under the Nazi occupation. I spoke to the citizens who were curious, using my new tolerable language. Some were too scared to respond. The rural people were not as glad to see us as the people prospering in Cherbourg.

I can't guess the distance we traveled. We stopped in the orchards; it was July and no artillery. The next day we had walked for three or four hours when I saw up

---

[6] Construction Battalion.

ahead the square center tower of a church. A signboard identified an approachable village as Beville. Soon there were clustered dwellings, a side road to the left, and a most magnificent stone church on the west side of the village. The church was between 800 and 1,000 years old and perfectly beautiful. In front of a white picket fence and a gate stood the priest and three nuns. I asked, in French, for Germans, when [the priest] said they had been gone for several days. He offered to do mass for our company. I had to explain that these were Norwegian Lutherans. He then graciously offered and escorted me to see his church. We rested there for an hour. The priest spoke no English, so confided with me. I said I was amazed that such a poor area could support such a fine religious facility. Silver and gold trappings, tapestries, and find cut-glass windows. He shrugged. Before the war, there were two priests and two more nuns. I couldn't hide my contempt at the whole tradition of high living for churches, and poverty for their providers. I will never get beyond that experience at Beville.

It was then July 24. We were officially under General Bradley's assignment, but a separate unit. This was about to change. XIX Corps consisted of three divisions—the 29th and 30th, plus the 2nd Armored (Tank Divisions). Early armored divisions were triangular, like the infantry, but armored commands, A and B, plus the 41st Infantry Regiment of three line battalions. When each armored command took infantry, one command had two battalions, the other only one. The 99th Battalion was assigned to 2nd Armored on July 27 and remained with them, as part of Combat Command B, all the way from Mortain to Aachen. The ancient capital of the Frank[ish] Empire of Charlemagne. This was the first German city to fall to any Allied force. The ancient city's name was Aix La Chapelle.

On July 24 [1944], 1,000 American bombers blew a hole through the German defenses at St. Lô, 3 miles wide and 4 or 5 miles deep. Nothing stood, nothing survived. This was the first time such a devastating force had been used against front-line defense.

XIX Corps was rushed through the gap and set up defense all the way to Mortain, at the base or south end of the peninsula. We were then motorized with C-C-B and went into defense at Mortain. On our way south, we sustained an intense air raid from what was left of the German air force. Once the flares were dropped, we all jumped clear of our transports and ran for cover, still hedgerow territory. The flares showed an opening and the raid was on. I was young and quick and [therefore] kept going across the first quad where a gate was finally visible. I didn't see the 1×6 boards of the gate and crashed right through them, falling to the earth and shaking from fear. I was trampled by many that followed. I wasn't seriously bruised, but scared to death and I suppose, legitimately wounded. This was a crushing and moralizing event. My first horror of war. There was one bomb run that shook the ground and destroyed several transports, followed by two strafing passes, then quiet and assembly. I don't think any who experienced air to ground will ever get over the helpless [feeling] and hatred for this kind of battle.

At Mortain, we were temporarily loaned to the 30th Division and placed among their defenses. The Germans always counterattacked after a loss. They tried at Mortain but were repulsed. All of this activity provided a highway for General Patton's Third U.S. Army. They streamed through and spread out to reinstate half of France to liberty. First Army proceeded around the German 7th Army and trapped them—the entire German army [stationed in Normandy] in what became [known as] the Falaise Gap. I believe the St. Lô breakthrough to have been the greatest single American victory in the war in northern Europe. We, with 2nd, helped secure the greatest battle victory in the war in northern Europe. We then made the end run, all around the enemy to the Seine River. We were the absolute left of the American "Blitz." Other Americans of XIX Corps all but closed the gap. We went 200 miles, while Montgomery failed to go forward from Falaise to prevent escape. Because of his ineffective leadership, it is estimated that 40,000 [Germans] got out for no military excuse. Eisenhower should have fired him right there and saved several more blunders by this supreme ego. The German loss in Normandy was, in total, over 300,000 service persons, plus tons of material and armored equipment. The Allied losses were somewhere near 150,000 personnel. General Rommel's command car was struck from the air by a British typhoon.[7] He was badly wounded and did not serve again.

We approached the Seine River, with Canadians somewhere to our left. It was now mid-August and we were gaining on freeing 20 miles of France every day. The Germans escaped at Falaise, were out ahead of the Canadians, but made no attempt to go south through Combat Command B. Every French village and farm showered us with flowers, bread, and wine. I remembered this when I saw the great Mauldin cartoon of the guys in a 6×6, throwing eggs and tomatoes at the officers in a command car in front, while the flowers and bread were reaching the personnel carriers. The glee on these grunts' faces, as only Mauldin could display. You may doubt, but that is how the expendables felt about command officers above our platoon leaders. We detested them. They covered their white stripe on the rear of their helmets with mud so they wouldn't be shot from the rear. A wise, but probably unnecessary, precaution.

Normandy was like a West Point football game. The First Army was the line, and Patton's Third Army the backfield and wide receivers. The First Army did the dirty work and Patton got the glory. It was the U.S First Army that won this great victory. General Patton didn't destroy very much and returned liberty to all of western France; he joined General de Gaulle as a hero for them. Paris was opened with modest engagement, and the celebration was on. We learned of all this a couple of days later, while engaged at Elbeuf, a city of [approximately 8,000–10,000 citizens], halfway between Paris and where the Seine River empties to the sea.

---

[7] British fighter and ground-attack aircraft used in the latter half of World War II.

Our approach to Elbeuf was over the precipice that made a perfect barrier—a three or four hundred 60 degree drop.[8] Armor could not enter by the southwest road until the city was taken by infantry. This was mountain infantry work. Colonel Turner sent A Company to the left, B in the middle, with C on the right. The colonel and staff went over the brink with B Company. I looked out over commander Lt. Slocum and [with] the 300 radio[9] I had been issued, too. He helped get it on my back and I, with just the radio and M1, then just went down the cliff. I was C Company's 300 operator because the tank people couldn't understand the Norwegians. The static, poor transmission, and foreign accent had forced a change near Falaise, so now I had a new vocation. The radio (30 lbs.) had a sharp metal bottom; by leaning against it, I had a break. Gliding down the precipice was much easier for me than the others. The entire steep cliff was covered with 3- or 4-inch hardwoods. The men controlled descent by hanging onto these trees that may have been an erosion-control project; [there were] too many and too uniform to be natural. I more or less followed the battalion staff [so they would have easy access to the radio].

At the bottom of the precipice was the west side railroad, and just beyond a parallel highway or city street. In a bulge between these was the railroad station, converted to the town hall by the German occupiers. I was told to leave the radio and rejoin my platoon. Lt. Keegan sent me on to the 3rd squad, which was facing a Panzer tank waving his 88 side to side, but not firing it or the machine guns.

There was heavy shooting to our left in B [Company's] section. A short time later, Keegan sent for me. Col. Turner needed a radio operator and his staff couldn't get a response. I tried three locations and had no success. Turner was frantic. B Company took many casualties and Panzer tanks were covering every street vertical to the river. He ordered all front squads and platoons to stand down and find protection. The German tanks also seemed to welcome a stalemate. All quiet for the [moment].

At headquarters, Turner conferred with staff and they all were looking at the only grunt there. Finally, Turner said to me, "You are here to get word out, it has to be done, we are trapped, no help until information. You will go on foot until you find someone." He turned to the operations officer, who took me to the huge city map on the table in the main hall. He showed me the highway running past Lt. Keegan's last post. The street was lined with buildings on the east and the railroad parallel on the right. There was a main road going southwest, several streets down. I was aware of the probability of a Panzer covering that highway and the overpass. I objected to the assignment. "This ain't my job." "Don't matter," I was told, "you have an order. I will inform Lt. Slocum. Now get going! And fast, this is urgent."

The battalion staff was in disarray, encouraging my departure. I told Keegan, as I went by, that I was carrying the colonel's message and proceeded cautiously down

---

[8] It is assumed that the author meant a 300- or 400-yard drop at a 60-degree angle.

[9] This was a portable radio transceiver used by the U.S. Signal Corps in World War II.

the highway, hanging close to the buildings. I expected to be shot at with every step. This was no-man's land, or still [held by the Germans]. When I reached the corner building, I peeked. One hundred yards down the vertical street was the biggest, most menacing tank I ever saw. The overpass was jammed full of broken vehicles, including a burned-out tank.

I crept to the side of the railroad, which was shouldered by 12- or 14-foot concrete walls. I couldn't cross anywhere but over the pile of debris. Why I kept my M1, I will never know. I got rid of everything else: helmet, canteen, bandoleer, and even the spare clip. I took one last peek at the Tiger tank, ran for the barricade, as the motor revved; he was backing down for a better view of the road as it climbed out of the valley, or perhaps, he felt too exposed. If he wasn't paying attention, my odds improved. I ran to the pile and dove onto the hood of a vehicle, slid off the back side, and clamored over the rest of the wreckage. Once over, I lay on the road, using my skill as an observer.

There was a building close to the road with an alley between the next. I ran to that spot and again dove to the ground next to the stone wall. I still expected to be shot at by some enemy. I crossed to the south side, still protected by the pile of debris, and played hop-scotch between various buildings and cover, as the hill got steeper and, once again, I could see the Tiger well down toward the river street. While I was getting it together the Tiger fired two 88 shells. They hit the pavement beyond. Probably, test shells to hold any American thrust at bay.

The splatter sprayed the north side, so I continued up the south until I felt out of sight. Suddenly, I was captured by three men who turned out to be Free French fighters. One went ahead with a white towel on a long stick. The other two wrapped their arms across my back and vertically carried me up the hill to where a sentry greeted the front guy. Once he saw or heard, "American," he was on his phone. A captain arrived, heard my plea, and soon a lieutenant colonel [arrived]. He was glad that word finally got out of Elbeuf and was most interested in the debris pile. They had heard the two shells fired.

Soon a Sherman tank with a bulldozer blade arrived; then the full column lined up behind the lead tank. I was told to get in the command jeep with the captain and lieutenant, who [commanded] a platoon from the 41st Infantry, that would accompany the first Sherman tank. We all trailed the dozer tank. A full assault column followed. American ingenuity by the Corps of Engineers was a secret weapon. How they created [methods] to solve problems quickly had to frustrate our enemies. Carry a bridge and drop it in place, how they knifed through hedgerows, cleared hedgerows, and here [used] a Sherman tank that was a bulldozer.

After several pushes, the dozer had [created] a pass through the pile. The Tiger fired one 88 into the mass, trying to stop the dozing. If anything, it helped loosen the wreckage. When there was room, the two Shermans went through, followed by the infantry platoon, down by the river road. The Tiger withdrew, heading north.

When the captain's jeep reached the corner where I left my stuff, I pointed toward our HQ. Colonel Turner and staff were ecstatic, and told me I did a real service. The operation officers said, "Silver." I believe Turner repeated Silver when he slapped my back, yelled appreciation, and went on with the 2nd Armored captain! I was sent back to 3rd Platoon where Keegan shrugged. "Hey," he joked, "the war goes on."

The 2nd Armored cleaned up the rest of Elbeuf and helped hold the town until we all were replaced by the Canadians on our left. Elbeuf was over and forgotten, for all but our HQ, which was hit by artillery from the east side of the Seine. Col. Turner and several were wounded and evacuated. The colonel never returned and our Major Hansen had his battalion back. Turner was fine [as a leader], being a West Point officer and commander. But Hansen had created this national force and was most deserving to lead. We all were satisfied.

While I was on my mission, Major Hansen visited C Company's positions. The Panzer was still holding the road during the stalemate. Hansen went on into the street, walked toward the Panzer, and fired his .45 at the viewfinder. Incredibly, the tank did not respond and backed up 50 or so yards. The guys in our first two squads were positive witnesses. The major's fame spread for the rest of the engagements. Whenever there was a long duty, the call was "Let Hansen do it!!" Major Hansen was soon Colonel Hansen. He was a top-class leader, our commander for the rest of the war, and was saluted by all. He deserved to go home a celebrated hero. He was!

Shortly, we moved to the CCA pontoon bridge just opened at Mantes. It took these engineers half a day to bring up the pontoons and tracks, secure them, and reach the far side of the Seine River, about 30 miles north of Paris, or downstream. Infantry had a perimeter defense for the bridgehead and two divisions, plus 2nd Armored, were in line. Suddenly, to the approach came three huge cannons with their transportation. We had to wait for them to cross. The first long tom had written on the barrel "Marzie Dotes," the second, "Dozy Dotes," and the third, "Little Lambsey Divey."[10] This was such a light moment to remember. Not many of those. The 155s set up behind the perimeter; we were emplaced as a second line, further out. All night those cannons fired and the rings seemed to whistle over us. When morning came, we were off with a tank column.

The 3rd platoon did a perimeter out front of two Shermans, dug our slit trenches, when Major Anzjon and staff arrived. He had been Hansen's No. 2 when Col. Turner took over. Anzjon went, with our 60 men, [to join] General Bradley. Sort of liaison or excess baggage. He was detested by all and now back as No. 2. The 3rd squad was spread out front on both sides of the highway. Anzjon jumped out of his jeep and said to Sgt. Wilberg, "We are taking this spot." Someone said, "Not my hole!!" With that, the entire squad opened their fatigue pants and urinated in his trench. The major was livid [and] instructed his adjutant to get our names. He busted us

[10] This comes from a novelty song written in 1943.

all on the spot. We slept on the ground and he withdrew to somewhere among the tanks.

We made Valenciennes the next day. Company B crossed into Belgium. Company C, A or B turned sharply right, once we all crossed, and were moving on the city of Liège, that had fallen to other advancing American forces. The Brits and Canadians were doing the coastal area; west of Valenciennes, their progress was difficult.

The V-1 rocket launchers were not being used as much by this time. Britain was greatly relieved, but was still rocketed by the devastating V-2s which could be fired from Holland and even inside Germany. Company C stopped at Henri-Chapelle, left all our gear, and went north on foot through the central canal district of Belgium. The other three companies [were] adjacent to our right. A great arc there [and it] was tough going [especially] for the closest to the pivot. From my squad, we were furthest out, so I had to run to keep up. The Germans were retreating everywhere but fighting delaying tactics at roadblocks and defensible built-up areas. The 99th Battalion labeled this, "The Canal Drive." The entire area was canal transportation. I was without the 300 [radio] because we had no tanks. They could not negotiate with all this water. I was back as lead scout, crossed the small tributing canals by jumping in and wading over, perhaps 3 feet deep. We had no option, out there on the swing pontoon, until we crossed the main highway to road signs. Orders came to dig in and hold, next to the road, and we quickly did our position out front of the armored Sherman that ran out of gas. We were his protection and he was our artillery. Fine partnership! This Sherman had a 76mm cannon and a .50-cal. machine gun. Company D sent us a bazooka team and we were in strong shape. While Sgt. Wilberg was checking our positions, he was picked off by a sniper at least 150 yards away. He was hit through both arteries and bled to death before the medic got there. It wouldn't have mattered. While Wilberg was gone and 3rd platoon did little, the tank crew leveled the house that held the sniper.

[Later] I was called to company [headquarters] to interpret. Three Belgium free fighters, black and orange arm bands [joined us]. They reported that 30 some of them held the ferry, crossing the Meuse into Holland, 2 miles to the east. The road that we were holding led to the ferryman's house. After much consultation Lt. Slocum said, "Here we go again." He was again our acting company commander. He assigned his driver and the company jeep [to us]. The three Belgians all spoke at least some French and I joined the driver, and off we went to the ferry. I had a walkie talkie and confirmed to Slocum but it was as reported. There were about 35 soldiers; self-appointed liberators. The ferry was at its dock, an ingenious affair on cables from his station upriver. By setting the keel, it would go over to Holland; reset the keel and back it would come. Every day the [people from] Holland would bring food out to meet the ferry; the ferryman's wife was willing to keep feeding all of us, just so glad the Germans were gone. The word from Holland was that there were [no Germans] all the way to Cologne. The fight for Aachen to the south and

Arnhem to the north had taken every German. We could take the jeep and have a mass in the great cathedral.

All forces on the Siegfried Line approach were halted. The "bridges too far" fiasco was in full action. *Market Garden.* The inexcusable Gen. Montgomery, in his egotistic desire to get to Berlin first, had convinced Eisenhower to again waste the airborne troops. The Brits over the Rhine at Arnhem and the U.S. at Nijmegen, taking the bridge of the Rhine at Nijmegen, and clearing the way to the second Rhine bridge. Eisenhower was the Supreme Allied boss. He had witnessed Montgomery's failures before. This was idiotic. The Allies needed the port of Antwerp. Montgomery bypassed the port and its estuary to rush toward the grand stroke. His intelligence completely failed to estimate the numbers [from the German 15th Army] that had withdrawn intact. They still had a fighting force. The Americans paid a terrible price for the area and crossing at Nijmegen. The British lost eight out of every 10 airborne [troops] that were dropped over the Rhine. This was a murder of thousands of Allied young men and is considered the reason the war couldn't have ended before Christmas 1944. Just think of how many died between November 1944 and May 1945. This is on our ineffective top gun and adored English hero of El Alamein.

I reported our marvelous situation and opportunity and C Company reported this to Battalion [HQ]. Not anyone with any authority or influence came to C Company to confirm or investigate this bonanza. Could First Army have made it to Cologne? They probably were so tied down at Nijmegen that they couldn't even rescue our "out-of-gas" tank. I was told to hold fast, enjoy home cooking, but to stay where we were. Slocum didn't want us to use the gas, as the jeep wasn't loaded. I did speak with Slocum every day, asking where the opportunist army was. I never heard a word and we were withdrawn after eight days. I presume the Belgians held that crossing until the war ended. I always believed that if a West Point officer had been involved, there would have been a response. The 99th was withdrawn and put under direction of the 30th Division, with orders to close the gap at Aachen.

The U.S. "Big Red One" 1st Division was fighting its way around the city on the south side and 30th [Division] exited from the north from the positions we had just abandoned. We went through the dragon's teeth of the Siegfried defense line to Herzogenrath and Geilenkirchen, where our acting squad sergeant had his eardrums blown [out] by a Nebelwerfer. We were now under constant artillery [attack]. Third squad was a real democratic little group. We all agreed that second scout Vogelson should be our leader. Voggie never got confirmed, but was our guy, the best, until he was hit (in the ass) by shrapnel at Stavelot, January 1945. Our target or objective was to close the main escape from Aachen to Würselen, and to link up with the 1st Division [then] to close off any relief from entering. The shelling was so intense that we were imprisoned in the cellar of a three-story apartment house being reduced to rubble by direct fire from 300 yards across the quad. Lt. Keegan was taken back in shock; he had counted 155 strikes on our falling fort.

When we could finally attack, our three line companies advanced abreast up three separate lines of buildings on two separate streets. Company B on a street to the right, C Company in the middle during the line of buildings on the south side, and A Company on the line of attached buildings on the north. [This series] of attacked buildings, mostly residential, were linked by holes in their basement walls. The Germans could reach the last building from the first, all the way through the cellar windows. Second platoon guys would enter, after we had [thrown a grenade into] the next cellar. The Germans were withdrawing, hopefully, before the grenades were live. Then 1st Platoon would climb through the piles of rubble and gain the first floor where it was sufficiently intact; they also were working up the street side with A Company soldiers opposite; same routine.

As our scout, I was hiding as best I could, and making sure we were not hit from the front. As we reached the corner,[11] 3rd squad spread behind the buildings on the escape route, I reached the last building and our guys filled in. The Germans, tanks, and personnel had abandoned these buildings, probably because the escape road was so full of debris and fallen buildings that it was impossible for vehicles [to get through]. Hell's Corner fell to C and A Companies, while B was making history. Whenever an army encircles a target, there is an inner line and an outer line. The troops of the 30th Division closed the inner line with the Big Red One and Company B of the 99th Battalion linked beyond the escape road with another unit of [the 1st Division]. Aachen was now encircled, and the first German city would fall. The 99th was instrumental in this very important psychological and military triumph. This was devastating to civilian morale. Probably all of Germany, but Hitler's staff, knew the war was lost. The road to Cologne was open.

We were held in position for about two weeks. Our job was to prevent relief. The 30th Division prevented escape. Aachen was surrounded. This front was reasonably quiet, after the closing. The Germans always counterattacked; this came, fortunately for us, directly from the east and at the 1st Division. This was a very hard and tentative fight that the 1st Division prevailed [in]. There just was no quit from the German combat forces. There would be hard, hard times before the end. We were an exhausted battalion, relieved, and went on R&R at the little resort village of Tilff, south of Liège on the Ourthe River. All our gear was retrieved from Henri-Chapelle.

It was late fall, we played flag football in the school athletic field. A call came for an interpreter. A Belgian dignitary wanted a soldier who spoke French to be a guest for dinner at his villa. I was it! An employee escorted me to a very nice home at the edge of town. This was a well-off family, headed by a gentleman in his late 60s. He had a story he wanted told. His family was the manufacturers of the stained glass for cathedral windows for 800 years. A true traditional skill and heritage. The factory was by the railyard, and in Liège. One night, a year ago, 1,000 British bombers

---

[11] Later known as "Hell's Corner," and found in the city of Würselen, Germany.

struck the city and the railyard, with the main rail line that supplied the German armies in France and Belgium. Everything near the yard and line was destroyed. In 24 hours, the German engineers had the line open and trains [running]. When this was discovered, the British sent a second 1,000 bomber raid against the city and railroad. Once again, the line was open and used in 24 hours. The devastation was extreme; thousands of Belgian civilians were killed and maimed. Within a week, the American Air Force sent a low-flying A-26 medium bomber on a daylight raid, took out the bridge over the Meuse River, and the railroad was done for the war. The glass factory was gone, my host family would not be able to rebuild [it], they were done, but resentful of the British attitude about mass bombing of civilian targets, when there were far more effective ways. When Churchill was informed of the loss of life, he is said to have had no sympathy for Belgium. A form of revenge for their "no resistance in 1939." We, otherwise, had a fine visit and I returned for a second dinner. Yes, there was a daughter, about 22.

I was [playing] football the next Sunday afternoon when the game was called. We were told to get ready for something. Trucks arrived. By dark, we were traveling south with no lights, after much confusion. The 3rd Platoon [got off the trucks] on a farm ridge. This was December 16 or 17. Three of us went into a small barn and joined two cows and a horse. It was very cold and we were not dressed for winter. The animals gave off enough heat to sort of warm the building, so we slept between their abode, in a make-do rotation. About 4 a.m. the company gathered, [and] we hiked in silence down a long hill, through a village, and up the hill on the south side where we became sentinels on a ridge above a railroad track. This village was Malmedy. [The 99th Battalion was] spread over the various entries, roads, open fields, and the rail line. We knew nothing about what had happened. This was the German breakthrough of the Ardennes, to be known as "The Bulge." Twenty-two Panzer divisions had quietly assembled and attacked our green Fifteenth Army, crushing the 99th Division (not our battalion) and the 106th [Division, which had just arrived].

The Panzer columns penetrated, in three days, nearly to the Meuse River and our major supply base at Namur, a breakthrough that could have been tragic. The German columns needed three supply roads. They were denied the southern road by failing to take Bastogne. The northern road and rail went through Malmedy, and our battalion. With other [units, along with the 99th, we] held Malmedy. This made the Panzer attack force dependent on the center road through St. Vith and Houffalize, their only heavy traffic source. The weather was in our favor. It snowed steadily, was extremely cold for Belgium; constant fog and low cloud [cover] made our air to ground by the P47 and P38s ineffective. The situation was grave. Eisenhower requested help from Montgomery. He told the Supreme Commander, "Not unless he was given command of the American Twelfth Army Group." This was Gen. Bradley's entire force. Instead of firing Montgomery, Eisenhower buckled and turned the Bulge defense over to the asshole. Bradley had to agree.

The 99th Battalion, with the 291st Combat Engineers and a company of tank destroyers, set up roadblocks and a perimeter defense all around Malmedy. We were fortunate to have the railroad on the west side [with] a raised trestle. This was to hold the grade because of the hill south of town. The trestle height was 20 feet where the road west passed through the trestle, making a formidable barrier of defense. Two tank destroyers were covering that protected underpass. Our B Company was aligned on the trestle at [that spot]. Our platoon was next up from the trestle, at the roadblock, south road and the hilltop beyond the railroad as it skirted the village. Our A Company was at the east entry and with C Company on the ridge. We held Malmedy for 16 days with two hard attacks from Panzers from the Stavelot area to the west. These attacks were directly at B Company on the trestle. The tank destroyers destroyed the lead tank, a command car, and personnel halftracks. The men on the trestle repulsed the infantry. The remaining turned tail and disappeared in the fog. They regrouped and made a full repeat.

Voggie and I had a very extensive foxhole, out front of the trestle, 200 yards above the action at the underpass. The next day, there was a roar, [Junkers] Ju 88 came over at tree level following a Heinkel 111. Our BAR guy was ready for the Ju 88 and emptied his 20 rounds directly into the large target. It was reported, from A Company, who also had shots fired, that the Ju was smoking when it disappeared. Several of the German planes on the raid were shot down. Our incident was unconfirmed.

After 16 days, our battalion exchanged places with one of the 30th Division [units] at Stavelot. Once again, Voggie and I were out about 30 yards in a fine hole with railroad ties for a roof. We were very cold, did an hour rotation in order to keep moving. I had pleurisy and transferred[12] and had not washed or shaved for 32 days. It was from this hole that Voggie was hit in the butt. We put him face down on a stretcher. The aide bandaged his rear, and he went out singing, "London, here I come." He was waving, from his belly position, and we, to a man, were envious. I lost my companion, one great guy, and again, 3rd squad was without a leader.

On my 21st birthday, we were bypassed. The Bulge was over. The Germans, still alive, were trying to get back on that single road. The skies had cleared and the bombing by our Air Force was incessant. The Germans sacrificed 22 armored divisions on the gamble for Namur that failed, a loss of 90 percent of their equipment and 200,000 men. It was assumed that no more than 30,000 [German soldiers] made it out of the pocket. Montgomery was sent back to his command and Bradley was again Twelfth Army Group's top general. The real victory of the Bulge was that the Germans could no longer resist effectively anywhere. Once winter was over, the Allies would be moving forward on every front. The Bulge was so stupid, when the most

---

[12] It is unclear what Curtis means by "transferred" but he did stay with the 99th Battalion through to the end of World War II in Norway.

feared army and the most feared repercussion, was from the Russians. They had real reason to hate, and they surely did.

Once again, the 99th was taken off [the front] line for R&R. Staff headquarters was concerned that the SS troops and Hitler's administration would retreat to Bavaria and Berchtesgaden. We were taken back to Barneville, for the security there, while a new Ranger regiment was formed and prepared for a mountain push. This was the 474th [Infantry Regiment] and the 99th was the third battalion. The reconstructed 2nd and 5th Rangers made up the other two. Company C was now L Company. The Army created tent camps along the Cotentin shore for R&R, to retrain spent units, and to provide security. The Germans were still on the islands offshore, so it was necessary to protect the supply line from Cherbourg.

We soon reached the west coast from Barneville to the south and Couville to the north. C Company at Barneville, A in the middle, and B Company at Couville. Our mission was to prevent any raids from German-held Jersey or Guernsey Islands, 20 or so miles out to sea. We were protecting the new supply lines from Cherbourg, south to St. Lô, and First Army's line. Long-range coastal artillery could reach the beaches and ran patrols at shore. About every hour a shell would come in so we could claim front-line experience—of a sort. There was one raid on Couville, easily repulsed, but our force's first casualties. We at C Company only learned about the raid a day or two later.

When reveille was sounded the first day of our encampment, all of C Company (now L) refused to come out. Our captain, who had done all of five days with us now on the front, was suddenly back. For two more days he did not show. Finally, the new regimental team investigated. Our captain was removed and we received a tough soldier's soldier, Captain Hanna. Captain Moleen was, in a sense, promoted. He was given a desk job somewhere and the war he never fought was over for him. He was protected by the commissioned [officers] and would go home to boast of his fine C Company. We were just glad to have forced his removal. He received a Purple Heart for a cut on his arm from a falling cookie jar. This was the politics of the Army that so sickened the grunts. That and the pay scale that said some Remington Raider with Tech stripes[13] was worth more to the war effort than someone on the front risking his life by the hour. We lost a replacement lieutenant at Würselen who was with 3rd Platoon [for only] two hours when he was killed. We never even heard his name. Why was this 90-day wonder sent out to a hot front rather than promoting a staff sergeant that knew what he was doing? This death, like so many thousands, [would not have happened] then. The finest officer I ever have known enlisted as a buck private for Korea, stayed for 30 years, and retired a lieutenant colonel. These should be our first officers, the experienced men of the

---

[13] A Remington Raider is a pejorative term that refers to a soldier with administrative duties (literally issued a Remington-brand typewriter and whose duty is to write reports of actions). Tech stripes refers to an infantryman that is a technician that can be of various ranks or stripes.

ranks. The expendables who do and survive. This soldier should have been teaching plebes at West Point.

Once fully organized, the 474th was moved to Aachen, where we were made part of General Patton's Third Army. The U.S. 9th Division captured Remagen Bridge at the Rhine and established an enclave on the east side. This was the last devastating blow to German forces in the West. Once this area was reinforced and secure, Germany was wide open to exploit. The 474th was trucked to Bingen, upriver from Remagen, to where Third Army engineers had finished a pontoon crossing, approaching Frankfurt. We caught up with the spearheads and led our own, east to Erfurt. When the Americans and Russians met at the Elbe (river), we were sent south to do the Bavarian push. We passed through or possessed miles of territory until we reached the Danube River at Regensburg. Hitler and others committed suicide in his Berlin bunker, the Russians took Berlin, and the war was ending. Our Air Force had orders not to bomb; there just were no targets and no reason to keep killing. Company C was put on "search and destroy" at Regensburg. I, with two others, were breaking confiscated material—rifles, cameras, and blades—over a telephone pole, then tossing them in the Danube [River] when a staff car pulled up. There was a captain and his driver, also a sergeant. We were ordered to get in. At a farther station, two other C Company grunts were added. We then went to a farm on the north side of Regensburg where we surrounded the dwelling. The officials went to the front door. I, with two others, was sent to the rear [door]. Almost immediately, two tall Germans in trench coats came out the rear exit. They were apprehended without resistance. They were shoved in the back of the staff vehicle with our five, and off we went to some destination unknown to us. Our prisoners were deposited, and we were returned to our destruction point. The Army intelligence people never told us who our prisoners were—just of their importance. From the news, when we got some, we read of the capture of Vice Chancellor Arthur Seyss-Inquart of Austria at Regensburg.[14] He was tried at the famous Nuremberg trial of war criminals and executed.

World War II officially ended two days later, May 8, 1945. The 474th Regiment was immediately pulled out of Germany and trucked to Le Havre, France, where we boarded LCTs and sailed for Norway. After five days on the water, the 99th Battalion landed at Oslo, Norway. All our surviving Norwegians were home and had done so much to make an invasion unnecessary. The well-disciplined Germans honored the surrender and managed their own personnel until they were returned home. Our other two battalions were sent to Kristiansand and Bergen, but the 99th was the toast of Oslo, the capital, and very modern city of 1 million Scandinavians celebrating. We were their heroes of liberation! The British and the Russians also sent troops to claim their share of glory, but to the Norwegians, the 99th could own the country.

---

[14] Some Canadian forces also take credit for capturing Seyss-Inquart.

Over 100 million people were directly involved; the entire population of the world indirectly was affected. An astounding victory for individual voices being heard, that freedom was restored to so many. For those like me, proud to have played my part. Victory for our world. Everybody's triumph! My real win, a good personal win, was yet to happen.

The 99th Battalion occupied the German main city camps at Smestad, which included the school on Klostervein Street. There were two ice ponds in the park-like facility, a recreation hall, and underground bunkers. Fences all around and [everything was] fine. Company C (or now L Company) was housed in the school, converted for housing. The local young people soon had holes in the fences and were sort of allowed to roam around and talk with the Americans. Not very military, but good public relations. Security was very lax. Several of us, still young guys, used the holes [in the fences] rather than bother with getting a pass. We joined with the teenagers playing on a vast hillside on the south side of the camp. Most of their homes were in Skoyen at the bottom of the open and wooded area. We were all the guests and friends of Norway. A wonderful celebration was had by all; one that would last for longer than five months [while] we were there. Among the sports-loving young people were several schoolgirls that, joyfully, I got along with. By schoolgirls, [I mean they were] like sophomores in college here. There was one that would have been a high school senior in New York, she was 17. She was small, blonde, blue-eyed Scandinavian, the exact picture it could be imagined [of a typical Norwegian girl]. I bribed my way to the parties her older friends were [hosting] almost every evening. Even this younger girl would be there, and I became a welcome addition. This 17-year-old was Gerd Stenberg, who lived near the bottom of Klostervein. I had first seen her on the hillside with her classmates. By providing chocolate, I found she spoke good English, so the biggest hurdle of fraternization did not exist. We began dating. For the next four months I spent every moment I could with her. We prepared for a certainty, even with the very uncertain circumstances.

This was Victory

Several interesting events happened during our stay in Oslo. Our purpose was to guard the military installations and to be aides to the groups getting Norway back as a democratic monarchy. We did parades, and were grunts of gatherings. Our officers made political speeches, but mostly, [we] helped the police get up to date on work that the Germans did for five years. It was now summer, school's out, and the kids near the camp were inside, using the main ice pond as their private pool. The battalion administrator decided to use their water safety licenses. We also had a section on Bygda Beach at the fjord. We were rotated [between] the two areas. At Bygda, the soldiers' beach was next to the civilian strip, and for Army [use] only. Of course, there were no soldiers on their beach. The bikinis were a better attraction.

We lifeguards set up at the water's edge of the fence and helped our counterpart with a busy place.

When the season was over, a football league was started with the three American battalions. It was an opportunity to display the American way. The other two battalions had plenty of quality players, but the 99th were all soccer players; only the late replacements, and a few of the younger original force, had any experience. We played before a packed Ullevaal stadium. I was the blocking back, single wing on offense and had to go both ways on defense, where I took a terrible beating from a 200lb veteran lineman. It was a great escape, and so strange to hear the American game called in Norwegian over the loudspeakers. When the season ended, there was a call for 30 volunteers to remain for a time to dismantle and clean up our camp. Over 600 asked to stay. Oh yes, the war in the Pacific was over too.

While there, I [participated in] two parades. Our Fourth of July celebration and the Honor Guard for the return from Scotland of King Haakon and family. This had been incredible for me to understand. Some entity wanted 6-foot, blue-eyed, blonde, trim Viking types for the 60-man guard to parade to the palace with the royals. There wasn't that many, so the call went out for 6'1" then 5'11". The last let me be admitted. I was put in the center of the block formation and told to pull my helmet down so the audience would not see my black hair. This Teutonic move, by those who were very full of German Teutonic superior race crap. The irony was inescapable to the American/Norwegian soldiers. That government had gotten out of Norway when the Nazis arrived, remained intact in Scotland, all returning before or with the king. Norway almost immediately had a waiting government, which made our regulatory duties brief. This was a wonderful experience, real friends in a very friendly atmosphere. When we were on the Liberty ship and waiting for several hours to sail, I bribed a garbage barge tender to take me to shore. I spent a last and painful couple of hours with Gerd and her family. I walked up the gangplank, to the astonishment of the guards. They, and the Sergeant of the Guard, asked me where I had been and how I got off. I lied. [I said,] "I just walked down the plank." They all looked at one another and didn't want to find out who had been lax. That was all [that was] ever said.

The Victory ship sailed early the next morning, on or about November 10, 1945. There was a brief stop at Southampton to pick up eight nurses headed home. In order to guarantee exclusive protection for them, they commissioned ordered guards on access to the officers' quarters. The officers had the third deck, and the nurses were at least tenants. When we were again underway, the worst storm to hit the English Channel in generations struck. Our boat made no headway against the powerful flow, wind, and torrential rain. Liberty ships were very stable, but we rolled and listed plenty. Soon sickness predominated, even on the centered third deck quarters.

When morning came, the third day, Major Anzjon could not be found. Could he have gone to the rail and be thrown overboard by the storm, or some revenge seeker? He was surely despised by just about everyone. The guard was thoroughly questioned.

Those who had been on duty were positive no enlisted person or persons had been allowed access. When the officers began looking at each other it was decided "Man Overboard!" That ended the search and accusations. They soon decided the storm did it. That whitewashed the issue; and not a tear was shed.[15]

We landed at Boston, and the battalion was dissolved at Fort Devens, and all the personnel were sent to be discharged at their place of induction. For me, it was Fort Dix in New Jersey, and then home for Thanksgiving.

Eternal Triumph

When I left Gerd, she had two more years of school in order to graduate from their high school, which equals a two-year college degree here. There were six provisions, besides her own determination [to finish] school. A very difficult path for a permanent visa. Gerd graduated from the Ullern High School in late May 1947. We had completed the six requirements, [received] both nations' approval, [as well as approval from] both parents. Her father had reluctantly agreed, if she completed her education. He was too stubborn to go back on his word. My father had to agree to support us if I failed as a provider. The strangest was the Church of Norway and the law [that they had]. No teenager could marry outside the church before they were 21. Therefore, I had to have agreement from my church in Johnstown that our marriage would be performed there, and by the agreed [upon] minister.

On July 20, 1947, I stood with my father on the dock where the Norwegian liner *Stangefjord* had just birthed, along a sloping gangplank moved in place. This was a most anxious time. She sent word from Oslo that she had her passage, but we did not have any confirmation that she actually was on the boat. Passengers started off. Then suddenly appeared, a very Scandinavian blonde young girl in an angora sweater, carrying a suitcase and her skis. When those waiting saw this skier emerge in the heat of July, they clapped and cheered as she proceeded to the dock. Everyone realized she was the victory and that I was there for her. She was hugged and well wished by many who were probably all Norwegians of some manner. I was ecstatic, my father pleased, and we departed by car for Mt. Kisco, where we would stay with my father's Cornell [University] roommate of 30 years' past.

After six days of red tape and travel, we arrived in Johnstown and were married on July 26, 1947. Sixty-six years ago, all this wonder happened. This was, and it always will be, the greatest personal victory that any human being can have. To find life's partner, and through sheer determination, make it happen and before as long as both shall live. We had this happen and as of the present we live in the same house, the same town, and the same dedication. After 66 years—Eternal Victory is in sight.

---

[15] Foundation research indicates that Captain Erwin L. Anzjon passed away in 1987 and is buried in Montana.

CHAPTER SEVEN

George Hunsby

George Hunsby was one of the oldest members of the 99th, having enlisted at the age of 44. He had previously served in World War I and as he writes in the included text, he felt a call to duty to re-enlist despite the misgivings of his wife, Ruth. Hunsby's placement into the 99th was undoubtedly a consequence of his Norwegian heritage and knowledge of the language, but seemed accidental to him. The grueling training in the mountains of Colorado put him to the test.

Hunsby's father emigrated from Norway to Michigan in 1884 and after stints working in the timber industry in Michigan and Minnesota, he moved to Whatcom County, Washington where Hunsby was born in 1898. The Hunsby family was deeply involved in the early days of the logging and timber industry in the area.

Hunsby was a prolific writer of historical events, including several writings about the history of Whatcom County in and around Bellingham, Washington. He also wrote a booklet titled "My How Time Flies" that was published in 1977.

Hunsby covers the time period starting with the 99th's initial training through to several of the large battles on the European continent. The initial training at Fort Snelling gives a sense of the community pride that supported the formation of this special infantry battalion. He shares that local residents would come on the streetcar to watch them in formation and that many soldiers were welcomed into St. Paul and Minneapolis homes for dinner on occasion.

The toughness of the 99th was illustrated by the hundreds of men (700 by Hunsby's account) that dropped out due to the extensive training in the high elevation in Colorado. The high dropout rates were a testament to the rigorous training and the stoutness of the thousand men that resulted in the final unit.

While stationed in England, Hunsby was transferred into the 99th's medical detachment to serve as a medic. While not entirely to his liking, it did provide a unique perspective to many of his experiences.

It is Hunsby's accounts of specific incidents within France and Belgium where he provides witness to the horrors of war. This witness includes burying 800 fatalities in temporary graves over the course of 10 days in Cherbourg, watching an old couple returning after a battle to find their home destroyed, French women collaborators having their heads shorn in front of the public, and seeing a home demolished by a bomb and the family digging in the ruins to emerge with only the limb of a small child.

Hunsby also tells of heartwarming stories, including the aid that he was able to provide to a young frightened girl hit with shrapnel. The girl and her mother came back a few days later in much better shape to deliver a "wicker basket filled with cookies, cheese, sausage, and a bottle of wine."

Hunsby's time with the 99th ended in September 1944 due to medical complications brought on by the bitterly cold nights. While he wasn't able to stay with the unit, he experienced many things that are a treasure to read about and learn from. He returned to his wife in the Whatcom County area where he lived until 1996 when he passed away in his late 90s.

When Grandpa Went to War

It had been my fortune to have been born in a most beautiful river valley, in the Puget Sound Country. My first school was a small two-room wooden one, and it was located 3 miles northeast of our home. My sister and I had to walk each way, through heavy woods and over skid-roads to that school.

At this little school we were taught much about the beginnings of our country, and the struggles that our forefathers had to endure in order to form our government and to bring it to its present strength and prestige amongst the nations of the world.

Those early lessons about our government have always remained with me, and when the specter of war threatened our tranquility, it was only natural to me that I should take part. Many of our immediate family have served. All have been volunteers. And so I, the writer of this narrative, did during November 1942, enlist in the Army of the United States with full intentions of being assigned as a military policeman, since I had considerable past experience in that sort of work. But the Army, following its usual pattern of making a chef into a heavy-duty truck driver, and a truck driver into an Army cook, proceeded to make a ski trooper and mountain soldier out of me, who was 44 years of age at the time.

My wife felt quite bad at my decision to enlist. But like all the thousands of loyal wives throughout the land, she finally gave her consent, and I was on my way to Fort Lewis, Washington, where I had been released from the United States Army in 1919. At Fort Lewis, one day at mealtime, I chanced to be seated next to a young sergeant from the personnel section and whose duties were to place the new recruits into the proper niche that they were to occupy.

Now it happened that this young fellow was an old acquaintance of mine, and with whose family we had resided up in Havre, Montana, when I was stationed there while in the Department of Justice. He knew that I was of Scandinavian descent and was able to speak those languages. He recognized me at once and soon he said to me, "George, I have a swell outfit lined up for you, and it is right up your alley."

Then he launched into a fine descriptive lecture on the virtues of that particular organization which was still in its embryo stage back in Camp Ripley, Minnesota. I did not remonstrate with him, only to say that it was my hope to get assigned into the Provost Marshal's department as a military policeman or an investigator of sorts. He brushed off my remarks as being irrelevant and I let it go at that.

Within a few days I chanced to look at the recruit company bulletin board, and there found my own name as being scheduled to leave for Fort Snelling, Minnesota, the following evening by the way of the Northern Pacific Railway. When I received my travel orders I was astounded to see that I was slated to join a rough and tough Norwegian American ski battalion with the designation of the 99th Infantry Battalion (Separate), Army of the United States. It was to be a member organization of the Second United States Army, at least during the training period.

On the evening of my departure from Fort Lewis I wandered around the depot waiting room by myself, there, at least for a short time, when another apparently lonely young fellow showed up to join me. He proved to be an old friend and classmate of my hometown of Bellingham, Washington, and whom I had not seen for 25 years, since his removal to Seattle, when still quite young. We greeted one another happily, and soon discovered that we both were headed for the same organization.

When we arrived at our destination at Fort Snelling, he went to one company and I to another, and I have never seen him since. I have no idea what became of him.

I soon fitted into my company very well and in no time flat I made many acquaintances.

It had been the intention of the War Department that this battalion was to be made up of native Norwegians and Norwegian Americans who had some knowledge of the Scandinavian languages. That plan worked quite well until our ranks were decimated on the battlefields of Europe during the next two years following our training period.

We were not at Fort Snelling too long to get bored with its environs, but I can testify to the fact that we did plenty of running up and down along the banks of the Minnesota River and through every piece of woods around the fort area. I was soon reduced from a quite portly person to a slim 160-pounder, and I was not alone in that respect.

New men kept coming to us from all over the country, and a good-sized contingent came from the old 3rd Infantry Regiment, which had already been sent to Newfoundland. Those boys were tickled to death to get back to the Minneapolis area, since Fort Snelling had been the home of the 3rd Infantry Regiment.

Now our ranks had swelled to one thousand men and our battalion began to be a snappy-appearing outfit, when we stood retreat every evening out on the parade grounds. Hundreds of people came out from Minneapolis on the streetcars to watch us and listen to the band at those impressive ceremonies of retreat. All of us quickly developed a fine esprit de corps since, after all, each and every one of us from Captain [Harold] Hansen and down were each playing a part in the formation of a unique military organization that was to play a very important role in breaching the touted Atlantic Wall and Hitler's Fortress Europa. So, every man pitched in with a will to build a real tough military outfit.

The training was tough and rigorous right from the start, and many a night I crawled into my bunk, with sore and aching muscles, and in the morning when reveille sounded, I was not quite sure if I could make it out to stand formation. But, the more we trained the more flexible our joints became, and it seemed that perhaps the worst was over.

I was fortunate in having relatives of my wife living over in St. Paul and a good many times during the weekends I went over to east St. Paul on the streetcar, to their various homes. This was a fine diversion for me since I had not yet gotten entirely used to the hectic pace of the wartime military training program. All the folks over there in St. Paul made me feel right at home, and to this day we visit to and from our respective homes, although we live far apart in different states.

On December 17, 1942 our organization left our comfortable brick barracks at Fort Snelling and bid the Twin Cities goodbye forever. Our destination was the Mountain Training Center at Camp Hale, Colorado, set atop the Rocky Mountains at an elevation of 9,600 feet. To men from the East Coast and the Plains, this was a terrific change in altitude, and any great exertion would at times leave men lying by the march routes, gasping for breath and wishing they could die quickly and be out of their misery. How I lived through it, I will never know, and only on one occasion was I left in such a predicament. I finally pulled myself up to standing position and doubled-timed it back to my position at the head of the column as the number one man of the first squad, of the first platoon, of my company which led the battalion that day. I really felt guilty and mightily ashamed of myself at that degrading exhibition.

That occurrence took place on the day we were taking a 4-mile qualifying march with full equipment, at a scheduled time of one hour. We made it in 50 minutes, but at the end of that march, there were many blistered feet and aching joints.

Camp Hale was a brand new Army installation and the wooden barracks were all spanking new and equipped with showers and indoor plumbing. The ironic part of the whole training period up here was the fact that we were out in the cold and snow most of the time and sleeping in small, two-man pup tents, well cuddled up in our sleeping bags fully clothed.

The daily training routine up here was out of this world, and only the toughest survived, and here is really where the boys were soon separated from the men. In the several months that we spent up here at altitudes that sometimes took us up to 14,000 feet, we ran through our organization nearly 700 men who could not take it and had to be washed out of the service entirely or transferred to other Army units.

So in the final analysis of the makeup of our outfit, it took a lot of men before we finally had a hard and tough battalion of 1,000 men to meet and cope with the situations we were to meet later on.

The climbs up and down Holy Cross Mountain across Bellyache Mountain to Climax, and the 50-mile hike on skis and snowshoes, made in the fastest time ever performed by any military units in the world's armies, and which record still stands I believe, are things that I am glad are in the past.[1] It is the hope of this "has been" that future young soldiers will not have to be put through such grueling procedures, since to my own estimation, it does not really make one tougher, and possibly it might break down a comparatively healthy young person.

The average infantry soldier in today's modern armies seldom carries more than 40 pounds of weight in his pack. But we of the mountain infantry carried from 70- to 90-pound packs. We were saddled down with a lot of experimental winter equipment, which it was our job to test for the government to determine its worthiness. Much of that stuff was found lacking. One such item was a plastic water canteen that split in two when frozen, and whose water content tasted like carbolic acid when not frozen. Another item was canvas mukluks that soaked up all the water when the snow was wet. If the government had set all the Aleut women up in Alaska to making mukluks, they could have accomplished two things at that time. The Aleuts could have become self-sustaining and the Army could have had a lot of waterproof mukluks cheap, and we would have considerably less millionaires in the country.

So, the days wore on, experimenting and with building gadgets, long marches, cliff climbing, and building igloos. Of course, we had some fun too, went to Leadville, or Grand Junction, on weekends, and we even put on a few shows of our own right in camp.

Camp Hale was also a dog training center and hundreds of canines were housed and trained there. Our own battalion had a team of Huskies and one big St. Bernard dog who pulled a single sled by himself. That old St. Bernard was more of a showpiece and company pet than a military dog.

During our remaining months at Camp Hale, quite a number of men were hurt badly in skiing accidents, but the general health of the group was remarkably good and there were very few of the 99th Battalion personnel to be found at the camp hospital. Most likely it was the outdoor life that we led that kept us so healthy. On one occasion we were filmed by a movie outfit and actually were visited by some movie celebrities, who watched us pass in review.[2] On that occasion we were dressed in our white snow outfits and carried our skis across our shoulders. The only

[1] This record told by Hunsby is not able to be verified, but this account speaks to the pride of the 99th's training.

[2] It is assumed that this is in reference to a 23-minute War Department production from 1943 titled *The Mountain Fighters* that included footage of the 99th. It was played as part of main-stream movie releases as part of the Army's communication campaign.

personal medical attention I was given was to get a pair of bifocals, so I would be able to shoot better on the range. And when the day of the qualifying shoot came the range was covered with snow and a blizzard was blowing snow across the buttes and I was lucky to make marksman. However, I became a bayonet instructor and made expert in that art of warfare, and that made up for my lack of marksmanship. During the summer of 1943 I was fortunate in getting to go home for a few days, and that was the last time our family was together for the next two years.

During June 1943 a new unit was to be formed which was to be a combination Commando–Ski Trooper–Parachute outfit that had its mission to drop over Norway and cut certain strategic railway lines between Sweden and Norway, and which were the lifelines of the German supply lines to Norway.

It was to be made up of some of our men from the 99th and certain Canadian units. When it was being formed I had a talk with my captain and he told me that he was going to volunteer for that other outfit, which he later did, and he lost his life over there. He said to me, "George, you are too damned old for that sort of thing." I did not have any intentions of volunteering anyhow, since I understood that parachute jumping was involved and lots of air flights, and I disliked all of those things. That group was finally formed, and we lost 50 good men in its formation. The unit sometime later trained at Fort Harrison, Montana, and over in Scotland. I have the War Department's own records of the exploits of that unit, and our own also, both of which will be quoted later on in this booklet.

During June 1943, we lost Major Harold D. Hansen as battalion commander and gained a new one in Colonel R. G. Turner, a West Pointer and a regular Army officer. Major Hansen became the executive officer of the battalion.

While our training was still in progress, we were notified that we were to be reviewed by President Roosevelt at Colorado Springs soon. We went into a frenzy of shining up equipment and the day arrived to leave for that auspicious occasion, and we were in fine shape to be judged by so great a man as he. Our pup tents were lined up by company and all were in rows as straight as an arrow to be reviewed in company with a Greek American battalion, and if my memory serves me, that battalion supplied the band music. We lined up on the parade field with our colors and Color Guard in the center, and with my own company right next to the colors. This put us in a strategic position to view the President and his party.

His car stopped directly in front of us and I watched two secret service men place themselves on either side of the President and assist him gently over toward our battalion center. He stopped directly in front of me and remarked about the size and weight of my ski boots. He stopped several times as he was assisted along the battalion front, and it seems that he questioned each soldier that he stopped in front of. All this time the band was playing, "Hail to the Chief."

After that review we did not dally long but broke camp and departed for Camp Hale, again to take up some more rigorous training. During the balance of our

President Roosevelt talks to Major Hansen at Camp Carson, Colorado Springs. The entire battalion loaded onto trucks and moved to Camp Carson with their alpine equipment to set up their bivouac. The 99th and the Greek Battalion were reviewed on April 24, 1943, by President Roosevelt as part of his second wartime tour of military posts, naval stations, and war factories lasting two weeks. (Courtesy of the 99th Educational Foundation)

training period, I did on weekends have some opportunity to fish in the excellent mountain streams around Leadville. My partner whose name was Bjarne Aaning and I chanced to become acquainted with a married couple who owned a nice little cabin up on the sidehill in Leadville. We were invited up to their home once and it became our home away from home, during the months we were at Camp Hale. They were the Albin Ericksons. Mrs. Erickson's former name was Sue Bonney and she had been a trapeze artist with the large circuses. Albin was a hard rock miner and was retired since he had gotten leaded and was suffering from the effects of that malady.

Through this couple I chanced to meet a Mr. Fitzimmons and his family. He was the postmaster of Leadville and they lived over on the west side of town. Through those associations I met many old timers of the town, who in turn related to me stories of the past glories of Leadville.

The Ericksons were caretakers of the historic Matchless Mine, whose silver production actually saved the Union Treasury during the Civil War. Sue Bonney Erickson was the only real bosom friend that the old and senile Mrs. "Haw Tabor" had left in this world. Mrs. Tabor lived in a cabin at the mouth of the shaft of that famous mine and she was always certain that there was a rich lode in those workings. But the old lady's dream never came true and Sue Bonney Erickson found her there, up in her cabin one day, frozen to death.

On August 24, 1943 we left our beautiful Rocky Mountain country and headed for New York state and on to an area near West Point, known as Camp Shanks. Here we underwent inoculations for nearly all the diseases known to the human race or so it seemed. Some of our men became violently ill from the reaction following those shots, and I was not spared some discomfort, too.

At this camp we did some more speed marching every day up and down the paved roads that wound through that beautiful wooded countryside. We also practiced going up the sides of a simulated hull on landing nets. One big fellow ahead of me stepped right on my hand with his heavy combat boot. This was quite a strenuous training for something that we later on never had to make use of, since we marched directly into the ships and LST craft in all our future amphibious movements.

Those men who hailed from New York City and its environs, were permitted a little extra time off. I had a cousin there also but did not know it at the time. In fact, during later years, I have visited two first cousins who lived there at that time. I did, however, get my chance also to see the big city with a companion, and we dined on a half lobster each at a place on 42nd and Broadway. I have eaten some lobster since then but can't say that it stacks up to good old Washington Dungeness crab, which to my estimation is the ambrosia of the gods.

On September 5, 1943 we were trucked over a Hoboken dock and there boarded an old fruit-liner, the SS *Mexico*. Its galley was dirty and the cooks themselves were none too clean. I got a look into the lockers where the meat was kept, and what I saw there staggered me. Sides of beef with fuzz an inch long on them and rotten turkeys. We sampled some of that turkey later on and it was not fit for human consumption. To fill my belly, I bought sandwiches from some of our own U.S. sailors who were assigned to the galley, for the sum of 50 cents a sandwich. Those boys were most likely from the gun crew contingents who were assigned to all these convoy ships.

Our convoy was quite a large one and outside of rough seas and submarine alerts the trip was quite uneventful. We were at sea 11 days and there was much seasickness, including myself. My own dentures went down a scupper hole[3] into the Irish Sea. That one incident perhaps caused me as much misery as anything else that befell me during the entire war.

There was one sergeant in my company whom I actually think hated me since his remarks to me were always caustic, and my feelings for him were likewise. On

[3] This is an opening on the side of the ship which allows water to drain out.

the trip to England, I had the satisfaction of seeing his face turn green from mal de mer,[4] and I thought to myself that he has now met his master in old father Neptune's domain.

On September 16, 1943, we came ashore during darkness at Greenock and marched up to the railway station at Guroch[5] nearby. We [boarded the train] there and we noted at once that all the blinds were drawn and the coaches were in total darkness. Scotch women war workers came aboard and gave us tea and scones and some very pleasant smiles. The tea was fine, but the scones tasted like sawdust, and I have an idea that this is the way the Scotch liked them. We traveled for 16 hours straight, stopping now and then to take on coal and water, and the few minutes we were stopped at Sheffield, I pulled the [window] blind aside just a little and it appeared as if the whole city was afire. The scuttlebutt soon had it that the Germans had just pulled a massive air raid on that city.

When we unloaded at Tidworth, Wiltshire, we were both tired and hungry. We found ourselves in an old British Army training camp composed of well-constructed brick buildings, and soon we were assigned to temporary quarters. All the bunks here were built too short to fit the lanky bodies of the average American soldier, and even I, who am only five foot nine, was forced to build a 2-foot-long extension on my bunk.

Later on we were assigned by squads to other permanent quarters, and here we each had steel bunks and each one of us had a pillow for our heads. This camp was empty when we moved in and we had no sooner gotten settled when 15 or 20 dogs of all descriptions and breeds moved in on us.

It was not long till each company had a couple of mascots each. Those dogs probably fared a lot better than many English people when it came to the food situation. Most English households were limited to two eggs per person per week and meat, butter, and milk were at a premium. No one could use more than 3 inches of water in the bathtub in hotels or homes, and matches were almost impossible to obtain. Now it was apparent to all of us, what it was like to be at war. Our folks at home found out later about rationing, but not nearly as severely as the people of England and the Continent did.

We launched into a serious training program and lost our designation as mountain troopers. We now became armored infantry to ride the tanks and to act as the eyes and ears for the tank troops. We rode the tanks both inside and outside to familiarize ourselves with the workings of the armored forces.

We lay on our backs and gazed up into the sky to familiarize ourselves with the many various types of military aircraft, both of our own forces and Allied aircraft. I never considered myself very adept at the art of aircraft identification, but never missed identifying our old P-38s due to their double fuselages. The B-17 and

---

[4] French for seasickness.

[5] He possibly means Gourock.

the English Sunderland flying boats were also quite easy to pick out as they flew overhead. Many a time we saw American bombers returning from combat missions with missing engines and with their wings and fuselage shot up so badly that their pilots were lucky to come down in one piece.

While here, at what we came to know as Perham Downs, we participated in field exercises, maneuvers far back in the woods during wet and clammy weather, sloshing over muddy roads, and sleeping under our tarps in the wet and cold. I remember one particular rainy night when I was bivouacked under an enormous spreading oak tree that must have been hundreds of years old. In the early morning hours just as dawn was breaking a tremendous shower of water came down on my tarp from above, and I thought it must surely have been a cloudburst, but as it became lighter, I could see that the entire oak tree was festooned with mistletoe and that parasitic plant was hanging in great bunches above me. It seems that those bunches took up the rainwater and held it back momentarily until a strong wind shook the tree, and the shower of water was released at once. When I saw all that mistletoe I thought of home and Christmas time, and as it happened, we were only a couple weeks away from Christmas then. It fell on me to get a detail and go out into the same woods to look for a Christmas tree for our battalion party. I found a good tree, and lots of fine wild English holly, and believe it or not, a lot of mistletoe to hang over the doors and light fixtures in our recreation hall to lure the NAAFI[6] and land army girls underneath them. The shame of it was that only a few old ladies showed up.

During January 1944 we moved by truck convoy up to South Wales to a village called Crickhowell on the River Usk. Here we established a Nissen hut camp on an old baronial estate called Glanusk Manor. When first entering the camp area, and while traversing a small wooded area, I happened to spot an old steel boiler that lay in the brush alongside the roadway, and I kept that bit of information to myself, since I knew that later on, when we were assigned to our Nissen huts, that I would have to take the lead in making my own squad comfortable in our new surroundings. So, when we were given a hut, I immediately commandeered a jeep and two men, and we hightailed it right down the road to where my boiler was lying. We found a fine steel boiler that evidently had been cut in half with a welding torch and had been used for a stove previously by other occupants of the camp.

We had no trouble at all to get it on the back of the jeep, and when we got back to our hut we set to work making a base for our stove and filling the base with 6 inches of dirt for the fire to rest on. We soon procured smoke pipes and in a couple of hours we were ready to light our stove. It proved to be the best heating apparatus in the whole camp in the days to come.

We were fortunate in our squad in having a fellow who had been a cook on one of the big ocean liners and he supplied us with many tasty dishes between our regular

---

[6] Navy, Army and Air Force Institutes, which were created by the British that ran recreational centers for military personnel.

meals. A few samples were eels fried in butter, sugar-cured home-made bacon, eggs of all styles, and a few trout at times. We had a scrounging party, of which I was a member, and we got acquainted with two old bachelors, who operated a small grist mill across the river. That little mill was operated by a waterwheel. We were welcome there since both of those Welshmen were former soldiers. Here we had access to plenty of eggs, home-cured pork, and sometimes stone-ground grain bread. We, in turn, supplied them with plenty of beer and stronger stuff. There was no manner of entertainment here and what we got was by mixing with the townspeople down in the village of Crickhowell. Here our outfit was barred from entering the Bull Hotel and Bar, since some of the gang had caused a near riot at that place during our first week in Wales.

I had not been a drinking man, so that ban did not mean much to me.

This fine old manor boasted a beautiful stone castle which contained 90 rooms, with fireplaces in most of the rooms. This building became our battalion headquarters for almost six months. During April 1943, we lost 52 of our men, who were chosen to guard the First Army Headquarters at Bristol. These men were hand-picked for many reasons. If I remember rightly, all of them were to be six-footers. This was surely a great honor for the 99th Infantry Battalion.

Back at Perham Downs I had been transferred to the medical detachment since my personnel records showed that I had previously been in the Medics and had past training as a laboratory technician. The medical detachment was short one man and the battalion surgeon thought that since I was twice as old as any of the other men, that he was giving me a break. By this move I lost all chance to go up to staff sergeant since the tables of organization for the medical detachment called for only one of that rank and he was already there and on the job. So, the colonel said, we will transfer old Hunsby in rank, which was buck corporal, and the medical don't [sic] have buck corporals. There they are known as T2s or a sort of specialist rank. Up at Glanusk Park I had charge of a little camp hospital where all the sick, lame, and lazy turned in periodically. On certain occasions I was sent out with our soccer team as a first aid man, when they played the English Army teams. On one occasion, one of our men suffered a badly broken leg and it fell onto me to fix him up while we were awaiting the ambulance. I took two pickets off a garden gate and made two splints, secured them firmly, applied traction, and pulled the broken limb back into perfect alignment.

The Army doctor who handled the job of bone-setting later at the hospital, said that all he had to do was to apply the plaster cast. He sent word back to my battalion surgeon to commend me, but that was the last I heard of the matter.

While stationed at Glanusk Manor we had ample opportunity to visit the little and ancient town of Crickhowell, which was located down the River Usk, about a mile and a quarter from our camp. Here we attended the local Grange Hall dances, and we became acquainted with folks, whom we still correspond with to this day. In fact, after the war, I acted as sponsor for one maiden lady who wished to come to America to teach in an exclusive girls' school in Maryland. She came and did teach there long enough to build up a very nice Social Security account, as I understand.

In order to get a down-to-earth understanding of the Welsh people, I would often take off by myself, in order to see the things I was interested in, such as museums, cathedrals, and ancient ruins. Up at the town of Brecon, in Brecknockshire, I visited a small museum that was out of this world. It had the flag used by General Wolfe in his charge at The Plains of Abraham outside Quebec, at the time he was killed. His body had been wrapped in that flag. His regiment came from Brecon. Here were also artifacts in the form of arrowheads, spear points, Roman coins, and a large, well-preserved dugout canoe that had come from the bottom of a lake that had been drained. Many of those things were of Stone Age vintage.

During our stay here I was given a short furlough and went up to Liverpool and on to North Wales by the way of Birkenhead ferry. My mission up there was at the behest of a lady in New Westminster, B.C. who had written to me asking that I look up her daughter who lived at the village of Mold, North Wales. The little town of Mold was tucked away in such a location that it was rarely visited by the American soldiers. There were no attractions there to draw them. I located the lady at the police station, where she was doing her bit as an Auxiliary policewoman, and she was dressed in a fine uniform which she wore smartly. Her husband was over in Africa fighting Rommel. By meeting this lady, I was fortunate in being able to attend one of the famous pantomimes that are given over there annually. It was a revelation to me to witness the artistry that those young people were able to produce. The play itself was based on one of the popular fairy tales.

A little excitement entered into this trip in the form of a great fire at Liverpool. I had a chance to ride to Liverpool from Mold with a police sergeant in his police car through the great tunnel under the River Mersey. That policeman had been assigned to help with the investigation of the cause of the fire, which was attributed to the enemy. That ride through the tunnel I will always remember, and the sight of Queen Victoria's monument as we emerged from the tunnel mouth on the Liverpool side of the river.

On May Day, 1943, our battalion left our beautiful surroundings in Wales and departed for Ludlow, Shropshire. Here we established a tent camp just a short distance from the River Teme, which wound around the lower section of that city. In order to reach the city we had to pass over an old stone bridge that spanned the Teme. At the end of that bridge there stood an ancient pub called "The Golden Sheaves" and it had emblazoned on its front a golden sheaf of grain. Here our accommodations were minimal, and our eating space was non-existent since we ate our meals out in the open, during rain or shine.

The tables were constructed of two-by-fours driven into the ground of a nearby pasture, with plywood tops nailed thereon, and wooden benches to sit on.

The dining area was quite a long distance from our sleeping tents and necessitated quite a walk to and from our meals. One bad, foggy morning, I was on my way to our eating area, when I chanced to pass a tent that was connected with another organization, which had sandwiched themselves in between us during the night. It happened to be a small Signal Corps company, which was undoubtedly a Bastard Outfit like ours. To those readers not familiar with the expressions and terminology commonly used by the Army, a Bastard Outfit is one that, at the time, is not a unit of a larger organization, and that is operating strictly on its own.

On passing that particular tent I saw a soldier leaning against the tentpole at the front of that tent, who appeared mighty familiar to me. At first, I thought that something had gone wrong with my eyes and that perhaps that I was starting to see double. On my way back to our tent, I thought that I would take another look to make certain. There was no one in sight in front of that tent now, and the flap was closed at the entrance. So, I opened the flap and walked into that tent, which happened to be completely empty and devoid of any manner of furnishings. In going into the tent I noticed another one attached to the rear, so I continued walking into that one, and found myself in a large cook tent and there was my old friend and neighbor from South Bellingham, Washington, presiding over an Army cookstove and a lot of other culinary equipment. We greeted each other like long-lost brothers. To me this was indeed a miraculous meeting, since we were just two small wheels in the First U.S. Army of one million men, and either one of us had not met anyone from our hometown, up till then. My friend was Staff Sergeant Martin Reitan and he was in charge of the food department of his company.

That evening we two took off across the River Teme, to The Golden Sheaves and there took on a goodly load of foaming stout. We saw a considerable amount of each other until one morning in late May, as we were on our way to breakfast, to our mystification the campground of that outfit was empty. They had stolen away during the night, without any sound, and that was the last I saw of Martin till long after the ending of the war, and we again met in our hometown.

During our nine months or so in England, I had occasion to visit London and many other cities large and small and I was astounded at the diversity of the natural surroundings found in a country so small, and where no person is ever more than 80 miles from the sea wherever he may live. It is little wonder that the Englishman has such a fine love and respect for his homeland. My attention was also drawn to the fact that here I noted that there was a greater respect for law and order than I had ever known at home in America, and I liked that atmosphere.

After having enjoyed the hospitality of having dinner with some of the farmers who lived in the vicinity of Ludlow, and having seen the oldest dovecote[7] in all of England, and the oldest stone cider press, we left this idyllic setting early in June

---

[7] A structure found in England that houses doves or pigeons. They can be freestanding or built into the end of a house or barn.

for a small village called Uffculme, situated on the River Culme in Devonshire. Here my squad got quartered in an old abandoned brewery. Here we spent perhaps three or four days when we [got on the train for] Plymouth on the east coast and marched up the hillside to the large embarkation camp located at a point looking at the entire city of Plymouth.

Here we were issued gas-repellent clothing that was quite uncomfortable to wear since those garments were donned over our wool O.D. trousers and tunic. One late afternoon in June we were marched down to the docks at Plymouth and onto the decks of the good ship *John Henry* which had been built by Kaiser at Portland, Oregon, and which had already weathered some terrific storms, since the pilot house had already broken its welded seams where it was fastened to the deck, and angle irons had been placed all along the deck points where the breaks had occurred to brace the ailing structure. That was a good lesson in what happens when a nation tries to prepare for war in a hurry.

We steamed out into the English Channel in darkness and joined the thousands of other ships that crowded the channel waters. A tremendous storm was raging and we were forced to steam around for some days until the storm blew itself out. Each night out there we were treated to a pyrotechnic display [that I] hope the world will never see again. The sky was full of bursting shells and the eerie blue light from the starshells[8] fired by the Germans to lighten up the armada so it could be easily seen by the Luftwaffe.

We were finally transferred from the *John Henry* to an LST landing craft and we lay there for a few hours. That night we got another dose of pyrotechnics and I remember one shell bursting directly over our LST and the fragments fell into the deck well where our vehicles were parked well inside the deck combing.[9] I was in between two of the vehicles and thought to myself, here is where I got my first war souvenir, since a large piece of shrapnel had landed close to me. I reached out and grabbed that piece and believe me I let go of it in a hurry, since it was red hot yet.

We landed out where the surf was breaking and when I jumped off the ramp I went clear up to my ears in the icy cold channel water of Omaha Beach. As we left that scene behind, I will always remember the great battleship *Nevada* which was nearby when we were lying out in the channel. That very ship had been badly damaged and sunk at Pearl Harbor and she was in our convoy coming across from New York and here she was again to guard us in the channel crossing. That small incident brought to my mind the strength and determination of the spirit of Americans, and it has made me very proud to have had the opportunity to be born an American.

---

[8] A type of artillery used as a means to illuminate the battlefield during the night time.

[9] He possibly means "deck coaming," which is a vertical surface on a ship designed to deflect or prevent entry of water.

In our landing operation the barge carrying some of our motor pool equipment capsized in the still turbulent waters and we lost our repair shop truck with all its tools and equipment. This was a catastrophe, but somehow, we got hold of a German Army truck repair outfit and it was carted along for some time until it was finally discarded. It was a bulky vehicle and it had been fueled with the ersatz German gasoline which emitted fumes that stunk to the high heavens and no other driver wanted to travel behind it.

After bypassing many ruined buildings, pillboxes, tank traps, and whatnot we finally found ourselves after dark that night about 3 miles inland and on the top of a sort of mesa. I was dog tired and wet and quite hungry too, but rest was uppermost in my mind. Each man in our medical detachment picked a spot for himself to dig in on but since it was now pitch dark, we just had to feel around with our hands to feel what kind of a terrain we were on.

I finally found what felt like a good spot to dig and my entrenching tool was soon at work and dug myself a good and roomy hole and crawled into it. Now the fireworks commenced in earnest with starshells, Screaming Meemies, and high explosives passing over us and mainly directed at the invasion craft out in the channel. The whole night long this continued, but it didn't bother me since I slept like a log.

When day began to dawn, I was awakened by a terrific odor and could not imagine what was causing it. It was still too dark to see around me, so I just lay back and took another catnap. When I awoke the second time it was broad daylight and the sun was rising in the east. I crawled out of my hole and believe it or not, I was surrounded by three large and very dead German artillery horses that had lain there for several days after the initial landings of the Americans. Much farm stock was also killed during those terrific bombardments that came mostly from the warships and, of course, the air force strafing did terrible damage too, but mostly to the German truck convoys and other military targets.

The next day we went by our own truck convoy to a town called Colombières, where we bivouacked and became attached to a Ranger group which was called the 4th Provisional Ranger Regiment. Our attachment with them was only of an administrative nature. While camped out in the brush near this village, we sneaked into the village one evening and had the fortune to find a nice bistro, where we had a few bottles of wine and were presented by the owner with several small wooden casks of the famous and very tasty Colombières cheese. It looked a good deal like our Philadelphia cream cheese, but it had a very fine and distinctive flavor. On June 29, 1944, we moved to a place named St. Joseph on the Cherbourg Peninsula and which was very near the city of Cherbourg itself. On the last day of June we entered Cherbourg, which had been badly damaged by the first assault troops. We were to be billeted in a large old school building, and when we pulled up in front of that building we found it still occupied by the German garrison troops who were right in the middle of preparing their breakfast of rice [filled] with raisins, Pumpernickel bread, Limburger cheese in tubes like toothpaste containers. When the Germans saw that they were being dispossessed they formed in orderly formations and marched down to the beaches under guard as prisoners.

We immediately made ourselves at home and in entering the kitchen part of that building I found a battery of large copper cauldrons full of that steaming rice and raisin mixture, and all of us had a mighty fine breakfast. I retrieved all the Pumpernickel bread, Limburger cheese, and German Army vegetable stew that I could carry and took it all to my pad for safekeeping. That hoard lasted me for many a day. We remained in Cherbourg for approximately 10 days and while there I was assigned to a very disagreeable duty.

During the siege of Cherbourg, the attacking American troops, in their efforts to dislodge the Germans, had killed hundreds of Germans and also lost many of our own in battle. Those dead were lying scattered all over the city. Many bodies were imprisoned in the pillboxes where they died manning their machine guns, some died inside houses where they were during the house-to-house and street-to-street fighting. Many were dead or dying in one or another of the city's hospitals, namely the Pasteur and the French Marine hospitals. It was important that the dead be assembled as quickly as possible and interred properly. The Graves Registration Army Unit were still over in England and time was of the essence. A Captain Grant, [who was part] of that service, had been sent over to Cherbourg to size up the situation, and when he came to our commanding officer for help, he saw that immediate action must be taken. He requested a detail right now and received such in the form of seven men with two jeeps and two trailers to pick up the dead.

I was one who, together with Sergeant Knute Knutson, were picked for that detail, and in our work during the next 10 days we garnered up almost 800 corpses and transported them out to two temporary cemeteries several miles from the city. At those burial points there were both U.S. and German chaplains, whose duties were to identify each soldier as well as they could under the conditions under which we were working.

It would not be well for me to describe the scenes that met our eyes, but even one old case-hardened German Army doctor told me that "War is sure hell." He added further that "It will only be a matter of days, and our Panzer divisions will be landing, and that will be the end."

The Panzer divisions did land, but it took many more months of fighting at the cost of thousands of lives to breach Hitler's Fortress Europa.

Within a few days after the liberation of Cherbourg, the residents began to straggle into the city, looking for their homes, and in some cases those homes were only a pile of rubble. I witnessed one poor old couple standing in front of their own pile of rubble, with their arms around each other and weeping silently. Being quite soft-hearted, that scene stabbed me to the heart.

While still in the city of Cherbourg, I saw a French woman seated on the top of a tall scaffold, which was erected on a principal street. She was seated on a makeshift barber's chair. Her hair was cut off with scissors and her head shaved, by a barber who wielded both a huge pair of shears and a calcimine brush covered with lather of some sort. To me this was a disgusting exhibition. A news photographer was up in a nearby window taking pictures of that scene. I and the soldier with me got caught in that picture and, believe it or not, I was identified by some of our friends down in Tacoma, Washington, who viewed that picture when it was shown there. They, in turn, sent word to my wife that they were certain that it was me that they had seen.[10]

The first place of business that really got going full blast was the local brewery, which had been undamaged during the entire siege period. It was not long till beer could be gotten in the local bistros. Another type of business soon going full blast were the brothels. All the girls had been commandeered by the German Army doctors to help in taking care of the wounded in Cherbourg. The German doctors and some of their medical personnel remained at the two main hospitals in this city, until it was fully controlled by the Americans.

The sights of horror and the stench of war that we medics witnessed in Cherbourg will forever be etched in our minds. The latter days of June we assembled our gear and marched up the hill past Fort du Roule and on to other adventures.

In fast-moving modern warfare, the assault troops move swiftly, and in such movements many small bodies of the enemy troops are bypassed. It was our mission to intercept such groups, disarm them, and turn them over to the Military Police, and to be eventually taken down to the sea for transport to England.

When we were still in Cherbourg, many of those German prisoners were forced to help bury their dead. This was a sort of a punishment our side dealt out, and it had some value, inasmuch that it put the fear of God into some of those young Nazis. Some of those prisoners were guarded by a group of Negro soldiers from a very tough regiment and they were scared to death, since the word had been passed out to them that those black soldiers would skin them alive, if they made one false move or tried to escape. Those groups generally got one day of burial duty before being carted down to the beaches.

Our next bivouac area was at Hau de Haut[11] on the southern end of the Cherbourg Peninsula where we teamed up with the 2nd and 5th Ranger Battalions and the 759th Light Tank Battalion. We patrolled this area for 17 days, then made camp near a village called Tourtheville La Haye where we stayed put for 10 days and got

---

[10] It was fairly common, after formerly German held areas were liberated, that local citizens would find women who had been friendly with the Germans and would shave their heads. This was to mark them as being disloyal or as collaborators.

[11] The author may have meant Hameau de Haut.

some rest. Here I noted something very beautiful, which did not fit into a picture of war at all.

Here was the most beautiful forest of large rhododendron trees I have ever seen. There were several acres of them and they were in full bloom. When examined by me, I found some trees to be from 12 to 14 inches in girth at the ground level, showing them to be very aged. I do not know if they were in their natural habitat or if they had been planted there ages ago. It was surely a beautiful sight to behold, and a great contrast to what I had witnessed during the previous weeks.

The first few nights away from Cherbourg we were generally dug into the hedgerows and while lying safe and sound in our nice hedgerow foxholes, we could hear Bed Check Charley droning over us. Bed Check Charley was a German observation pilot and he always came after dark, at the same precise time, and he flew low over us. The Germans did not bring [their] air force out in great numbers after dark.

Another feature we had now was the broadcasts of Axis Sal[12] from Germany, who was telling all the Americans that they should be home taking care of their wives, and that the ones that remained home were doing that for us now. Those remarks gave everyone a big laugh. The Germans found out too late that this sort of propaganda was for the birds.

On August 14 we became attached to the 41st Regiment of the famous 2nd Armored Division under the Command of a Colonel Hines. We received some special training from them that we were in need of. While moving forward with the 2nd Armored, we came under shellfire on several occasions, and we were forced to dismount and take cover. On one occasion I got into the mouth of a concrete culvert and there I lay safely while shells were bursting overhead. We were at a crossroad at the time and such points were generally already zeroed in by the German artillery units. They would fire at such a point sporadically in the hopes that they could hit some American unit, and on many occasions they guessed right. While looking out from my point of vantage I saw one or two shells hit in the middle of a church graveyard and saw gravestones fly in all directions. I also saw a shell hit squarely in the middle of a small stone farmhouse, and it collapsed in a heap, and a cloud of dust rose from the ruins and enveloped the entire area where the building had stood. Within a few minutes several old people came from a nearby air raid shelter, running toward the rubble of their home. They all scrambled into the center of the rubble and began pitching stones to the sides and within a few minutes one old lady came staggering from the ruins, and holding in her two hands what appeared to me as a limb from a small child.

We were given the signal to get aboard our vehicles and departed with no opportunity to investigate nor possibly render aid to the stricken family. The scene

---

[12] Axis Sally was a generic nickname the American GIs gave any female radio personality that did Nazi propaganda shows in English.

which I have described was not an uncommon one during World War II and happened hundreds of times in various countries of Europe and happened to both friend and foe. This same night we were under artillery fire all night long, most of the big ones passing over us to explode far to the rear.

One afternoon, as we were passing through a small French village, I had the rare opportunity to see a real live town crier in action. He came out onto the village square ringing a large hand bell and carrying a large placard with his other hand.

He placed himself in the center of the square and rung his bell vigorously and shouting at the top of his lungs. We did not find out what the good or bad news was, but very quickly a good-sized crowd of villagers had collected around him.

That scene gave me an impression how it must have been back in Merrie Old England during the Shakespearean days when the town crier really held sway.

One evening shortly after we had dug in, a tremendous thunder and lightning storm broke overhead, and the rain came down in torrents. My foxhole partner at that time was Corporal Harry Nyhus, now a Seattle dentist. Harry and I had made ourselves as comfortable as possible down in our hole, with one shelter half under us and the other over us. We had no blankets at all. All of a sudden I felt water under me and in no time flat our foxhole was half filled with water. We had a roof over the top of our hole and we knew that the water did not come through there. So, we came to the conclusion that it must have seeped in from the bottom. Then we debated about if we should get up, but finally decided that if we lay in it long enough it would reach our body temperatures. So, we lay there till daybreak.

During this night a terrible artillery barrage was going on up in front of us, and between that and the thunder and lightning, we really had a good show. When the morning broke the sun came out bright and warm, and we took off all our clothes and hung them up on the surrounding bushes to dry. Chaplain Norris P. Holvorson was dug in alongside Nyhus and I, and when he arose out of his hole, he too was very wet and bedraggled, and a discouraged padre.

On the night of August 19, 1944, we were camped in a heavy patch of woods near Toureuvre. We had set up roadblocks at all the roads that traversed this area, and had also put out our perimeter guard around our entire encampment as is customary. During the early morning hours many enemy soldiers infiltrated our camp, not to fight us, but to beg for something to eat, since they had lost their units and they were completely demoralized. I don't know if the cooks gave them anything to eat, since military law says that a soldier can be shot at sunrise for giving aid and comfort to the enemy. We were in the process of stowing our medical equipment, preparatory to moving out, and I had already seated myself in the back end of our truck. I saw a truck coming into our camp, bearing the last of the perimeter guards and all their armament. They were approaching a point where I knew there were a number of mines laid out on the grass strip alongside the road. I had just been over there a half-hour before talking with the soldier who was guarding those mines. He, incidentally, was a very good friend of mine.

As I sat there looking at the scene that was unfolding before me, I saw a jeep leaving our camp and drove toward the approaching truck. It became apparent that neither driver understood the danger that lay before them. The driver of the heavier vehicle drove off the road to give way for the smaller jeep and drove over the several mines that lay in the grass. A tremendous explosion followed, and the heavy truck was lifted into the air by the force of the explosion.

The medical unit sprang into action immediately and we cared for 10 wounded right then and there. My friend and another soldier were killed outright.

From July 25 and up till August 25 our battalion operated with the 2nd Armored Division, and we did all those same types of movements that they did, moving from one village to another. We were fired upon and strafed constantly but managed to come through this period without anyone getting killed or wounded.

On the morning of the 25th, we were approaching the outskirts of the city of Elbeuf on the River Seine, and were skirting a patch of woods in order to be out of view of the German artillery spotters who were generally roosting up in the trees on the highest area around us.

We very carelessly came out from the woods and entered a large cow pasture, with the intention of crossing it into another wooded patch, and that was it. The observers had seen us and we were in the middle of a bracketing fire, where one group of shells are fired short of the target, the next burst over, and the third to hit right in the center of our column. At the first bursting shell we all scattered for cover, and I and another soldier found ourselves down in a cow wallow lined with sticky blue clay. Getting out of the wallow and up to a steep clay bank was quite difficult, but my first problem was to get my entrenching tool off my backpack, where it had been placed to conform to GI instruction manual regulations. It was soon apparent that the fellow that wrote those regulations had never been in such a situation as we were in now.

I damned near had to undress to get at that doggone tool. And from then on, we all carried our digging tool right on our belt, where we could grab them without a struggle.

The firing stopped abruptly after a half-dozen shell bursts, and again our outfit was lucky. But not so for one of the units that we were with. Some of their men were wounded during this little episode.

Our goal here was to seize the city of Elbeuf, and to especially capture and take control of the railway station. As our battalion got right up to the edge of the city, we discovered that the enemy had many tanks with which to repel us. I saw one Nazi tank knocked out by one of our machine gunners and the crew exterminated in attempting to get out of the hatch. Four enemy tanks were destroyed by our riflemen, before we received help two hours later from a tank destroyer outfit that had been sent to help us.

Our medical detachment had been instructed to dig in on the top of a bluff overlooking the lower portion of the city. Here we were to be kept in readiness to care for such casualties as we were certain would develop from this assault. The fighting was terrific but our riflemen, in less than an hour, drove the Germans out of the city and on across the River Seine to the north of town.

Our communications section, shortly after the initial assault, advised us that a large number of wounded were lying on the streets and in the alleys unattended, and that we had better be on our way. Captain Thorleif Gunderson ordered me to take a detail and go down into the city and care for those wounded, and on the way down to carry our Red Cross flag high on a staff, so it could be seen by the German snipers, who were hiding in many of the buildings. I felt kind of silly carrying that banner, but I was under orders and did as I was told. There were three of us in that group, but I just cannot recollect who they were. When we got down into the city, we found that all the wounded had been picked up by a litter squad of French Boy Scouts. I located one of those Scouts and asked him what they had done with the wounded, and he told me that they had left them in front of the large Catholic school nearby. That school had hastily been converted into a hospital of sorts.

We were quickly directed to that building and found everything there to be in a state of utter confusion. We picked up several of the wounded and brought them into the entrance of the building and laid them on the floor.

The enemy air force was strafing the building with several planes and the din of bursting anti-personnel bombs and anti-aircraft fire, coupled with aircraft fire hitting the cobbled courtyard, was really something. There were a number of Catholic nuns who were doing their best to help the wounded, and one little old priest with a kindly face and he was counting his prayer beads and praying silently.

One of the nuns motioned to us to carry the wounded down into the basement, where they would be safer. Another medic and I took several wounded down there, but in carrying the last one down, a bomb burst out in the courtyard, breaking a large window on the side of the staircase, and showering both the wounded and us with glass.

Down in that basement there was a scene not to be forgotten soon. The floors were littered with stretchers bearing wounded. We gave such first aid as was necessary. One of the men whom I treated was a young Lieutenant Berg from Everett, Washington, who I did not see again until October 20, 1975, at our reunion in Minneapolis [Minnesota].

In this assault we lost nine of our officers who were wounded, including our commander. We had seven of our enlisted men killed and 41 wounded. In this engagement our organization took 80 prisoners. After doing what we could for the wounded, our detail was ordered back to our position on the hill. Up there I had provided myself with two foxholes and had a concrete slab over the top of one of them, since we were being plastered by shrapnel bursts from the German batteries on the other side of the River Seine.

I lay back in my hole to rest a little when I heard an unusual noise coming from the woods behind me. I peeked out to see what might be the cause of it and out of the woods came a whole battalion of Canadians who were to relieve us. An officer from Vancouver came up to me and said, "What the hell is going on here? And where is all that firing coming from?" I pointed across the river, and he right then issued orders to his men to silence that battery, which was easier said than done.

I could see our men straggling up the hill and going to the rear after we were relieved. Captain Gundersen came up to me and said, "George, you and I are going to remain here until the last man is up the hill and safe." And we were the last of our unit to leave. In this battle we lost Pete Aadland from Custer, Washington, whom I knew quite well. Another hometown boy who participated as a scout and runner in this engagement, and many others, was Ned Kluken, Mr. Kluken lives at this time in Bellingham, Washington, and is my neighbor and fishing partner.

The Canadians who relieved us later lost Elbeuf in a severe enemy counterattack. We moved back a few miles to a rest area to lick our wounds and rest a bit. Here I got into a nearby village and bought a large horse-meat steak, which I fried over an open fire. It tasted very well but it was terribly tough.

On August 28 we became attached to Combat Group A of the 2nd Armored, and on the 30th we made a concrete attack and won six objective points.[13] [We then set] up our command post in the town of Villers that night.

We now lost our connections with the 2nd Armored and were given an assignment with the 7th Armored Group, XIX Corps, Reserve.

We set up a bivouac outside the village of Drucourt, France, and prepared a defense ring around that village. Here we ate well and got back some of the sleep we had lost while following the crazy tank drivers of the 2nd Armored.

One incident that I will remember was when we were stalled on the outskirts of Paris since we had no fuel for our vehicles. The story that came to us was that the striking oil workers back home had caused the delay in fuel delivery. On the two days we were in this location, I was living in a dugout made in a chalk cliff on a World War I battlefield. Here we found many empty shell casings from that war. By scratching the head of the casings we found what English firm made them. My chalk cave had been occupied by the English or Canadians during World War I.

It was in this area that we were visited by a group of supply planes, which dropped us a number of bales of clothing and some gasoline for our motorized equipment. Those bales fell in an open field and we all rushed out to open them up, and I got myself a wool union suit that was so large that I had to cut 6 inches off the arms and legs, so it would fit me. Here we got a few pairs of socks too. My shoes had not been off my feet for three weeks until we came to this place.

---

[13] Objective points refers to the goals of a military operation and in this case achieving progress on phase-line milestones to the ultimate objective at Elbeuf.

I went down to the river with my new underwear and socks and took a good bath in the icy water and felt much refreshed after that. We left one morning from a town called La Glanerie, heading for Mons, Belgium. Half of the time we did not know what country we were in, since the borders of some of those lowland countries come close together at certain points, and we could cross and re-cross from one country to another without knowing where we actually were at times.

The battalion headquarters, of course, knew where we actually were, but the average soldier did not. On our way out of France one day, while seated on the back end of our truck, and passing through a small French town, we hit a very deep rut in the roadway, and the resulting jolt dislodged my helmet and it fell to the roadway. I looked far back toward the end of our truck convoy, and I saw a French gendarme reach down and pick up my helmet, handing it to the driver of the last truck. I was just wondering how I was going to get me another helmet, and actually went without one for some days after getting into Belgium.

After our arrival at Mons, Belgium, we set up our aid station in a large old school building not far from the center of the town. One day a Belgian mother came through our guard post leading a very small and frightened daughter, who had received a nasty shrapnel wound on her right knee. It happened that I was alone in the aid station at the time and it fell to me to attend to the little girl. I cleansed and dressed her poor little knee, and during that operation she cried considerably and was quite frightened. I advised the mother to bring the little one back in a day or two for further treatment.

A couple of days later, when a new guard was at the gatehouse, the woman and child came back and the guard, not knowing of our previous arrangements, called for the corporal of the guard to check with me, and thinking perhaps that a spy was planning on entering our compound. The corporal came up to our aid station to find out what the woman and child were here for. I gave him the lowdown and he went back to the gate and told the lady and girl to come right in.

When they arrived, the woman was carrying a wicker basket filled with cookies, cheese, sausage, and a bottle of wine, which they gave me. The little girl's leg was much improved, and I gave it another dressing, and this time the little girl held back her tears and smiled the most beautiful smile, and mamma thanked me profusely. This was just one of the heartwarming experiences that one sometimes finds during wartime.

Before leaving Mons I had the opportunity to rub the head of the Iron Monkey[14] placed on the city hall entrance, and by doing so was assured a whole year of good luck, according to the legend that goes with that monkey. We also got into a large bistro in the city hall square and were treated to an evening of schnapps by a Swedish

---

[14] Located at the City Hall in Mons, Belgium is a small iron monkey statuette. Legend has it that rubbing this monkey will bring the person good luck.

stove salesman, who signed a chit at the end of the evening in payment for the wet goods we consumed.

In one of our movements by truck convoy, which took place sometime before we were in Mons, we got caught in a precarious spot by the Luftwaffe. [We] were in the middle of a small canyon, when two fighter planes swooped down on us. They had already dropped many magnesium flares, which had lit up the whole area so brightly that one could almost see a grasshopper jumping. When we saw that we were to be attacked, the order came to abandon our trucks. All the young and sprightly fellows sprang to life like they had a fire built under them, only the fire was up in the air above us all that time. In their mad scramble to get over the sides of our truck, I, being slower, got bowled over and found myself lying in the bottom of the truck, well entangled in the pack straps of the many packs resting on the truck bed. It took a minute or two for me to get myself free of all that equipment, and when I was able, I scrambled off by myself and crawled up a steep bank, and at the top, found myself in a recently plowed field.

The two enemy strafing planes were now buzzing around like a nest of angry hornets, and the din of machine-gun bullets hitting the ground and anti-personnel bombs bursting was something terrific. I dove into the closest furrow and drove my nose into the soft ground and lay very still. When the danger was over and the enemy had departed, I saw my comrade and neighbor Ned Kluken arising from a furrow just a little beyond me.

At the time of this close call we were being transported by the Cannonball Express,[15] whose drivers did not relish the idea of having to make too frequent trips where things were really hot, and the driver of our truck was no exception to the rule. When I first saw him after the attack, he was standing up against a tree and shaking like a leaf. When he got into the driver's seat and behind the wheel, he shook so bad that one of our boys had to take the wheel until that driver was sufficiently calmed so that he could resume his duties. He was not alone in being scared. Our battalion again [was] fortunate in not having any casualties, but some men belonging to another organization traveling with us were hit this time.

The middle of September found us far away from Mons and down in the canal country. Here again we were with the 2nd Armored Division on a combat mission. Now we were in an area where part of the time we were in Holland and part of the time in Belgium, since the Willems Vaart Canal and the River Maas formed the boundaries of those respective countries here. We set up an aid station in a small concrete building after first going through the windows instead of trying the front door which might have been booby-trapped.

I was sent farther up ahead with another couple of men, and since shrapnel was breaking around us, we got into a nearby brick oven for shelter. Here the three of us

---

[15] The author most likely means the "Red Ball Express."

stayed that night where it was nice and warm, since that oven was being fired by a caretaker who lived on the other side of the canal in...I don't know which country.

Our entire battalion participated with the 66th Armored Regiment of the 2nd Armored Division in the entire Canal Drive, and our riflemen gained a healthy respect for the tankmen and they for us. From September 14 to September 28, when our participation in the Canal Drive was finished, we had been strafed and bombarded by everything the enemy had to offer. The 99th had in turn dished it out generously to the enemy and had captured 565 prisoners. We lost three officers killed, two wounded, nine enlisted men killed, and 75 enlisted men wounded. None of the 99th men were ever taken prisoner.

Some of my friendliest recollections of my minor participation in that war were those I have from the city of Valenciennes, France, where we were sent on September, 8, 1943, to act as a buffer against an anticipated attack by a large body of the enemy which were attempting to break away from a British encirclement northwest of Valenciennes.

Here we were quartered in an old French Army Post located near the center of this city. A group of young underground fighters known as the Maquis or Maquisards[16] were attached to us to act as informants and be our eyes and ears.

Some way or another I got in with a gang of those young Frenchmen, and even was invited to eat at their mess building which was also one of the old garrison buildings at that Army Post. It seems to me that I was the only American soldier at that particular mealtime. We were all seated opposite from each other at a long table in the center of the dining hall. At either end of the table were the two lead men of this group of Maquisards.

Each man had a very long and sharp dagger stuck into the table alongside his soup bowl. I soon discovered the real purpose of having that knife in that particular position, since there was no other cutlery except a very large soup spoon at each setting.

One of the leaders got up and introduced me to the group. He then barked an order and two flunkies appeared, with each bearing a large iron kettle full of steaming pea soup. These flunkies passed from man to man and ladled into each bowl a goodly portion of that thick soup or rather gruel, since it was not of the watery type. Soon several bottles of wine and beer appeared, and several long loaves of French bread, each loaf about 3 feet long. The loaves of bread were passed from man to man and here is where the big toadstabbers came into play in carving off a slice. I reached into my own scabbard and pulled out my own toadstabber and did as the rest had done.

The bottles of wine were passed from man to man, each one taking a swig, until we ran out of drink. There was much joking and laughing amongst those young

---

[16] French for a member of the Resistance or a guerrilla unit.

fellows, and all through the meal one or another would break into some rollicking song, and they would all join in song, till the whole resounded.

While the meal was in progress, I had picked a piece of meat out of my pea soup, and when chewing it I bit into something very hard and sharp. I removed the object from my mouth and lay it alongside my bowl, and I felt that all their eyes were watching me, and soon they all laughed uproariously and the young fellow seated next to me informed me that it was nothing but a piece of shrapnel. Before the dinner was over I had a sizable pile of that hardware alongside my soup bowl, and so did the rest of them.

During the bombardments that took place when the invading Americans and British soldiers hit the beaches, thousands of cattle were struck by shrapnel; some died instantly and others walked around wounded, possibly for days. Those enterprising Maquisards were not going to see perfectly good meat go to waste, and they systematically hunted up such creatures and dispatched them humanely. Another thing about these young guerrilla fighters, they did not have any services of supplies as organized armies have. Each unit scrounged for themselves.

The reader must remember that at this time there was no French Army. No Frenchman who lay down his arms could again serve as a soldier. The only units that were still active were the 2nd French Armored Division and a few ships of the French Navy, and they were either in England or elsewhere.

While we were yet in Valenciennes a few French officers from England showed up, for the purpose of commencing to organize an entirely new French military force. It was my privilege to see my friend Rene Baert, and many of the other young guerrillas, sworn in as soldiers of the New French Army, and that group were most likely amongst the first ones. After my return home I continued correspondence with Rene Baert and others, and my wife and I are godparents to his first child, and she was named by us.

Rene Baert served with the French occupation forces in Germany after the war. Back home in Valenciennes he worked in a carbide factory and was partially blinded in an explosion there and is now on pension. Our families still communicate, and our goddaughter is married and has her own family.

My mementoes of Valenciennes include a French homemade flag with the names of several of those brave young Maquisards written thereon by themselves.

So many scenes passed before my eyes and so many incidents occurred along our march into France, Belgium, and Holland during the few months that I personally was in the combat area, that it would be impossible to enumerate all. And therefore, I am only giving the high points as I observed them.

The last two incidents that I remember well was one in particular when we had set up our aid station in the courtyard behind a large brick house in a little village in Belgium. Our own mortar section had located themselves just across the road from us in a small apple orchard.

That mortar section naturally drew the attention of the German observers, who were either up in church towers or other high points. Only an hour prior to the time the Germans sent their first shower of mortar shells over on us, I had talked to a young doctor who had joined us only an hour before. He had been sent down to us from the nearest field hospital in the vicinity to take over the duties of our battalion surgeon, who was to be sent to another outfit to take over greater duties.

I had barely gotten acquainted with the new captain and he and I were sitting on a small haycock in the compound to the rear of our aid station talking, when the first burst occurred above us, knocking a few tiles off the roof housing our equipment. I thought I had better get out of there while the going was still good, and therefore I dashed down into the cellar beneath our aid station building and took cover there. The captain, however, remained sitting right where I had left him. I had no sooner gotten under cover until several more mortar bursts came almost simultaneously, hitting our roof and sending down a shower of roof tilings. I took a quick peek out from my hiding place and saw our new doctor lying on the ground beside the haycock. The last burst must have evidently broken just over him. He was killed instantly.

A contingent of Belgian FFI[17] men came within a few minutes and picked up our captain and I heard that they buried him in the village churchyard. During this time, we had 300 of those Belgian guerrilla fighters aiding us in that area.

One of the last incidents prior to me being sent back to a field hospital, is one that clings to my mind very strongly. It occurred when one of our medics was treating two German wounded. He was down on his knees beside two of the enemy and dressing their wounds, when he was shot in the back by two snipers who hid in the brush nearby.

Our riflemen soon surrounded that pair and they were brought up to the scene of their atrocity and exterminated right there and then. All us medics were well marked, our helmets bearing red crosses, and each wore a Red Cross armband. We felt that we were well protected by the pact drawn up under the terms of the Geneva Convention protecting medical personnel. The Germans were signatories to that pact, but they did not always adhere to its provisions.

We had traveled by truck convoy for hours without lights of any sort. Toward the end of our journey as we were crossing a flat plain, which had low hills on either side of it, we suddenly were fired on by enemy artillery. We could see the gun flashes on the hillsides and hear the scream of shells overhead. We passed through that area harmlessly, and an hour later we pulled into an area where we were to bivouac.

I found what I thought to be a good spot for my foxhole, but the ground was full of large stones, which made the digging poor. However, I finished a sort of a dish-shaped excavation, put my shelter half in the bottom thereof, and lay down

---

[17] This probably refers to the Belgian Resistance fighters.

with my pack for a headrest. I soon fell asleep and slept like a log. When I awoke the sun was shining directly on my face, and not being quite fully awake, I had a sort of an eerie feeling or a premonition that someone was watching me closely.

I woke up with a start and directly before me stood a tall, rangy, and bedraggled man with three small children alongside him, and him holding a very large and kicking hare by the ears, with his left hand. With a long and bony right-hand finger he pointed down toward my feet and spoke the words "Solie, solie." I understood that he was interested in my shoes and wanted to trade that large hare for my shoes.

Now as far as I can reconstruct this happening from the beginning, I must say that I did actually have an extra pair of shoes in my pack. I have an idea that some of my comrades who knew I had those extra shoes, and who were out of the sack ahead of me, had steered that fellow over to me.

That pair of extra shoes were too big for me anyhow and only that much more excess baggage to carry. I looked at the poor old fellow and got the shoes out of my pack and gave them to him. He then handed me the large and struggling hare. I had a hell of a time explaining to him that I had no way of preparing the hare just then. It took a smattering of French, German, Norwegian, and English to put my message across to him, and he very reluctantly took his hare back, and with a face filled with smiles; the last I saw of him and the kids, they were winding their way up that Belgian hillside to their farmhouse on the top of that hill.

The last incident I will relate before going into some statistical information relative to our outfit is as follows:

This was also in a little Belgian village. I had run into two German soldiers lying by the roadside, both badly lung shot. Their breathing was labored, and they were in much pain. I prepared a very large dressing for each of them and used my sulfa powder[18] liberally on their massive wounds. About that time a Belgian village doctor came onto the scene and he wore a large butcher's apron which was blood spattered.

When he saw that I had taken care of the enemy quite well, he had a look of utter disgust both for me and them. [He then continued to break the stocks] off many rifles lying by the roadside. He accomplished his task by smashing each rifle over the end of a projecting road culvert. As I disappeared down the roadway from him, I could still see him swinging rifle stocks onto that concrete culvert.

The end of September had come and the nights were getting colder and colder, and one bitterly cold morning I could not arise from my foxhole. My principal joints were locked stiff, and it took four of my comrades to get me out of that hole and onto a stretcher. That was the end of my participation with the 99th Infantry Battalion.

My next stop was the nearest field hospital, and from there to a great base hospital at Liège, Belgium, from where I was flown to a hospital somewhere near Lands

---

[18] Used to treat bacterial infections.

End, England. After a day at this hospital we were all loaded aboard a Red Cross train and taken to a large Army hospital near Malvern Wells. While here a group of us were taken on a bus ride to visit Stratford on Avon, Kenilworth Castle, and Warwick Castle.

The mayor and mayoress of Warwick were our hosts and they presided over the dinner which was given us at Warwick's leading inn.

For many weeks I received much therapy, X-rays, and vile-tasting medicines, in several Army hospitals. The great day came when one doctor said to me, "I am going to schedule you for Zling." He explained to me that this meant I was to be sent to the zone of interior, meaning the good old U.S.A.

We who were on our way home soon found ourselves back in Scotland again, but this time Glasgow, and out there in the firth lay the great gleaming *Queen Mary* which was to take us back home.

The voyage itself was quite uneventful and this time I did not get seasick. But many did, and once or twice during the crossing only a handful were in that great main dining hall at one time. At New York I was sent to the great Halloran Army Hospital on Staten Island, across the bay from the city. Here I enjoyed a fine Thanksgiving dinner.

My last post was in the hospital known as The Baxter General Army Hospital at Spokane, Washington the night before Christmas, 1944. This ends the story of one old man who went to war and lost his helmet in France and got it back again in Belgium a week later.

CHAPTER EIGHT

Harold F. Plank

Harold F Plank wrote about his experiences in a 26-page booklet titled "Memoirs of World War II: The Story of a Tioga County Soldier" published in May 2002. The writings included below pick up shortly before Harold was added to the 99th Infantry Battalion (Separate) in October 1944.

Prior to joining the 99th, Plank was part of the D-Day invasion on the beaches of Normandy—the heroic scene storming the beach and scaling the cliffs at Pointe du Hoc that has been played out in numerous movies and books. Out of the 235 men in his unit, he wrote that only 87 were able to walk away from their experience two and a half days later. For his efforts in this battle, he was later awarded the Bronze Star Medal.

As became common, more and more members of the 99th were joining as reinforcements. Plank is just such an example and became part of the non-Norwegian contingent of the group. He had been a member of the naval gunfire liaison group to direct gunfire from naval ships. Once the beaches at Normandy were secured, that role diminished in need and consequently soldiers such as Harold Plank became available for reassignment.

Plank writes of several key events that the 99th were involved in, including the Battle of the Bulge where he spent 28 days outside in the frigid and tense environment. His one day spent indoors was on the occasion of his 21st birthday when his captain pulled him from his foxhole to spend the day inside a barn with a fire to warm himself by.

Upon returning from Europe, Plank went home to Pennsylvania and soon married Hazel Houghtaling. Harold passed away in 2008 at the age of 84 and is buried at Champlin Cemetery in Westfield, Tioga County, Pennsylvania.

Digging Foxholes

After we were no longer useful as the Naval Shore Fire Control Party, I was transferred to the XIX Corps headquarters and did guard duty there. I dug foxholes to stay in whenever artillery fire came too close and lay there lots of times, watching our bombers go over. Man! The sky would be chuck-full of them, mostly heading to bomb St. Lô, so that we could finally break out and head toward Paris. From where we were, we could hear the bombs whistle down and land in and around St. Lô. The ground would just tremble. It was quite an experience; but eventually the breakout did come, and the XIX Corps headquarters kept following along as closely behind the advancing troops as possible.

I remember riding in the back of a big Army truck on a dirt road. We were coming to a curve, where the wheels threw dirt and dust out to one side. I noticed a dead German soldier lying there, and his lower half was almost covered with sand and dust thrown from the wheels of the trucks. His face was looking up at the sky, and his eye sockets and mouth were just literally crawling with maggots. It was not a sight that I like to remember. We kept following the lead troops for the next several weeks, coming close to Paris at one time.

Late in the summer of 1943 the Germans deployed their so-called secret weapons. Among these were long-range rockets launched from deep in Germany. They rose very high in the sky and fell without warning on the coastal cities of England. Another weapon was one we called the "buzz bomb." It was shorter range and launched from mobile launch pads close behind enemy lines. An unmanned winged bomb with a motor to propel it, it could be aimed at railroad yards or villages with highway intersections and would carry just enough fuel to get to the target. It was very inaccurate. The noise from the motor would set up a vibration of the tile roofs on sheds and outbuildings that would make a scary rattle. If you heard one, you looked for a hole, a ditch, or a cellar. If the motor stopped, you knew it would hit close by. If the motor was still running when it passed, you breathed a sigh of relief because it had missed you.

During these stressful times, it wasn't unusual to see small groups of GIs gather together in sheltered spots to dig out their New Testaments or prayer books and engage in Bible studies. The New Testament that I carried was given to my father by his grandmother when he entered the Army in World War I. He carried it during his tour of duty, some of which was in the same section of France. He gave it to me when I was drafted in January 1943; and I carried it during my service in World War II. Years later, I gave that same New Testament to my son, James, to carry into Vietnam. The New Testament returned, but my son gave his life in that war.

Finally, the Allied troops had broken into Germany; and on October 16, I was taken to the front lines and put into the 99th Infantry Battalion, a Norwegian American Ski Troop outfit. They had worked with the British Commandos, so they were similar to the Rangers I had been with. At the time I joined them, they were just outside of Würselen, Germany, located on a highway being used as an escape route by the Germans encircled at Aachen. We were sent to secure the roadway and cut off the escape of the Germans from Aachen. The 1st Infantry Division was closing in from one side and the 30th Infantry Division from the other. For at least five days, we were constantly under artillery fire, tank fire, mortar fire, and bombing by the Luftwaffe. It was hard to even get warm food. Because of the battle at Würselen, I was recommended for the Combat Infantry Badge.

"No Letter Today"

Eventually we were relieved from that post and moved out to Henri-Chapelle, Belgium, where we spent a few days in rest and then went back into training. We then went to Tilff, Belgium, where we were housed in really good apartment buildings. It was a nice respite from some of the things we had been through. That wasn't going to last forever, because on December 17, 1944, the blitz started by the Germans in the Ardennes offensive; and we were loaded onto trucks and rode all afternoon and into the night from Tilff, Belgium, into the outskirts of Malmédy. There we took up roadblocks and made some reconnaissance patrols, trying to locate the Germans. We picked up a few engineers who had escaped what would later be known as the "Malmédy Massacre."

When we were not scheduled to man the roadblocks, we took shelter in an abandoned cafe nearby. There we discovered a jukebox and a stack of records. Only one record was in English, and it was played over and over. It was very appropriate for the situation we were in. The title on one side was "Worried Mind," the other, "No Letter Today."

We spent December 17 through Christmas in and around Malmédy. Shortly after Christmas, we were on a combat patrol in hopes of at least capturing one German to find out what outfit we were opposing at that time. We were going up a roadway in a ravine and came under fire. We were pinned down for a short time, but eventually we made it through and into a little village. At that time, I was ammunitions bearer for a fellow with a bazooka. If we ran into any tanks, we could fire at them with it. He was just a short fellow, and the bazooka was longer than he was. It was comical, keeping up with him pulling that bazooka along.

In this little village, we had had an artillery barrage by our own side to prepare it for entry. We came upon a stable that was on fire. There were live cattle in it that we couldn't rescue, so we stood outside and shot as many as possible to keep them from suffering in the fire. We went on a little ways, and I remember seeing some Germans in overcoats running across a field into a woods. They were too far off for us to even bother to shoot at. When we came back from this combat patrol, it was said that we had captured one German and killed 30. We did identify the unit that we were opposing there.

A few days later, in January 1945, we were moved from Malmédy to Stavelot in Belgium; and there we continued doing practically the same things we'd been doing around Malmédy, only it was a little more forested. Lots of times we were near enough to Germans that we could hear them talking but couldn't see them. It was bitter cold with up to 2 feet of snow, and most of the time was spent in foxholes until January 18. On January 13, when I turned 21 years old, the captain of the company, knowing it was my birthday, pulled me out of my foxhole; and I spent the day at company headquarters in a barn with a fire in a barrel. That was the only time during 28 days in the Malmédy and Stavelot area that I spent inside.

On January 18, we were pulled from the line there and went back to Tilff, Belgium, where we'd been stationed before. Not too long after that, it was decided that the 99th was going back into France to be put into a new outfit and trained for the invasion of Norway. I believe it took us 72 hours by train all the way back to Barneville, France, on the west coast, south of Cherbourg. There we started training again and were united with all the remnants of the Ranger battalions that had been fighting in Italy and France, as well as the remainder of the First Special Service Forces that had been fighting in the mountains in Italy. We were now part of a regiment called the 474th Infantry Regiment (Sep.). Of course, the 99th Infantry Battalion also had "(Sep.)" after it because we didn't belong to any larger outfit. But now we were with the 474th Infantry Regiment (Sep.). It was later decided that things were going so well in Europe that we no longer needed to think about invading Norway. The outfit was shipped, partly by rail and partly in convoy, back to Aachen, Germany, where the 99th would detach from the 474th. We went south into Germany and followed closely behind the advancing troops. We were split into company areas, where we searched out wooded areas, villages, farmhouses, and anything that could hide either officials that might be wanted for war crimes or soldiers who had dressed in civilian clothes. We were also picking up anything that could be used as a weapon.

I Visit a Castle

During this time, we had moved into the Bavarian Alps. One day I was driving a jeep with an officer, followed by a couple of armored vehicles. We went into the mountains and up a dirt road that reminded me of a place back home in Pennsylvania, going from Log Cabin Inn up to Colton Point, only it was heavily wooded with more pines and hemlocks. There we eventually came into a courtyard of a castle. It was just like a storybook castle. We parked in the courtyard, and the officers went inside to talk with the people. The courtyard soon filled with pages in tight black britches and white socks. The britches came to just below their knees and the socks went above, and they were wearing bright red coats with red tails. They just stood around and didn't cause any trouble whatsoever. Also, there were maids who wore starchy aprons and skirts and bonnets. It was just like something you'd read about in a storybook. That was a nice experience.

It wasn't long until we were in Heroldsbach, about 15 miles north of Nuremberg, and the war had ended in Europe. Occasionally we were still picking up some bypassed bands of Germans and freeing foreign prisoners who had been jailed by the Germans. On May 13, we started back from Nuremberg to Le Havre, France. We went through many places that had big names during WWI, such as Verdun. We were in a camp near Le Havre for several days until ships came into the harbor to take us to Norway.

On May 29 I boarded an LST. It was loaded mostly with motorized vehicles, armored vehicles, tanks, and military equipment. We set sail for Norway. When we started up the fjord toward Oslo, our LST stopped at Drammen, some distance from Oslo. We unloaded the ships and I got to drive an armored vehicle from there to Oslo. It was six-wheeled and had either a .50-caliber machine gun or a 20mm anti-tank or anti-aircraft gun in the turret behind me. We didn't have any problems in the convoy into Oslo. There our vehicles were turned into a motor pool, and I was taken to a camp in Smestad, Norway where I would stay.

It was at this camp that I got a "Dear John" letter from my girlfriend in the U.S., and she said that our engagement was off. It had been off for some time, but she didn't want to notify me for fear that I would be in a war zone at the time of receiving it and I would not react to it properly. I recovered quickly and got acquainted with a Norwegian girl who lived right near the camp we were staying at by Smestad. She was a cousin to one of the fellows in the outfit. From where we were camped, it wasn't far by electric train into downtown Oslo and we were able to go there quite often. The Red Cross had set up canteens and places to stay. This young lady from Smestad was a good guide to show me the sights around Oslo.

Most of our time in Oslo was spent guarding warehouses that the Germans had used for storage, guarding some war criminals who had been captured, getting in touch with the German Army camps, and preparing those troops to be transferred to Germany by ships. We had a few big parades in Oslo. When King Haakon VII returned from exile in England, we had a parade for him and formed up in the castle grounds. He inspected us, and so I got to see a king.

Sailing Home

Time went on, but finally the USS *Bienville* docked in Oslo Harbor, our troops were put aboard, and we sailed away on October 16. We let some British troops off in Southampton, England, and then left the next day and started out through the English Channel into the Atlantic Ocean. We ran into a very severe storm; but we were too far out to go back and take shelter in some harbor, so we rode it out. I believed I was on my way home, so I wasn't too concerned about it.

Finally, on October 31, [1945] we landed in Boston Harbor and were taken to Camp Myles Standish. There we got rid of some of the equipment, and we were sent by train to Indiantown Gap. We went through a lot of paperwork and were finally discharged on November 7, after which I went to Harrisburg and took a train to Williamsport.

My honorable discharge shows that I was awarded the Bronze Star Medal, Good Conduct Medal (if you can believe that), Distinguished Unit Badge, Combat Infantry Badge, Europe-African-Middle Eastern Campaign Medal with six bronze stars and bronze arrowhead, and World War II Victory Medal. The six bronze stars represent various battles and campaigns. They were Sicily, Normandy, northern France, Rhineland, and Ardennes, Central Europe.

On the train ride to Williamsport, I was talking with some civilians, and one fellow asked me where I was going. I told him, "The Wellsboro area." Well, he was a salesman headed for Wellsboro, so if I wanted to, I could ride with him from Williamsport to Wellsboro. That was really a godsend, and so I made it into Wellsboro probably around 11:00 at night; and he let me off on the corner by the red light, where the Wellsboro Diner is now. I walked down the sidewalk a little ways toward where Dunkin Donuts is now, and there I sat my duffle bag down and stood there wondering what in the world I was going to do next. I hadn't been there too long, when a car pulled up, and the driver said, "Where are you headed, soldier?" I said, "I'd like to get to Westfield." He said, "Well, we're from Elkland and didn't intend to go that way, but we can just as well." He said, "Climb in," and I told him after I got in that I lived between Little Marsh and Westfield and that was OK by him. It was election night, and the driver had taken election returns from Elkland to Wellsboro, and they were now on the way back home. I tried to get him to let me out at the mouth of the road that goes up to where my folks' place was, but he wouldn't have anything of that. He took me right up and parked me in the driveway at home, then left.

A Family Reunion

I took my bag and got onto the front porch, and I could hear a dog in the house just a "yippin'" and "yappin'" away. I didn't know what kind of a dog it was, but I tried the doorknob and it opened. I found the light switch and turned the lights on; and it was only minutes until footsteps were galloping down the steps from the sleeping quarters overhead. My sisters, Margie and Eileen, and my mom and dad came "a barreling" down the steps to greet me. It was after midnight at that time, but I don't think we did anymore sleeping. It was the first time in two and a half years we'd been together. It was quite a homecoming. I think we just sat there and drank coffee and visited. I do remember the next day getting my picture taken outside with my parents. Margie, knowing that I would be home soon, had gotten my old '32 Chevy out and shined it up and had it all ready to go.

From there on, I was home. *Praise the Lord!*

CHAPTER NINE

Luverne Ostby

As the written history below indicates, Ostby was a member of the 99th from the early training at Camp Ripley, Minnesota and Camp Hale, Colorado. His narrative provides additional perspectives on nearly all the major campaigns that the 99th was involved in through to the time spent in Norway. As with many others, this time in Norway included reunions with relatives.

Ostby's grandparents emigrated to the United States in the 1880s from southern Norway and settled in Swift County, Minnesota after arrival. After the war, Ostby returned to Minnesota and worked for the Swift County Telephone Company installing lines, setting up phones in people's homes, and later conducting repairs until he reached retirement age.

Ostby married Adeline Danielson in 1949 and they raised their five children in Benson, Minnesota. He died in 2011 at the age of 88 and is buried in Glenwood, Minnesota. He received the Bronze Star during his service in the 99th.

Timeline of the 99th

Luverne Ostby was born on July 23, 1922 and was raised in rural Minnesota. He left for military service in September 1941. After being sworn in at Fort Snelling, he was sent to Camp Claiborne, Louisiana for his basic training.

Early on in his training at Camp Claiborne he was called aside and confronted by an officer that asked him if he spoke Norwegian, upon which his reply was yes. The officer asked, "Why don't you answer in Norwegian?" and pointed to a large tent instructing him to go there. Inside was a tent full of Norwegian-speaking soldiers including a neighbor, Bob Stay. The group was sent to Camp Ripley, Minnesota to begin training.

Ostby was chosen to become a part of the 99th Battalion (Separate), a unit specifically made up of soldiers able to speak Norwegian. The plan was for the unit to help with the Norwegian occupation, code-named PLOUGH. Four objectives were expected to be obtained in this mission:

"C Co, 3rd platoon ready to board the trucks to Camp Carson to meet FDR. We have to lean like that because the pack is so heavy, (I'm) third from the left," reads the handwritten label by the 99th's Kristian Brun. Packs of 75–90 pounds were common at Camp Hale, Colorado. The presidential inspection of the Norwegian and Greek Battalions at Camp Carson was reported publicly. (Courtesy of the 99th Educational Foundation)

1: to eliminate Norway as an economic asset for Germany;
2: to force Germany to keep large numbers of troops on occupation duty in Norway and away from other active fronts;
3: to limit the ability of German troops in Norway to attack Allied convoys transporting to the Russian port of Murmansk;
4: to prepare for the future occupation of Norway, and create a link through Norway to Russia.

In December 1942, the battalion, including Luverne, was transferred to Camp Hale, Colorado. They were expected to receive extensive winter training and Ostby was issued skis. Shortly after being issued them, he had to turn them back in. He never even wore them.

After the snow melted in the spring of 1943, they began training on rock climbing. On Easter Sunday 1943, President Franklin Delano Roosevelt personally reviewed the battalion. In the spring of 1943, it was determined that the possibility of a Norwegian invasion was not possible. The invasion of Europe was determined to be better coming farther south, in France. About 100 men from the battalion were recruited to form OSS teams to help with the Norwegian resistance and conduct unconventional warfare operations.

On August 24, 1943, they received orders to move to New York by train, arriving in Camp Shanks to await being shipped to Europe. They boarded the SS *Mexico*, a steamship, and departed for Europe on September 5, 1943.

Luverne and the battalion arrived in Scotland on September 16 and boarded trains for the 16-hour ride to Perham Downs Camp, in the Tidworth area of Wiltshire, England. They began training and preparing for the eventual invasion of Europe.

In January 1944 they moved to a new site at Glanusk Park in Wales where they continued with more mountain training. On May 1 they moved again to Hereford, England. Luverne remembers during this time before the invasion receiving orders to begin "waterproofing" their jeeps to prepare to cross the English Channel. For that they installed extensions to the exhaust system to bring it above the water line and coating all mechanical and engine parts with a waterproofing agent to protect against the saltwater. Ostby takes pride in the fact that his jeep was one of the few that continued to work after the landing on the beach.

On June 17, 1944, 11 days after the initial assault on the Normandy beaches, Luverne and the 99th Battalion boarded a ship for crossing the English Channel. Due to the poor weather, the beach head waters were too violent to land. The men spent days on the ship waiting and almost all became seasick. They arrived in sight of Omaha Beach and were transferred to a landing craft for the final trek to Normandy on June 21.

Luverne drove his jeep off the landing craft into about 8 feet of water. The vehicle stayed afloat for a short time before finally sinking in the channel. Luverne sat on the back of the seat while the waves from the channel slowly pushed the jeep forward until he could get enough traction to drive onto the dry ground.

As soon as they landed, the jeeps would need to be stripped of their "waterproofing" and prepared for battle.

Most of the heavy fighting was done by the time the men of the 99th landed, but they still sustained artillery shelling from the retreating German Army while on the beach. Luverne says that the beach was strewn with broken and burned equipment and dead soldiers.

The battalion was attached to the battle-stricken First Army. Near Cherbourg, France, Luverne encountered his first taste of combat. Although the landing force had taken the city and moved on there was still much resistance there. A three-day battle ensued before the men of the 99th defeated the Germans.

After fighting in Cherbourg, Luverne and his unit pushed inland in a southerly direction, continuing to meet and fight the Germans. Near Cherbourg, Ostby recalls seeing German 90mm gun emplacements aimed at the English coast. These guns were fully capable of reaching England, but it appeared that they never had the chance to use them. He recalls them as an awesome site and with field glasses could view the English coastline from this position.

Luverne traveled the distance of about 50 miles meeting sporadic resistance all the way to Caen, France. In July they engaged the Germans near Hau de Haut,[1] where they stayed for some time fighting and continued their training exercises. They conducted rear area security operations with the 759th Light Tank Battalion.

In the middle of August 1944, Ostby was attached to the 2nd Armored Division, along with the rest of the battalion. They battled [their way through western France], gaining praise from the 2nd Armored's commander [who claimed they were the] only infantry unit that they couldn't keep up with. On August 25, they were engaged in heavy German resistance near Elbeuf, on the Seine River. This location was important to the Germans as it was one of only two locations for the retreating Germans to cross the Seine.

Through September, Luverne and his unit continued to fight with the 2nd Armored Division and saw heavy combat near Maastricht, Holland and into Belgium. They were attached to the 30th Infantry Division in mid-October and were assigned to attack Würselen, Germany to cut off the German retreat out of Aachen. They served as the First Army's rear reserve for defense against any German airborne operations.

On December 16, 1944, Germany launched its offensive in the Ardennes, known as the "Battle of the Bulge." The 99th was positioned around the town of Malmedy. A German unit, commanded by SS Colonel Otto Skorzeny, launched a mission to pose his men as American soldiers and have them infiltrate American positions to cause as much damage and confusion as possible.

Skorzeny's plan failed, but it did have an effect on the 99th Battalion. Many of the men of the 99th were direct immigrants from Norway and spoke poor English. In the confusion of arresting the German infiltrators, some of the men of the 99th were also arrested because they were thought to be the enemy due to how poorly they spoke English.

On December 21, 1944, at around 10:30 p.m., German Panzer Brigade 150, led by Skorzeny, attacked the 99th Battalion's position. For 11 days the battle raged in what Luverne described as mud, snow, and extreme cold in what was one of the worst winters in the history of that region. Heavy casualties were sustained on both sides, but due to the defensive efforts of the 99th Battalion, Skorzeny's attack failed. Ostby says that thousands of Germans surrendered and were taken prisoner. He was on the very edge of the German lines near Liège, within ½ mile from the breakthrough when the Germans finally surrendered.

After the defeat of the Germans at the Battle of the Bulge, Luverne and the men of the 99th were sent to Tilff, Belgium for some R&R (Rest and Relaxation). On January 22, Ostby and the 99th loaded into French 40 × 8 railroad boxcars[2]

---

[1] He probably means Hameau de Haut.

[2] French boxcars that had these numbers on the side denoted that each one could carry either 40 soldiers or 8 horses.

for the 72-hour ride to Barneville, near Normandy, where the war had started for them months before. Here they were reinforced and rolled into a new unit, the 474th Infantry Regiment. They also received a new directive for their operations in the war. They were directed to move out and round up German units that had been passed by, clear out hiding Nazis, and demilitarize the civilian population.

Along the way they met up with Patton's Third Army near Aachen, Germany. There was a huge celebration amongst the men. Luverne recalls the men drinking German beer but they soon determined that it wasn't to their liking. Eventually, they found a stock of vodka and continued their celebration. Vodka was new to most of the men, and many became sick from it.

In Aachen, Luverne lost his friend Bob Stay during a sniper attack. From a nearby burned-out factory a sniper fired into a group of medics, killing Stay. Luverne, and a number of other men, began firing at the window, silencing the sniper.

Luverne [and the 99th] continued in their push toward Berlin. He witnessed companies of German prisoners and civilian refugees all along the way. He also saw many of our own American POWs being liberated as well as the prisoners from the concentration camps. He says it was a terrible sight to see along the road, "eyes sunken into faceless heads, legs the size of a woman's arm…looking like walking skeletons."

Luverne came close enough to see the outskirts of the city of Berlin when it was decided by the High Command that the Russians would be the ones to enter the city. The men of the 99th also had the task of transporting Nazi gold and stolen art treasures from the Kaiseroda salt mines in Merkers, Germany to the Reichsbank in Frankfurt. Total retrieved items were valued at around 2.1 billion dollars.

On May 7, 1945 Germany, defeated, surrendered to the Allies. The war in Europe was all but over. Luverne and the 99th Battalion received orders that they would be going to Norway to assist in the disarming and demobilization of Germany's 300,000-man army there. They headed back to the coast, through Luxembourg, for Le Havre, France. They spent some time there preparing before departing for Oslo, Norway.

They were garrisoned in Camp Smestad, a log cabin camp just outside of Oslo. Luverne states that there were still some enemy forces to be cleaned out, and there were a few skirmishes, but he did not have to participate in any of them.

Although the 99th Battalion received some replacements during their time in battle, a majority of the men in the battalion, like Ostby, had relatives in Norway that they wanted to look up.

Still being on active duty, but a generous leave and pass policy was allowed, Luverne took his time to meet up with many of his relatives that he had never met. He met many cousins, uncles, and other relatives. He says that they were thrilled to meet a relative from America. He also met his grandfather's brother for the first time. The man's memory was impaired, but he could still be out and about. Luverne first saw him from a distance, in the pasture working with his bull. Luverne was recognized as an Ostby, even though the man suffered from memory loss. The man's son served in the Swedish underground resistance throughout the war.

At the U.S. Embassy in Oslo, Luverne was told that a man thought to be his nephew[3] was working as a conductor on the railroad. The depot was nearby, and Luverne thought that he might find the man waiting there before leaving for duty on the train's return trip. He found the man asleep like he was told he might be, and he woke him up. The man, bleary-eyed and startled awake, looked at him and said, "You must be Uncle Erick's son." Luverne said, "No, I am his grandson."

Luverne met up with many of his relatives and word about him spread quickly through the family tree. He said that he spent many weekends at their homes and was treated to much fine Norwegian cooking and Norwegian hospitality.

Luverne and the entire 99th Battalion left Oslo on October 16, 1945 and boarded the SS *Bienville* to set sail for the United States. They arrived in Boston on November 1 and they were sent to Camp Myles Standish where the battalion was demobilized on November 2. Luverne traveled to Camp McCoy, Wisconsin in December where he was discharged as a private first class one week before Christmas, 1945.

---

[3] The author possibly means Luverne's grandfather's nephew.

CHAPTER TEN

Anonymous

Among the many written reflections that have been collected from members of the 99th Infantry Battalion (Separate) are a number that had no author or name associated with them. Three of these anonymous contributions are collected in this section, with each providing a compelling and engaging account of the actions of the 99th.

Anonymous—A Close Shave

The following account of a reconnaissance patrol to find the enemy provides a frightening glimpse into a brush with death that can occur at a moment's notice. In this case, there is also a direct view into the type of heroism that defined Major Harold Hansen. He had been the original leader at the formation of the 99th and then later resumed command and was promoted to lieutenant colonel after the injury to Colonel Robert Turner.

Hansen was known for his bold and audacious actions in the face of danger—and for his dry humor. This garnered a strong following from the men and legendary status in their stories.

A coded message from "higher ups" exacted a strange order for the 99th. Col. Turner was ordered to dispatch a reconnaissance patrol consisting of two commissioned officers and two enlisted men for the purpose of establishing the exact location of the enemy!

Volunteering for the patrol was Major Hansen and his driver, an A Company commander and his radioman.

The jeep hadn't driven more than half a mile before it was stopped by combat MPs. The MPs asked: "Sir, what are you doing on this road? The Krauts are only a couple miles ahead of us!" Explaining the assignment, Major Hansen added: "We'll just mosey on down and see what happens."

In the dead of night, the jeep purred down the road, rustling up its own breeze as it went.

Lt. Col. Harold Hansen during 1945. He joined the battalion in late August 1942 as the captain selected to command the battalion. He had been promoted to major by May 1943 when Lt. Col. Turner was given the command and Hansen became his executive officer. When Turner was wounded at the battle of Elbeuf, Hansen resumed command of the battalion for the remainder of the war. (Courtesy of the 99th Educational Foundation)

None of the occupants actually heard the shell as it hurtled by, but it passed so close to the jeep that Major Hansen and the radioman felt the compressed air and the heat of the projectile.

"Stop the jeep!" yelled the major. "Let's turn around and get the hell out of here!"

The four occupants were on the roadway simultaneously. Grabbing the jeep by the rear end, Major Hansen singlehandedly lifted it off the ground and swung it into an arc sufficiently wide for a quick exit.

A parachute flare popped above, saturating the darkness with its brilliant light. The driver made good use of the illumination. Taking an opportune corner on two wheels, he charged into a grove of trees.

After a few moments of blissful quiet, Major Hansen cleared his throat, and in a hushed tone, spoke: "I suppose the Germans wanted to see if we were closely shaven. They're such sticklers for sharp military bearing, you know!"

Even as the four occupants in the jeep had sported a week's growth of whiskers, they had had as close a shave as they ever wanted!

Anonymous—Canal Drive & Würselen

In this unattributed narrative, there is a detailed accounting of the critical role that the 99th Infantry Battalion (Separate) performed in the Canal Drive of September 1944 and into October and November for the intense battle at Würselen.

In the span of just a few days, during the Canal Drive, the 99th Battalion had an estimated 40 casualties while at the same time capturing 440 German prisoners.

The writer then shifts to telling of the time spent in October as they entered Germany. Specifically, the move into Würselen that was in support of the critical pincer move to surround the Germans in Aachen and cut them off from re-supplies, which forced a surrender due to a lack of any means for a retreat. For nine days, the 99th Battalion was engaged in a nonstop period of intense foxhole fighting with little sleep, much confusion, and heroic actions.

While on the Canal Drive and moving forward with the tanks of the 66th Armored Regiment, the objectives were taken and the battalion reorganized and held strong points to meet the never-failing counterattacks. Estimated casualties for the period, by the 99th, numbered 40 enlisted men. One hundred and eleven prisoners were taken. Casualties for the operation from September 16 through 18 for the 99th were one officer killed, two officers wounded, eight enlisted men killed, 75 enlisted men wounded, and 10 enlisted men missing in action. The 10 men missing in action were later accounted for. During this same period, 440 prisoners were taken. It was at this period of the war that an officer in the armored force was heard to say, "This is the only damned infantry outfit in the world that tanks have to worry about keeping up with."

Now at this time, between September 19 and 28, the battalion's front lines were reinforced by over 300 Belgian F.I. men that proved to be invaluable to the unit because of their work behind the enemy lines, sabotage, and information obtained by them through espionage activities. They also served as guards to handle Nazi sympathizers and prisoners within their own districts. It was mainly due to the work of these Belgium F.I. men that our battalion was ready and up to the task when they brought the news that a strong enemy counterattack was reported to be forming to the battalion's direct front on the morning of September 20. However, the concentrated and accurate fire of our own 99th 81mm mortars combined with the artillery support on the right, and the British artillery on the left, discouraged the attack from the beginning and the enemy withdrew to the vicinity of Roermond. The remainder of the battalion's time on the line here consisted of activity limited to patrol classes and artillery.

On September 30 the battalion moved to a wooded area about 2 miles southeast of Eupen, Belgium. The battalion had been relieved by the 7th Armored Division. We stayed here [only] one night, and the next day we marched ahead to an area about 2 miles south of Montzen, which was near Aachen. While in this bivouac area the men got some well-earned rest, ate hot food, and tried to forget about the rain that kept falling all the while on our area which became a sea of water and mud, which to most people would have looked anything but pleasant, but to the tired soldiers of the 99th, the place almost seemed to be perfect. During this time, the men were kept busy with getting supplies up to issue, cleaned their equipment, fired new weapons, and adjusted all weapons that had malfunctioned during the previous operation.

Our rest period ended abruptly when on October 12 the battalion was attached to the XIX Corps and moved into Germany, near Marienberg. Our stay there was very short, because four days later the battalion moved up to Herzogenrath and was attached to the 30th Infantry Division. As often happened, that same day the orders came to move again. That move was to Würselen and our mission was to attack and close the gap between the XIX Corps and the VII Corps. The town of Würselen was located just outside the city of Aachen. The gap we were to close was about 600 yards. (That is the length of six football fields, and it may not seem now to be so big, but in the conditions we faced it was more like miles.) One side of the gap was held by the 30th Division and the other side was held by the 1st Division. A division consisted of many thousand men, while our 99th Battalion, at full strength, was only 1,000 officers and enlisted men. By this comparison you can start to see the task which our battalion had laid out before us. Now to add to the work assigned to us was the terrain. The terrain was very rough with many buildings. The Germans were at a tremendous advantage, because as we moved up on October 16 to attack, we faced a murderous crossfire from all the well-planned enemy positions. They had pillboxes of concrete, dug-in tanks, and so many foxholes on the commanding ground, which gave them a tremendous advantage over our advancing force, but in spite of the advantages they had, the mission for the day was accomplished and the objectives secured before nightfall. Keeping this gap open was of utmost importance to the German forces which the Allies had surrounded at Aachen, and if this gap was closed, they were all trapped. This was their last remaining escape route to Cologne.

So, after nine days and nine nights, side by side with other famous fighting units, such as the 30th Division, the 1st Division, and the 29th Division, the gap was closed. All the advantages the Germans had prepared were of little use. They fought with all they had to keep the gap from being closed and we, the Allies, fought to close it and we won. The enemy's stubborn resistance was so intense it was nigh unto impossible to get goods and water forwarded to the fighting men. Words cannot describe what these men went through for those nine days and nights. All that time lying in the cold, sticky mud of their foxholes, and under constant attack by the Germans. Sleep was virtually impossible during the period, and with the cold rain, constant shelling, lack of food and water, and the perpetual counterattacks, the growing tension was beginning to tell on even the hardiest of the soldiers. Combat exhaustion was the main cause of casualties in this mission. So, it was with great joy that the battalion accepted the news of a move to the vicinity of Henri-Chapelle, Belgium for a well-deserved rest. The final count of the battalion losses in this last mission was: five officers wounded; two officers killed; 26 enlisted men killed; 40 enlisted men wounded. Four soldiers were reported missing. One hundred and five enemy were captured.

Even now, after all these years, just the mention of "Würselen" brings back bad memories to most of the soldiers of the 99th Battalion. It is a nightmare yet to all who were there and came out of it alive. There was always a danger lurking over us because of the always-present mines put out by the Germans, and it was at Würselen that we had a medical aid man from A Company, who stepped on a Schu mine, which resulted in one of his feet blown off. This was the first casualty from this source in the battalion.

I mentioned earlier how difficult it was to get food and water up to the men on the front line. The Germans had the area completely observed both day and night and their artillery made the work of those bringing ammunition forward to the men on the line extremely difficult and dangerous. It was not a task that many would like to undertake, but someone had to do it, so it was done.

On October 24, at 1730 hours, the 99th was formally relieved by elements of the 116th and 119th Infantry of the 30th Division, and after remaining in reserve for a few more days, the 99th Battalion moved to the vicinity of Henri-Chapelle, Belgium for a well-earned rest. The city of Aachen had fallen, and the mission had been completed.

On October 30, the battalion returned again to the area 2 miles south of Montzen. Now the battalion found complete rest and [new uniforms and equipment were] given to the men, where needed. This rest was sorely needed as the nerves were frayed and morale was at a new low. It is surprising what good rest will do, because after a few days the spirit was back, and all the battalion seemed in good shape.

The 99th Infantry Battalion (Sep.) was billeted in the Henri-Chapelle area from November 1 through 25. At this time the order of the day was to get back to the usual training. That consisted of firing weapons, conditioning marches, and training films. Here again the weather was what we called "dreadful, without enemy fire." There was still that continual rain and mud to contend with. It was not the type of weather the pup tents were made for, and besides the rain the temperature was dropping with each passing day. It became a priority for each of us to get permission from a farmer to stay in one of his buildings, preferably in the hay loft above his cattle. I happened to be one who got that permission and slept very well away from the rain and mud. The farmer did, however, have rules that we had to abide by: no smoking in the building; no one was to use the barn as a toilet; we must, no matter the weather, use the always-handy "slit-trench" out back. Everyone gladly complied with his rules. The family on that farm were so kind and helpful to us. A great family.

As I said earlier the morale was again high after a few days' rest away from the front lines, and Col. Hansen wanted, without fail, to keep the morale where it was, so he ordered that the men must be paid on time. That was no easy order to fulfill, as the only place out of the rain that we had to set up our typewriters was in a rickety old shed where the farmer kept some machinery. We set up the best we could as far as getting the typewriters where we could use them, but this being November, and the days were rather dark and dreary, how were we going to be able to read all the fine print in each soldier's service record? There were no electric lights, no oil lamps, or lanterns. What to do? I don't remember now how we managed to get our hands on some ordinary wax candles. We lit the candles and maybe you remember how one could tip the candle and drip wax on the surface where you want to set the candle to provide the most light? You guessed it. We lit the candles and dripped wax on the cover of the typewriters and set the candles right there before our eyes, but that didn't warm the old shed in the least. So, we would type a little and then clap and rub our hands to get the circulation going in them. While we were struggling to fulfill the colonel's order, the youngest son of the farm family came into the shed and said, "Mama has said for you to come in the house and write." He spoke German, but with his voice and the wave of his arm toward the house, we fully understood his beautiful invitation. What a great feeling when we entered that warm house and the mother showed us into the dining room and welcomed us to use the dining room table for our typewriters. At that moment we knew there was no excuse for the men not getting paid on time. Thanks to that wonderful farm family.

Thus, the payrolls were all completed, and it was then brought to the company for each individual soldier to sign his name in the proper place in order to receive his pay on payday. Those who did not sign the payroll would not be paid until the next day. As you would guess there was no difficulty in getting their signature, and they could also see if all was correct as to insurance, allotment, bond purchases, etc. All this was kept in the individual service record, but sometimes recent changes were not entered in time for the payrolls being printed. Payday was usually always a very happy day, except when I first entered the Army and received 21 [dollars] a month. That was bad.

Anonymous—Ardennes

This account is one of the few that steps back from telling of the specific actions of the 99th to conjecture at the larger view of the European campaign and the lack of aligned planning between the Americans and the British. Specifically, it details the supply and logistical challenges due to having only one port—Cherbourg, France—available to the Allies, and the desperate need to establish a more effective supply port at Antwerp, Belgium.

The author brings that lack of aligned planning back to the hardships faced by the soldiers in the field and the window of opportunity that the delays gave to the Germans to regroup and prepare for their surge in the Ardennes known infamously as the Battle of the Bulge.

The battalion had been billeted in the Henri-Chapelle area from November 1 to 25. Although the weather had not been great, we were at least away from the constant German artillery and gunfire, which was appreciated by all. As we spent those days in the Henri-Chapelle area, we thought the war had shut down, so to speak, because of the nasty weather. We were so wrong. We had advanced so rapidly that our supply trucks could no longer keep everyone supplied, and without fuel for the vehicles there was no way to continue moving forward. Ever since the breakout from the Normandy area at St. Lô it had been a steady forward movement. With vehicles it isn't so much an aggravation, but for the infantry it was annoying to move forward to an area and get "dug in" in our foxholes. We would just get to the point of we could crawl in for some protection, and the word would come down the line for everyone to prepare to move out. This happened so often that some took the extra risk of procrastinating long enough, so they didn't get much digging done by the time the "get-ready-to-move-out-in-15-minutes" order came down. They would feel that it was little use to dig a hole that they would never get to use. If we did by chance get to stay in an area for a day or more, then some of the foxholes got to be quite comfortable, but that happened only on rare occasions. It didn't happen often for sure.

After the breakout at St. Lô our supply source (the Red Ball Express) was running day and night. This was a fleet of American trucks and American drivers hauling supplies from our only port for supply ships to land, and that was Cherbourg. The trucks were always on the road, just the drivers had to be relieved for some badly needed rest at times. The only time the trucks stopped hauling was when they would break down. This happened often enough so that there was a shortage of trucks at times. These trucks were now traveling about 250 miles from Cherbourg to the front lines. Therefore, General Eisenhower deemed it necessary that we take Antwerp. The Allies were in desperate need of a nearer port for our supply ships to land; the port of Antwerp was much closer to Great Britain, which meant quicker shipment across the channel, and it shortened the distance to the front lines by many miles. There was talk of a gasoline pipeline being constructed, but it progressed very slowly.

General Eisenhower had called a meeting of his high-ranking generals, but as usual General Montgomery did not attend. He sent one of his aides in his place. At this meeting General Eisenhower discussed the urgency of getting control of the port of Antwerp and sent word back to General Montgomery asking him to drive the Germans from the port. This meeting was in the early days of September 1944. General Montgomery was already in the northern area, and it should have been quite simple for him to concentrate on securing Antwerp, but instead he continued with what he thought was more important. It was not until November 26 that the first convoy of Allied supplies arrived and were unloaded at Antwerp. This nine-week delay by General Montgomery brought our entire Allied army to a halt because of the supply shortage, and as we see later it will cause the loss of life for hundreds of American soldiers. That delay also gave Hitler time to amass his great forces for the breakthrough at the Battle of the Bulge. If it had not been for that delay the Allies might have driven through the Ardennes area, and by so doing it would have taken away Hitler's chance of building up such a large force in the area which was so difficult to defend.

Anyway, I better not get ahead of myself and stick with our move from the Henri-Chapelle area. The stay at Henri-Chapelle had been trying in some aspects, and yet comforting to be away from the fighting for that long a period. I believe everyone was ready for the move out of the haylofts, barns, and buildings of many [types]. With the war having slowed we were all hoping for something more comfortable for the upcoming Christmas, and with our arriving at Tilff, everything certainly looked more to our liking. It was now November 25 and things were looking good.

When I say that things were looking good, I'm speaking of a cozy little village on the outskirts of the large supply center for the Allies, namely Liège, Belgium. Liège was a very important rail center, making it the ideal supply center for the Allies. The Germans thought it was a very important city too—and they wanted very much to regain control of it.

Our mission now was to serve as a reserve unit for the First Army guarding against enemy airborne attack, infiltration tactics, and guerrilla warfare. But, with winter weather having set in, the advances had slowed and most of the Allies at the front were, more or less, settled in waiting for the winter to pass and the warmer spring weather to arrive when the pressure would once again be applied to the retreating German Army.

The 99th was happy to be where we were. Now, those of us who were billeted in Tilff had the good fortune of being invited into the homes to use their baths. What a luxury to get into a bathtub again. It had been a long time coming. The battalion had a dance for the whole battalion, and a lot of civilians attended. Like old times for those who danced. Myself, I had never danced before, and then either, but I enjoyed watching all those GIs with their combat boots making that dance floor bounce. It seemed that these civilians enjoyed the evening too. Maybe they had never had a fun-loving group like the 99th Norwegians in their village before.

The battalion, [in order] to fulfill their mission in the area, were spread out in the area from Liège to near Bastogne, a distance of almost 40 miles. They were guarding sawmills, they set up roadblocks, and to fulfill their mission they were assigned to guard duty throughout the entire area. We had been alerted to the fact that the Germans were in the process of dropping spies by parachute into our area, and these spies were dressed in American uniforms. I recall having a company jeep driver take me all through the area wherever there were Company A soldiers in order to let them sign the payroll again. I only regret that I don't still have a map of the area that we traveled that day to reach all of the company, because the very next day the Germans ran over that area; that was the very beginning of the Battle of the Bulge.

A few nights earlier I was assigned to outpost guard with one other soldier, whose last name was Olson. We were sent out with a jeep as the only means of contacting the headquarters. We were told that "If anything happens in your area come in and tell us." Sure, as we stood there, who knows how many miles out we had come to man the post we were assigned; it was so dark we couldn't see each other. As often happened at night there would be planes going over from time to time. And that happened that night also. As a plane came near us it dropped flares which lit up the entire countryside. We had also heard something hit the ground with several faint thuds. That was caused by smoke bombs, because as quickly as these flares lit up the sky, these smoke bombs filled the area with smoke so thick we were unable to see 5 feet from where we were standing. We had this large tree near us, and I told Olson to stand with his back against the tree on one side and I did the same on the other side. If anyone came out of the smoke, they would not come from behind us. Well, we were lucky. No one came out of the smoke, but in the morning, we found parachutes in the trees with straw-stuffed dummies attached to them. Now if there were any enemy soldiers that came down, we do not know. It may have been just a war of nerves being carried out, but we do know that the very next time we heard of parachutes, we also heard of German soldiers behind our lines dressed in American uniforms. I never did really enjoy guard duty. I wonder why????

Another time I was an outpost guard with one other soldier, when the artillery was flying over from both the back and the front. Those big guns would fire a round and soon you would hear that swoosh, swoosh, tumbling sound pass overhead, then would come the ground-shaking explosion sound. It wasn't fun, and my guard partner said, "We can't do anything against that stuff, so I'm getting out of here." I said, "We can't leave our post until we are officially relieved." He said, "Watch me." And he was gone. Needless to say, I made it through the night safely.

Like it or not, life in the Army consisted of constant guard duty assignment, so life at Tilff, Belgium was no different. As I stated earlier, the battalion was spread over a wide area. In many cases units of A Company were assigned duties quite a distance from the rest of the battalion. They were supplied with their own kitchen, medics, and supplies. They operated as an individual unit. Usually the work was interesting; the food was also usually good as was the quarters they lived in. In other words, "it was not such a bad deal." Guarding the "enemy ammunition dumps" was a little on the hairy order, but all in all it was a good deal compared to what the battalion had been through earlier.

In the Tilff area, the battalion experienced something new in that the Germans were intent on destroying Liège, and they rained "buzz bombs" steadily day and night. Several of these buzz bombs dropped near Tilff. At night you could see the exhaust flame for miles and the steady drone of their noisy motors carried almost as far. It is hard to explain the feeling one would get when the motor noise stopped. Then the bomb would nosedive toward earth and explode upon contact. As I remember there were almost 90 of these buzz bombs that dropped on Liège in just one day. You could see the strain and fright in the eyes of the civilians as well as the soldiers. When the motor sound would reach their ears, the civilians would shout, "Robo-Robo,"[1] then they would drop down beside a building or along the curb and wait for the explosion and the concussion that followed. Then, slowly they would rise up and look around with their terror-stricken faces before leaving to return to their homes or to air raid shelters. It was not uncommon for those people to live in those air raid shelters for weeks. Many of the people had an air raid shelter dug in their backyard. It was the safest place to be, as these bombs came day and night and there was no relief from them except to stay in those shelters. On one such night a group of us soldiers huddled in one of those makeshift shelters with some timbers over us covered with dirt. As the ground shook, the dirt filtered down through the timbers over us. After quite some time all became quiet and we sat there waiting in silence when John Olson said, "Vell, I tink dat is all now, I tink dat day have left." From the other end of the shelter Sven Martinsen asked, "Are you sure about that John?" But he said it in Norwegian: "Er du sikker pa det John?" and that broke the tension, and everyone started laughing. The frightful thing about those buzz bombs was after the motor stopped, you knew it was going to hit the earth in 30 seconds or less. It would appear as [if it] were going to fly right on by when the motor would suddenly stop, and we would just hold our breath. It has been said that any place is the right place to pray, and it has certainly proved true for U.S. soldiers in war, because at times prayer seemed to be our only open door to be saved. After the heavy bombardment by the buzz bombs the German stopped the attack on Liège. Because they heard by way of the grapevine that Liège was in a state of complete ruin. This is what the Germans stated in their newscasts. As soon as they learned differently, they resumed their attack on Liège at even a faster pace than before. This stepped-up attack happened just prior to the German breakthrough in the Ardennes.

---

[1] Buzz bombs (German V-1s) were considered a robot bomb due to their self-steering feature. Robo-Robo is slang for a robot bomb.

CHAPTER ELEVEN

Stan Anderson

This section is from a letter that Stanley (Stan) A. Anderson wrote to Morten Tuftedal after one of the 99th's reunions and is dated January 3, 1991. In his opening page Stan apologizes for both his typing ability and his memory. He also wanted to give a "salute" to the medics of the 99th and the role they played during the war.

Despite the 45 years that had passed by the time Stan Anderson wrote his letter, he shares many specific incidents. Each incident provides more insight into both the daily life as well as the milestone moments for a private such as himself. This includes near-death moments and an encounter with a Malmedy Massacre witness.

As he shares in his letter, Stan was with the 99th from June 1944 after the 99th had landed at Normandy through the end of the war and the time spent in Norway. As with many of the members of the 99th, Stan was able to visit relatives and shares a few intriguing stories of the departure of the Nazi forces and leaders in Norway.

Stanley A. Anderson received the Combat Infantry Badge in October 1944.

C Company and Headquarters Company

"I Remember When…"

Some memories stay vivid after 45 years, some good, some bad, and some we don't speak of.

I came to Normandy in June and joined the Rangers. At an orientation they asked if any of us were Norwegian. I smelled a trip to Norway and joined the 99th. At the lecture we were instructed to NOT salute "in the field." In C Co. I shared a tent with Iver Johnson and "Swede" Windh was in the next tent disassembling German mines. I wondered what crazy outfit I had joined but forgave all when I tasted the better than average chow.

I remember a training problem where we had an outpost in an ancient watchtower near the beach. I was amused to see inscribed over the fireplace in Latin, "Holy Mary protect us from the fierce Northman."

I recall going through St. Lô at night with the remains of the town still burning, an eerie sight. The smell of cordite and death was everywhere. The race north with "Hell on Wheels"[1] was on.

Near Domfront we had taken a few prisoners who seemed glad to be captured. They were hungry and still in shock from our air assault. When I gave them K-rations in the rain I said in German "Bad weather!" A prisoner replied in English, "Yah, too many Lightnings and Thunderbolts!" (P-47s and P-38s)

We once bivouacked next to an all-black artillery unit and were impressed at their efficiency. They would load and fire counting cadence. When all guns fired as one, they would shout in unison, "Hitler, count yo children!"

The Canal Drive and Würselen

For a while the 99th was the connecting unit between the British and American forces. Our S2 section[2] was liaison with them; their food was poor and when their group ate with us, they wanted to join the 99th. We didn't tell them we ate C- and K-rations half the time.

Rode shotgun on several truckloads of prisoners who hoped to be sent to America, but they were cursed and spit on by the Belgians as we drove through Maastricht. The Belgians were equally hard on their own people who had collaborated. Women had their heads shaved and had to publicly apologize for their activities.

Our section had acquired a .45 Thompson for our jeep weapon. George Troseth used to borrow it for combat patrol or raids. I'm sure he could have cut many notches on it as the ammo clips were always brought back empty.

Closing the gap at Aachen was a nightmare. The enemy seemed to have an endless supply of artillery and mortar shells while we were rationed due to the extension of our supply line. After several days the shortage was corrected. I remember officers from the 30th Div. coming to our forward CP to have us watch a night display of "Time on Target" firing. We saw the flashes of the 155 and 240mm cannons. As the shells [flew] overhead the 105s and mortars cut loose. The highway out of Aachen exploded in a flash that shook the ground.

I happened to be at the battalion aid station when Col. Hansen had his wounded foot treated. He asked me to help him with his gear. We had two or three blocks to the forward CP. We wound up limping down the middle of the street while everyone else was ducking from doorway to doorway. He seemed oblivious to ongoing mortar bombardment. But that was Hansen…boy, talk about a bear with a sore paw!

---

[1] Nickname of the U.S. 2nd Armored Division.

[2] S2 was a unit's intelligence officer and gave all security clearances.

A Nazi sniper was caught behind our lines who had [just] shot one of our men. Another GI and I delivered him to a collection point near the rear CP. We had to go the distance on foot as the road was under fire. Later we asked an MP there what had become of the Nazi. "Hell," he said, "we shot him the next day."

Another bad moment for me was when I took a much-needed nap at a narrow coal-mine entrance. I awoke to see a German coal miner standing over me with a raised hatchet. I grabbed my carbine and luckily there was no shell in the chamber. In the meantime, he really quickly explained that he hadn't seen me and was chasing a runaway chicken for food. He later came back with the chicken to show me.

Malmedy: The Ardennes

I celebrated my birthday on December 15 in Tilff. I went to sleep happy as a First Army colonel had told us we were going to the beaches of France for R&R. I had a Christmas tree in my room and a touch of champagne. Later we were rudely awakened and sent to Malmedy. One of our first nights there was spent in a hydroelectric plant. There I brought rations and a blanket to a wild-eyed straggler who told of the [Malmedy] massacre. I doubt if many believed him until the ugly truth was discovered later.

Our billets were good the first few days downtown. Our section even made potato cakes on a new iron range. Col. Hansen smelled them and ate his share with butter and sugar. We were unhappy with the 30th Div. who took over our quarters and we moved to a farm overlooking the town. It was lucky for us though as our Air Force thought the town was in German hands and sent squadrons of B-26 Marauder bombers to flatten the town. The 30th Div. and local civilians suffered many casualties. It was ironic to me as I had spent the two years preceding my enlistment helping build Martin B-26 bombers.

Four of us left the Malmedy area with a load of ammo to be delivered to an ordnance dump. We also had the personal gear of our casualties on board. The ordnance non-com showed us where we should unload and proceeded to return to his warm hut. Our versatile GI [found a] helmet with [an] officer insignia and dressed down the non-com. In short order there were six men unloading our ammo and we were on our way to Tilff.

Aside from sailing home, my most happy moment was our return to Tilff. Kai Ostby and I were met by our landlady Rozy and Dr. and Madam Perant. The Perants invited us to their home for a hot bath in a real tub...and we were scroungy! Then we were served a T-bone steak dinner with French fries and apple pie. Where he got T-bone, I can't imagine. I have letters of thanks from our friends in Tilff that I treasure.

From Barneville to Regensburg with Patton

Barneville was cold and dreary. Some of us were sent to "mine and booby-trap" school which was held in a vacant beach house. The instructor had a lot of information but lacked experience. He was to show us how to breach through a wall with explosives. When his first attempt failed with grenades, he placed a German anti-tank mine against the wall and pulled the pin. We all ran out the door; the instructor dove behind a garden wall. Sgt. Jakobsen yelled, "Keep on going!" We got about 50 yards away when the entire house went sky-high. The instructor, [who had only served in the] Army rear [area] was embarrassed and almost buried in plaster and shingles. Col. Hansen was not happy with him but we thought it was hilarious.

The race into Germany with Patton was a change of pace. We were impressed with Third Army's efficiency. Our free PX rations were always on time and all there. The German people were puzzled by our "no fraternization" policy but it had the desired effect.

Shortly before the war ended we were called to a roadblock to pick up a German staff officer who believed he could keep his carload of belongings and his orderly with him. His car was shoved in the ditch and he was told to just take his musette bag. He proceeded to scream orders to his aide what to pack. The aide asked us if he would go with the colonel. We said, "No," whereupon he delivered a solid kick to the rear of the colonel, smiled at us, and said, "Danke."

VE Day: two of us came upon a farm sale disposing of homemade potato schnapps. We filled a Mermite can[3] for 50 marks. You could burn the stuff in your cigarette lighter. The timing was perfect as we got the news we were waiting for and had schnapps for the entire company. It was a good VE party.

Norway

When we landed in Norway the people lined the streets of Drammen in welcome. Kai Ostby and I visited with two little lads while our jeep was stopped and Kai tossed a nice fresh orange to the younger boy who dropped it and ran away screaming. His older brother told us the lad thought it was a grenade as he had never seen an orange before. Later when I visited my cousins in Bergen their five-year-old boy hid under the bed as he thought me a German. A Hershey candy bar made us friends however.

We drove several German staff officers to Fornebu airport on their way to the trials at Nuremberg. They had to ride unceremoniously behind the jeep in a luggage trailer. German officers had been allowed to keep their sidearms. One Navy officer spoke to me in perfect English: "Soldier, there doesn't seem to be a formal surrender of arms, would you like to have my pistol?" To this day I wonder if it was Admiral Raeder.[4]

---

[3] An insulated metal container that the Army used to bring meals in.

[4] Admiral Erich Raeder was one of Germany's top naval commanders throughout the war.

In Norway I visited an aunt who had cared for me when I was born. She is still alive in 1990 at the age of 102. I also met a cousin, Harold Hammer, who flew a Spitfire in the Norwegian wing of the RAF. He had escaped the Nazis from Bergen, trained at Little Norway[5] in Canada, and flew air support for us at both Elbeuf and Aachen.

---

[5] Little Norway was a Norwegian Army Air Service/Royal Norwegian Air Force training camp in southern Ontario during World War II.

CHAPTER TWELVE

Harold K. Hanson

As with many other members of the 99th, Harold was recruited from existing Army units into the battalion due to his Norwegian background. In his article, H. K. Hanson writes of the early days of the 99th's formation at Camp Ripley in rural Minnesota to Fort Snelling in the Twin Cities—and of the strenuous training at Camp Hale, Colorado, which caused a high turnover rate.

He recounts harrowing and humorous stories from throughout the 99th's time in Europe. This includes the time that members of the 99th were in charge of protecting (and consuming) captured liquor, as well as the incredibly difficult time during the Battle of the Bulge when temperatures plummeted and the 99th unfortunately had little of the cold weather gear that they had trained with in Colorado.

H. K. Hanson ends with an accounting of the death of the popular and well-respected Osmund Skarning during the Canal Drive—just one of many tragedies that befell soldiers during their campaign in Europe. Hanson received the Bronze Star for his service with the 99th.

H. K. Hanson had a long and productive tenure leading the 99th's veterans' group. This included organizing reunions, assembling speaker panels, publishing newsletters, and ensuring that the veterans and their families were able to maintain meaningful connections. His efforts and commitment to the 99th made him a legendary figure.

Harold K. Hanson married Crystal (Lee) in 1943 and died in 2010 at the age of 90 and is buried in Orland, South Dakota. Their son, Harlan Hanson, who was also instrumental in the 99th's veterans' group, passed away in 2018.

Corporal Harold K. Hanson Recalls the 99th Infantry Battalion[1]

I went to college for one year, and then things were tough, so I stayed out. I was going to make some money and go back to college again, and then the war came along, and I got my final notice for going into the Army on about October 16. I thought,

---

[1] First appeared in *Vesterheim*, the magazine of Vesterheim, the National Norwegian-American Museum and Folk Art School.

Harold K. Hanson and his wife Crystal Hanson at the entrance gates to Camp Ripley in Morrison County, Minnesota in 1942. Company Clerk for Company A, Harold and his son Harlan were tireless in their work with the Veterans' 99th Association. They also assisted with the creation of the 99th's Educational Foundation that took over telling the saga of the 99th. (Courtesy of the 99th Educational Foundation)

"Well, I'll be leaving before Thanksgiving," but I didn't go before Christmas, I didn't go before New Year's. Right after New Year's in 1942, I got orders to report.

I was stationed at Camp Gordon. Miles Green and I got a job of cleaning Cosmoline off weapons. These big crates of guns were packed in Cosmoline. A lieutenant came along and said, "Private Green, come along with me, we're going over here," and they marched off and I kept cleaning. Pretty soon Miles Green came back and the officer told me, "Private Hanson, come with me," and he set me down in front of a typewriter and gave me a copy of something and said, "Type me a copy of this." I hadn't typed since I was a freshman in high school, and here I was, 21 years old. So, anyhow, I went pretty slow and he said, "That's enough," and we went back, and he said, "Private Green, come with me." He got shipped off to Africa. [In Africa they needed a clerk that could type. Green got the job. Hanson never saw Green again until after the war.]

I went with the 4th Division on summer maneuvers up through North and South Carolina. Shortly after our maneuvers, I went into the orderly room to pick up a pass to go into Augusta, Georgia, and the sergeant of quarters said, "Hey, you're getting transferred," and I said, "Oh no, what outfit?" He said, "I don't know," and I said, "Where is it?" and he said, "Minnesota, someplace," and I said, "When do I leave? I'm ready to go and get out of Georgia!" And so, I got transferred.

There were eight of us that left there on the train and went up all the way to outside of Little Falls (MN), and we stopped out there in the country, and they said, "Okay, all you guys going to Camp Ripley, get out here." So, we got off with our barracks bags—we didn't have duffel bags yet, just barracks bags.[2] We could see buildings out in the distance, and we got out and started walking.

We lived in tents up there. First, we had to cut the grass down—it was knee high or better. So, Lieutenant Harold Larson said, "Well, we got to cut the grass out here," and we said, "Well, what do you mean, how are we going to cut the grass?" And he said, "Well you all got bayonets don't you? We'll chop it down." We brought up just clouds of mosquitoes, those big old Minnesota state birds. And they loved that Norwegian blood!

In the latter part of September, we got a big snowstorm and our tents collapsed from the heavy, wet snow. So, the quartermaster got a bunch of trucks out and hauled us into Fort Snelling. Think about moving from tents in the snow into Fort Snelling—those big stone buildings up there— it was like moving into a Holiday Inn—just terrific.

The training wasn't to the liking of our battalion commander. He thought that we ought to have better training facilities. And the social life was just taking the guys' minds off of training completely, because they had so many invites to go out for dinners. Our chaplain's assistant was getting all these telephone calls—they wanted so many boys to come. We kept getting complaints from the battalion commander that he couldn't train troops under those conditions, because the men wouldn't come back. About one fourth of the company would be missing for bed check at night. They would be out socializing and forget about bedtime. Our first sergeant in Company A had roll call in the morning and, when he took roll call, he had about 11 guys missing and so, talking just like they were out there, he said, "Now, you guys that are missing this morning, you had better be here tomorrow morning!" And those guys were far off enjoying themselves, not paying any attention.

All of a sudden, all of this social life ended and we got orders that we were moving out on December 17, the week before Christmas. Just about everyone had plans for Christmas. But we got on the train and didn't stop until we got to Colorado. We got off at a little shack on the railroad track—not much more than 12 by 24 [feet], just a little building—and we wondered what in the world we had gotten into now.

We had a tremendous turnover in personnel because they couldn't quite take that strenuous training in the mountains. We had a lot of guys that were 38 years and better and they would be transferred into a less strenuous service. Our major in the medics kept contacting Washington, D.C., saying, "Hey, you know you got to get these men out of here, or you're going to ruin their health, because they are all inhaling this smoke," because all of the buildings were heated with coal. The smoke

---

[2] A large cloth bag for carrying clothes, equipment, and personal items. Often called a duffle bag.

would rise up and then just settle back down into the valley. You'd cough and it would be black like tar, and then, after a while, you'd be spitting up blood with it. Just about all of us ended up in the hospital during our stay there.

Our tour of duty ended there and we shipped out of the area. Ended up in Camp Shanks, New York.

One day, they said, "All right, you guys, all those who have family, or relatives and friends in New York may go on pass tonight, and then the rest can go on pass tomorrow night." We had guys that didn't come back, and then, next morning, all passes were canceled, and we shipped out. We had to mark all of those guys that didn't come back as deserters. And all through the war, working at the dock, were those that we had marked as deserters. When they saw us loading the boats to go, they said, "Where you guys going?" and we said, "We are going to Norway." That's where they had wanted to go in the first place, but because they were labeled as deserters, they missed out on the chance. Some of them were Norwegian sailors, experienced at sea, so they were well qualified to work on the docks there with the shipping and stuff, but that's the penalty they had for not coming back when they had a pass.

We trained in Great Britain for nine months, shipping back and forth, back and forth. We first settled in a camp in England, and from there we went to Scotland, and then we went to Wales, where we lived in an old castle, just a beautiful place. The officers had one half of it and the enlisted men working in battalion headquarters had the other half.

We had it good, living in that castle, but the rest of the battalion didn't have it so good. They lived in these huts. The huts had been housing sheep for quite some time. So, the guys had to start shoveling that stuff out of there and cleaning those places up. They had those places really in great shape by the time we moved out of there, so the group of soldiers that moved in there after we left found it really nice. The guys had made up stoves and had put in flooring and doors and had it really quite comfortable. But our tour ended there and we shipped back into England, and we found out later that, all the while we were shifting around there, Hitler had been moving his forces back across the channel to correspond with our movements to resist any attempt at invading.

We ended up going to Omaha Beach, but we were there two weeks after the initial invasion. There was a fair amount of beach captured at that time, so we went in there and made a right turn and went down to Cherbourg, which was a big base for Hitler's submarines. The Germans had these tremendous caves dug into the mountains there—we called them mountains because they were more than little hills. They were massive and had stuff stored in them—everything you could imagine in the line of food supplies—even live hogs, and they hadn't had a chance to butcher them, monstrous big hogs. They had the liquor stored in there and we had guys assigned to guard it, and we always chuckled over that—having

Norwegians guard the liquor was kind of a funny situation. The guys always talked about it later. It was the best duty they ever had in the Army. Those guys would go out to guard duty with a jeep and, when they'd go home from their duty, they would load up some liquor and take it home with them. The officer in charge of the guard group had to sign for the liquor, and when we were called to move on, he had to turn it over to the British. So, a British officer came, and our American officer said, "You have to sign for this," and he said, "Okay," and never looked at what he was signing. So, we always wondered what happened to him when they found all those empty crates underneath the full crates. Somebody had to take that loss down the line, I imagine.

At Saint Lô, working at battalion headquarters, we were out there pulling guard duty like everyone else. So, I was on guard duty and all hell was breaking loose. There was a guy, a corporal just like me, and he said, "We can't do anything against this stuff," and I said, "We can't leave until we are properly relieved. If we leave, we could be court-martialed," and he said, "Watch me," and he took off. It was dark at night and the only light we had was the flashing of artillery. So, he took off and, had I turned him in, he would have been court-martialed for sure. But I thought, "Why turn him in? He wouldn't have done any good, had we gotten in trouble out there—he was too scared."

It was spooky standing out there, doing guard duty at night. If you held out your hand, you couldn't see it in front of you. I had an Army watch that had a luminous dial and it was shining clear as day, and I said, "Oh, I need to cover that over, because some German might zero in on that!" You get those feelings, you know? People ask, "You ever get hit?" and I say, "No," and they say, "Well, how close did you get, how close were the shells?" How can you tell? If they go right by you, you can't tell how close they are. One time, we were really getting shelled bad as we were coming out of this brick building. We crouched way down low and we were going along the side of this building and all of a sudden, a machine gun went off and just shattered those bricks right above our heads. And that's when you know how close those bullets are.

You get spooked out there in the pitch dark. You have those orders, "Don't leave your foxhole at night, because you are just asking to be shot." We were dug into foxholes and one guy heard this noise that sounded like somebody walking close to him, probably two people. He just kept listening and listening, and it sounded like someone talking, so he just stuck his rifle out there and fired away. The next morning there was a dead cow lying there. He had thought it was a couple of soldiers coming. But that's what they said: "If you get out of your foxhole, you are taking a chance. Somebody is going to shoot you." And it could be your own buddies, you know.

After the break from Saint Lô, we got into the Canal Drive in the Netherlands. From there, we went to Elbeuf, where we had our first really bad casualty list. Even our battalion commander was wounded and evacuated, and officers were killed.

They aimed for the command post. Colonel Turner was evacuated then, and Hansen took over again—he had us from the beginning at Camp Ripley, but he had been replaced by a higher-ranking officer in Camp Hale. Hansen got back the control of the battalion and he was a great commanding officer.

We moved on from there to Aachen, Germany, and there was another vicious battle. We had to close up the escape route for them, and I know the engineers loaded a freight car with explosives and sent it down at a rolling incline into the city. When it stopped, they rattled off with bullets and set off a big explosion, just as bad as a big bomb. It blew up everything around them—just from that one freight car, loaded with explosives, rolling down into the city.

The next battle was at Würselen. Our Company A was sent out ahead, out of their foxholes into the open area, and they were zeroed in on from all sides. The Germans got behind them, so they were cut off from the rest of the battalion, and we had guys that were gone for three, four days, working their way back. They crossed this canal—they had to crawl through waist-deep water and crawl back up the bank on the other side, trying to find cover somewhere, because they were out in the open. So, they would try to find buildings. They left real secure positions and the men wondered who in the world gave the orders for them to go out there in the open like that, because the Germans just had the place zeroed in. We had a lot of casualties and a lot of guys missing, but they showed up three or four days afterwards, so we got the company assembled.

Then it [turned into] fall and things slacked up. Everyone thought that the fighting would lighten up and just be sporadic until next spring. This was in late November and so everybody was just kind of settling in. Everyone thought that this would be time to relax and work on your equipment. So, we got to December 17 and all hell broke loose. Hitler had this big last gas attack and, had it worked the way he had planned, the results of the war would have been a lot different. But thanks to the efforts of a lot of people, they were able to stop him.

The Russians had reversed the trend on the Eastern Front. They were driving the Germans back to Germany from there, and they had been on the edge of victory in Russia, when winter set in for them there. So here we were in the same situation in the Battle of the Bulge. We had had this beautiful equipment up in Camp Hale, Colorado, in the winter training there, and here we were in warfare at the Battle of the Bulge and we weren't prepared for winter at all! We had these men running fuel to the front of the line 20 hours a day and we thought that we had everything under control. They were rushing up the fuel, but all of the supplies like winter clothing were held back. We had had the beautiful camouflage equipment when we were in the mountains in Colorado, and here we were in the war and we didn't have that. For some sort of camouflage we were confiscating sheets out of the hotels and hospitals as a way of trying to hide ourselves in the white snow. With your dark uniform, you were just a real good target.

At the Battle of the Bulge we were told that it was only going to last a couple days at the most. We were ordered, "Don't bother to pack, don't bother to pack, don't bother to pack." So, guys didn't have a razor with them, they didn't have a lot of stuff they would have had with them for what turned out to be 31 days on the line up there. It was a shabby-looking bunch of guys. Their clothes were bad. They had bad frozen feet. They hadn't been able to shave or have a bath or anything. It was a really horrible situation, but as it turned out, the German big invasion didn't work out the way that Hitler had wanted it to.

I pulled guard duty at the time of the Battle of the Bulge, and I had a guy with me, and they sent us out with a jeep. We parked in front of a building, where there was a big tree, a monstrous tree. It was pitch black, and all of a sudden, a plane came over. A little bit later, these flares just opened up, and so everything was just bright as day. Then, shortly afterwards, you hear this thud, thud, thud, thud, and it was smoke bombs. They burst and then you couldn't see anything. So I told old John, "Okay, you stand on that side with your back against the tree, and I'll stand on this side with my back against the tree, so if anybody comes upon us, we'll be ready for them. But nothing happened. The next day, we found parachutes with straw dummies hanging in the trees and we wondered then how many real soldiers they had dropped by parachute. We had German parachutists dropping behind our lines and changing the signs. If the sign would be pointing west, they would change it to point east, and if it was pointing north, they would have it pointing south.

At the Battle of the Bulge, finally, we got the Germans turned around and headed back toward Germany, and so our duties from then on were with the 2nd and 3rd Armored Divisions, working with the tanks. As the Germans were being driven back on the Western Front by us and on the Eastern Front by the Russians, we were with the 3rd Division, falling deep into Germany, when the war ended.

Everybody was out shooting rifles and machine guns into the air when they got word that the war was over. It was like a Fourth of July celebration. They were shooting tracer bullets into the air just as fast as they could…oh, it's hard to explain the feeling, you know. It's just like a big relief comes over you. You just took a big breath and you felt relieved. For a few days after the war ended, we remained in the area, where we were supposed to search for German stragglers, because their main force had been driven back. There were still stragglers in pockets left behind. We'd get those and get their weapons from them.

We got orders that we were to go to Le Havre, France, and that we were finally going to go to Norway. We got on LSTs (landing ship tanks) and went across the channel, followed the British coastline north, then cut across the southern end of Norway, and went up the Oslofjord. All the while we had the minesweepers ahead of us because the waters were heavily mined. We got into Norway and we wanted to get off the ships, but we had orders that we had to stay on one more night. We were supposed to move into Camp Smestad, but the Germans weren't out of it yet.

So, we stayed on one more night and they gave us a pass to get off the ships and to walk into Oslo a little ways. There were people greeting us. It was like getting home.

Our main thrill was that we were chosen to be part of the honor guard for King Haakon. He was celebrating his return to Norway on the exact date that he had left Norway five years earlier. There was a parade and celebrating and dancing in the streets. We were so fortunate, those of us that survived and came through, and we think of all those good buddies that are lying in graves over there. It's sad to think of the guys and how they met their last.

Osmund Skarning was in Company A where I was. Another Harold Hanson in Company A was riding on the tank with Osmund Skarning, and they had been on the tank for several days. So that morning, as they were taking off, Osmund and Harold said, "Hey, let's change sides, to get a different view for a while." They changed sides and hadn't been going far before a bullet hit a turret on the tank and ricocheted off and hit Osmund Skarning right across the stomach. He slid across the tank and his innards just gushed out. Harold Hanson jumped off and held him in his arms and Osmund said, "They got me, Hans," and those were his last words. He was gone. He was the nicest, friendliest guy, smiling all the time, and everybody missed him. He was an amazing accordion player. His dad had an all-accordion band in the Midwest and played for dances all the way through Minnesota, the Dakotas, and Wisconsin. It's sad to think about the ones that didn't make it home with us, but we have so many here and we've had such great reunions through the years.

Harold Berndt

The material was handwritten on 99th Infantry Battalion (Sep.) letterhead by Harold Berndt of the 99th's Company B. Some of the content was written in rough shorthand, so has been edited for clarity. Additionally, some of the locations have not been able to be verified.

It is not clear if Harold relied on his personal journal in these writings; he likely used a compilation of sources to create this timeline of events spanning from the formation of the 99th at Camp Ripley to the close of the war and the time spent in Norway.

His accounting of actions includes brief mentions of many momentous events. This includes the 99th being credited with capturing 1,900 enemy soldiers in the Canal Drive at a time when they had a force of 500. On another occasion, he describes being in a small unit that had gotten ahead of the front line and was into enemy territory with friendly fire coming at them. He also briefly tells of the chaotic scenes at the Battle of the Bulge where Germans were impersonating American soldiers and the 99th's medical team cared for the scarce survivors of the Malmedy Massacre.

Harold also shares short snippets regarding the 99th's role in guarding Nazi loot at the salt mines (Merkers Mine), time spent at the Siegfried Line, and their role in the successful advancements with Patton's army. He closes with a few accounts of his time in Norway before the eventual return to the United States.

Record of Events

A brief history of the 99th Infantry Battalion before overseas shipment:

10 July 42: The 99th Bn was activated at Camp Ripley, Minnesota, by special request of the President of the United States.

1 Oct 42: Unit moved to Fort Snelling, Minneapolis, Minnesota.

17 Dec 42: Unit moved to Camp Hale, Colorado, in the heart of the Rocky Mountains. Here unit received ski and mountain training. Elevation 9,000 ft.

Received honor of being reviewed by the President [Franklin D. Roosevelt] at Camp Carson, Colorado. Unit was wearing ski equipment and clothing when being reviewed.

24 Aug 43: Unit moved to Camp Shanks, New York, prior to overseas movement.

5 Sept 43: Sailed from NY on SS *Mexico*.

15 Sept 43: Arrived at Greenock, Scotland at 0300. Remained on ship till noon time following day. Then debarked and rode train through Scotland and into England. Went through Edinburgh, etc. and pulled into Tidworth. Lived in brick barracks till January 44. "Perham Downs," Wiltshire. Furlough.

20–29 Dec 43: London.

12 Jan 44: Alerted, moved to Crickhowell in Wales. Lived in Nissen huts, officers in the old castle. County Brecknockshire.

17 April 44: Alerted for departure.

29 April 44: Departed Glanusk Park via truck in the morning and arrived at Ludlow Park bivouac area. Tent life (eight men), very good food, rations, and lots of fun in Ludlow. Several passes to Hereford, including visit to the Norwegian Club. Ludlow Castle, County Shropshire.

11 June 44: Left Ludlow by rail and arrived at Uffculme, Devonshire 1330. Company spread all over the city. Room in ordnance building, soft beds, etc.

16 June 44: Left camp D-5 via truck at 1700 and arrived at transport X-3 at 1800. Liberty ship. Falmouth Harbor, England.

18 June 44:[1] Arrived Omaha Beach, Bayeux, France at 2000. Rough weather and high seas.

23 June 44: Debarked at 2200 in LCT. Stayed at transit camp all night.

24 June 44: Left Omaha Beach and rode to Colombières. Pup tents and 10 in 1 rations, cider, etc. Connected with Ranger Group HQ.

---

[1] Dates for the 99th Battalion landing on Omaha Beach varied from June 18 to June 22. The soldiers did not all land on the same day.

28 June 44: Left in trucks for St. Joseph and stayed overnight in the bivouac area.

29 June 44: St. Joseph by truck 1200 arrived Cherbourg 1330. Police of city. Assisted by 101st Airborne. Fourth Division had just pulled out. Cognac, wine, etc.

8 July 44: Left Cherbourg, arrived at Hau de Haut.

25 July 44: Left Hau de Haut,[2] arrived at Teurthe Hague,[3] German training camp. Had regular garrison life there. USO shows and all the trimmings. Also trips to Cherbourg.

7 Aug 44: Arrived at Le Mesnil-Herman.

11 Aug 44: Arrived Buais, were bombed [on the way to] Brécey, scared the dickens out of us. Lucky that they didn't strafe more.

14 Aug 44: Arrived at Barenton.

17 Aug 44:[4] Arrived Essay, traveled 50 miles.

20 Aug 44: Arrived Toureuvre.

22 Aug 44: Arrived Bois Biot.[5]

23 Aug 44: Arrived Le Failly.

24 Aug 44: Arrived Cesseville.

25 Aug 44: Arrived St. Croix de Martin 0400. Departed 1100 for Mission Elbeuf. Captured town. This was our first taste of actual combat, except for the bombing. In Elbeuf it was hot! The 88s had seven holes through our CP building before we moved out on the morning of the 26th. Quite a few casualties in the Company. Col. Turner's CP knocked out. Met Canadians when we pulled out, they would hold town. Assisted by the 28th Div. and 4th Armored.

---

[2] In both cases, the author may have meant Hameau de Haut.

[3] He is possibly talking about Teurthéville-Hague, about 8 miles from Cherbourg.

[4] Dates varied from one person to another within the 99th on specific events. This may have occurred on August 19th instead of the 17th, or the members of the 99th arrived on a range of dates.

[5] Unable to validate this location on modern maps.

26 Aug 44: Arrived back at St. Croix de Martin 1800 and bivouacked.

27 Aug 44: Pacy-sut-sure.[6]

29 Aug 44: St. Martin La Renne[7] (on Seine). Arrived there over pontoon bridge and slept in deep sit trenches dug by 79th Div. Heavy artillery fire throughout the night. Pulled out in the morning at 0630. Cold and damp. Ate breakfast [and] started on [the] mission. Rode scout car on this mission manning the .30 cal. in the rear. We had plenty to drink once we got started. Too much! Took six objectives in order. Germans had cleared out at 0530 that morning due to the heavy artillery concentrations. Had plenty of cognac and finally got lost from the company. We were in unknown territory for several hours ahead of the company with artillery going off on all sides of us. Later heard tanks but found that they were American tanks catching up to us!

30 Aug 44: Left Villers en Arthies and marched to Sailly. Stayed at big French chateau.

31 Aug 44: Arrived at Le Perchay, 14 miles.

1 Sept 44: Lost 1st Sgt. Thompson.

2 Sept 44: Arrived Arronville, 23 miles.

3 Sept 44: Arrived at Bray sur Somme. At this time gas shortages started to slow us up. 2nd Armored Division, to whom we were working, felt it badly.

5 Sept 44: La Glanerie, 72 miles.

7 Sept 44: Arrived at Mons, Belgium. What a town! Lived in a big green school. Beds, kitchens, showers. Had lots of fun in town—plenty of beer, cognac, etc. The people had been throwing flowers and fruit at us for days. Even bottles of wine—good too! Hundreds of flags greeted us everywhere. People were lined up along the roads for miles to see us pass. Also passed miles of German vehicles and armament that had been strafed by the Air Corps—Air Force Typhoons.

9 Sept 44: Left Mons and got into Valenciennes. Just as good a town as Mons. Operated patrols in all directions from here. At this time the Germans were surrendering right and left for they were cut off and had no place to go. We lived

---

[6] Pacy-sur-Eure might be more accurate.

[7] Unable to validate this as an accurate location since it is outside the region in which they were operating.

in German barracks, more or less a garrison. Town good and lots of fun. Also, big steaks—horsemeat. Spent lots of money but it was worthwhile.

11 Sept 44: Capt. Bjornstad left us to be Bn S3. Lt. Gunderson took over as CO and Lt. Svendsen as exec.

13 Sept 44: Hasselt area.

15 Sept 44: Left Hasselt area. Continued mission. Contacted the enemy at Eijsden.

16 Sept 44: Street fighting in Eijsden. Enemy snipers. Pulled out of Eysden during the morning and returned to the bivouac area in the woods. At this time, we ate and relaxed. At three in the afternoon [we] mounted trucks again and started another attack. Dismounted on the outskirts of town and pressed forward under terrific artillery and mortar fire. The boys in the apple orchard took the worst beating. Then [those of] us in the dispensary area. Finally, managed to cross thru the town and approached the wooden bridge over the Willems Canal. Bridge was under 88 fire as well as under machine-gun fire from the other side. We managed to cross the bridge, formed on the other bank, and then advanced. Around nine that night we pulled back into a defensive position.

17 Sept 44: Sunday. Arose at dawn and surprised with a machine-gun attack the first thing [that morning]. We all dove for our holes and the tanks went ahead and blasted the MG nests with 76s. Attacked all day. Suffered severe casualties. 2nd Armored Div. supported us with around 30 Sherman tanks, so we had tanks advancing every 40 feet, side by side. This gave a very strong front and intense firepower. Sniper action was bad here. Kotem was finally secured toward evening. In this attack the 99th Bn was given credit for taking 1,900 prisoners, while only 500 of our troops were used in the action. B and C Co. were on the attack. A Co was in reserve. WP shot landed next to me.[8]

18 Sept 44: Continued outpost security in Kotem and Uikhoven area. Holland was a very picturesque place. Took German prisoners in civilian clothes. CP was in Mechelen. Brick factory and Temp Bridge.

19 Sept 44: Continued outposts and motor patrols.

22 Sept 44: Moved CP to Lanklaar. School Building. Free Belgian CP was there too. Had many Nazi sympathizers in area with all hair cut off. Washed mess kits and clothes. Motor patrols continued in Stockheim.

---

[8] WP shot refers to a tracer shot that commonly used White Phosphorus as the burning element.

23 Sept 44: Patrols to Maaseik. Continued until 28 Sept 44.

28 Sept 44: Left Lanklaar, Belgium at 1800. Marched to the assembly area and got in trucks. Arrived near Eupen, uneventful. 63 miles. Stayed in heavy woods during the night. This was directly on the Belgian side of the German border.

29 Sept 44: Marched from bivouac area to Henri-Chappelle [Belgium]. Went through Herbesthal on the way. New area was on a farm. Pitched tents…and made it permanent. Here we stayed till the alert on 13 Oct 44. After a while we got the CP set up in the building, and some of us moved into the barn, which was a lot better than out in the fields—especially since there was so much rain at that time. Kitchen was set up and we lived on B-rations. Had shows in Eupen several times, movies in building near RR station. Also, Clubmobile with doughnuts, coffee, etc.

13 Oct 44: We left Henri-Chappelle late at night. Trucks were not permitted lights so several went off the road and got stuck. Arrived at Marienberg which was the first time that we were actually on German soil. This town was on the outskirts of the pillboxes of the Siegfried Line. Everything was ruined. Bivouacked here for four days. Strafed by Germans in an American plane during supper one night. CP set up in a brick building.

16 Oct 44: Pulled out and arrived at Herzogenrath in trucks. Marched to Bardenberg through a continual artillery bombardment which was directed against us. Stopped over in a factory for two hours during the worst period. Then proceeded to Würselen. Here we remained until the 24th. It was directly in the middle of the Siegfried Line and we were under continual artillery fire all the time. The result was many wounded and a large percentage of combat fatigue cases. The company CP was in one of the pillboxes. Bn CP was in town. Became messenger after the young kid was killed by the sniper. Horn, too. One major counterattack occurred during this period. Artillery stopped them, also D Co. mortars. During this time A Co. had its massacre, losing quite a good deal of the Co. Due to withdrawal of the 1st Division without proper notification. A Co. was in a gully with 88s from tanks shooting down on them from above. Company was withdrawn. Looking at the "big picture," what was actually happening at this time was this: The Bn was used as a link between the 30th Division on one side and the 1st Division on the other side, the purpose of the action being to cut across the gap that existed on the southern side of Aachen. At the time of the A Co. deal, the gap was bridged with A Co. in the middle. As a result, the 99th Inf. Bn received credit for closing the Aachen Gap.

24 Oct 44: Withdrawn from Würselen and marched to Bardenberg and bivouacked in a big house. Occasional artillery followed us while there.

30 Oct 44: Left Bardenberg and arrived at Montzen. It was nice to be back again.

30 Oct 44: Back at Montzen life was enjoyable again. Kitchen was set up between the house and the barn. We made beds in the hay and had it nice. In the coming days we enjoyed movies, haircuts, shows, etc., at Eupen and at the RR station. Doughnut wagon made several visits.

15 Nov 44: We moved to new quarters in houses again. Fixed up the place and made it comfortable. Had a three-day pass to Verviers in Belgium and had a lot of fun. Bought ice cream for the first time since we came overseas. Upon coming back, the company was alerted, and we were ready for the next move.

23 Nov 44: Left Montzen at 0800 and arrived at Tilff, Belgium several hours later. Rode in the scout car. Arrived at the old chateau on the hill and things looked fine. It was a huge place with a beautiful view. People were friendly and swell to us. B Co. had its own bar in town, and we had merry times there. Cleaned up the house and made it nice. Even had a spring bed there. The only bad element was the buzz bombs going overhead. They were aimed at Liège [Belgium] which was 5 miles away, but due to defects many landed in our area with devastating effects. It was quite a sight to watch them going over and starting to dive.

17 Dec 44: The beginning of the Battle of the Bulge. We were alerted in the afternoon but didn't know the reason why. At six an MP escort picked us up and led us to Malmedy. Never in my life have I seen such traffic—going the other way. Even First Army Headquarters in Spa was packing as we passed. At midnight we arrived in cold Malmedy. We were the first infantry to reach the town and immediate roadblocks were put up. Held these roadblocks until the 21st.

20 Dec 44: While holding the roadblocks we took several prisoners, mostly disguised as Americans. One American jeep even tried to drive through the roadblock. It was blasted. Gradually we got some 76s to back us up, but at first we were pretty weak. Prisoners of the Germans that had been shot were helped by our medical detachment. Over 100 had been shot instead of being taken to the rear. While we were holding the 30th Division was building up the front lines behind us, about 600 yards. Saw the Air Force over Houffalize knock out two German armored columns heading for Malmedy. It's a good thing they did!

20 Dec 44, continued: During the evening of the 20th we were moved back to the front lines where we had a company position about 600 yards [toward the] front. CP was in the big building. After moving in I went with [Ray] Helle to town. While there we saw artillery rain down on the roadblock we had evacuated hours before. A local attack was taking place there now. We returned to the CP where the night was spent in making preparations for the coming attack.

21 Dec 44: Signs of the enemy were discovered at three a.m. Sgt. Smyth's OP heard vehicles and was evacuated. Flares were sent up and three light German vehicles were seen with a handful of infantry. MG and 76 fire finished them shortly. Later the full weight of the attack was felt when we were attacked by a company of tanks, and one company of infantry directly in front of us. The attack lasted about seven hours, but the enemy was repulsed. By this time, we had gotten attachments from every unit around us. The company strength was approximately a thousand men. Afterwards, seven tanks that had been knocked out were examined and found to be American Sherman tanks,[9] which the Germans had captured and were using for the offensive. The German infantry also were dressed in American uniforms, with dog tags, etc. It was a nerve-shaking experience to be there for one never knew what the next one was. The American hospital across the street, which had been evacuated, was a source of food and clothing for the entire company for the coming week. We lived well. Set up a rear CP at the fork of the road. The building next door was bombed in half while I was on guard duty one night. Four civilians killed. Evidently, [they] noticed our scout car in front of the CP for we were strafed afterwards.

27 Dec 44: Went into Bn Support in Malmedy itself. Found some beautiful artillery and overhead MG fire for protection. For the first time the proximity fuse was used on our front. No Germans taken.

30 Dec 44: Occasional German air activity from Heinies.[10] During the period from the 21st to the 26th Malmedy had been bombed by Americans three times. This was due to the ever-changing positions of the front lines. *Stars and Stripes* had reported Malmedy was in the hands of the Germans several times and that seemed to be the general opinion at the time. Casualties were suffered because of the inaccurate information. The bombing power of American planes was much greater than that of the Germans.

---

[9] Some historians have argued that these tanks were actually German tanks made up to look like ones from the U.S.

[10] A derogatory term for Germans that originated during WWI. Likely in reference to a style of short haircut.

6 Jan 45: Released from Bn Support and placed in front lines at Masta, Belgium, several miles from Stavelot. This was a defensive position, with only artillery and rockets to disturb us. We had over 100 miles of wire laid covering the company front. Casualties were high due to the intense artillery concentrations. We in turn were employing the proximity fuse and found it very successful.

15 Jan 45: Stayed in this defensive position while troops around us were building up in strength and equipment. Gradually they pushed ahead and finally cleared all the land in front of us so that actually we were not the front lines anymore. This action was completed on the 15th. This was the last day of the Bulge for us. We had been on the front continuously since before Christmas. (17 Dec 44).

16 Jan 45: Packed up and prepared to leave for the rear.

18 Jan 45: Finally got started and on the way. Rode scout car with Co. HQ. We arrived back at Tilff at 1500. Instead of finding the chateau we had formerly had we found nothing but ruins, for a buzz bomb had crashed and exploded 50 feet from our building. The fortunate thing about it was that the bomb had landed just two hours after we had left the chateau for the Bulge! Had we been at the building, casualties would have been high. We fixed the place up temporarily but couldn't do much [because] it was intensely cold. As we knew we were not going to stay there long we did not bother further.

20 Jan 45: We now started our trip from Belgium back to Cherbourg in France, a trip of over 600 miles. We were sure it was for the job of invading Norway, so excitement was running high. I rode in the scout car in the back and had it nice and comfortable. The company which rode in the 40 × 8s started ahead of us. We saw a lot of the countryside which we never had time to enjoy before. It's a grand ride. Stopped in a chateau the first night, ate and went to bed. It was quite cold. Drove through Charleroi, Colombières, Valenciennes, Mons, etc.

21 Jan 45: We started out directly after a 10 in 1 breakfast. Drove all day and pulled in a camp near Rouen, France at four-thirty. Hot meals prepared by the English were waiting for us when we arrived. Reason was that we had entered the British zone. We went to town that night but did not find much of interest there. We got to know the city pretty well though.

22 Jan 45: Drove all day after an early start and arrived at Barneville on the coast of France, a little southwest of Cherbourg. It was quite a disappointment to see the place for it wasn't what we had expected—some hopes had run as high as to have

a boat waiting for us to take us to Scotland, and then to Norway. Tents had been pitched and we got to bed.

25 Jan 45: On this date Co. B, 99th Inf. Bn (Sep.) was redesignated as Co. K, 474th Inf. Regiment. We remained intact, but in a larger unit, the Bn to be known as the 99th Bn (3rd Bn). The first and second Bns were composed of the First Special Service Force (FSSF) and Rangers. We were motorized and made highly mobile, with a much greater firing power than ever before. It was presumed that we would be employed as commando troops thereafter.

26 Jan 45: We remained in Barneville, France until the 2 April 45. During this time, we were alerted several times due to activity of the Germans on Jersey and Guernsey Islands, which were only several miles from Barneville. One landing was made at Carteret with light artillery. The reorganization was taking place continually and we had much new equipment. Barneville was poor for passes, but we were within 20 miles of Cherbourg.

2 April 45: We took off for Aachen, Germany again, riding the well-known 40 × 8s. Weather was good so it was enjoyable. Saw a lot more of France so we were rather well acquainted by now.

5 April 45: Arrived at Aachen, which still consisted of a pile of rubble. Hiked through town and settled in some buildings which had not been damaged so badly. Here we waited for an assignment which came around 10 April. We were assigned to HQ, Third U.S. Army, to guard General Patton's headquarters. We visited the old hunting grounds in the Siegfried Line and found things there a lot more peaceful. Some of the old pillboxes were still standing.

11 April 45: Started for Hersfeld, Germany, crossed the Rhine near Mainz, then proceeded for Frankfurt. Then on the autobahn till we arrived at Eiterfeld. This town was a short distance from Hersfeld where Third Army HQ was located. Immediately sent out motorized patrols. From then until the end of the European war we moved with the Third Army. A few days before they moved we would go ahead and clean out the area, taking all suspicious civilians in for questioning, confiscating all weapons, cameras, etc. It was a lot of fun while it lasted. We stopped at Heroldsbach for some time, living in an old beer hall. While at Eiterfeld the Bn had the honor of guarding the gold found at Hersfeld (in a salt mine) to Frankfurt where advance SHAEF HQ was located. This shipment was worth millions of dollars and every care was taken to see that it arrived there safely. Even had air protection over the entire route. One tank for every two vehicles carrying troops.

Our last stop before the war ended was at Regensburg, on the Danube River. The company stayed at Kallmünz, a swell place. We were here when the capitulation came and immediately received alert orders. We were separated from the Third Army, and now assigned to HQ, SHAEF. We were now part of Task Force "A," with Norway as our next destination.

13 May 45: Started north from Regensburg in a motor convoy. Rode jeep with [Herbert] Leidahl. Passed through ruins everywhere, crossed the Rhine again near Karlsruhe, then proceeded into France through Metz, Verdun, Rheims, Rouen, and ended up at Camp Twenty Grand, Duclair, France.

15 May 45: In bivouac at Camp Twenty Grand, making preparations for the sea voyage. We received all new clothing and equipment, and also had all the luxuries of the rear echelon troops—for once.

29 May 45: Left Camp Twenty Grand and rode in big QM trailer trucks to Le Havre. The docks here were still in ruins so the LST had come all the way to shore and had dropped the big gate in front to let us enter the ship. Vehicles and men loaded at the same time. Boats were Navy operated and therefore clean and neat. Good food, etc.

30 May 45: Convoy formed and we set off for the Straits of Dover. Followed the coastline of France all day.

1 June 45: Sighted the coast of England, and Straits of Dover. Weather was good, seas a bit choppy.

3 June 45: Sighted the coastline of Norway late in the afternoon.

4 June 45: Arrived at Oslo after a long trip up the Oslofjord. Very beautiful scenery all the way. After the boats pulled in at the docks, we were issued passes for the evening. Boats anchored at Grønlia. Went to the center of town on a streetcar and had a nice evening. Visited the Grand Hotel, and the "Kongen."[11]

5 June 45: Landed with all vehicles and equipment and rode up to Smestad, which consisted of a group of log cabin barracks which were to be our homes for the next months. It was a beautiful camp, built by the Germans with all the comforts of home. Hot running water, heating system, small rooms for two, etc. A better-planned camp did not exist. The other two battalions went to Drammen so we had the city

---

[11] He possibly means the King of Norway.

pretty much for ourselves. Being of Norwegian extraction most of the men had the time of their lives.

7 June 45: Our Bn [served as] the Honor Guard on the arrival of the King. I have never seen such celebrations as were evident that day in all my life.

4 July 45: Another parade, this time only by Americans, to celebrate Independence Day. The best parade Norway had ever seen. Review[ed] by the King, etc.

1 Sept 45: And so it went for the rest of the trip. Task Force A and the British were assigned duties by SHAEF and [we] carried [them] out. Mostly guarding Germans and German installations. It remained quite pleasant. Everybody of Norwegian extraction had a furlough and had a chance to see the old homesteads again.

10 Oct 45: We were alerted and preparations began for the trip back to the States.

14 Oct 45: Most of our equipment was given to the Norwegians, so we had an opportunity to get rid of many things before we left.

15 Oct 45: Embarked at 1400 on the SS *Bienville*, a Navy transport. Again, we were blessed with a good ship.

17 Oct 45: Departed from Oslo, Norway at 0930, and the pier was jammed with people. I imagine it was the greatest sendoff that anybody had ever gotten. Steamed into the harbor and we were on our way. We had some Limies[12] on board so our next stop was Southampton, England.

21 Oct 45: Landed at Southampton, discharged some troops and picked up some Americans. We left after several hours and were now on the way to the United States.

1 Nov 45: Arrived at Boston early in the morning, around 4:30. It was a grand sight after 26 months overseas. Landed, had milk and doughnuts, and then started for Camp Myles Standish, about 28 miles from Boston. Here we had the famous steak dinner, and all the milk we could drink. Processing started and continued until we left for Camp Dix, New Jersey (Separation Center).

3 Nov 45: Arrived at Camp Dix at 1700, detrained, and had something to eat. Processing started again and continued until time of discharge.

6 Nov 45: Discharged from the Army at 1500 this date.

---

[12] American nickname for the British.

The following is a list of the different units that the 99th Infantry Battalion has either been assigned to or else attached to for a period of time:

Mountain Training Center
10th Light Division
V Corps
VII Corps
1st Army HQ
Ranger Group HQ
101st Airborne Div
Cherbourg CAC, ASCZ
4th Division
2nd Armored Division
XIX Corps
7th Army Group
29th Division
30th Division
12th U.S. Army Group
XVIII Corps—Airborne
Normandy Base Command
474th Inf. Regt.
CIC
3rd Army Hq.
SHAEF

CHAPTER FOURTEEN

Robert T. Bjorgum

Robert Bjorgum was drafted in 1942 and started off with basic training in Texas and Officer Training School at Fort Benning in Georgia before joining up with the 99th at Camp Hale in December 1942. His Norwegian heritage made him a natural fit for the unit and he was drawn to the group. The small rural Midwestern community that he grew up in was typical for many of the members of the 99th.

Bjorgum entered France on D-Day+16 (his third wedding anniversary) and was wounded in Elbeuf in August 1944. He returned home as a consequence of his severe injury after several months' rehabilitation in England and Wales. He was an active member of the 99th's veterans' group and was a lifelong supporter.

He received the Norwegian World War II participation medal (Deltagermedaljon) in 2011 and was approved for the French Legion of Honor Medal to be awarded posthumously. He and the others that received the Deltagermedaljon award met with the King and Queen of Norway.

Robert Bjorgum was born November 18, 1918 outside of Fergus Falls, Minnesota. He married Genevieve Doris Nelson in 1941 and spent most of his adult life in Faribault, Minnesota before passing away at the age of 94 on September 7, 2013.

Bjorgum—Part 1

This first section first appeared in Vesterheim, *the magazine of Vesterheim, the National Norwegian-American Museum and Folk Art School.*

My life started on the farm in western Minnesota near Fergus Falls. My folks were of Norwegian extraction. My grandparents had purchased the farm that I was born on. I lived there and went to country school and I went to high school in Fergus Falls. I started with The F. W. Woolworth Company in 1939. I worked for them for a while and was transferred to Valley City, North Dakota.

At that time, we were required to sign up for the draft. I signed up in 1941 and then, in the spring of 1942, Woolworth's transferred me to Fargo, North Dakota.

Capt. James Rice, Lt. Elmer Undlin, Lt. Charles Askegaard, and Lt. Robert Bjorgum of Company C pose in a Coney Island photo studio on their 12-hour pass in New York City before they boarded the SS *Mexico* to sail for Europe. They also visited the Latin Quarter nightclub that night, a Times Square nightspot competing with the famed Copacabana. For the 40 percent of the 99th Battalion who had entered the Army from the New York City area who received a pass that night, home, family, and friends were the priority. (Courtesy of the 99th Educational Foundation)

That's when I got my call from Uncle Sam. My original home was Fergus Falls and my wife was from Fergus Falls, so I asked them to transfer me to Fergus Falls so I could bring my wife to her mother. I went into the service there and went to Texas for basic training.

I spent three months in basic training, and at that time, they were sending everybody to the South Pacific. As a Minnesotan and a Norwegian, I didn't want to go to the South Pacific if I could help it. I'd rather go to the European Theater. There were three of us who felt the same way, so we figured that there must be some way to prolong our stay until they needed some help in Europe. We applied for Officer Training School and, at that time, we had to wait for about a month before we were accepted. We were sent to Fort Benning, Georgia, for Officer Training school.

This was a 90-day course, and during that time, I happened to look at our Army newspaper, called *The Stars and Stripes*, and lo and behold, there was an ad in there for people of Norwegian extraction to apply for the 99th Battalion, which was stationed in Camp Ripley, Minnesota, just a few miles from my hometown.

I thought, "That's worth a try." So, I applied to the commandant of the training camp at Fort Benning and, sure enough, when I graduated, I received my orders to report to the 99th Battalion. But by that time they had left Camp Ripley and they had gone to Fort Snelling, Minnesota, and then to Camp Hale, Colorado, for skiing and mountain training. I had done a little bit of skiing, but no real skiing like we trained for there. I had never been a mountain man by any means, being brought up in Minnesota, but here you were, right in the middle of the mountains and training with an outfit that proposed to go to Norway.

We were kind of a unique outfit. I think the best thing about the whole unit, which consisted of approximately 1,000 men, was that everybody was of Norwegian extraction or from Norway. So, we had a feeling of oneness, I think. I don't think there was anyone in the military that was as close as we were. People from all types of nationalities got together but did not feel as one unit as we did. Even amongst the officers and enlisted men, we were a close-knit unit.

Very few people knew anything about mountain and winter training. Several units had gone in to fight the Nazis, but they were not capable of sustaining themselves in that type of terrain, that type of weather, so we were an experimental group training ourselves for combat in that type of situation. One of the things the unit was trying to do was to transport people and supplies in mountainous snow country. This was something the Army had no experience in at all. We tried many different types of transportation and none of them really worked in snow. They experimented with many different types of snow vehicles and they found out that they weren't capable of handling themselves in that type of terrain. The only thing that we had that was anywhere near usable was the Snow Weasel.[1] This was quite acceptable in snow country—unless you went up a steep mountain because there was too much weight at the back of the vehicle. It tipped back when you went up a steep slope.

We did a little experimenting with dog teams and we found out that it wasn't very practical. We did a little bit of training with mule teams and found out that wasn't practical. So, we ended up working on skis. The talk was that we would be coming down through northern Norway and would come down on skis.

We went over to Europe in the fall of 1943. We were in a convoy and, at that time, we still assumed that we were going into Norway. We went into England for training and spent many months there training, especially endurance training. We had many odd jobs there. We took a ration test for ETO Headquarters and we were out for 15 days on the moors of England, experimenting and testing the different rations they would use when the unit went into France with invasion troops.

We trained in southern England for quite some time and then we were shipped over to Wales to open up a new camp. We were doing endurance training, still

---

[1] A Snow Weasel is a transport vehicle with tracks designed for use in the snow. Otherwise known as an M29 Weasel, they were created for Operation *Plough* to be used by the 1st Special Service Force.

with the impression that we were going into Norway. It didn't work out. Of course, when the invasion came on June 6, we expected to go any time, but we didn't get our call until about June 16 or 17. By that time, the invasion had proceeded and was going into France. When we did go across, we were greeted by a storm, so we had to lie off the coast of France for three days. We were worried about the nights, because we were still seeing a few German planes going over at night. We went into France and saw some of the terrible things that had happened during the invasion. The troops had been moved in and there were no casualties anymore, but we did see the wreckage. I guess we were very fortunate that we didn't have to go in on D-Day.

The wreckage was just about everything you could imagine: ships lying damaged on the shore, and trucks, equipment, and everything that you could imagine that would have been left there, damaged. They hadn't been cleaned up at all. I can remember the first night we got ashore. We had to dig foxholes. The Nazis were still sending over planes, so we were under some fire occasionally, especially at night.

We went into France and we were assigned to armored units—tank units—and some of our men had to ride the tanks to protect them, because at that time they were still experimenting with the hedgerows that are very common in Europe. The tanks were having quite a problem with them, mainly trying to climb over them—they exposed the belly of the tank, which made the tanks very susceptible to enemy fire from underneath. Tanks are not protected on their bottom that well. So, we rode the tanks and protected them. Being a separate battalion, we were assigned to many units and, wherever they needed a little help, they'd call us in.

We went down as far as Saint Lô in France and then we were called back to Cherbourg, which had just about surrendered. For the Allies it was very important that they get Cherbourg as a port of entry into the country, so they could get their supplies in for all of their troops. Cherbourg fell that day. We were not the unit to capture Cherbourg, but we went in the day after and tried to clean up, and it was there that I was sent out.

I was told to take 18 of my men from my unit to the breakwater across Cherbourg harbor. We didn't know what we were going to do out there. There is a huge breakwater 2 miles long across Cherbourg harbor. This had originally been built by Napoleon. It was about 25 feet wide and about 25 or 30 feet high in most places. It was a very solid structure, built of stone and mortar. The Nazis had built three forts on it: one on each end and one in the middle. There were two stories under water and three stories above water.

I had 18 men and was sent out there and we got hold of two Frenchmen with boats. We divided up into the two boats. The first boat headed out into the edge of the harbor, and the one that I went in went straight across the harbor. The fellow who steered this boat motioned to me to come up in the front with him—he was steering the boat from the front and stood up and looked out. He was zigzagging back and forth and he said, "There's a mine, and there's a mine." These huge mines were about 6 or 8 inches under water and, when you got close enough, you could see them. Well, we missed them all, thank goodness. But it was kind of scary for my men and me.

We got on the breakwater and we stayed there for three days. The German unit that had been on the breakwater was just taking off before we got there. The Allied forces had tried to bomb this breakwater, but the forts they had built were concrete, 10 to 12 feet thick. The bombs the Allies had were not sufficient to damage them. They'd chip off some corners, but they really didn't knock the forts down at all.

With the three forts, I had six men in each fort. I found an old bicycle out there and would ride back and forth to my three forts to check on my men. We didn't know what we were going to do out there, if something happened, but nothing did. We watched the minesweepers come in and clear the harbor, which was quite an interesting process. This, of course, had been the main submarine base for the Nazis. By that time, the town of Cherbourg was pretty well cleaned up of the Nazis and the Germans, so then we were sent into France again.

Some of our unit were guarding a tunnel and I know, after talking to some of the men who had cleared it out, they took 33 2 ½-ton truckloads of liquor out of that tunnel, which the Germans had stored in there. The tunnel was visited by many of the Allied officers of rank.

A number of men were taken out of our battalion for guarding. From what I hear, Eisenhower or Bradley had come up to some place at one of these tunnels and had asked to go in. The guard that we had from our unit had said that you had to have a permit from our chief to get in, and he wouldn't let him in, and this man was quite angry. But he did go back to one of our officers and he said, "I want that man and some of the men like him to guard me, to provide guard for our headquarters," and that's one reason why we got some of the men picked out of our unit to guard this higher officer.

We then went into France further and were used as guides and to find German units, until we finally got orders to capture the little town of Elbeuf. There were two or three units assigned to it. That was probably the first real battle that we ran into. We had had small encounters, but nothing such as we had there. I can remember walking around the corner of the building and having machine guns firing at us from the German unit that was in there.

I had light machine guns and 40mm mortars and I had those assigned out to the rifle companies. So, I was pretty much alone with my platoon sergeant and we were assigned to follow and report back to our platoon headquarters on the progress our battalion was making.

We got up to the center of Elbeuf. Most European towns have a town square with a stone fence around it, and we got up to the stone fence in the center of the square. Here stood this big Tiger tank and he saw us over the stone fence and he turned around and fired at us—one shot, and it clipped the telephone pole next to us and it was right above the fence. So, my sergeant, Johnny, from North Dakota, set up this 40mm mortar in back of this fence and aimed it by guess (he was pretty good at that) and dropped in three mortar shells and they landed all around the tank. All of a sudden, the turret of the tank popped open and three Germans jumped out and ran, and left the tank with the turret up, and when we got to it, the motor was still running. They had run for the river to get across it and away from us. They didn't know what we had and we didn't know what they had.

My next orders were to report back to battalion headquarters on progress that was being made. I had with me the company chief, his driver, and there was one other lieutenant. An artillery shell went off just about a room's distance from me, where I was sitting on the right side of the jeep. This artillery fortunately went down in a pile of rubble and exploded and threw up a huge piece of concrete and it caught me on my leg. I felt a sudden jolt but could not feel any pain. When I looked down, my foot was turned around. I knew I was down, so I said, "You'd better take me to battalion headquarters," where the medics were. We had to go up there anyway, so we started up there, and then they started dropping shells on battalion headquarters and that is where we lost our battalion commander and a couple of other officers.

So, I said, "We can't go up there," and I knew, as we had come into town, that we had seen a medical unit setting up at the edge of town. I knew it wasn't our unit, but it was a medical unit, so I said, "You'd better take me up there, because I think I'm done." So, we headed up this long grade, up to the edge of town, and pretty soon the artillery shells started falling in front of the jeep, and in back of the jeep, and in front of the jeep. There was a nice, deep ditch, about 3 feet deep, alongside of the road. I said, "We'd better stop and get in this ditch." So, my driver and my officer jumped into the ditch and I tried to climb out and I couldn't do it, so they helped me into the ditch. We sat there for 10 to 15 minutes, until the shelling stopped. They lifted me back into the jeep and took me to the medical unit, then went back to report to the battalion.

That was the final day of my experience with the 99th. I stayed there overnight and the next morning they flew me back to England. I can remember just barely flying over the treetops. They didn't dare go any higher because of the enemy airplanes. They took me to a hospital in England and I stayed there for about a week. Then they sent me over to a hospital in Wales and I was treated there. It was shortly before Christmas and I was loaded on a hospital ship and was sent back to the States.

This happened on August 26, 1944, and I was released on August 25, 1945. I spent one year, to the day, in Army hospitals. I lost most of my hamstring muscle and I had an overriding fracture, which they couldn't correct, because of the big skin graft I had on my thigh, and I had infection in there and they didn't dare to operate. I ended up with my leg three-quarters of an inch shorter than the other. I do wear a lift on my shoe to offset some of this.

The officers and men got along wonderfully together. There was, I think, in many military units, quite a difference between the officers and enlisted men, but we were one big family, really. Sure, the men obeyed our orders, no problem at all. But we were together: we ate with them, did things with them, hiked with them, and that was so surprising.

Bjorgum—Part 2

This second section consists of a writing from Bjorgum's journal, written primarily while the 99th was in England, an interval of nearly 10 months. His writings begin as the 99th is preparing to embark from New York to Scotland in August 1943. He captures the anxiousness of the soldiers not knowing what is in store for them as they traversed the Atlantic. That ocean journey aboard the S.S. Mexico *and in a convoy of other ships was just the beginning of their experiences.*

Among the various stories he shares is one about the field test conducted by the U.S. Army to determine whether American or British rations provided better sustenance. This and other stories from Bjorgum's experiences provide an insider's perspective into the tremendous logistical operation that was unfolding as the American forces were building up in anticipation of their formal entry into the European Theater.

A recurring responsibility for Bjorgum during his time in England was billeting, which consisted of the work required to plan and outfit a location so that it could be ready to receive several hundred or up to 6,000 men fresh off of boats from America. His responsibilities grew with each successful billeting exercise and included opportunities to go to new areas of England where he was met with a warm reception by the locals.

"Across the Pond"

On July 17, 2005, I ran across a series of notes I had begun to keep in the fall of 1943 when we headed across the Atlantic Ocean in World War II, not knowing where we were going to land. Of course, we all were of the opinion that we would end up in Norway, as we were the 99th Infantry Battalion (Separate) or more commonly referred to as the Norwegian Ski Troop Battalion. We were formed and trained in the mountains of Colorado for such a task.

CAMP SHANKS and NEW YORK, NEW YORK
We left Camp Hale, Colorado, on August 24, 1943, by train, having no idea what our future would be, only assuming we would end up in Norway. The train was crowded with our unit and supplies and [was] not comfortable. We ended up in Camp Shanks hoping to have a few days of rest. After we arrived, we found out all [of the] unit were eligible for 12-hour passes, one half of the unit each night for

the next two nights. I ended up the first night going with Capt. Rice, Lt. Undlin, and Lt. Askegaard. We were first interested in a good meal. Our taxi driver took us to the top nightclub called "The Latin Quarter" with good food and dancing girls. After that we made a deal with our driver to show us as much of New York as he could. He knew it well and we saw a lot of the city in 12 hours. We finally ended up in Coney Island, the large entertainment center. Here we had our picture taken at a photo center. When our 12 hours were up, and we got back to Camp Shanks, we found out plans had changed and the second half of the unit would not get their leave.

THE SS *Mexico* (A Caribbean "Banana Boat")

An overseas story must naturally begin with the ride over the blue. It was a thrilling experience for me, as I had never even seen the ocean before. To me, it didn't seem possible that there could be so much water in one place.

I left for POE (Port of Embarkation) with an advanced detail on Sept. 3, 1943, for the docks in our great New York harbor. After a ferry ride across the river, enjoying the scenery of a busy harbor, we pulled up at our docks. I might say here we saw the famous *Normandie*[2] lying on her side. To me all this was very interesting as harbors and harbor life was new to me, my experience with such being limited to some lake resorts and a rowboat in Minnesota. Quite a change I must say.

Two ships were moored to the pier where we stopped, one being quite a large liner and the other a smaller cargo ship built mainly for use in the West Indies and coastal trade. We were almost sure of going on the large one but to our disappointment that was not where we were led. She was almost dwarfed by the liner beside her.

Our cabins had been assigned to us and we spent the time looking for them and making ourselves as comfortable as possible. I had a cabin with Lt. Berg and Lt. Brevik and we were quite fortunate as it was not a bad one. The day was spent roving over the entire ship and watching her being loaded. Our duties were to arrange for routes and areas for our respective companies and supervise the loading when they came on.

That evening after trying 101 times to get permission to go ashore and found we couldn't, we played cards and watched the harbor's life. I slept late the following day as the troops were not due until afternoon. When they did come most of the day was getting them situated in their quarters and arranging the equipment so it would not be in the way. Everyone was more or less tense trying to think of what lay ahead. Maybe we would never see these good old United States again or maybe not even the other side.

---

[2] The French ship *Normandie* was seized by the U.S. and renamed USS *Lafayette*. In 1942, while being converted to a troopship, the liner caught fire and capsized onto her port side and came to rest, half submerged, on the bottom of the Hudson River.

Our destination was not known but we were quite sure it would be Scotland. The only thing we could think of that looked good was that we were drawing overseas pay but money didn't mean much there.

Before dawn the next morning we heard the tugs drawing near (September 5, 1943) and felt the ship moving. We of course got up to see it all. I'll always remember that view of the Statue of Liberty. She looked mighty good and it did something to you. How long before we saw her again? Everyone looked at the last look of land with a sad expression on his face…and not much was said.

Water, water, and more water—where did it all come from? Gosh would it seem good to see land again. Our interest was kept by watching the convoy form. Troopships, cargo ships, tankers, destroyers, and our one and only battleship. She really looks swell and we hope we could be right beside her always. Our little banana boat looked very small beside the others, but she was a sturdy and powerful little craft and she plowed right along with the rest. My first trip over the bounding main was quite an experience, [one that] I'll never forget. It does make one do a lot of serious thinking out there with nothing around you but water and plenty of it, especially as a submarine threat was quite great at that time. You think if you ever get on solid land again someone is really looking out for you. The planes that patrolled overhead look mighty comforting too.

I was waiting to get my introduction to seasickness at any time but was fortunate enough to avoid it. Seems funny how it affects people so differently. Some were sick the moment the boat started moving, some did alright until we hit rough weather, and some missed it entirely. To my belief a lot of it is due to the mind, as some were so sure they would get it even before going aboard. I had to laugh at some cases although I shouldn't have done it. The mess hall was a favorite spot for it to hit. Some would come down for a good meal, have it set before them, take a look at it, and make one streak for the door.

During the day we conducted a training program, mostly to occupy the minds of the men, and it helped pass the time. Of course, poker games flourished and the bones rolled.[3] We had a library, music, phonograph, church services, and many things for our comfort. I spent most of my spare time during the day and evening on deck. Somehow, I felt better in the fresh air and some nights I even slept out there. Blackout regulations were enforced, and I can remember the voice over the loudspeaker. ("Attention: Blackout regulations are now in effect. Close all portholes and doors leading out. There will be no smoking on deck. Repeat…")

Of course, for a bit of excitement once in a while the alarms would sound—some of them were practiced and some were not, although none of them developed into anything. A few of them were some interesting incidents though—such as the night

---

[3] Reference to playing dice.

when one of the Air Corps officers, who went over with us, was found after an alarm, sitting in a lifeboat with only his pajamas and lifebelt on.

For several days we had rough weather and it was not fun and I felt sorry for the men who were in the hold. They had to be kept off deck to prevent them from being washed overboard. It was hard trying to stay in bed without being tossed out. A lot more became sick then, too. One of the men in C Company, while on deck, had to run for the rail and lost all of his dinner plus his false teeth![4]

Once in a while the gunners would check their guns and let go a few rounds that caused us to find out what was up—and every so often a depth charge would start a few rumors flying around. Several days we had fog too and you couldn't see across the deck. I was afraid of running into another ship as they all closed up in the fog. Our position in the convoy, for most of the trip, was the "Famous Graveyard Corner"—the left rear of the convoy that seemed to be the favorite spot for submarine attacks. My only consolation was that I didn't believe they would pick on such a small ship as ours. Subs were reported in our vicinity several times, but we were fortunate to have a large covering force.

Scotland

Our first sight of land was the coast of Ireland and it really looked good. We followed that for a while and cut over to Scotland where much of the convoy broke up. We awoke in the morning in the harbor near Glasgow. I'll always remember the view we had at sunrise. The green hills, fields, buildings, and such felt like looking at a picture postcard. We unloaded after dinner onto a tug and were taken to a dock. It was interesting, our first view of a foreign land, the people, their clothes, and everything.

Several bands were there to meet us and that helped our spirits too, but soon we were on a train, our first English train. They are much smaller than ours and consist of compartments with an aisle on one side. All compartments have two doors, one on the aisle and one to the outside; quite a convenience in loading and unloading. We found out we were not to stay in Scotland but were going south for some distance as we were not due at our destination until nearly morning. We were all tired and dirty after our trip across and sick of traveling so we tried to get a bit of sleep, but the train was crowded and cold.

We were notified about 4:30 a.m. that we were soon due and had to get ready. We pulled into the station and were met by Lt. Stube who had gone across sometime before. Then a long hike to camp at Perham Downs, as it was known, which was quite nice to look at as it was an old British military school and had large brick barracks. We found out however things did not look so good inside. No equipment

---

[4] A possible reference to George Hunsby who recalls a story of this happening to him in his chapter.

except some battered bunks and such. A nearby unit had prepared a meal for us and we had our first introduction to dehydrated foods. The eggs were terrible, but we were hungry and ate them.

Our first few days were used entirely with making our quarters fit to live in and drawing and issuing equipment, and the rest of the week was spent improving the camp area. It really looked quite different at the end of that time and we were feeling a little better about the whole thing. Of course, there are a complete set of regulations and rules that had to be read, learned, and practiced by all troops new to the United Kingdom. By that time, we had our own mess halls going and drawing rations that were quite good. It wasn't long before we were ready to start our training schedule, much to our disappointment. Some time had passed since we had done any and we were not anxious to start it again. Our first weeks were devoted mostly to conducting marches and exercises and orientation and finally a review of marksmanship and basic subjects.

Some weeks passed before we could have passes and it ended up that I finally managed to get a 24-hour pass in the fourth week we were there. The enlisted men fared much better however (but more about that later); as our training advanced, we spent much of our time in night work and tactics, most of it done in training areas some distance from camp. About half the day was spent in going to and from the areas, but conditioning held a high priority still. We often made a 30-mile march in one day and ran into other problems as well. Our worst problem was rain. England seems to be blessed with an almost continuous rainfall and fog. It's cold and very disagreeable much of the time. Frankly, I don't see how anyone could get used to it but living in it all your life and not having anything else helps a lot.

About the middle of October C Company and A Company were selected to make a ration test for ETO (European Theater of Operations) headquarters. The results were to determine the proper ration and distribution for all Allied forces when the invasion of the continent began. We were trucked to one of the most desolate sections in England and I mean desolate. This was the Dartmoor Moors. These moors are the bleakest, coldest, wettest spot I have ever seen. We were there for 15 days and it rained every day and every night, not continually but off and on. There is very little vegetation except short grass resembling tundra and, on occasion, small bushes. Mostly the terrain is rolling with large swamps in all low ground and even on high ground. At any time, you are apt to step on perfectly solid-looking ground and sink to your knees or hip in the mire below. We slept, hiked, ate, and cussed in rain and mire the entire time.

We were weighed every morning, half undressed in the cold fog or mist. Our Co. was divided into groups, each group trying a different ration or combination. I was unfortunate enough to be in the group who were eating the British ration and I never have been so sick of tea, powdered mutton, and English chocolate. During this time, we were required to march at least 15 miles a day with full field pack and usually it was up in the 20s and even up to 30 miles. It was truly the roughest time of two weeks I have spent but, of course, that was the idea.

I don't know how I kept from catching pneumonia or something as I went to bed many nights soaked. It got so wet that very few days were we able to dry anything more than to wring it out. Capt. Melin and I slept together in our pup tent. We had lots of fun though, trying to sleep, eat, and doing nearly anything in those little pup tents. And we seem to have many an unfortunate incident [such as when he would touch] his head on the tent over his bed [which was] like having a hole in it when it rains.

[There was] one night I will always remember in my mind. I finally consented, after a long argument, to pitch our tent in a nice spot out of the wind, but on low ground, in fact a ditch; however the ditch had been blocked off and the water had been turned in another direction. We had a downpour during the night and the ditch washed out, suddenly leaving us lying in nearly a foot of water. If there ever was a record for tent pitching, we broke it when we moved ours that night in the rain. One day we walked nearly 30 miles to take a bath, the only time that we were able to. We were nearly as bad when we got back to our starting point as when we left. It was worth it though!

Actually, I enjoyed the whole trip, aside from being miserable, and felt better than I had at any time before. You should have seen the appetites though after getting back. They were enormous. At least it had broken the monotony of training. Up until this time we had little opportunity for amusement, except for our club room where we had a ping pong table and billiard table. The rest we provided ourselves, but we didn't have much spare time. Many of our evenings were taken up by night problems, classes and such. Of course, we had several theaters within walking distance so that helped. We had very nice quarters there too so spent much of our time sitting by the fireplace writing letters and reading. We had one dance in our officers' quarters with girls invited from the Bank of England and later some of us were invited to one of their dances. It all helped to pass the time away and to make it more agreeable.

The first part of November I received my first 48-hour pass and went to London. Lt. Rystad and I went together. It was quite a trip and we enjoyed it a lot. Our train left about 5:30 in the afternoon and we were in London by 6:45. I can remember the air raid alarm sounded—our first experience with such where it caused any concern on our part. Everyone seemed to disregard it and went on their way, so we did the same, being concerned with getting a cab more than anything. We ran for the taxi queue (which is a waiting line).

You have to get in a queue for nearly everything and people are very used to it as a matter of fact. Back home people try to beat someone or get impatient if they have to wait in line for something. We got a taxi finally and went to our rooms that we had reserved at one of the Red Cross clubs. The Red Cross had done a wonderful job over here by establishing these clubs. There are many of them in London and any large town. They provide you with beds, meals, entertainment, and such things as sightseeing tours and any information you may desire. They are almost a home overseas. Our first evening was spent at one of the nightclubs there. We were very fortunate to get a table as it is next to impossible without a reservation. Anyway, we had dinner and enjoyed ourselves as it was quite a treat for us. We went to bed quite early that night as we planned on a busy day the following day.

The next morning was spent in the stores mostly in Oxford Street and getting a few things we needed. In the afternoon we hired a cab and went sightseeing. Our driver was quite interesting, and he [showed] us a very good time, and explained to us many of the places of interest. It was quite a busy day and it so happened that it was a very foggy one. We really found out what the London fog was and frankly I didn't like it. That evening we met several more of the officers who just came in and so proceeded to see the nightlife of London.

The next morning, we were off for camp again, our first trip to London over. So, back to training again. We were of course always [going] to some school of some kind. They were having a lot of them, to get away from camp and see more of England. I finally got to go to a weapons demonstration given by an English training school. It was quite a ride down as it was some distance from Plymouth. One officer and one NCO from each company were selected to go. We went through all the methods of instruction and simplified form. It was very interesting and nearly half a day was spent in firing all types of English weapons. We also ate with them [during] the time we spent there. It consisted of a large number of British and American officers of high rank so you can imagine what a show it was.

We also had a fair opportunity to see Plymouth and its wreckage from bombing. Block after block had been leveled to street level and it really made you think a lot. I had seen the same in London but in a large city it did not appear as bad. Also, in London as soon as possible they clear the areas, including streets and sidewalks, and the areas are leveled off. In many cases flowers and vines are growing where a short time ago a building [once stood]. Many buildings are not leveled but if you could look a bit closer you could see they were unused inside, merely a skeleton standing.

Also, while near Plymouth, we spent one evening in a small coastal village named Looe. We had to walk to get there and did not get to stay very long. Anyway, we got to see another village; it's all very interesting as you never know what may turn up. Most of our training at this time was confined to tactics and we almost had too much of it. The officers had a rotation plan on passes, and also leaves, which had not started yet. So once our pass was over, we didn't have much to look forward to for some time. [Not until] the latter part of November, on what later proved to be some very interesting and much long[ed] for assignments. There were various billeting details we were called on to do. They [were] lots of work but at times you didn't mind that, if it's a change from our previous work, and a chance to be on your own more or less. Also, an opportunity to see some part of England you had not seen.

Billeting Detail

Capt. Rice was in charge and we had quite a large group of men, nearly 100 to be more explanatory. Besides Capt. Rice and myself there were Lt. Vannig, Lt. Olsen, Lt. Heald, and Lt. Trosvig. The day we were to leave, our convoy formed and of course something went wrong with one truck so I was assigned to stay behind until it could be repaired and then come alone. I was nearly two hours behind the convoy but of course could make much better time than a convoy could, so I wasn't too far behind at the end.

We went to Gloucester, which by the way is pronounced Gloster. It took some time to say that but after being corrected by quite a number of local people we finally got used to it. The idea of these details was to prepare a camp for use by incoming U.S. troops. It included furnishing everything a new unit would need until they could get operating on their own. Some of these details are explained more fully later on. As this was our first detail it was necessary to concentrate a bit more on the process of obtaining various items and services.

By the time I got in, it was growing dark and I was mainly interested in getting a place to sleep for both my men and myself and, of course, getting something to eat. The group that had gone on ahead had almost finished getting their quarters and eating, so they helped us out and it wasn't long before we were settled. Naturally we were anxious to find out a bit about Gloucester as it was a fair-size city, and we were in the mood to see a little nightlife. It was dark by the time we had changed and got ready, and we had made our beds and were ready to crawl in when we got home. We had found that preparation was always well worth the time it took.

It was only a short walk to the bus stop and we had a ride down to the center of town. From there we were hoping to find someplace to go. To be in a strange town in a blackout is quite an adventure. Most of the time the first night was spent wandering around trying to find what places were open and if we could get a little scotch and someplace where there was something going on. All the places close at 10:00 p.m. so you really have to get an early start unless you know just where to go. We found one place that was open after 10:00 and that was a canteen so we could get something to eat.

By that time we were ready to head for our barracks and get a little sleep before a hard day. It took a little time to make our way home as it was dark, and we didn't have much of an idea of our way as we had come by bus and hadn't been able to see any. After asking our way a number of times we finally made it. You know, asking an Englishman for directions to someplace can turn out to be quite a complicated discussion, and it usually is nine times out of 10. Here is a sample: "Oh, it isn't far—about a 15-minute walk. Go down to the bottom of the hill, take the second turning to the left and up that street. You take the fourth turning to the right, then you come to a roundabout. Turn left and it's about a five-minute walk from there—you can't miss it." But the trouble is you can and plenty easy. We made it though, [and] often [had] a lot of fun finding it. [We then] crawled in for a good snooze and visions of a busy day ahead.

We had plenty too. The camp was quite large and not ready for occupancy by any means. My main job was to secure beds and straw for the mattresses. I had to draw nearly 1,000 beds and after finding how many we had that were usable had to arrange for the rest through the local British authorities. Found out I had to travel some distance to get them so I planned on leaving the next morning. That evening we got an early start downtown, but I was quite tired, and after seeing a stage show nearly through to the end, I and one of the other officers went home. Anyone who can sit through one of those shows and listen to an Englishman's sense of humor surely can take anything. At least I got a good night's sleep, that meant a lot, and I was going to need more as I later found out.

I got a fairly early start from my trip the next morning and was lucky as it was a long ride and I really had a hard time finding it. First, I had to locate an English officer who gave me permission to secure them and then I had to find them. Reached the place just before noon and then after getting something to eat we started loading the two trucks. These were English beds and only amounted to three boards that lay on two horses. Just about the same as lying on the floor except you were off the floor.

I loaded over 500 on the two trucks and that was the limit. Found I had to come back with a truck the following day. We made it home and got them unloaded in time for supper, so we were sent for a full evening. Off we go for the city again, trying to make use of all the chances we had. They came very seldom while we were back at a regular camp. That night was spent in some of the pubs we knew and also in exploring for a few new ones. Guess it was about 2:00 [a.m.] before we got there but that didn't worry us.

The next morning, I went after the remainder of the beds and in the afternoon went out to locate straw to fill the mattress. I had a contact through the British office but by that time I had driven about 50 miles. Spent the rest of the day working in camp and going back after more straw. I had two trucks but had to haul three tons—I piled the bales as high as I dared and got back safely but quite late. Another evening downtown, but home early.

Another day was spent hauling straw and filling the mattress sticks and arranging them on the beds and the various barracks. That night the troops were to arrive, at least quite a number of them. We had three trains to meet at two different depots and had to get trucks from a nearby unit and have them part in a convenient way so as to facilitate loading. I had charge of the baggage on the first train so was busy. Everything went off quite smoothly and it wasn't long before we had the men in camp, eating a hot meal and in their quarters. It's quite a job to handle several hundred men who are sleeping and tired and in blackout at that.

The next train was due soon after, so we had to hurry back. Here I had charge of loading the men in the trucks and seeing that they were loaded. The last train was due just before daybreak, so we were a busy group that night, not getting a wink of sleep or even having time to think of it. So was the following day a busy one, taking care of a number of smaller jobs that we hadn't had time to do, and that night we had to meet two more trainloads, both after midnight. It was useless to go to bed and get right up again so we went downtown for a few hours getting back in time to meet the trains. They were met and we succeeded quite successfully, having things run quite smoothly.

By this time, we were getting quite tired—I [didn't] sleep for two days and two nights. I was hoping for a chance to sleep that day and a little celebration in town that night but several of the officers, including me and the majority of our men, were to go back to our camp that day. It was almost noon when we left, and after a cold ride we were at camp in time for chow and a welcome hot bath and a good night's sleep. The next day was spent cleaning our equipment and as we had a party that night, we of course prepared for that. Our parties always were successful with a good feed, the orchestra, and a good place to dance with everyone enjoying himself or at least seeming to. The next several weeks were spent in training again so we were back in the old swing again.

About that time another billeting detail came up and I was one of the officers selected again. This was a different type as all the camps [that needed to be prepared were] spread over quite an area, so one officer and about 20 men were assigned to each. My detail was near Oxford and it was the only one where I really worked hard all the time as I had to handle all the details. I had very little chance to go out except to see some of the country in my travels to procure what was needed. Our first day was spent mostly in traveling to our new location and finally our camps that were under British control. We located them and then got to work repairing our kitchen so we could have a hot supper and such. The men were very willing to work, and I had promised them a good time if they were willing to work. I spent my time looking over the work I had to do and such. It was quite a job doing all that alone as there were so many places to go and so many things to do.

I had to arrange for cots, rations, gas, mattresses, coal, and furniture and dishes. I only had one jeep and one 2 ½-ton truck so they were busy nearly every minute of the day and part of the night. I was gone most of every day, only back in time to outline the work and see how things were going. Every night I sent a truckload of men to Oxford on pass and although I never got to go in for an evening myself, I was in several times during the day. Lt. Berg had a similar place just a mile or so away, so we were fortunate in being able to combine a few of our duties to save time and driving. Our troops were due in Oxford early one morning and we had arranged for transportation to get them to camp. I was detailed to take our men back to base camp the day our troops arrived, so I got back before some of the others.

By this time, it was not far from Christmas, but our training was just the same. We planned for a big dinner and party on Christmas Eve. We were also invited to go to a party given by a neighboring unit. It was quite a success, and everyone had a good time. The following night we had our own big blow-out and it was quite successful with dinner. Of course, we had our dance with our own orchestra playing. We had the place decorated up quite a lot [for] Christmas [with] local-grown holly and such. It was quite a lonesome eve, though, as it made me think of home and our loved ones. Also, what we may have ahead of us before we could celebrate another joyous holiday. It was sort of hard to look ahead at that time when we were so uncertain. Christmas morning, I went to church and in the afternoon I left on a 24-hour pass.

This pass was spent at the home of an English family. Eleanor Barraclough had invited me; her mother and sister Hilda were down from London with Hilda's husband to be. The home known as the "cottage" was near the small village of St. Mary Bourne, a few miles from Andover. The evening was spent before the fireplace with games and conversation. It seemed quite good to sleep in a bed again and in the morning I was awakened to have hot tea delivered to my bed, which was a pleasant surprise for anyone in the Army. Of course, I had a nap after that and had breakfast about 10:00 a.m. Eleanor had gone to work in London, but Hilda, Alex, and I spent the day wandering around visiting the pub and taking a few pictures.

I left early enough to catch a bus and get into camp early. This 24 hours was a very pleasant one because it was the time to be in a home and not in the Army barracks. And so back to training. It was the same old thing—hikes, problem solving, and actual firing operations. About the middle of January, the day I had had my first leave in England approved, we were alerted to move. At first, we did not know where or what our duties would be.

Wales

After leaving our camp at Perham Down we began our train ride to our new destination. Did this mean an embarkation area? Rumor had it posted as such. No, it couldn't be. Invasion rumors were not yet floating around. We knew that we were headed for Wales. What would it be like? What were we to do there? Time alone would tell. Our train left at an early hour and we were fortunate to be in early, having the pick of the rooms, barracks, and everything we could lay our eyes on. [We were also] able to be moved by a platoon or more [at a time]. We were allowed to take our bicycles so therefore we knew it was more training. Why, we'll be worn out before we see combat.

Crossing England at a speed that varied from a crawl to a roller-coaster pace can be both interesting and dull, usually dull. That is due to the high embankments and hedges that seemed to border all English roads and rail routes. However, trying to catch a glimpse of the countryside, villages, and waving to the English girls passed the time quite fast. The rest of the time was spent trying to catch up on lost sleep, playing blackjack and poker, [which was] sometimes a costly pastime. Through many small villages we pass—past Bath, Bristol, and then darkness came. Where were we? Under the Bristol Channel? Windows were quickly closed to keep out the smoke and cinders. It's impossible to keep clean on a troop train, that's an established fact.

Light again—now we are in Wales—not much different is it? But it gradually changes. Everything seems much greener, fresher, and peaceful. You would never believe there was a war on just by passing through here. People seem more friendly; they all move and cheer and appear very happy. The countryside changes from the level "Salisbury Plains," to a rolling, cleaner, brighter view. We wind through valleys miles long that are truly beautiful. Then the skies darkened and rain was falling and we know why everyone carries an umbrella or raincoat as the suddenness of it all would never allow you to run for shelter as it may be over by the time you reached it.

We are told to get ready as we are nearing our destination. A scramble to pick up our belongings, to get your heavy pack on with helmet, rifle, gas mask, binoculars, and everyone in your way. Now we are pulling into a beautiful village. Looks good—not many Yanks here—maybe we'll have good pickings here. Wonder if we can get a pass tonight? There is a nice-looking pub (by the way a pub is an English bar or saloon). "What village is this?" we asked the conductor. Abergavenny, Wales, is what it was but every one of us had our own pronunciation of it and later we had many versions of it. Some we had best forget but an example was Aber-ca-dab. Anyway, anything that couldn't be pronounced fit quite well with the Welsh names. They are impossible.

Into company formation we go; some fun in a pouring rain but you aren't a civilian anymore so forget it. Off we go in a column of twos to align [with the] English lorries. By the way, we take one of our own trucks to England and it becomes a lorry, but to us it is still a truck. We wonder why all the drivers are there as it's nearly teatime. Oh well, they will have late tea today. By the time we are loaded the rain stops and the sun [comes] out, but the mud stays. Off we go; how far, we wonder. Soon we find out, for we go on a beautiful ride up and down hills, around curves, and through another small village. "What is this?" we ask and find out from our driver it's Crickhowell—we are soon there, they say—we go to Glanusk Park, the estate of Lord and Lady Glanusk. Boy, we're getting into royalty now and will have something to write home about for a change.

Into the ground surrounding the building—Well, well! Now we move into Nissen huts; that's what we see among the large stately trees. In case you don't know what they are, they look like a piece of huge pipe cut in half and boarded up on either end and really quite comfortable though. Say! What is that up ahead? A real, honest-to-goodness castle? Must be as big as Buckingham Palace! Looks awfully

Rolf Simonsen in front of a Nissen hut with drainage, gardening tools, and rubbish bins. Harold K. Hanson recalled what the enlisted men found on arrival at the old baronial estate called Glanusk Manor at a village called Crickhowell on the River Usk, in South Wales. "The huts had been housing sheep for quite some time. So, the guys had to start shoveling that stuff out of there and cleaning those places up. They had those places really in great shape by the time we moved out of there." (Courtesy of the 99th Educational Foundation)

old and shabby though. And what's that sticking out the doors—straw? Have they turned it into a barn? No, it's merely a storage place for the straw we are to sleep on.

We are issued a palais—that is a mattress cover or tick and we will fill them with straw in order to hit the hay at night. It takes an experienced hand though. Usually you pack it full and figure the more straw the softer, but wait until you sleep on it—or I should say try to stay on it without rolling off several times during the night. Our new home at this time didn't appeal to us as much as we first thought. This was due to a number of things. First, we were quite hungry, dirty, and tired. We had no fixtures such as beds and everything looked dirty and trash was piled up everywhere. It was raining and it was muddy and that in itself was plenty discouraging.

Secondly, this moving into such a messy spot went against the grain as we had been out on a number of billeting parties and took pride in having clean quarters, beds, and a hot meal ready for incoming troops. Why couldn't we have had such a welcome or even been permitted to send a larger detail ahead to do it for us? The rest of the day was spent trying to salvage a few pieces of furniture, getting something to sleep on and trying to start a fire with coke[5] and very little wood in one of those miniature fireplaces, and I mean trying. That's about as far as it got or anyone could get. I had been assigned a room with three other officers on the second floor of the castle. Not too bad as we had high hopes of fixing it up enough to make it livable.

Our vehicles, which had come by convoy, arrived, and we finally were able to dig out enough food to keep the cooks busy preparing it. It wasn't much but it sure hit the spot. Of course, we had to supervise the men of the company who were assigned to the Nissen huts. As usual C Company received the worst group of huts and the ones furthest away from our quarters and the orderly room. But in the Army, you take what they give you because if you complain to the right sources you may get something worse. That can be learned only by experience. Most of us slept in our clothes that night and felt better in the morning.

After a few days were spent mainly in cleaning, scrubbing, raking, shoveling, and such you could never believe such a change was possible or that anyone could leave a camp in such a mess as the former occupants did. On our third day I was given an order (a pleasant one for a change) to take two trucks down to Newport on the southern coast of Wales for lumber and supplies. I had to find a guide from a small man in a given unit nearby. I found the man who was supposed to know the exact spot. [What I later discovered was that all he knew was the] road to get started on. [Unfortunately,] I didn't find this out until we were on our way.

If there's anything that's hard to do it's to run around some of these English cities with several 2 ½-ton trucks, down streets so narrow you scrape through. Reminds me of the time I had a convoy go through a town and got caught in a narrow one-way street, the wrong way. That's the most traffic I ever tied up and had to talk fast and nice to the bobby[6] on the corner. I was enjoying this trip though as I was one of the first to get out of our new camp and see what the surrounding countryside looked like. Finally found my supplies and loaded up. Never dreamed I'd make it. Got the assistance of a crane to load it and it was so high it scraped the underside of several bridges and I came close to cutting more overhanging wires than ever before. While passing through a town everyone stopped to look at the load and shook their heads. Was I ever glad to get home that evening.

Training schedule, to our dismay, was to start two days later. So, I put in for my leave again that had been so rudely interrupted back at Tidworth. Yes, it went through

---

[5] A coal-based fuel.

[6] Nickname for a British police officer.

OK so two days later Lt. Clarence Trosvig and I took off on our long-awaited leave. We caught a ride with one of our trucks into Abergavenny and planned on a happy six days of leisure and sightseeing. We had no special schedule to follow but bought a ticket for Gloucester, having been there before and knew the pubs. Finally, [we] reached there a little after noon and got a room and proceeded to rest and take it easy. Spent that night there and decided to take off for London the following morning.

London

We arrived in London the next afternoon and our first problem was to find a room. Our first Red Cross club was full, as reservations were usually needed. Well, there are plenty of hotels and that would be better anyway. Money was of no consequences at that time. One doesn't get to London every day. The Shirley—Savoy—Barkley and the best were all tried but no luck. Finally got a lead from one of the doormen. He gave us an address of a hotel a ways out. We of course grabbed it and I think disappointed the brass-button fellow when he received our tip. Got a taxi and our bags and took off. It was quite a drive, much further than we had hoped, but we had more to do than look for a room. It was across from Hyde Park and quite an old section of London. The hotel as I said wasn't what we expected but somebody said there was a war on so we decided to be satisfied. A bath and short rest did the trick and we were ready for a full evening. Where to go? No place in particular, just take the Tube[7] to Piccadilly Circus and start out from there. No one else knows so just follow your conscience.

I think London deserves a few words from their wonderful subway system or the "tubes" as they are known there. They are so much better than New York's in my estimation. So simple, fast, and easy to get where you want to go. You never have to ask for instructions and when you do that in England you get lost for sure. It has caused quite a joke among the Yanks but let me tell you that some other time. I'm telling you about the tubes now. The tubes are quite far underground and nearly all the stations have escalators so you don't have to exert yourself. To change from one line to another is simple and any person who can read can do it easily but we are headed for Piccadilly Circus, not explaining the subway system.

Piccadilly Circus to England is what Times Square is to New York. Piccadilly is a monument and fountain now boarded up for the duration. Seven or eight streets meet there although at times I'm sure there were at least 15 or more of them. Traffic is quite busy but the sidewalks are crowded. You wouldn't think there was a war on; everybody is busy and seems quite cheerful and that is a lot when you see some of the things they have gone through. One can stand on a corner and see uniforms from every Allied country in the world in a few minutes. The streets are not too

---

[7] London subway system.

wide but wide enough. The buildings are not high but look old and shabby. The shops as a rule are small and with the exception of the larger department stores in Oxford Circus (the shopping center) seem to carry on a business from their windows as once you get inside, they seem to have very little merchandise.

We know where to get a meal though and a good one. That's at the American Red Cross Club so that's where we go. By this time we're ready for a walk in the night air and it's as dark as can be. You would never dream where you are. What to do? Keep walking until you run into someone and then back up and start again. If you haven't a torch (that's a flashlight over here) you are out of luck—surely you will run into a lamppost or step off a curb. One thing that helps is that no one sees you. But what you don't hear in a blackout. A pleasant evening could be had standing in a doorway and just listening to the sounds around you. Of course, someone else is bound to try to take your place and an MP or bobby will probably come up and stick a light in your face and find out what you are doing if anything. You grope around in the dark trying every door that has a light [coming from it] or looks like it might lead someplace.

Finally, you find a bar and that helps considerably. All of them are so full though that it's nearly impossible to get to the bar and find out that their ration is gone. So, you decide to settle for a glass of bitters (beer to you). It comes in any number of varieties—pale, mild, stout, and such—but one is just as bad as the other, so you ask for the first one that comes to your mind. Maybe we can go to the cinema and see the flicks. Over here you go to the theater to see the movie but it's all the same. No, every place is sold out and we are too late. We didn't know they started so early. The second show is over about nine. That's to get home before the tubes and buses stop running, as everything is over early now that blackout is in effect. We finally end up in the Barkley Hotel for a few drinks and then to the underground for a ride home.

In the tube stations you see a pitiful sight—hundreds of old people and children lay on the hard floors and bunks with their only belongings, a blanket and the clothes they wear. Their homes have been destroyed, parents killed, and they've lost everything.

Back at our hotel we decided to have a "spot of tea" before we go to bed and have a chat with the manager beside a warm fireplace in the lounge. And so, the day was over. The next day we again do what every serviceman longs for—sleep as long as you feel like and does it ever feel good. Another day has begun and we better get going if we are here to see London. After breakfast we feel like a walk so decide to walk downtown.

When reaching the Queen Victoria Monument we meet a professional guide and strike up a bargain to show us the city. From that time on for the rest of the day we don't say a word. But that was because we don't have a chance. Our guide put England's history from hundreds of years back into words and that makes a full day. Wish I could have had him beside me in history class. And to top it off we found out that he was an Irishman. A few of the places we visited were Westminster Abbey, Big Ben, Buckingham Palace, St. James's Palace, St. John's Cathedral, House of Parliament, and any number of famous places you have read about. That evening was spent at a movie and later at a dance at the American Red Cross Nurses' Club and so on home to bed. We were tired but having a good time.

Our next day consisted mostly of wandering around London. Spent quite a lot of time in the stores and trying to get a reservation for a table at a nightspot. But that in London is almost impossible without two weeks' advance notice. So, we had to head for our favorite, "The Barkley," but tonight we ventured further than the bar. Had supper with two American nurses who were also there. What a pleasure to talk with American girls again. Almost took you home but not quite. After arguing with everyone including all the waiters, the headwaiter, and the manager, we got into the ballroom. Seems like every time you sit down, they slap a cover charge and about three or four others and [then they ask you] to tip if you have to order something. And to dance is a problem. I never saw a dance floor over there that was large enough for three couples. Yet you never saw less than 15 couples on it. And so [we decided to head back] home before the tubes stop for the night.

The next day was Sunday and a good morning for sleep. On reaching the street that day we were properly stopped by an Englishman who asked us what we thought of the air raid last night. I asked him what raid and he showed me the paper telling about quite a number of Nazi planes shot down over us. Seems as if all the anti-aircraft guns all around us had been doing quite a lot of shooting and even the streets were littered with shell fragments. And we both had slept right through it all. My first air raid, and [there was nothing] to it. Little did I know that months later I was to hear the terrible sound of planes droning overhead and the terrifying sound of bombs whistling down to their target.

The afternoon was spent sightseeing, taking pictures, and visiting the ice skating pavilion, the only one in London that we could find. Also spent some time at the Red Cross and then a movie we had wanted to see. We left the next morning for Newport and planned on spending the night there, but no luck as not a room in town was available. So, what could we do but catch a bus to Abergavenny and stay at our favorite—the Dugel Hotel. We slept late the next morning, covered the town, took pictures, and planned on staying there for the evening as we weren't due until midnight. However, we met one of the officers and he informed me I was to leave the next morning for central England on a billeting party. I had lots to do then before I could leave so decided to ride back with him. It was swell to get some good food again. The only good meal we had since we left was the one we had in the Red Cross Club in London. Little then did I realize that I was leaving the next morning on one of my most pleasant assignments in England.

On to Leek

The following morning, we took off for our new duties. The men were all looking forward to these billeting details as they meant seeing new areas, freedom from the training schedule, and a chance for a few evening passes to explore the villages, pubs, and meet a few girls. Our hopes were always on these trips to get to someplace where the Yanks had not covered. And this time we connected.

Our orders were simple and we were more or less on our own, from supervision of the higher ranking officers. The detail consisted of Capt. H. C. Melin and a select group of 30 men from my platoon and the 4th. We had 2 ½-ton trucks and Melin and I a Jeep apiece. The drive was about 150 miles and that in England is a long way. The camp we were going to was near Leek and that's as much as we had to go on. It was rather interesting however to find these camps and decide yourself what work had to be done, including possession of the camp, lights, water, barracks, beds, mattresses, blankets, coal, wood, food, and supplies for the new unit to get a start on. Also post office facilities, vehicles, and meeting of the unit at the train, providing transportation of the unit to the camp, and also 101 minor details. Really quite a job when you don't have anything to go on.

We arrived in the middle of the afternoon and found quite a nice set up. A new camp under construction with only the part we were to get ready finished. We were also quite fortunate to find a small group of Signal Corps men there and obtained quite a store of information from them. Our work sized up for the next day, and [after having] a little something to eat, we were ready to explore the village of Leek. What a town—close by, plenty of pubs, no American troops, transportation, and no Military Police or anything to worry about. We were on our own. That evening was spent finding out what we had to look forward to during our stay there. And that was all we could ask for, an initial paradise after what we had seen on other details. Home late, and everyone happy.

However, we had lots of work to do the next day. No reveille either, another blessing. From that day on we had no trouble getting our work done as the men were so pleased with the prospects; all you had to say is "no work, no pass," and you could have had a week's work done each day. In fact, we accomplished the first day what we had planned for two days. Barracks became shining as if by magic, a truly surprising operation. The largest job was contacting the different British officers to arrange for many of the articles and services we needed and that requires the patience that very few men can find in a lifetime. You start out with good intentions and call on your man early in the morning before he is busy, only to find he doesn't come to work until about 9:00 [a.m.]. Well, you decided to come back in the forenoon only to find out he is out for the morning and won't be in until 12:00. Now that's lunchtime so you will [come back] at 1:00 only to find they have their lunch from 1:00 until 2:00. Well, you start working on something else and trying to go down about 4:00. He must have some work that keeps him in—uh oh, you forgot about teatime again. By this time, you decide to leave it until tomorrow. That is plenty discouraging when you drive 40 to 50 miles to see someone. I went down to a village some 50 miles away that day to draw supplies and get back about dark. Couldn't draw everything so that meant a trip back. Some fun. And we expected our troops to arrive in a few days.

That evening was spent in town and at a dance there. Now there was a dance every night and you'd never believe it to have a few Americans walk in, not an everyday occurrence there. It was an unusual experience to step in the door and to watch the girls on the sideline edge around and finally you would have a circle around you, all hoping they would be the ones asked to dance. And I might add that the word "unusual" does not cover it at all. If you were slow in selecting a partner the girls would soon take it in their own hands to ask you. In fact, it was the opposite of all dances we had been to since we received our greetings from Uncle Sam. Army dances have always been a ratio of 15 men to one girl but here was exactly the opposite. You would plan a dance with some good dancer but before you finished you danced with them all. They cut in every few steps. There was truly a manpower shortage and these girls were starved for male company, especially Yanks. And if you never danced to the majority of British orchestras, you have never missed anything. No life at all but strictly monotony.

The next day we went to our base headquarters to inquire about a number of problems and such; as it was over 70 miles, most of the day was gone. And if you can find anything colder than riding all day in England in an open jeep I'd like to know what it is. Capt. Melin that day became sick and after supper I persuaded him to be taken to the hospital. There was no American hospital within 100 miles so took him to a British hospital in Leek. The nurses were so thrilled over having a patient and especially a Yank that I had to hurry out before they had me in bed too. I had all the work to handle now so didn't dare stay. Found out that Herb was not seriously ill, so I decided to get some wood and after that was accomplished went down for a drink.

Capt. Bjornstad came up for the evening so I took him down to see Capt. Melin and then to our favorite pub. A pub in England is more of a social spot than a place to get as much to drink as you can. The older people drop in for their daily beer or whiskey and spend the rest of the evening talking. We got in the circle and had a wonderful time. Everyone had to buy us a drink and at one time I had seven shots of scotch in front of me. That's English hospitality. I was invited to more things that evening than in the rest of the time I spent in England. As an example, at least six couples invited me up for dinner, was invited to the Golf Club, tennis tournament, and even some of the large factories in that area. One of the old men when he found out we couldn't get eggs ran home and brought us each one. And by the way, they were rationed one egg per person per month! I think he had a few chickens someplace. It really was an enjoyable evening though.

It's a good thing they closed when they did or the stool I had wouldn't have been enough to hold me. By the way, I passed out several packages of cigarettes that night. Even one old lady (she was 72) had to have a smoke with me. They all like our cigarettes very much; it's easy to understand after smoking a few of theirs. After that we went up for a few dances and then home. The following day was spent in making a trip for additional supplies and working around the camp. Much of our work was done by telephone and the English phone system is terrible now. However, a military call went through much faster. Much of the time was spent keeping in contact with the RTO (Rail Transportation Office) to be sure as to when our troops would arrive and arrange for transportation from the stations to the camp. It was a movement that had to be timed exactly and must follow that timing also.

Capt. Melin was released from the hospital the following day after he had argued himself almost to exhaustion and I had stated to the doctors and nurses that I absolutely needed him. I believe the nurses would have kept him there yet if he wouldn't have [left] that day. We had to promise however to drop in to see them and accept an invitation to a party they were going to have. Our work at camp now was almost finished and several days later our troops arrived. They were several days late but that didn't bother us a bit. I met our transportation and had them parked so we could unload the train and have the men in trucks in 10 minutes. This is a fact that takes lots of planning and some efficient help. Remember this was done under strict blackout conditions. The troop trains usually arrive from midnight to daylight. Everything went quite smoothly and we had our troops in warm quarters and had a hot meal ready for them.

The following day we sent most of our men home, keeping only a few. Up to this time I had been in charge of all supplies, had a new camp capable of holding 6,000 men, and thousands of dollars' worth of supplies under my name. I can be fortunate there was no slip up or I'd be paying Uncle Sam for the rest of my life and then some. I lost no time in signing it over to the new unit commander. The following day I was to take our new CO to Army Headquarters in Bristol, a drive of 175 miles. Upon our arrival we found out that they were not assigned to First Army but to VIII Corps, so our trip was a wasted one. We stayed there overnight and then left for camp headquarters at Kidderminster the following day.

After our business there was accomplished, we were on our way home. A relief it was to get away from the brass one finds at any such place as we had been. [Once] this was over with, we were supposed to be on our way home, but base headquarters had not been able to get the requisition for vehicles through so we waited several days. It was a pleasant wait however as we assigned all our duties over to the new unit and took life easy. When we did get our requisition through we used an extra day getting these vehicles, and the following day, took off for our base camp. By that time we were getting very anxious to get back as we had overstayed our expected absence by some time.

I had not been on duty since early January, that is, on a regular training schedule. It was really a vacation for me but expected now to settle down for a little work again. In fact, I had seen very little of our new home in the castle. The second day I was back I received the surprising news that I was to go on another billeting detail—truly surprising! All the officers wanted to go, and they were split up quite early, but here I was to go on my fourth one. This was to be a longer one with four officers and approximately 100 enlisted men. The location was not so good, but we were glad to go anyway. It was near our first camp.

We took off the following morning and reached our location that evening. After quite a lot of running around we found the area and took stock of our task that confronted us. The following day we went to Tidworth and Andover to draw rations and arrange for supplies. That was a job that took all day and [we] stayed home that evening. The following day we worked in the camp and spent the evening out. We found a suitable pub and thoroughly enjoyed ourselves. Capt. Melin won a chicken in a raffle and it caused quite a lot of enjoyment. The following day we worked in the camp area. I was to make another trip for supplies but at noon we were notified that Army Headquarters had made a mistake and we weren't supposed to be there at all. Quite a disappointment but at least we had a few days of pleasure. Next morning, we were off for home again.

And on to Normandy…

These incidents were nearly as stated. Remember though that I am recalling them entirely from memory and [it] is nearly a year later. A great many things happened since that time in England and Wales.

CHAPTER FIFTEEN

Norris J. Gustafson

Norris Gustafson wrote this recollection of his time at Camp Hale, Colorado, and in Wales, United Kingdom on 99th Infantry Battalion (Sep.) stationery on July 28, 1986. Before he told his story, he wrote the following: "Dear Kjell.[1] Dee is out visiting relatives in the country today so thought I'd reflect some. Stensby had told me that if he did undertake the task of writing about the outfit, he would like to inject humorous incidents into it. His call for help in this regard went unheeded. I failed also to help in this regard."

Gustafson's stories reveal the lively side of the 99th. The men and Norwegians of the 99th developed a reputation for alcohol consumption to go along with the many heroic acts on the battlefield. Gustafson was in the 99th's Company B and received the Combat Infantry Badge as well as a Purple Heart.

Gustafson was born in December 1919 and passed away at the age of 74 in December 1993. He is buried at Fort Snelling National Cemetery in Minneapolis, Minnesota. He was married to Delores Elsie Witte Gustafson.

Recollections: Camp Hale

For those of us who went to Camp Hale on the advanced party in Dec. 42; it was a long wait in the train depot before we got on our way. Gus Weberg and I noticed a Tavern neon sign flickering across the street from the depot and after several quick trips to the Tavern, we boarded the train. On the train we had a real jovial porter whom we talked into getting us a bottle several times when the train stopped. Needless to say, when we arrived at Camp Hale, we were feeling no pain and as they poured us off the train we fell into the arms of the 10th Div. welcoming party headed by a colonel. We were billeted with the 87th Inf. and the next day some of us were put on a detail where we were given long iron bars to remove wooden blocks from around jeep wheels so they could be unloaded from flatcars. Not realizing we were at a much higher altitude, and not knowing how it would affect us, we thought that the reason the work was so difficult and we tired so quickly was because of the booze

---

[1] He is probably referring to Kjell Nilsen.

we had gotten from the porter on the train. As we walked to the barracks that evening, we were much relieved when a fellow worker from the 87th explained that we were in high altitude and it would take some time to adjust to it.

Some of us do not want to take out GI insurance and have approximately $6.00 taken out of our pay while we were still relatively safe in the States, so in order to convince us, we had to attend many evening lectures on the matter. Many finally signed up as it was interfering with our beer drinking at the 99th Post Exchange. We would have to stand in a long line to get a bottle of beer after which we would gather around the jukebox which had a few Norwegian tunes on it, and under the direction of Einar Eliassen we would break out in song.

At times, when beer was reported to be in short supply, 99ers would be posted outside

99th soldiers ascend a mounting trail above Camp Hale's 9,300-foot elevation, with Mt. Elbert (14,440 ft.) and Mt. Massive (14,439 ft.) in the background. The Camp was built in a valley and all the training areas were uphill. Week-long 50-mile hikes were part of the grueling training program in 1943. (Courtesy of the Minnesota Military and Veterans Museum)

of the PX to keep persons from other units out, and needless to say, this resulted in an occasional fray with members of the 10th Division.

No one liked to stand in line to get a beer so when it was discovered that a case of beer could be obtained by writing: PLEASE GIVE BEARER ONE CASE OF BEER and signing an officer's name to it, we were delighted. In B Co. this beer was drunk in the long cadre room second floor of 3rd and 4th Platoon barracks. All went well but we were a little worried when we were standing at our last inspection at Camp Hale before going overseas. There was an entrance to the attic in this room and we had thrown many not-quite-empty bottles up there. As we waited for the inspecting officer, beer began leaking through the ceiling.

Fortunately, the inspecting officer wore dark glasses and barely stuck one foot in the door, spun around, and left.

Weekend passes from Camp Hale were eagerly looked forward to and many of us looked forward to going to Grand Junction on the train which would stop just up the mountain side alongside camp. There were only two hotels in town so getting a room could be a problem but in our group the problem was solved by having one person jump off the train and run like mad to a hotel and get us registered. After a few drinks and a meal in town, many of us wound up at a large dance hall on the outskirts.

On Sunday afternoon, before getting on the train for the return trip, we would stock up on bread and sausage to enjoy on the train. We weren't always all sober on the return trip but we were straight as we entered camp which, on one occasion, I was in my stocking feet, my shoes having been thrown out the train window.

On one weekend I was kept from going to Grand Junction. My roommates nailed my shoes to the floor and lightly sewed my pant legs together. This made me late for reveille. Einar Eliiassen enjoyed reporting the absent and I was made Charge of Quarters[2] over the weekend.

Going on pass to Leadville was asking for trouble. The town was seething with Military Police and many places were off limits. One time, several of us went there and two MPs seemed to follow us everywhere we went. With most everything off limits, we soon became disgusted, bought a bottle to take back to camp, and decided to try and find a place where we could get a hamburger first. We finally went into a place where there was no off-limits sign in the front window or if there was we didn't see it. We entered and were told the restaurant was in the rear. We no more than got there when the MPs entered and told us we were in an off-limits establishment. We argued to no avail. Eliassen had handed our bottle to a civilian and asked him to hold it till one of us came back. Eliassen, then speaking Norwegian, told me that as they started to load us in the wagon he and the others would make a fuss at which time I was to escape, work my way back, and get the bottle. I did escape, dodged in between cars with an MP firing his pistol over my head. I returned to the Tavern but could not find the gentleman to whom we had entrusted our bottle. The others who had spent the night in jail were quite displeased when they finally came back and found I had been unsuccessful in recovering the bottle of booze.

A story long and probably yet remembered in Leadville is when a robust group from Co. C of the 99th, enjoying themselves in the Silver Dollar Bar, got tired of being annoyed by the MPs, rose up, and threw the MPs out the plate-glass window. I visited Leadville's Silver Dollar Bar several times in the '50s and when they found

---

[2] This is when an enlisted man is ordered to handle administrative matters in a unit especially after duty hours.

out I had been a member of the 99th, I was a hero and couldn't buy a drink then or anytime later when I came in, even though as I explained, I was not in C Co.

***

While at Camp Hale, we were convoyed down to Camp Carson at Colorado Springs to a parade for President Roosevelt. We set up our two-man mountain tents on a flat area in camp and we were given passes into Colorado Springs.

We were not accustomed to the 12:00 curfew so on the second night in town my buddy and I decided to go back to camp. We were waiting on a corner for a bus which seemed long in coming so being right by a coffee shop we decided to have a cup. Just as we started to drink our coffee two MPs came in and told us we were violating curfew. We refused to go until we finished our coffee. They were back minutes later with help and we were taken to the Colorado Springs Jail where lo and behold a good many other 99ers occupied cells. We learned that they would soon truck us back to Carson and turn us over to our battalion commander. If this happened, we felt we may be privates again soon!! We all had these mountain knives. Our plan was that we would cut the canvas and as soon as the MP wagon stopped for any reason we'd be gone. The truck didn't stop until we got into camp. It was a dark night and before the truck was completely stopped, we were on our way (having already cut the canvas) and the MPs had no one to turn over to Col. Hansen.

I remember another fellow who didn't want to go to town and get in trouble, so he stayed in camp and someone brought him a bottle. He got drunk in his tent and set his hair on fire, lighting a cigarette.

***

Wales

At Glanusk Park in Wales, several 99ers bought bicycles. When you went to town to a bar, often after only one drink, they would hang up a "Spirits Off" sign, which meant they had sold all they could that day. It was found that if you had a bicycle, you could ride out to a pub in the country and drink [for a] much longer period, [but] we found it was not easy to ride a bike after drinking, and as a result many injuries were sustained to body and bike on the return to camp.

Norwegians have their priorities: recall dances at Glanusk Castle when Lt. Knutson brought girls in from town to dance. The girls sat around while most 99ers just hung around the beer keg.

CHAPTER SIXTEEN

Melvin C. Hammerstrom

This section contains a letter that Melvin "Sarge" Hammerstrom sent to Yngvar Stensby for Stensby's proposed book manuscript. The letter was written February 4, 1986 and was written on 99th Infantry Battalion (Separate) stationery.

His writing is focused on specific aspects of the early battle in and around Elbeuf, France. This was the scene of the 99th Battalion's first real action and was a test of their skills and preparation.

Hammerstrom was born in August 1912 and grew up in Glencoe, Minnesota. Hammerstrom met his wife at Fort Snelling in 1939 and they corresponded and courted during the war years. On November 1, 1945, Louise Caroline Hoppe married Melvin Hammerstrom at Presbyterian Church in Moorhead, Minnesota.

Sarge Hammerstrom made a career in the military, and through various moves, transfers, and promotions, they were stationed at Fort Bennington, Georgia (one year), Fort Jackson, South Carolina (three years), Berlin, Germany (three years), and various posts throughout Germany and Fort Leonard Wood, Missouri (two years). Sarge was also sent to Korea for 16 months.

In 1958, Sarge retired from the United States Army and they made their home in Glencoe, Minnesota in the family homestead on the "railroad lot" where Sarge grew up. Sarge died at the age of 88 in July 2001. Louise entered her eternal rest in October 2013. They are buried together at Fort Snelling National Cemetery in Minneapolis, Minnesota.

Hammerstrom was awarded the Combat Infantry Badge in October 1944. He also received a Bronze Star for his actions.

Elbeuf

My knowledge of what happened at Elbeuf is limited to what I can remember mainly about the 2nd platoon of B Co. I cannot recall who was on our right or left or what the lineup of our companies was, nor the company set up, as we moved into the town.

Melvin Hammerstrom, seen here after the war, was one of the 28 soldiers that transferred to the 99th from assignments with Newfoundland Base Command in early November 1942. Arriving as a staff sergeant, he served as a technical sergeant in Company B, and received a Bronze Star Medal while the unit was fighting under the 30th Infantry Division. He was one of the few 99ers to continue a military career after the war. (Courtesy of the 99th Educational Foundation)

I remember we approached the outskirts of Elbeuf at night and we were all herded into a long low tunnel. It was so low we almost had to crawl. We stayed all night in this very damp and dark spot. I suppose I recall the tunnel because I found that I had spent the night on a pile of human waste. I'm not sure if any of our officers spent the night in the tunnel as I don't recall seeing any of them enter.

The next morning was beautiful and sunny as we gathered up our gear to move out. In addition to our regular equipment, most men had two bandoliers of ammo and a good supply of hand grenades. In addition, I had pyrotechnic flares and a gun.

As we moved out, I noticed cattle fences off to the right which would have to be crossed by the flank patrol. I was also concerned as I felt that our point and advanced party were not far enough out to our front and I felt we were carrying too much equipment to move properly. I mentioned my concern to the company commander and his only comment was, "Sergeant—remember we are in combat now."

As we moved along, all was quiet and peaceful and we began to feel that there was no enemy around but!—as we neared the center of town all hell broke loose. Enemy artillery and small arms fire rained in on us. One of our weapons and ammo carriers was put out of commission, wounding several men.

During the thick of it, someone in the 2nd platoon reported that there was an underground tunnel up to the front. I quickly followed him to see for myself. It was big enough for vehicles to come through. I knew the location of Col. Edwin Walker—CO of 2nd Armored Infantry—so we both ran back and told him about the tunnel. He thanked us and said he would put a few tanks at the entrance of the tunnel and fire some canister rounds into the tunnel and that should stop the enemy from using it.

We were under extremely heavy enemy fire in Elbeuf, so we moved back to high ground and set up a defense in this position. Someone in the 2nd platoon said he could see the enemy on the high ground across from us.

All of a sudden enemy artillery started hitting our position and it was concluded that reflection from the field glasses gave our position away.

We stayed in this position until late afternoon at which time it was decided that we should try and re-enter the center of Elbeuf which was on low ground on the Seine River. Everything was very quiet, and the platoon leader of the 1st platoon said he thought things didn't look natural. He told me he was moving out of the city to higher ground. He led his men out very quickly and I followed him with the 2nd platoon. Just as we got out of town the enemy hit the town with a heavy barrage of artillery fire, so we concluded that we saved ourselves a lot of casualties because it was a very heavy barrage.

When we finally got over the embankment to higher ground, my platoon leader and I had to report to the company commander who said that we should not have left our position without his permission. But God knows what would have happened had we stayed. I have learned later the platoon leader of the weapons platoon of B Co. told his man that the battalion had been ordered to get out of the town because units on the Bn's right and left had pulled back and the 99th was alone.

Our kitchens were set up to give us a hot meal in the rear area but I don't know if we got fed or not because as we were lined up for chow, German planes came over and strafed us and everyone scattered in search of cover.

CHAPTER SEVENTEEN

Ray Helle

This collection of anecdotes was written by Ray Helle and contained in Yngvar Stensby's materials for the unpublished manuscript Stensby was creating.

Ray Helle was a lieutenant with A and B Companies of the 99th Infantry Battalion (Separate) and played pivotal roles throughout the 99th's campaigns, including a commanding role during the action in Malmedy as part of the Battle of the Bulge.

Helle had a role in the design of a monument in Malmedy that was dedicated in 1994. It is located near the railroad embankment where members of the 99th held their positions against the Germans. This position was critical as it was a concerted focal point of the Nazis as they attempted to keep the northern section of the bulge moving under the aggressive leadership of Hitler's favorite, Lt. Col. Otto Skorzeny. The monument is on a street that has been named Avenue De Norveig (Avenue of the Norwegians).

Helle's account of the 99th's leader, Colonel Hansen, in the Canal Drive battle as well as a misadventure with a toilet in Norway gives a good picture of the bold, courageous, and devil-may-care attitude that Hanson had. It matches with the reputation shared by others and helps to confirm the culture that existed within the 99th for courage and a penchant for action.

In Helle's section on Merkers Mine, where the 99th Battalion had a key role in transporting stolen Nazi loot, he writes about the 99th being "involved in everything but never really knew what was going on." That statement captures the pervasive nature of the 99th Battalion in numerous significant and critical events of the war.

Helle's profession before and after the war was as an illustrator and cartoonist. His work appeared in many publications, including Colliers, The American, *and* The Saturday Evening Post. *He also created several serial comics including "The Flibbertys," which ran in syndication for nearly 20 years, "Sam and Ellie," which ran for decades, and the series, "Box Seat."*

Helle started the 99th Battalion's newsletter and organized it until his health started failing in 1999. In addition to the newsletter, Helle would create illustrations for the 99th's reunions.

Helle was born in May 1917 in Brooklyn, New York to Norwegian immigrant parents. He died in September 1999 and is buried at Bay Pines, Florida.

Glanusk

Checking the guard on a cold night, I spotted a solitary figure racing across the grounds, in his long johns. Taking a shortcut to the tree he leaped over the little creek, or runoff; whatever it was. Landing on the other side he stopped dead in his tracks, slowly took off his long johns and proceeded to wash them.

Seems he had met the unseen enemy, diarrhea, and lost.

The Canal Drive

Midway through the Canal Drive a brigadier general told me he wanted to see Colonel Hansen right now, and even assigned his staff car to me to speed things up. As I approached the front lines to ask about the Col., the Germans laid a load of artillery fire in the area. The 99ers, from their foxholes, and using all the courtesy due a staff car flying two stars, politely told me to "GET THAT DAMN THING THE HELL OUT OF HERE." The general then assigned me a tank to find Col. Hansen. Using the backwoods I reached the same area and was told that Hanson was out in front somewhere. Since the major in charge of the tank refused to go beyond the safety of the 99th rifleman I had to walk. What seemed like miles and ages (probably several feet in a few minutes) I came up on the colonel, standing next to an overturned German ration wagon. He said, "Taste this, it's good." So while a brigadier general fumed somewhere, we enjoyed the next 10 or 15 minutes having a "Cheese Tasting party." Somehow, probably because of his self-assurance and relaxed attitude, "tasting cheese" in the middle of the mess they called war, seemed like a most natural thing to do.

Norway

We were playing poker at a British officers club in Oslo. Col. Hansen excused himself and left the room. He came back a little later dripping wet exclaiming, "DAMN TOILET! I stepped on the pedal and it squirted back at me." Then suddenly realizing what had happened he burst into laughter, sat down, and resumed playing as though nothing had happened. Seems like nothing could faze the colonel—battles, bombs, bullets or "bidets."

Merkers Mine

Letter to Les Carlson on December 2, 1996 that was found in Yngvar Stensby's collection. Ray Helle wrote it on 99th Infantry Battalion (Separate) stationery.

Dear Les: thanks for the information you sent me. It brought back memories. I was one of the officers assigned to that trip.

I had a rough idea of what was in the trucks but did not realize that teeth were a part of the cargo.

I do remember all the sheepskins that were used to protect most of the artwork. I also remember the area around the bank in Frankfurt was cleared of civilians.

This is the kind of stuff that the 99ers like to read about. After all they were involved in everything but never really knew what was going on.

It seems amazing but the 99th, besides its fighting, somehow managed to get involved in everything else. Somehow I was always a part of these strange goings on. Guess they did everything they could to keep me out of mischief.

Ray

CHAPTER EIGHTEEN

Lars Larson

Lars Larson was born September 20, 1910 in Brocket, North Dakota and farmed until joining the service in 1942. After the war, he worked for the Johnson Store in Larimore and later purchased the Johnson Store in Portland, North Dakota where he worked until retirement in 1977. Lars died on January 20, 1984 at the age of 73.

Lars joined the 99th at the outset as they initially assembled at Fort Snelling in Minneapolis, Minnesota. His family indicated that Lars was very excited about being with other Norwegian descendants and some local friends from back home.

In a series of letters and postcards that Lars sent to his parents, we get a view into the life of a soldier in the 99th from his first experiences at Fort Snelling to Camp Hale, Colorado, and on to Europe. His firsthand account of the challenges of training in the mountains in Colorado—at high elevation, in deep snow, with heavy packs and ski equipment that the soldiers weren't used to—lets us see the hardships that they faced in training.

His letters continue into England and then France, Belgium, and eventually Norway. Lars' accounting leans more toward observations of rural farm life and comparisons to home. This includes several letters that show us his interest in the status of farming, back at home. In one letter he writes of visiting historic sites in England, including the House of Commons, House of Lords and No. 10 Downing Street. He writes that the "English take pride in it all. As far as I am concerned, they sure as hell can have it." As with many other members of the 99th, the time spent in Norway at the close of the war was a chance to visit relatives, which for Lars brought him to his relatives in the town of Ål, part of the Hallingdal region.

Lars received the Bronze Star for his actions as well as the Purple Heart for an injury received; however, in one of his letters home he emphasizes the minimal nature of the injury so as to not worry his family.

Larson's Bronze Star citation reads:

> *For heroic achievement on 17 September 1944 in Belgium, in connection with military operations against the enemy. During action in Belgium on 17 September 1944 at about noon, Private First Class Larson, Browning Automatic Rifle man*

Mark Nelson recalls his 99th veteran: "My great uncle Lars L. Larson (lived) outside of Lakota, ND after the war. He let me drive his truck as a pre-teen to check on the sheep out in the pasture. He never talked about the war, other than the time he was shot and helped a fellow 99er seek cover." Lars is seen here in early 1943 at Camp Hale with his rucksack, skis, poles, polarized goggles, and his Garand rifle, ready for the rest of the hike back down to Camp Hale, in a valley at 9,300 ft. His Purple Heart is on display in North Dakota. (Courtesy of Mark Nelson)

of his squad, was wounded. He refused available medical aid and evacuation, stating that his wound was slight and that his services manning the Browning Automatic Rifle were too urgently needed by his squad. Private First Class Larson then laid fire on the enemy, causing twelve Germans to surrender to members of his platoon. His courageous spirit of self-sacrifice and his devotion to duty were an inspiration to his comrades.

Fort Snelling, St. Paul, MN

December 4, 1942

[Postcard]

Dear Pa,

Well I am here in Fort Snelling and I think I'll be here for some time. I am in the Norwegian Battalion. I told them I could read & write & speak Norwegian, so I suppose they figure I could do my best here. They talk Norse here everyplace, but of course they talk English to us; I mean the officers. Will write a letter soon, when I get time.

Lars

***

Fort Snelling, St. Paul, MN
December 13, 1942

Dear Pa,

I am still here at Ft. Snelling and am in this Norwegian Battalion. It is only Norwegians in this group and all from New York to California. Quite a few have only been in the U.S. a few years; have not run across any from Hallingdal[1] yet; they are mostly from Bergen and Oslo.

We are treated OK. Our officers are easy on us, yet tell us we have to try our best. It is going to be harder after a while. Sometimes they talk a little Norse to us and among us. In the barracks, it gets to be quite a bit of Norse talked.

I've been running up and down these darn halls till I am sore & stiff in my legs. One day we went out on the rifle range and shot eight shots with our rifle. I did not make out so bad for being the first time.

Last Wed. night, I went up to the Farmers Union Convention and saw R.O. Moen, C.F. McErlane, and M.J. C.A. Moe was given a ticket free and got in on the banquet. The orchestra played a number for me, so had quite a time and last night I had supper with S.J. Lillehaugen. M.J. and C.A. Moe were still here.

It is not as cold as I hear it has been in N.D. It is more snow here though. I have not seen a cow or horse for two weeks, so it is a different life. I'm not lonesome, nobody here seems that way. Here they are bad to drink beer, these Norwegians. No real tuff [sic] guys, so I think I am lucky to get into this outfit.

---

[1] The region in Norway where his family originated from.

No, can't think of anything else just now. We have been warned not to write anything that might be information to the enemy, so it is hard to know what to write about, but just let you know I am OK and don't mind it a bit.

We are going to move this week as I understand, don't know where. They have shipped our supplies, so I'm sure we will be going soon. I'll let you know when we get to our new place. Then you better write me.

Lars

Camp Hale, Colorado

December 20, 1942

Dear Pa,

We left Thursday night from Ft. Snelling on a troop train and got here at four o'clock Saturday afternoon. So, I am a long way off now. I've seen a lot of country. We went through Minnesota, Nebraska, Kansas, and Colorado and I'm way up in the Rocky Mountains, 10,000 feet above sea level. They say it is something like Norway.

This camp is about 3 or 4 miles long and ¾ of a mile wide and is surrounded by mountains. The sun rises about 9:20 and at four in the afternoon, it gets behind the hills. The hill on the west side of camp is darn high; don't think anybody can climb it, too steep.

It took us about seven hours from the time we got into the mountains to get here and the last 75 miles, they had two locomotives on. In places, it didn't go very fast. The track follows a river and in some places you could look down on the one side of the coach, down about 50 or so feet to the river and on the other side it was straight up for I don't know how high. At times, the train was in a perfect "S" shape. Sure seen some scenery.

We are to be trained as ski troops. I suppose I will break my neck. The air up here is light, feels like you cannot get enough air and you play out very easy. Yesterday, we marched from the train to our barracks and some of the older men dropped out on the way.

They are all Norwegians in this outfit. At present there are about 600 men. Some come from New York, some from California, a few from Minnesota and N.D. A lot of them here were born in Norway. I have not run across any from Hallingdal though and nobody from around home that you know. There is going to be 15,000 men here soon. But I saw today that there are a few Indians here and there is supposed to be a bunch of Finns here too. There is most everything here—road machinery, trucks, mules and what not. If I can get a camera, I will send you some pictures of this place.

There are deer and bears up in the mountains, so maybe I will see a bear after all. There are four slides somewhere around here and then we will have to climb up these hills on skis. I will write more about this when I have tried some of it. Not much snow in camp, but there is supposed to be about 10 feet or so on top of the mountains.

Can't think of more just now, so will close. Didn't do much at Ft. Snelling; just fooled around. We were supposed to have moved before, but for some reason or other, we didn't. How is everything up north? Have you much snow yet?

Lars

***

Camp Hale, Colorado
January 17, 1943

Dear Pa,

Well, I am getting used to this country, so like it better now, although it is not very healthy to stay in camp too much. The buildings are close and very little wind, so the smoke from furnaces and stoves lay over the camp just like fog. At times, a person can't see the other end of camp for the smoke. The snow gets black, like it hasn't snowed for two weeks and things on the ground are almost black. Today it is snowing to beat the band.

A week ago, we were out on the firing range, practice and record fire. It was kind of cold out there; they said it was 10 to 25 below. Every day it doesn't seem as cold at 25 below as it does in N.D., but it was plenty cold. We left here at 7:30 a.m., came back at 6 p.m. and had our dinner out there. We got some on our plates, sat down in the snow, and ate away. We had to shoot 221 points out of 340 in order to qualify for marksmanship. I qualified; those that didn't had to practice more.

Last Wednesday and Thursday I was the fireman for Co. B. There was one more besides me. Anyway, at night I had only 15 furnaces and stoves to take care of. It's quite a responsibility at night. Thursday evening, the old fireman came back, and I sure was not sorry. It's an awful dirty job.

Friday night, we were on a compass hike. They turned a bunch at the time loose, up a way in the mountains with a compass. We had to go so many degrees one way, then in another way. They had some papers tied to certain trees, so you see we had to follow the compass close. We at least came out on the right spot.

It sure is nice when you get up a ways so you can see around a little. One peak sticks up here and another there, covered with trees and snow. I thought for sure we were going to get to the top of the one we climbed, but heck, didn't get more than about half ways. It sure doesn't look far to the top, but just start climbing and it sure is quite [far] away. I haven't done any skiing yet. We haven't gotten any skis.

Last night, I ran across a guy from Hallingdal. He is in the Co B. He came over in 1924 and is from Tørpe. His name is Herman Opheim. He also had an uncle in Norway by that name. His Dad's name was Knut Opheim. Do you know this guy or his dad? He has heard of Bjella, Helling, etc., but didn't exactly know any of them. He knew Anders Haug. He had heard about a fellow by the name of Erik Bellehus Haakensen. Erik had used a knife and cut the throat pretty bad on a fellow by the name of Anfin Sando. Was that Erik? He also knew Lewis Njøs and that he was married to Erik's sister. I asked about Lars, but he didn't know him at all.

This Herman O. is 40 years old. I don't know if these names are spelled right. When you write, let me know if you know this guy. I imagine he will be gone by the time you answer because all men over 38 years are being kicked out. Those that at least want to, and it seems that they all want to get the heck out.

I suppose you heard from home about Lester's operation for appendix and tonsils. He had them both removed at the same time. Tollef had his tonsils out a week or so before Christmas, so they both should be in pretty good shape now.

Benny Rortvedt is in this camp, but entirely in a different outfit though. I was down to see him about two weeks ago. He has gotten leaner than he was. He doesn't look quite so husky. Hilda wrote that Charley Pouzor is here also, but I have not seen him yet. Otherwise, I am as you may say, all alone. But I am in a good bunch, so have no kick coming. So, this better be all, and when you find time, write.

Lars

***

[Postcard to O. B. Larson dated January 5, 1943]

Dear Pa,

Well I'm taking it easy just now. I had my appendix & tonsils out last Thursday. It's the second spell I had and it was plenty bad, so I thought it's best to have it out. I guess Rudolph Nelson is over & helps Tollef, so he gets along OK. Not much to write about, just to let you know I'm OK. I guess I go home on Saturday.

Lars

***

Camp Hale, Colorado
January 30, 1943

Dear Sis, L. & kids,

Everything is quiet with the exception of a poker game, so have no excuse for not writing. We have Saturday afternoon free; even so, I never get started writing until evening.

There has been nothing new around this week. Sure hope we get skis soon. We are to have 40 half days of skiing and I get tired of hanging around these barracks day after day. I was up the trail yesterday afternoon, otherwise it's classes.

Gena's birthday brought me my first KP since I came to the 99th. They post all such notices on a bulletin board and some of the boys have had KP two and three times, so they watched the board when my name was printed there. They sure let me know about it. I expect guard duty soon.

I can't locate Charley Pouzor. If you find out his barrack number, I'll find him. The address Lionel sent doesn't help much as I would have to look all over camp in order to find him. I wrote him a week ago but have not received a reply and also about C. Grove, you sent me his address also. Last Sunday I was over to see Ben and asked if he would go with me to Colorado Springs some weekend. He said he would later on.

[The letter ends here—missing a page]

Camp Hale, Colorado
March 7, 1943

Dear Pa,

I will write you a letter now as I have a few hours for letter writing this afternoon.

We got our skis a week ago and have had two days of skiing, but I have a heck of a time. I want to sit down too much. If they would only let us go down the hills straight, it wouldn't be bad, but instead we ski down sideways sort of in a "S" shape. It's hard to make the turns and they are rushing us too much too. They take us up the hills which are plenty steep, and we are supposed to go down them and 90 percent of us can't handle the skis properly yet. The 87th Bn has been training all winter and even now they don't go down any steeper hills than we do.

We left camp Tuesday noon and had along tents, food, etc. We camped out till Friday morning. We sleep in tents with about 5–6 feet of snow as a mattress and cooked our own food outside the tent. It is rather cold in the morning. It was about 10–15 below one morning, so you know just about how it is cooking our breakfast. We have sleeping bags and they are plenty warm once you get them warmed up.

Friday morning, we left where we camped and were on skis for three hours with about 70 pounds strapped to our backs before we got back here. Was a damn hard trip the last 4 miles or so. We were going through a snowstorm. It wasn't blowing so very hard, but it sure was snowing. So, they are sure letting us have it. As I said before, the 87th is just starting to carry a 70-pound pack now. But I suppose the snow here too will go in another six weeks or so, so haven't much time for ski training. We are leaving again tomorrow at nine for another three or four days out camping.

Otherwise, this life isn't bad. We have plenty to eat, may at times not get all a person wants of meat and such, but can always fill up on something else. The bunch I am with are as decent boys as can be expected in Army camps.

You mentioned about getting me home again. I will say it's pretty hard. The men over 38 years sure have to go thru more red tape to get out than I ever care to go thru. Everything has to be just so. It usually takes them a month or so before they finally get their discharge papers.

I suppose you hear from home sometimes. Guess the boys feel better when they got rid of their tonsils. Tollef has been bothered with them quite a while, but you know how [easy] it is [to] always leave it [for later]. Lester also has had trouble with his stomach for about a year. He was to the doctor a couple of times and was told that it was ulcers, but it wasn't that after all. Anyway, I understand they have been putting on a little more weight this winter.

Lars Espegard is about 80 to 90 miles from here. So, some weekend I am going to get a pass and go and see him. We have very poor train connections, so can only spend about six hours with him. Will find out about busses and see if that's better. A weekend pass is from Friday night till midnight Sunday. Lars wrote that he is working about four hours each day. So, can't be very strong.

So, guess this will have to be all, as we are supposed to get all set for tomorrow. And when you write, you better ask questions if there is something you want to know that I don't write about.

Oh yes! I had the measles about three weeks ago. Very light and had to go to the hospital. I was up and around all the time, stayed five days and then was sent back. Just as I got back, the fireman got sick, so I was fireman for a week. I fired from 10 at night till six in the morning. I had 15 stoves in four different buildings to take care of. I had plenty to do at night but had the other 16 hours for myself. I didn't do anything else, but can't sleep decent in the day, so it throws a fellow off balance in a way.

No, this better be all, and I'll hear from you again.

Lars

Doing anything with the barn yet?

***

Camp Hale, Colorado
June 13, 1943

Dear Pa,

It's been a long time since I wrote, got your letter the first of May. We usually go on hikes during the week, kept on with the damn skis till about the middle of

May. Yep! It's hard to get used to them. We haven't had so very much practice as far as learning to handle them after a week's training. We went on long hikes with our packs on and it took almost all a person has to carry the packs, not to mention balancing on skis. Imagine we will have more of it next winter and winter starts here again the first of October. Had 6 inches of snow June 3 and [there] is snow yet up the side hills and quite a bit on the high peaks.

We were all in Colorado Springs during Easter. The President looked us over. We had our ski uniforms on, something the President hadn't seen as he asked about our caps, shoes, etc. While there, we stayed in Camp Carson. That Saturday afternoon, we were off, so I went to see Lars E. He is in Colorado Springs. He looks good and weighs 170 pounds and works for an electric company [as a] "bookkeeper." He still has a little spot left on his lung.

I was down there last weekend and he took me around there. Saw a lot of funny things, sort of lots of "wonders of the world" there. It's very nice around too and down there a person can see civilians, cows, green grass; here it's soldiers, mules, dogs, and snow. Oh, it's getting green here too now. We are [up] high, you know, 10,000 feet and when we hike, we are usually up 12,000–13,000 feet. The air is pretty light up there.

I understand you have had plenty rain in N.D. Tis better that way than it was in 1934–36. The grass will grow at least. I am going to try to get a month leave in August or so, to help out at home if I can get it. I don't know how it's going to go. I had to sign up for furlough last week and we were told that we better take it when we can or not at all, so may be home next month unless I get a month leave in August. We were supposed to go on six-week maneuvers June 14, but that's been called off.

We were supposed to go on maneuvers with the 87th, but they got notice a few days ago to be ready to pull out by Sunday "today," so most of them left yesterday, possibly overseas. They have had the same training as we "ski troopers," so it goes quick sometimes.

Didn't feel any too good the first month here, but after that, I got used to the climate and these last months, I've been putting on more weight.

No, guess it's all for this time and may see you in the future.

Lars

***

Camp Hale, Colorado
August 1, 1943

Dear Pa,

They didn't give any furloughs in July or August, so I guess I won't be home till it's all over. We will be leaving this camp in the near future for parts unknown.

We are supposed to get all affairs straightened out, which I have done before I left home, except insurance, which we carry. I took out $10,000 insurance and it's in your name. So if the next guy should be quicker with the trigger than me, this insurance will be paid to you, so much each month. As I wrote home, I wish that each of my brother's and sister's kids would get a little to start out with, so if you wouldn't need it, I would want you to have $2,800. Then it would leave $1,200 to each of my brother's and sister's kids. All in all, I expect to come back, but just in case, you'll know how I wanted it.

It's long since I heard from you, expect you are busy. Hear it's plenty of rain in N.D. Too darn much to be in good humor at all times.

Here we have climbed almost every hill within 20 miles. To me they seem to grow, crossed over the top of one here a couple of weeks ago with snow along the east side of it, which will last another month. West of camp about 40 miles there is a lot of snow left yet on the so-called Holy Cross Mountain. It stays cool up here too, but on the south side of the hill during the day, the sun is hot if no breeze, but when the sun goes down, it gets right cold.

A guy who had gone thru Hallingdal showed me about how the mountains look there. As a rule, they are quite a bit steeper here. The day may come when I'll be able to compare them.

How is the barn coming? It should be finished by now. Crops good, they [family and friends back in North Dakota] write, but too much water.

No, it's about all I can write, except you better not write again till you hear from me, so you get my right address.

Lars

England

December 19, 1943
[V-Mail]

Dear Pa,

Wrote you a letter a long time ago but haven't heard from you. Perhaps the letter got lost. I suppose you are having colder weather, snow, etc. Here the ground is not frozen yet, grass is still a little green, but it's sure raw weather. It's foggy and misty most of the time, very little sunshine.

We are well taken care of, plenty to eat, plenty work, and kept on a jump most of the time. I believe this to be good farming country. I see cattle out in the pasture every day and as far as machinery is concerned, they seem to have modern stuff. There are lots of tractors, see very few horse outfits, only thing is their threshing machine, they are way behind. They have to feed it by hand, also stack the straw. So far I have only seen one with a feeder and blower on it.

Expect a furlough soon, so will see how people live there in the city. I will write you when I get back.

Merry Xmas,
From, Lars

***

February 20, 1944
England

Dear Pa,

Received your letter some time ago and see that you are as spry as ever. Yes, I bet that new barn is very nice to have. Sure getting a good price for the livestock.

I had my furlough some time ago and spent my time in London. Sure is a lot of old stuff, such as buildings, ways & means of living, and saw quite a few buildings 700–800 years old. I also saw the House of Commons, House of Lords, and No. 10 Downing Street, etc. English take pride in it all. As far as I am concerned, they sure as hell can have it.

I got in contact with quite a few Norwegians, so you know what we talked about. I didn't see anybody from the valley, but was told it really isn't too bad up there, although they have lost quite a bit of their property. Otherwise, they are left alone. Cities are not so good. Guess they really slugged it out up there and at one time, they were giving them all the trouble they could take care of. Not much damage done by air.

I am not at the same place as at first, but I like it better here. It's nice country, grass is still somewhat green, seldom the ground freezes, so you see it's not cold, but usually fog or rain and raw wind.

As far as Army life is concerned, we sure can't [complain], get enough grub, fairly good huts, and not working very hard. The boys are a good bunch to be with. At times, it gets a little tiresome to go on with the same training day out and day in, when a person feels he could be somewhere else doing something. But, then again, I suppose we really don't know how lucky we are so long as we can stay here.

Hear from the boys quite regular. They have cleared the farm and have about $5,000 besides not counting the bonds they bought. So they are not doing badly at all. They wrote and asked if they should buy the barber land. Fargo Loan Agency is asking $3,040.00 for it. I told them to do as they want to. As far as I am concerned, I made up my mind not to go back and farm. I told them whatever is there, both land and property is theirs. I will never claim anything. Don't know if they bought it or not as yet.

I like this kind of life almost better, sure feel free, nothing bothers me, and I get three meals a day and a place to sleep. It is good enough and if I get out of it, I can always find something to do. If not, I won't have any more to worry about.

No, lights will soon be out, so will close this time.

Goodnight,
Lars

France

July 7, 1944
[V-Mail]

Dear Pa,

Haven't heard from you for a long time, but imagine you are quite busy. Besides the stock, I suppose you have to look after the rest of the farm and by now haying is in full swing. Boys wrote that crops look very good. Guess they have been plenty busy shearing.

Suppose you know that I am in France. It's a surprise to you as well as myself. I hadn't quite figured it out that way. Have seen a few towns and they are reduced to quite an extent and it sure isn't much for the civilians to move back to. The country is very nice. The farms and fields look pretty good. Stock is in good shape.

Well, I thought that perhaps you were wondering about me as I haven't written for some time. Everything is OK and I expect it to remain so. When you find time, write a little. Have you finished the barn yet?

Lars

July 10, 1944
[V-Mail]

Dear Sis & Family,

Received your letter some time ago, so will write you this time. On the quiet order around here now and the boys went out for a little stroll. Guess they have something lined up for me tonight, so am going to write letters till I'm blue in the face, which is easy as I spend six hours on the first one, copy the rest.

Yesterday it rained, so I slept nearly all day. Today it seems to start up again. Suppose you saw the letter I wrote Gena, so it's no use writing about that again. It's about the same all over in that respect. Haven't heard from Oswald, but am sure he is here somewhere.

Excuse my handwriting as my knees serve as a table and my only seat is the one attached to me. Everything is OK.

Greet all,
Lars

Belgium

September 24, 1944

Dear Pa,

Some time ago since I got your letter and glad to hear from you. I understand you to be just as busy as ever, but imagine it's handy in the new barn. As they write, I guess it has been plenty rain there again and seems to come when a person just as soon have it dry. I haven't heard from anybody for nearly a month, so do not know how threshing turned out. The mail has been a little slower lately, but expect to hear from somebody soon.

Here it's quite a difference than what I was used to at home. In France, I saw a few binders, mowers, etc., but here I have not seen any. They do almost all their work by hand. They cut, tie, and then stack their crops. The little they have of it plowing, dragging, etc. they use one horse or some have two horses. Others still use oxen and the oxen are sure in no hurry, so it goes rather slow.

The people are very friendly and they sure show their appreciation. They come with apples, pears or whatever they have. A few can speak English, so it's quite interesting to hear their stories. Well, I hope this war will end soon. It's holding longer than most of us expected some time ago.

Oh, had a letter from Oswald Thompson. He came in on D-Day and said it was plenty ruff [sic]. He has seen more than most fellows have. Just now, he is in England. He got malaria, so perhaps he may not be sent back.

No, it's not a hell of a lot to write about, so will close. All is well and expect it to remain so. Sure hope it won't last much longer. I'm afraid it won't be any too good if it is to last thru the winter. When you find time, you write me a few lines.

Sincerely,
Lars

***

September 28, 1944
Belgium

Dear Pa,

It is not so very long since I wrote you, but having time, I'll write a few words again. I am sending you a little box which you will receive later. So far I have not told you or anybody else what I am doing at times, but will tell you in hopes that you keep it entirely to yourself. You are the type that doesn't worry very much, which is the only way to be. With my brothers and sisters, it's different and I'm afraid they would worry some.

Here in Europe there is a war going on and sometimes a person can't help but run into the Germans. They just as soon shoot you as to look at you. One day we ran into a bunch that was a little more stubborn than usual and I got hit by some shrapnel. I got a little in my leg and it put me out for a few minutes. But I got up and took off again, so all it amounted to was a good scratch. Anyway, I received the Purple Heart which I am sending to you to keep for me until I come home.

If my sisters would get a hold of that, I got the Purple Heart; most likely they would think that I am all shot up minus a few legs and so forth. So keep it entirely to yourself and tell no one because I am entirely well now. My foot hurt for a week, but now it's just as good as before and why worry those that do worry. If they find out about it, they will figure that as long as I have been in it once, I'll go again, maybe and maybe not. No one knows; if I go, I go. If I don't, I don't. There's nothing I can do about it, at least I'm not worried a bit and feel I can take care of myself.

Well, when you get it, let me know. It may take a while. Anyway, I am interested to know if it got home or not. Nights here are getting a little colder and can notice that fall is here.

Suppose it's getting colder in N.D. by now.

Sincerely,
Lars

***

November 5, 1944
Belgium
[V-Mail]

Dear Pa,

I received your letter a few days ago. Everything is OK with me, taking life easy again. Now, after my last trip up there, I got a little excited and wrote Gena a little of what I have been doing. I'm darn sorry I ever did, sure hope Tollef doesn't find out about it. It's hell when a person is up there, but after you shake the dust off your clothes and see how few got hurt, it sure is nothing to worry about.

Had a letter from Lester's wife and she said they finally finished threshing Oct. 13. Guess it was a mean fall, but they had plowed quite a lot, so they were ready for winter. Here grass is green. We had frost one night so far. It rains so darn much here that frost doesn't hurt.

Well, all for now. That package won't come for a while yet. It takes about two months.

Lars

France

January 28, 1945
[V-Mail]

Dear Pa,

Just a few lines this time to let you know everything is OK with me. Now I am way back in France away from noise and everything, so it's not half bad over here now. We are living in tents with a stove in each, so can't complain about anything. I only hope this darn mess will come to an end soon. The Russians sure are going good. As far as I am concerned, I don't care if they keep on till they hit the French coast. I'll get out of their way, that's for darn sure.

Had a letter from Selma and she said they had been up to see you and that you are kept plenty busy. Bet it's nice with that big barn in every way and suppose you have plenty feed for the stock.

Well, all for now. I will write you a letter later on.

Lars

***

February 25, 1945
France
[V-Mail]

Dear Pa,

Just a few words to let you know I am still in France. I'm not doing much of anything. We do some training every day and that too gets tiresome going over and over again, but then we sure are lucky being back here.

I had a pass to Paris some time ago. It sure is a nice city, not much damage done there, and every little thing costs plenty though. On the way up, the farmers were busy in their fields. They take good care of their patch. Close to Paris I noticed some good-sized fields.

I suppose you are busy with your stock. I've heard quite a few remarks that you are working too hard. You better ease up. You have done enough hard work in your days. No use to keep on that to the last day. I've seen that happen to one person.

Well! Take care of yourself and let me hear from you.

Lars

***

March 11, 1945
France

Dear Hilda and family,

It's about time I answer your letter. I am really slow in answering and have no reason for it. You have plenty to do, so do not blame you a bit, so do not expect to hear from you so often. Everything is as usual. Still back here doing the same each week, so have not much to report. You said in your letter that you knew where I was on Sunday, Jan. 21, but I'm afraid you were mistaken as I was back here. You get this outfit mixed up with the 99th Division and doubt very much if you ever hear anything about us over the radio.

I do not remember if I ever thanked you for the Christmas package I received. It came thru OK, well, thank you. It's a shame but I think I forgot to thank a few I got packages from. I let it go so long before I wrote, so am sure I forgot. I saw a picture of Clifford Grove in the *Herald* and didn't know for sure if it was him or not as nobody wrote about him. Once in a while there are pictures of boys I know. Saw in the *Walsh County Record* about a Lt. Swenson whom I knew very well. He was our boss for 4–5 months. He sure acted [like] and was just one of the boys. He did more than his just share for us. No matter how bad things were, he would be right up there with us. We respected him as he was a leader, afraid of nothing. I believe it was in the Jan. 25 issue of the *Record*. I told Sig to save the clipping if he had the paper yet. Perhaps some of those up "North" know his wife because she is from Adams.

Today, it's been quiet as usual and no place to go. There is a show some evenings, but so crowded that it's no fun to go there either. I went to services this morning and after dinner. I was going to write letters but instead I had a little too long a nap, so got off with a slow start.

I notice you have been on a not-so-pleasant trip to Minnesota, but you got away from your daily routine. I guess it's pretty nice down there. Hate to admit it, but it's rather bare in N.D., haven't got the trees as they have other places, but hardly think I'd trade the prairies for any other place though. Here it's getting very nice as it's getting green trees and all.

No, I haven't written anything so far and have no more so will close. You better not work too hard. I know you have plenty on your hands with the bronco busters (boys). In a few years, you'll be able to just sit around and boss.

Well, all for now. Everything is OK. Hope this finds you the same.

Greet the bunch,
Lars

***

March 30, 1945
France
[V-Mail]

Dear Pa,

Just a few words to let you know I am still back here in France. Taking life easy and not doing much of anything and enjoying nice weather most every day. The little fields they have here are green and it has been spring for the last month. I suppose they are ready for spring work back there too. You didn't have so very much snow according to reports.

I had a pass to Paris a couple weeks ago. It's a nice city and they carry on as if nothing had gone through. There's not very much damaged. Everything is high priced. They sure broke me in a hell of a hurry. I went by train, so got a good view of the country and it's quite nice all the way. Nice farms, etc.

Well, this will be all for now.

Sincerely
Lars

CHAPTER NINETEEN

Dr. Raymond Minge

Dr. Raymond K. Minge served as the medical doctor for the 99th Infantry Battalion (Separate). He joined the unit in 1942 at Camp Hale in the Colorado Rockies at the age of 29 just a short time after getting married, having a son, and starting a career as a town doctor in Clarkfield, Minnesota.

Minge was born to Norwegian immigrant parents in Fergus Falls, Minnesota, in 1913. As was typical with many of the members of the 99th Battalion that grew up with family members who spoke Norwegian, he understood, but was not fluent in, the language.

As the doctor assigned to the 99th and as the leader of the medics, his wartime function was operating a critical field hospital/triage unit at or just behind the front lines. He also attended to the aches and pains of the soldiers when at rest.

During the war, Minge wrote a series of letters to his wife and parents and five of these letters are included in this chapter. Some of his letters were also published in the Fergus Falls newspaper as a means of keeping the local community informed of the war effort.

Among these letters are startling accounts of the horrors that he and a handful of 99th Battalion members experienced while visiting the Nazi work camp, Buchenwald, shortly after its liberation. His letters also tell of the reception among the French citizens, including of giving candy to Belgian and French children.

Among the many experiences during the war, there were various stories Minge shared through the years. These stories include the death of a fellow doctor who was hit by shrapnel while standing near him, intense action during the Battle of the Bulge, and seeing women being publicly shamed for having fraternized with German soldiers.

One of the stories that was recorded relates to the Malmedy Massacre in which 84 American soldiers that had recently been captured were killed by Nazi machine-gun fire. Minge treated one of the few survivors of this massacre, Staff Sergeant Henry Roy Zach of Wisconsin. Zach's harrowing story is told in the book, Fatal Crossroads: The Untold Story of the Malmedy Massacre at the Battle of the Bulge, *by David S. Parker. In this book, Captain Minge is quoted as telling Zach that his injury would be sending him home—an understatement, as Zach's leg had nearly been shot off.*

Interestingly, Raymond Minge was not the first from his family to have stories of the Nazis. Minge's older sister, Margaret, had moved to Germany in 1931 to further her piano studies, perform at concert halls, and compete in competitions. As such, Margaret was in Germany during the rise of the Nazi Party and witnessed the increasing ugliness toward the Jewish community and anyone that opposed Hitler. She occasionally attended events with the U.S. Embassy staff, and at one event, quite unexpectedly Adolf Hitler paid a quick visit.

Margaret Minge and her fiancé, George Perret, took part in underground efforts to assist the Jewish community. This included helping to smuggle money (especially jewelry)

Captain Minge was the battalion surgeon, and the battalion medical section commander. His section was attached to the battalion and immediately responsible to its commander. He is seen here in front of a ¾-ton WC-52 ambulance marked with 474th Infantry bumper markings and the regiment's distinctive pentagon on the hood and bumper. It was one of four possessed by the 474th in 1945 and each had a heater and room for a driver, four to seven patients, plus a medic. (Courtesy of the 99th Educational Foundation)

out of Germany to Switzerland for Jewish friends. One time, the German Gestapo boarded a train on which Margaret and her fiancé were riding. The Gestapo inspected everyone's luggage and chose to perform a total-body search on George. They found nothing, but were suspicious that the violin he carried was actually being smuggled out of the country. George said, "No, I play." The Gestapo asked him to prove it, so George warmed up and tuned the violin and played Bach's "Partita." After 10–15 bars, they indicated that was sufficient and moved on to the next search victim. What they didn't discover was that George had a secret compartment in his violin case with hidden jewels.

Margaret and her fiancé left Europe via Italy on May 26, 1940 on the SS Manhattan, reported to be the last ship to leave Italy before they joined with Germany to form the Axis. Accounts of the couple's experiences and views on Nazi Germany were published in newspapers across the United States.

Raymond Minge would return to Germany four years later as part of the Allied effort to defeat the Nazis. His experiences provide a bookend to the rise and fall of the Nazi Party.

Upon returning to Minnesota after the war, Minge maintained connection with the 99th Battalion through reunions and through various personal connections. On one occasion in 1947, the Minneapolis newspaper reported on a reunion that Minge had with a fellow veteran of the 99th Battalion who had been brought into the Minneapolis General Hospital emergency room as a prisoner with injuries from a police chase. To the amazement of the police and the hospital staff, Minge and the patient recognized each other, and the two of them spent time reminiscing about their time together in the 99th.

After living in Minneapolis and becoming a surgeon, Minge moved to Worthington, Minnesota with his wife, Elsie, and continued raising their family. At the end of his career, he pursued his calling to serve as a medical missionary in Liberia for several years and then later in Bangladesh, where he suffered a fatal heart attack in 1981 at the age of 68 and was buried at the rural hospital compound.

London

I returned from London last night after two very interesting days in that huge city. We left here by train Thursday—late afternoon, so when we pulled into Waterloo Station in London it was very dark. We were unable to get a cab so asked a copper where to find the tube (London term for subway). He very courteously told us and within about 15 minutes we were out to Piccadilly Circus. That's a spot something like Seven Corners in Minneapolis. Our officers club (the American Red Cross Reindeer Club[1]) was supposed to be only four or five blocks from here. Well you have no idea how pitch black everything is at night.

We wandered around Piccadilly Circus bumping into people, telephone poles, and whatnot. I found a man on the corner selling blackout flashlights so immediately

---

[1] This is the name of the specific club.

bought one. We groped about some more and finally found a copper who directed us to the reindeer club, but even after his most explicit directions we had some difficulty. The streets are also crooked and confusing and totally dark. (Ordinary darkness plus heavy fog.) We finally found the club. It is operated by the American Red Cross and staffed chiefly by British volunteers; we had made reservations beforehand.

The whole atmosphere at the club was one of marked friendliness. After being shown where our room was, we went to the dining room and had supper—roast lamb, potatoes, vegetable salad, tea, and apple pie—and seconds on anything, including apple pie. The whole meal cost only two shillings (about 40 cents). That's the maximum price for any meal at the Red Cross Club. The rooms were three shillings a night. None of the service boys over here can give too much praise to the Red Cross.

It is impossible to get any hotel accommodations in London, and the food in London cafes, because of the wartime restrictions, is very poor and expensive. So the Red Cross Club is really a life saver. There are three officers' Red Cross clubs in London and about 20 for enlisted men. Well, after supper, we went to our rooms and went to bed because we wanted to get a good start the next morning to see the city. The beds were comfortable and no air raid sirens blew so we had a very good night's sleep.

Friday morning, after breakfast, we made a B-line to Buckingham Palace by a taxi cab (cabs are very easy to get during the day). The cabs are very funny looking and are driven by old men. The cabs look like a Model T Ford, 1918 model, but really get you there and the rates are very cheap—one shilling and three pence (about a quarter) took the two of us to Buckingham Palace. Buckingham Palace, of course, is the home of the King and the Queen. They were both in—the flag was flying above the palace to designate that they were home.

The palace is an immense structure surrounded by a huge iron fence and very closely guarded. No visitors are permitted to enter during wartime. We were standing by the huge statue of Queen Victoria in front of the palace quite awestruck and wondering just how we should proceed when a stranger came up and asked us if we'd like to see London; he had been a guide for 18 years and knew the city, so we said, "Let's go." He insisted on walking wherever we went so we really wore out some shoe leather.

He first showed us all about the city, with detailed explanations of everything. We then headed for Parliament Square, passing by Westminster Abbey for the time being. We gazed upon the House of Commons and the House of Lords and heard Big Ben strike. Big Ben by the way is on the House of Commons. Near Westminster Abbey we passed a statue about a block away. The guide said, "If you don't know who that is I won't take you any further." Luckily we recognized Abraham Lincoln and proceeded onward.

We crossed the Thames via Westminster Bridge. From that bridge we had a beautiful view of the Parliament buildings, Big Ben, London Bridge, Lambeth Bridge, and the Tower Bridge. Next we headed toward and visited Scotland Yard—a very impressive layout. We continued along and stopped at the old Curiosity Shop, the shop of Charles Dickens; the guy took a picture of the two of us looking in the window.

We then continued onward to St. Paul's Cathedral, still standing there in the midst of the wreckage and destruction caused by the blitz three years ago. It was one of the most impressive places I have ever visited. The domes on so many of our state buildings are modeled after St. Paul's. We saw the two points where the bombs had struck the cathedral, one of them unexploded. Remember all the publicity given the rescue party for removing this bomb? An Army officer supervised that work; he apparently capitalized on his work and was discharged from the Army. The repair work to the cathedral will have to await the end of the war.

The cathedral still stands there for worship and prayer and is a symbol of Britain's faith during these awful days. After visiting the cathedral we walked across the famous London Bridge (and it shows no sign of falling down). And then across the Tower Bridge to the Tower of London. This consists of 12 acres of buildings and was built seven or eight centuries ago. Here many queens and other notables were imprisoned and lost their heads—literally speaking. Our trip through here took one and one half hours and was quite spooky at times. The guide—a man who had worked there about 40 years—was very interesting and seemed to delight in pointing out spots where such and such a person lost his or her head. He said one queen got three blows on her neck with an axe before she was finally "executed."

The London Tower is now closed to everyone but servicemen for sightseeing. A short distance from the tower is a place called Tower Hill; every day at noon people gathered there to air their views on any subject. Men will get up on a soapbox and start to narrate and orate on any subject—religion, politics, economics, etc. It was very interesting to listen to them; I thought at times they might come to blows.

By the time we had gone through London Tower it was almost four o'clock; our guide left us here and we took a tube back to Westminster Abbey. We got back there just in time to make another tour. It is a truly magnificent structure. A very impressive ceremony was going on when we arrived. The whole place was lit up with candles, and the beautiful gold sword which the King of England is going to present to the people of Stalingrad was on display. An opportunity was being given for the people of England to see this sword before it is sent to Russia. We saw the Tomb of the Unknown Soldier, Poets Corner, the inner sanctuary where the King and Queen are crowned and where royal weddings take place, the cloisters, as well as numerous tombs, etc.

It was now after five p.m. It's beginning to get dark. We had a ticket for the theater at 6:30 p.m. so we hurried back to the Red Cross, washed up and ate, and got back to the Colosseum theater in time to see the performance *Foolish But Fun*. This theater rather reminded me of Northrop auditorium. There are many such theaters in London; the people go to the theater rather than the movies or cinema as they say. The acting was good and the orchestra excellent. And so ended our first day in London. We were really ready for bed Friday night (our second night in London).

Saturday (yesterday morning) we went again down to Buckingham Palace to see the Change of the Guard ceremony. It's a very impressive ceremony held every 24 hours in peacetime and every 48 hours in wartime. At each guard change, a large band takes part and the new guards of the palace take over. The people think very highly of their King and Queen. During the blitz one bomb landed uncomfortably close to the palace but the King and Queen stayed right there and took it with the others. I forgot to tell you that we also walked past Churchill's hangout—No. 10 Downing Street. After seeing the Change of the Guard ceremony we went to a smaller gift shop operated by an American Red Cross Nurses Guild Club.

This is the only place in London where any silks or linens may be purchased by soldiers without coupons. So here I bought you a birthday and Christmas present. It was quite a procedure. I had to get several forms filled out in triplicate for the desired items, take them to two stores, with which the Red Cross had special agreement, pay for the articles, get receipts, and then go back to the Red Cross and have the gifts wrapped. I was glad to get a chance to see these doors. They were simply magnificent and no doubt two of the best doors in London. The silk item was bought at "Jacqmars" and the linen at "The White House." I shall not tell you anymore, only hope that everything reaches you in time for Christmas.

After this little shopping expedition, it was time to get back to pack up and go down to the train station and hit back for camp. I truly enjoyed the trip. On my next 48-hour pass I shall try and visit Oxford and Stratford upon Avon. So if the war should suddenly end I'd make a B-line for the coast and take the first ship back to the U.S.A. and to you. The British by and large think we're a bunch of upstarts and we think they live too much on tradition and the glorious past, but in spite of differences, the British and American soldiers get along quite well together. So "Good-day," as we say in Britain.

France—Reception

Several days ago I came upon one of our American jeeps that had been turned over and injured three men. I gave what first aid I could and sent them back to a clearing station. While I was working by the side of the road about a half dozen French civilians gathered about. They were so very sympathetic toward the injured. They brought a pail of cold water, a pail of milk, and some cider. They placed cold towels on the foreheads of the injured and held branches over their faces to keep the hot sun away. One of the ladies even presented us with a few fresh eggs.

It seemed so queer to see these civilians right in the combat area. They must be immune to war. Artillery shells made land only a hundred or so yards away and they carry right on with their work while soldiers hit for the nearest foxhole.

Yesterday a little French boy came crying up to our aid station. He had burned his hands and arms. I fed him some of those chocolate-covered nuts while we worked on him; it was a perfect anesthetic. He said he was going to bring us back some eggs. By the way, you can send more of those chocolate-covered nuts anytime.

Here's a good one. One night we were moving into a new bivouac area about 3 a.m. Some American patrols heard us moving in and heard some of our men chattering in Norwegian. I guess they thought it sounded like German and radioed the artillery to set the guns on our positions with orders not to fire until it was definite that we were the Germans. Luckily for us the misunderstanding was soon clarified, and we were spared being fired upon by our own artillery.

Last night after going to bed the chaplain Svendsen and I had a little argument [in regards to] just what some rumbling and flashing in the sky signified. We concluded it was a bombing attack and artillery firing in the distance. But the argument was settled about half an hour later when we found ourselves caught in the open in a good old-fashioned thunderstorm. I can now almost appreciate the conversation between two PFCs when one remarked to the other, when told a certain noise was exploding bombs, "Thank goodness, I thought it was thunder."

After a little experience of being on the receiving end of a few German bombs I really feel sorry for the Germans who have to live through the horrible air raids of our Air Force. What the Germans gave us is not even a drop in the bucket compared to what they received. My constant prayer is that the Germans will soon ask for peace so this insane business can end.

France—In Pursuit

August 22—we are on the constant move, and I'm glad to say forward. Much has happened since last I wrote you. We have done a little in the war effort. We've had a few casualties, some serious and others not. We were very busy one morning when one of our trucks loaded with men struck a mine. The truck of course was blown to bits, but fortunately not so with most of the men; it was a horrible mess. We put on bandages, applied splints, and even administered some plasma. One of my very best friends was a casualty, but I can't disclose his name as yet. His injury was serious, but I trust will come out OK.

We've done so much night traveling of late it's pretty hard on the drivers as we always have to drive with dim lights. France has so many dense forests and oh how dark they are at night. However, what Germans are left in these forests do not, as a rule, fire at us. They rather shout "comrade" and give themselves up. We've taken a few prisoners, but I have not seen them as they were not wounded.

The part of France we are now in is so very pretty and much like parts of Minnesota and Wisconsin. There are many nice fields and the harvest is pretty well along. We are on the heels of the Germans most of the time and sometimes are the first Americans the French civilians have seen. What a welcome they give us.

Right now there are a couple dozen civilians visiting and telling us how less than 24 hours ago the Germans were on this very spot. They hate them intensely and cannot do enough to make us feel welcome—bring us vegetables, cider, jam, eggs, etc. I had a little accident with one of my eggs, crushing it in my pocket, but I still have one good egg left. We're living entirely on K-rations again so what we received this morning tasted very good, especially the cherry jam.

Keeping clean continues to be a major problem. We travel on dusty roads and across fields and open vehicles and after about an hour are as black as a Negro. We are happy that we are motorized so we don't have to do any hiking. Hiking was one of the biggest things stressed in our training and now we don't do any of it at all.

You would think every vehicle in the United States was in France the way the highways look. One convoy after another in both directions. When we drive through the towns and villages, civilians line up along the street throwing flowers and kisses.

The American flag is seen flying in practically every town we passed through. The land and towns in this section of the country had been so much better preserved than in Normandy. It was so very depressing to see all the leveled towns and uprooted countryside. I hope Paris will not be damaged too much. I should very much like to see that city, but of course, we have to go where we're told.

August 23—Good morning. We took off again in a hurry, traveled more in the dark, and got in a few winks of sleep. In a few minutes we'll be off again. The last few nights we bivouacked in wheatfields. We dig our holes right under a shock [of wheat]. If I learn nothing else over here, I have at least learned how to use a pick and a shovel, so if things get too bad in the field of medicine I can do a little ditch digging on the side.

Over here I feel that our lives are so entirely in God's hands. Of course the same holds true in civilian life, but dangers certainly do draw us closer to God. Church services are irregular. We get together whenever opportunity presents itself, and then of course much time for private devotion and prayer. Talk about morale builders, nothing compares to the boost one gets from a few passages from the Bible and a short prayer.

August 24—just a few lines. I have to write now when opportunity presents itself. We've been racing through France at breakneck speed—on the go almost night and day. I don't mind missing sleep at night as long as we continue to advance; but this night travel is quite nerve-trying with the German planes and flares. You should see what a mess it was last night after diving into a muddy slit trench with nothing but my shorts on.

It seems to rain almost every night, but the continual successes on all the fronts keeps up our spirits. Our lives are so entirely in God's hands; never have I felt so utterly helpless, but yet so strong, knowing that our Heavenly Father is watching over us night and day.

The French civilians jam the streets as we drive through and shout—"Long live America." They toss flowers, apples, and kisses at us. I saw a very sad sight yesterday; a French home had just been hit and a woman and two men were frantically digging in the debris. The woman became hysterical when she uncovered an arm of what appeared to be a small child. Yes, the poor civilians over here are surely going through the horrors of war. I believe the ties between France and America will be more binding than ever after this war. If only all nations could be guided by Christ's teachings in making the peace.

September 1—These have been some rather hectic days, so I have not had [the] opportunity to do much letter writing. We have been living in the mud like a bunch of pigs, on the move almost constantly and experiencing the true h— of war.[2] I am most thankful that I am unscratched and in good health. The Germans are retreating so fast it's hard to keep up with them. Yet, even in their hasty retreats they do manage to make things uncomfortable at times for those in pursuit.

We have treated some German wounded. Most of them are very humble and most grateful and also happy to be out of the war. They are no longer the supermen Hitler pictures in *Mein Kampf.*

We continue to live on K-rations fortified at times with vegetables we find along the roadside. The French civilians extend us most hearty welcomes as we move along, tossing apples, tomatoes, flowers, and whatnot to us.

France—Demoralized Germans

August 7, 1944

Dearest Mother and Dad,

We are now bivouacking in a cow pasture, but it smells much worse. There is such a mixture of foul odors around here—must be a combination of decaying flesh and all the other aftermath of war. You know war is really much more horrible than I have ever imagined from what the movies portray it to be. Some of the country is so completely devastated I can't imagine how it can ever be reclaimed. The poor

---

[2] Captain Minge censored his own language in this section of the letter.

French have and are going through things that no one here can appreciate—and for the second time in only a quarter of a century. But they love America for again coming to her rescue during the dark hours. At times I am almost happy to be here just to see how grateful they are as more and more of their country is liberated.

You would have laughed if you had seen Capt. Svendsen and myself hit the ditch last night. A German plane came over (no bombs dropped) and anti-aircraft only a few feet off the road along which we were riding opened up. It was such a terrific racket I thought it was bombs falling. Anyway, we were both lying on our stomachs in the ditch in a twinkle of an eye. Svendsen was smoking a cigar when he hit the ditch but could find no trace of it when he got up again. Night time is about the only time a few German planes dare appear and you should see how the sky lights up with anti-aircraft from every nook and corner, like a tremendous display of fireworks at one of our Fourth of July celebrations.

This little leaflet I'm enclosing is one dropped by our Air Force. (The leaflet published in English and German reads:)

SAFE CONDUCT

The German soldier who carries this safe-conduct is using it as a sign of his genuine wish to give himself up. He is to be disarmed, to be well looked after, to receive food and medical attention as required, and is to be removed from the danger zone as soon as possible.

I guess they have had quite an effect on the German troops by decreasing their willingness to fight. Some smart boy over here last night predicted Germany's surrender in another 96 hours. Statements like that sort of make us feel good although we don't believe them.

More and more B-rations are arriving. For supper tonight we had delicious chocolate cake with boiled chocolate frosting. I took an extra piece back with me. I shall go for a little walk to see if I can find some little boy or girl to give it to. Having been deprived of all forms of sweets the past four years they go almost crazy over anything with sugar in it.

I washed clothes this afternoon. We usually find some French woman to do our laundry. We furnish the soap. They seem very pleased to do the laundry for us and believe me it's quite a job washing clothes over here. They don't have anything over here resembling a washing machine; they get down on their hands and knees and scrub away with cold water. It's a very common sight to see little concrete pits constructed and some little stream for washing clothes. They hauled the clean clothes back to the house via wheelbarrow. It's such a typical sight over here I should try to get a picture of it. Perhaps the people living in the largest cities have more modern conveniences. Also, a great share of the country folk wear huge clumsy wooden shoes.

I don't see how they make them stay on. The little boys up to the age of 10 or 12 wear dresses. Isn't that terrific? I have yet to see a building that's not constructed of stone. Everything is typically European; that's the way I imagined Europe to be. Most of the men wear tams.[3]

I suppose your letters will soon find me again. I'm looking forward to seeing you and being with with you again. Give my best regards to all the folks.

The letter from Capt. Minge continues, but is dated Aug. 17, showing that he had to complete his initial letter home a few days later.

August 17, 1944

Today marks two months since we came to France. The progress of our armies since that time has certainly been wonderful. Perhaps another two months we will see the end of the war in Europe.

The average captured German soldier is completely demoralized, and the whole picture seems hopeless to him. Yet the resistance [that] the Germans can continue to offer in the face of disaster is almost unbelievable. Of course, it's the Nazi war machine that keeps them going.

We've had some rather anxious and tense moments over here. Things change so quickly that we can't plan for more than a few hours ahead. We've been fortunate in having wonderful weather, so nice we haven't been using our tents at night. But we did get caught the other night in a thunderstorm and got thoroughly soaked, sleeping bag and all. The boys that really have it tough are they who have to be all night long in their foxholes with rain and shells dropping all about. It's surprising how well a person can stay, living this type of life. I don't even seem to catch colds anymore.

With much love, May God keep and bless you.

Horrors of Buchenwald

This letter to his wife was also published in the Fergus Falls, Minnesota, newspaper. In a short intro to his letter, they highlight that his description of the camp is the first eyewitness story of conditions in Germany told by an Otter Tail County man and fully corroborates the stories that have been written by the various war correspondents.

April 22—Trying to keep up with the rapid advance of our armies across Germany doesn't give much time for letter writing. We have just moved into a fine German

---

[3] A "tam" is a round, flat hat that the French call a beret. The word "tam" is the Scottish word for this type of hat.

Several groups of 99th soldiers witnessed scenes like this at the Buchenwald Camp and other sub-camps like Ohrdruf, where 99th soldiers met infamous *Life* magazine photographer Margaret Bourke-White who took photos of the camp the day they were there. Several of the soldiers wrote to their families about the atrocities, including letters that were published in local newspapers. The 474th Infantry Regiment arrived in Germany in early April 1945 and was assigned directly to Third U.S. Army Headquarters. The unit's mobility and security mission gave its soldiers the opportunity to experience more of wartime Germany, including an impactful witnessing of the horrors of the Holocaust. (Courtesy of the 99th Educational Foundation)

house and believe it or not the occupants cleaned it up for us before they took off. After a long session of tent life it is a real treat to again live indoors and enjoy such luxuries as electric light, heat, and running water.

The smaller German towns and villages often escape the destruction of war and life seems to be almost normal amongst the civilians. They are well fed and have fine clothes; the women seemed to have a bounteous supply of silk stockings.

The little children, at first afraid, then shy, finally become quite bold and ask us for candy and gum. Of course, any type of fraternization is strictly taboo and a court martial offense. I feel sorry for the little children (and there is no end to them in this country) for they're certainly innocent, but the older folks must be treated very sternly.

Not long ago I had the opportunity to visit one of Germany's recently liberated concentration camps. It was a real eye opener. Any doubt I ever had as to the justification for sending American soldiers overseas was completely banished.

I've heard much about the horrors of the concentration camp, but no story can give the true picture as the actual site of starving children. We were guided through the camp by one of the liberated prisoners, a German citizen who had been at the camp for two years. He was first arrested in 1933 because of his anti-Nazi activity, but managed to escape to France. There he married a French girl, established a home, and lived a happy life until the Gestapo knocked at the door two years ago and took him away. He was never offered a word of explanation as to the reason of his arrest. He spoke fine English, having lived in Philadelphia [for] four years and seemed to be a most refined and intelligent sort of person. He was ashamed to admit he was a German and was now eagerly awaiting transportation to his "home" in France. He said he was never again going to meddle in politics. How different the situation is in the States where a person can speak his true mind.

The camp was a huge affair and had been constructed entirely by slave labor in 1934 and 1935. Adjacent to it was a large factory for war equipment to feed the Wehrmacht. Here the prisoners were forced to work without pay and without necessary food to sustain life. Our guide had the greatest admiration for the American air force. Last fall it completely demolished the factory area but had not touched a single building housing the prisoners. Although the prisoners had access to no news other than a little Nazi propaganda, they did manage to gather bits of news and knew that the Americans were making good progress across Germany. Their hour of joy came on a certain afternoon when American machine-gun fire was heard; they then knew their hour of liberation had arrived. The majority of Hitler's Elite SS super coward troops guarding the camp managed one of their strategic withdrawals and escaped capture.

After passing through the heavy iron gates of the camp the first thing to greet us was a tall monument constructed the day before by Americans; it was made of cardboard and had the number "51,000" printed on it; above the number was a large wreath. It was put up in memory of the 51,000 who starved to death at this camp.

Nearby was a large whipping post and next to that a scaffold where men were hung by their hands, tightly bound behind their backs for two or three hours. We were next conducted to a crematorium, but before reaching that passed a heap of about 50 bodies of men who had died from the effects of starvation the preceding night. It was a ghastly sight. Beside this pile of starved bodies were two dead SS troops who were found hanging; the SS insignia was tattooed on their bodies.

We then entered the crematorium, which contained five large crematory furnaces; bodies were being cremated at the time the Americans arrived, but the process had been cut short—charred bones and skulls still filled the furnaces. Numerous urns, packed and addressed, were piled on shelves ready for mailing to the next of kin, to be followed, of course, by letters of condolence that Mr. So and So had unfortunately died of appendicitis or some other natural cause.

On the floor below the crematorium was a large room with numerous hooks in the walls for suspending prisoners for various forms of torture. When they had breathed their last, they were put on an elevator and conveyed to a crematory furnace. No detail was overlooked in the systematic mass human slaughter.

We next visited a large, modern, and beautifully equipped experimental pathological laboratory where numerous experiments were carried out by the camp doctors. The laboratory contained many mounted and preserved specimens—all of the work inspired by a fiend. Many of Europe's best men met their death at the hands of these doctors. The sick were terrified whenever any of these doctors paid them a visit.

We were then shown through one of these so-called hospital wards; never have I imagined such a pitiful state of affairs could exist in a civilized nation. Lying on the floor with hardly sufficient room to turn around were many hundreds of men too weak from starvation to stand or talk beyond a faint whisper. Their arms and legs were like toothpicks and their faces really not human. Many were lying in a semi-coma and nearing the end. Some were a little stronger and smiled as we walked by. A few could speak English. I especially remember one man of about 50. He was a living skeleton, deeply jaundiced. I stopped a few minutes and talked with him. He spoke good English. He had been a prosperous lawyer in Vienna, and anti-Nazi. Four years ago he was arrested and removed to this camp. His wife had managed to escape to New York City. After these four long years he at last again had hopes he might get word of her welfare. He was so very happy and thankful that the Americans had arrived; now he seemed ready to die in peace.

All ages were represented. Even small babies had been brought in with their fathers and given the same starvation regime. The total daily diet consisted of 300 grams of bread and a bowl of fatless broth. Three hundred grams of this coarse and heavy German bread is not much.

Women prisoners were taken to a different camp; only 18 were kept in this camp for immoral purposes. The men were allowed to visit them once a week after having been in the camp six months, but very few men did so. The men in the camp were political prisoners and comprise the educated and cultured classes who dared oppose Hitler. There were professors, lawyers, ministers, doctors, musicians, etc. All nationalities were represented—German, British, French, Belgium, Dutch, Czech, Russian, Poles, Danish, Norwegian, Italians.

I asked if any Americans were there. There had been 20 fliers interned there. They had all mysteriously disappeared and it was believed they had all been shot. Escape from this camp was all but impossible with the guard system set up. There were three rings about the camp; the first contained 500 well-trained police dogs, and the other two of 2,000 SS troops armed with machine guns. Of course, there were the usual electrified barbed-wire fencing, searchlights, watchtowers, loudspeaker system. What chance would one have? Only SS troops were allowed to guard and enter the camp.

It was located near a city, so I thought surely the civilians must have realized what was going on but apparently not so. All they knew was that it was a political camp;

a large band played every day and the outsiders, hearing the music, thought that the prisoners must really be having a fine time—and what a fine time it was—slow, sure death from starvation.

To date 51,000 had died of starvation in this particular camp. How many similar camps exist through Germany and Nazi-occupied countries remains to be seen. I am now thoroughly convinced we have a good reason, in fact an obligation, to be over here fighting the Nazi system and playing a part in the liberation of these poor victims. I cannot conceive of a civilized nation subjecting its own people or any other people to such inhuman treatment. Our guide insisted the whole German nation was guilty. I cannot believe that the bulk of the German people would approve of the treatment accorded the inmates of a concentration camp; their guilt rests chiefly on the fact they permitted men like Hitler and Himmler to gain power and in their attitude of indifference at the policies these men adopted to achieve their goal. The German nation is now suffering the consequences in the loss of their men in battle and the destruction of their cities.

We visited one of the barracks where the man slept; it was a building for 100; but 1,800 were quartered in one of these buildings. They slept on boards without blankets or heat. One winter morning 600 dead were removed from these barracks. The commandant of the camp was an SS colonel, one of Himmler's stooges.

The colonel's wife, in all her splendor, used to ride through the camp on horseback each day. The prisoners were supposed to bow and remove their hats when she approached. If she didn't like the manner of a certain individual, she reported his number to her husband. (Each prisoner wore a metal tag on which his number was stamped.) The poor victim would disappear mysteriously and soon his ashes in an urn would be on the way to the next of kin—another death from appendicitis.

American doctors and nurses, medical supplies, food, Red Cross facilities, and all we have to offer have now been placed at the disposal of this camp, but even so about 50 continued to die daily from the effects of prolonged starvation. The Americans are real heroes in the eyes of these people. If they hadn't arrived, death by starvation or some violent means was the inevitable fate of every man and child. Now they have freedom to look forward to; those whose health has not been entirely broken will be nursed back to health and the hopeless will at least be offered relief from suffering during their remaining days.

Our guide was jubilant that day as he had just gotten a message through to his wife in France and was expecting to be on his way home again shortly. He says he will never in all his life forget how his heart leaped for joy when he heard American machine guns; but he believes we are too kind. He wishes we had immediately shot the 200 SS men that were captured instead of making prisoners of them. The day after liberation of the camp, civilians from neighboring towns were forced to march through the camp and see for themselves what had been going on. Many of them had to be revived with smelling salts. These were the people who had boarded the bandwagon when things went well in the Reich. Now of course, they all decry Hitler.

Just the other day we picked up a man in civilian clothes who cursed the Nazis. His clothes were forcibly removed and under his left arm was tattooed the lightning insignia of the SS soldiers. He had probably been one of the guards at this concentration camp.

It will undoubtedly take some time before the full story of these camps comes to light, but I have already seen enough to justify sending American troops to fight in another European war. It now looks as if the war is getting into its final stages.

CHAPTER TWENTY

Arne T. Thomassen

Arne T. Thomassen was born in Grimstad, Norway, on June 9, 1921 and moved to Brooklyn when he was a boy. He returned to Norway for a little over a year and then moved back to Brooklyn.

Arne writes about his experience as one of an estimated 13 members of the 99th that visited the Buchenwald concentration camp shortly after its liberation. Most of those from the 99th that visited were medics; however, their role at Buchenwald was focused primarily on witnessing the atrocities. As with Dr. Raymond Minge's account in the previous chapter, Arne's information came primarily from a personal tour provided by a prisoner that had at one time lived in Philadelphia. Arne's accounting of their visit reveals that shock and horror that they witnessed.

Arne Thomassen received the Soldier's Medal for heroism not involving actual conflict with the enemy in France. The award was accompanied by the following text:

> *On 20th, August 1944, when a 2.5 ton truck loaded with men, while passing another vehicle on a narrow road, struck an anti-tank mine, Thomassen, without hesitation and with utter disregard for his personal safety, entered the burning truck accompanied by two other enlisted men and removed several seriously wounded soldiers. Thomassen's exemplary courage and heroic actions reflect great credit upon himself and the Military Service. This tragic event marked the first deadly casualties that the 99th sustained and was on the eve of its first action at Elbeuf, on the Seine, North of Paris.*

For many years, Arne would attend the annual gathering of veterans of the 99th. He loved the 99ers and through his involvement with the national reunions, as well as the annual luncheons in Minnesota, he indelibly perpetuated the memory of the 99th Infantry Battalion (Separate) in the hearts and minds of his family.

Arne died on June 29, 2006 at the age of 85. He was married to Alice Louise Thomassen, who passed away in 2009. They had three sons, Roger, George, and Curtis. Arne became a minister and served communities in Wisconsin, Iowa, New Jersey, Massachusetts, and Minnesota.

Arne Thomassen, lower right, wearing the four six-month overseas bars on his left sleeve that attest to two years away from home, with fellow members of the 99th Medical Detachment wearing their Combat Medic badges on their left breast. They also wear the 99th Viking Ship Patch on their right shoulder as a "combat patch" and the 474th Spearhead on their left. This picture was possibly taken on their arrival at Camp Myles Standish near Boston, in November 1945. (Courtesy of the 99th Educational Foundation)

A Report of My Visit to the Buchenwald Concentration Camp in April 1945

They marched them out in the morning to the strains of music, so the people in the surrounding territory would think it was a cheerful place to live in, so our guide told us, who had been a prisoner there for two years. "Buchenwald" means a forest of Buchen trees.

The political prisoners had to cut the trees and build the shacks in which they were to live. There were people who were opposed to the rule of Hitler. These people had principles, who would not live under or support a group who had as its aim "the mastery of the world." Hitler realized that they were his opponents, so he had them removed. These peoples suffered physical and mental agony during those long years of internment and HOPED that their suffering would not be in vain.

In August 1944 they were thrilled by the MUSIC OF THE BOMBS which were screaming from American planes, and they saw the war planes which were close to the concentration camp destroyed. You could ask them, the few who remained, and they remembered the very hour of the bombing. That day in August 1944 and the 11th day of April 1945 were two days they would never forget. It was on the

April 11, 1945 that they heard the chatter of machine guns. The inmates of the camp knew the Yanks were coming, but they didn't expect them so soon. The SS, Hitler's pride and joy, began to feel out of place now since others had machine guns too. The SS didn't fear when they were in the driver's seat so to speak, but now their position was being threatened by some GIs, so some proceeded according to plans to go to the rear; others stayed and were either killed or captured.

As we entered Weimer (the city near the camp) on our way to Buchenwald, we saw men in strange attire walking the streets. They didn't seem to care if others were eyeing them, for they were now FREE MEN once more, like a bird out of the cage, they were spreading their wings so to speak and were no doubt thinking of the FUTURE, wondering if the world had anything to offer them.

The road to the camp was cluttered with German civilians who were on the same mission as we were, to see for themselves the "HORRORS OF BUCHENWALD." As we stepped out of the jeeps, we got into a conversation with a man who had lived in the camp. He had also spent four years living in the city of Philadelphia. He offered to show us around and explain things to us.

Out in the open yard were hastily made replicas of the famous beating post (the Germans had destroyed the originals). Here men were beaten and hung up for disobedience. As we walked along I saw a man standing on a box, looking over a fence. He was sketching something on a scrap of paper. I wondered what it was that had caught his eye, but being in a group, I didn't go over to satisfy my curiosity. We walked by a barking dog, one of the few remaining dogs the SS guards had used to guard the prisoners.

Our next sight was one all the world should see. It was this sight the man was sketching as he looked over the fence—there in the yard lay HUMAN BODIES stacked like cordwood. They had died for lack of food and due to sickness. Their bodies were nothing but skin and bones. They would have been burned in the furnaces, [but] the SS did not have time to dispose of the bodies before the GIs came. We went into the building where the ovens were and we saw the hooks on which the men were hung. There was also a club which looked like a large potato masher which was used to beat out whatever life remained before being put into the oven.

I have an article written by a staff correspondent of *The Sunday News*, Graham Miller (April 22, 1945) which describes in graphic detail the horrible treatment given the prisoners of the Buchenwald concentration camp. May this inhumane treatment of human beings never be repeated.

CHAPTER TWENTY-ONE

Les Carlson

The content in this chapter was among the materials that George Stensby had collected with the intention to include in the manuscript for the 99th Infantry Battalion (Separate). It is included separately here.

Lester Carlson's role as motor officer including detailed planning of the Merkers Mine operation where gold, artwork and other valuables looted by the Nazis were being moved from the Kaiseroda salt mine to Frankfurt, Germany. This included logistical planning for two convoys sent from the mine, with the first convoy handled by the 1st Battalion of the 474th and named Task Force Whitney. The second convoy was led by the 99th and named Task Force Hanson.

While the Merkers Mine operation did not involve the entire 99th Battalion, there were likely over 100 men from the 99th that were involved. Carlson's short summary is very focused on the tactical items. There are other accounts from members of the 99th Battalion included in other chapters of this book that provide different angles on the operation.

An earlier example of Les Carlson's work includes the effort to move the 99th Battalion within Minnesota from Camp Ripley to Fort Snelling. Carlson, as the motor officer, was ordered to organize the motorcade. He reportedly called a cousin with the Minnesota Highway Patrol to arrange with all the towns along the route to have local law enforcement stop the traffic when the 99ers' vehicles group arrived in each town so the 99ers' vehicles would not have to stop along the way and drive straight through to Fort Snelling that day.

Carlson grew up in Rushford, Minnesota. After the war, Carlson returned there. He was active in planning reunion events, and participated in official events including a ceremony with the Norwegian Chief of Staff at the Norwegian Embassy in Washington, D.C. in 2011. Carlson died in 2012 at the age of 94.

Merkers Mine

Another act of unusual duty the 99th Infantry Battalion (Separate) participated in during the tour of duty in the ETO.

Lester Carlson's "boys," here with his drivers, with Lester on the right in October 1944. His 36-man Service Platoon, with drivers, mechanics, cooks, supply, and administrative soldiers was one quarter of Headquarters and Service Company. The service and medical elements made the separate battalions self-sufficient, though QM truck units would still be needed to move the entire battalion. (Courtesy of the 99th Educational Foundation)

I was told to go to Third Army Headquarters to meet an officer in regard to some movement of something, no idea of what was in the plans. After meeting him, we went to a room with five officers, a Col., a Lt. Col., and two Majors. The first question was how many vehicles we had available. After listening to what we had, they thought it was satisfactory.

Then they explained the operation. We were to furnish protection for 12 trailers, [which were to be used to transport] art, and the same for another trip of gold, from Merkers, Germany to Frankfurt.

They gave the formation they wanted:

1 M8 scout car with each 3 trailers
1 6×6 with a squad of men with each trailer
1 officer and jeep in the lead
2 6×6 and 2–5 guards for rear guard
1 maintenance truck and mechanics in rear

If any tractor or trailer had to stop, the unit of three trailers, three 6×6, and an M8 would stop together. The only problem we had was a flat tire on a trailer which we found when we had a rest stop. Maintenance crew changed the tire and the convoy went on together.

The QM delivered the tractors and trailer to the Kaiseroda salt mine at Merkers, Germany. We were not permitted to enter the mine. As they were loaded, they came out and we formed a convoy as they wanted the formation.

When all the trailers were loaded, we took the convoy out to the autobahn. There we had one of the rearguard trucks stop all traffic going south until the convoy was all on the autobahn. From that point, no one could pass for the 80 miles to Frankfurt.

We had our radio communications within the convoy, and I had a radio contact with a cub reconnaissance plane who had contact with four P-47 fighter planes who circled within a 10–20-mile area over the convoy.

On arrival at Frankfurt Bank, we unloaded in the basement to a vault. All men were on guard around the bank and [in] the streets, until the last trailer was empty.

The artwork was moved on the first trip and two days later we moved the gold.

With about 35 vehicles in the convoy, I told the lead vehicle to set a 35mph speed. In turn, we got a huge buildup of vehicles behind us. The rear guard got all the complaints, until a Col. from some MP BN wanted to know who was in charge. They called me on the radio so Hadley Jenson was with me and we stopped until the rear caught up. I went over to the Col. and he wanted to know how I could block the autobahn? I said, "Sir, I have orders." I handed him the orders, signed by General Patton. He read it the second time and pulled back in line the rest of the way to Frankfurt.

CHAPTER TWENTY-TWO

Kjell Nilsen

Staff Sergeant Kjell Nilsen joined the 99th and was a very respected sergeant in 99th's A Company.

In a letter that Kjell Nilsen wrote, he vividly describes a collection of incidents that occurred at milestone moments. One such incident is the death of the well-liked Ozzie Skarning during the Canal Drive. Skarning's death is recalled by several members of the 99th, including several references in this collection.

Kjell wrote an excellent account on sealing the Aachen Gap at Würselen, Germany. This battle was often referred to as the 99th Battalion's "nine days in hell" where the 99th was a critical component of the pincer movement around Aachen in October 1944. Nilsen's writing captures the strategic nature of their role at Würselen while also giving us a detailed front-row perspective into the heroism and tragedy that can come at a moment's notice. As an example, he writes of the capture of a German outpost behind enemy lines, followed by a harrowing return confronted by friendly fire. This story illustrates the figurative fog of war. Additionally, these and other stories paint a vivid picture of the action seen in this intense period: "For nine straight days and nights we had endured the greatest concentration of firepower directed against American troops since D-Day in Normandy."

Nilsen closes out with a short accounting of the time the 99th patrolled the Ardennes in November 1944 just weeks before the beginning of the Battle of the Bulge.

Kjell passed away in 2005 at the age of 84.

Canal Drive

When we were moving up to join the 2nd Armored for the Canal Drive, S/Sgt. Ozzie Skarning and some of his men from his mortar section rode in the same truck with me and my rifle squad, and we had a chance to talk. Then we got off the truck and mounted the tanks and that's the last time I spoke with him.

A couple of days later, as our tank column was moving along the Willems Vaart Canal, the bushes on the far side, to our left, erupted in a storm of machine-gun fire, strafing our whole column. We all piled off on the right side of our tanks, so that they would shelter us as we walked along, keeping our heads down, trying to get out of this ambush. The lead was flying hot and heavy and zinging as it ricocheted off the tanks.

Then I heard someone pass the word back from the tanks up ahead, "Ozzie got hit!" Thinking he only got wounded, I thought to myself, "Well, I'll call him Purple Heart Ozzie the next time I see him." As we continued along, crouching behind our tank, someone said, "There's Ozzie." I looked to the right and there he was, stretched out on the ground on his back with a big, bloody hole in his abdomen. His skin looked like wax and he was so long and thin, with his nose sticking up so high, I could hardly recognize him. I guess all his blood had drained out. Beside him lay the body of the medic who had tried to help him, shot right through his Red Cross.[1] That scene is seared into my memory forever. We had to leave them there, as the Krauts were still giving us hell, but we vowed to make them pay for this whenever we caught up with them.

It must have been a couple of days later that we crossed the canal and caught them at Lanklaar. They were dug in outside of town, and after the

A formal portrait of Kjell Nilsen of Company A, taken at the Hartsook photo studio in Seattle, after his discharge in late 1945. Soldiers were authorized to wear their uniforms after discharge until they could get civilian clothing. On his right breast we see the Honorable Service insignia that was issued at his discharge, also known as the ruptured duck. A lapel device was also provided to wear on a civilian coat through a buttonhole. Kjell, born in Sweden, was one of eight Nilsens in the battalion and he had worked in the Puget Sound as a lumberman, raftsman, and woodchopper before he joined the Army in September 1942. He joined the battalion at Camp Hale by 1943. (Courtesy of the 99th Educational Foundation)

tank shelled them for a while, we overran them. They were just a bunch of young Luftwaffe cadets, with a few paratroop noncoms, fighting as infantry.

Talking with some of the guys who were on the tank with Ozzie, I learned that he had been hit by a ricocheted bullet off the tank from the first machine-gun burst. That's why it made such a big wound, and he bled to death so fast.

---

[1] The Red Cross insignia on his helmet.

In your account, Yngvar, you stated that he disappeared off your tank without a shot being heard. Evidently then, he was bounced off of your tank and later picked up by another, where he got shot. I hope this clears up the mystery for you.

Aachen Gap—Würselen

After the Canal Drive was completed, Sept. 28, we were sent back to Eupen and Montzen, where we rested for two weeks. On Oct. 12 we moved to Marienberg, Germany, and four days later we heard that we were attached to the 30th Inf. Division. American forces including the 30th, 29th and 1st Inf. Divisions had surrounded Aachen, except for a narrow gap N.E. of the city along the Cologne–Aachen highway at the town of Würselen. Our mission was to reinforce the 30th and help close the gap between them and the 1st Div.

We moved up through the town of Würselen at night in a column of twos, one column on each side of the street, as artillery was coming in and we could duck into the deserted houses, if it came in close. Suddenly, we were stopped and we heard a disturbance up ahead. Soon word was passed back that we had come up behind a German outpost and what must have been the most surprised soldiers in Hitler's army were taken prisoner. Somehow, we had missed a turn and had marched right out through the front lines into no-man's-land and stumbled into this outpost. Now we had to make a turn to get back to our lines, but when we got close enough to be heard, units of the 30th Div., thinking we were Germans, opened fire with machine guns and anti-tank guns, pinning us to the ground. It took a lot of shouting back and forth and explaining before we could pass on through and move up to our designated sector. This incident seems comical now, but it must have caused considerable consternation in the German command post to have a whole American company walk up behind their outpost and take it without a shot.

When we arrived at the area where we were supposed to relieve some of the 30th, we found foxholes dug in front of a row of houses, but nobody was in them. On searching the houses, however, we found that some of the 30th guys had locked themselves in a room in the basement for the night, and we had to nearly hammer the door down before they would come out. They seem to be pretty undisciplined and disorganized; quite a contrast to the sharp, efficient 2nd Armored Div. that we were accustomed to working with. I later learned that they had suffered nearly 4,000 casualties among their rifle companies near St. Lô in Normandy when our bombers blasted them by mistake. That included many of their experienced officers and non-coms, and they never recovered from it.

Heavy artillery kept coming in all night, so we took turns manning the foxholes, while the rest stayed in the basements. When daylight came, we could see that our positions were dug in on the crest of a hill overlooking a valley through which the Aachen–Cologne road ran. That was the gap where the Germans in Aachen were trying to break out, and German troops from Cologne were trying to break through to help them.

For the next few days and nights, we endured almost constant artillery fire, making it tough to get any sleep. Then one night we got orders to move out. There was no moon, and a steady drizzle was coming down. Not knowing where we were going we just plodded along in the darkness, going downhill, until we arrived at a road at the bottom near a farmhouse. Capt. Svarstad came up and told us to set up a roadblock and that the enemy would be coming from the direction of Aachen, so evidently, we were right down in the gap. We placed our minds on the road and dug in alongside, then settled in to try to get some sleep. Capt. Svarstad had said that we would get support from anti-tank guns on the main line up on the hill that we had descended and the artillery was going over our heads instead of landing around us, so I dozed off the rest of the night, even if it was still raining.

At daybreak I got out of my hole and was walking around to check our position when suddenly German tanks came charging in firing their 88s and machine guns. But they didn't come down the road from Aachen as we expected. They came in slightly to the rear of our left flank over some low hills and they were shooting directly into our foxholes with their 88s. I didn't have time to get to my hole, so I [dove] into the nearest one on top of somebody. We looked up the hill toward our main line, expecting to see the anti-tank guns giving us support, but all we could see was tracer bullets from machine guns and unbelievably they were firing into our positions, too. We heatedly cussed out those "dumb so and so's" who didn't even know we were down here.

Our situation was now impossible, so the only thing we could do was run for it, and everyone who was still able jumped out of their holes and ran toward the hill where our main line was. I remember passing a guy in his hole whose head was half blown off. He was a new replacement that joined us just a few days before…I didn't even know his name yet.

At the base of the hill was a shallow ravine with a creek running through it, bordered by trees and brush. It offered some cover, so we waded into the knee-deep creek to get down as low as possible. But the 88s were still whistling over our heads, and now we could hear "Burp guns," which meant they had infantry with them, so it would be only a matter of time before we were flushed out or blasted out. That's when we threw away any German "souvenirs" that we had, just in case we were captured. I dumped my prized Hitler Youth knife.

There was a small group of guys around me, and we didn't know how many of the company had escaped, so not seeing any officers around we decided to wade downstream a ways to get away from the tanks, then climb up the hill to get back to the main line. The hill was wooded nearly to the top, but when we came to the clearing where we could see our line, our own machine guns opened up on us.

I quickly stepped behind a nearby tree that was about 2 feet in diameter, and made myself as narrow as possible, as the tracer bullets were flashing by on each side of me. Other guys were pinned to the ground. When the firing slacked off for a second, I turned to get out of there and discovered that another guy was behind, covering me perfectly. That's one time all that close-order drill really paid off.

We all ran back down the hill to the creek again, trying to figure out what was wrong. The only answer seemed to be that the Germans had taken our main line, and here we were, trapped between tanks and infantry below and now a German line above. We waded down the creek as fast as we could to get away from the artillery that was crashing in the trees behind us. It seemed to be following us.

Suddenly we broke into a little clearing where one creek ran into what I thought was a larger creek. The guys ahead of me ran along the bank to the left toward a bridge, where a group of our men were crossing, when rifle fire started coming from the right. I figured I wouldn't have time to reach the bridge, so I jumped into the larger creek to wade across. However, it wasn't a creek, but a canal with vertical sides, and I went in over my head. Coming to the surface, I swam to the other side, about 100 feet, where I could see someone struggling to pull himself out. I just barely managed to reach a bush growing on the bank, and it was all I could do to pull myself out of the canal. It had been raining that morning, so I had on my raincoat, combat pack, rifle belt full of ammo, hand grenades taped to suspenders, canteen, shovel, rifle, bayonet, and helmet, and full of water. I felt like I weighed a ton. Turning to the other fellow, I saw that it was "Curley" Peterson, our platoon messenger. He couldn't make it and was weakened rapidly, so I pulled him out and dragged him into some bushes. The rifle firing continued, but I couldn't see anyone. We had to get out of there, but Curley was exhausted and couldn't go on, as we had a steep hill to climb. I figured I wouldn't be doing anyone any good if we both were taken prisoner, so I told him to catch up when he got his strength back. Peeling off all my wet, heavy gear, I took off up the hill with just my rifle and helmet.

Near the top I ran into Capt. Svarstad and about 50 or 60 of our men. Some of the guys didn't even have their rifle or helmet. For all we knew, this was all that was left of A Co. At last we were out of the artillery fire, so we could rest up some while Capt. Svarstad considered the best course of action. Meanwhile, more men came straggling in. We didn't know how much of our line had been taken over by the Germans, so he decided to keep moving along roughly parallel to the line until we found a position still occupied by Americans, where we could get back through the line.

Forming into a combat patrol formation, weapons platoon Sgt. Elias Peterson advanced as first scout, and I followed as second scout. We cautiously moved along through the woods and fields until late in the afternoon, [when we] spotted some troops across a clearing about a quarter mile away. We weren't sure they were

Americans, though, until Capt. Svarstad checked them out with binoculars. Then he sent a small patrol ahead to make contact, and we finally got back into friendly territory. I believe they were the 29th Div.

At last we felt safe again and I was glad that Curley had caught up with us along the way. But now it was getting dark, and we had to get back to the rest of the battalion, so we set off, trudging through the streets between the deserted buildings. Suddenly, a formation of planes, that at first glance appeared to be our Thunderbolts,[2] flew by overhead. But then they circled around and dove down, strafing and bombing. Messerschmitts![3] We all took off into the basements of the buildings for protection. When it let up a bit, we tried to resume our march but the planes came back and attacked again, so it was back to the basements. Finally, Capt. Svarstad said that he had to find battalion HQ and report to Col. Hansen, so telling the men to wait where they were, he told me to come along.

By now it was completely dark as we hurried through the streets. The bombing and strafing was still going on over different parts of town. I don't know how far we walked, maybe a mile or two, until we ran into some men of the 99th who directed us to Bn HQ, in a building. As Capt. Svarstad went in, he told me to, "Go back to get the men AND BRING THEM HERE."

Somehow, I found my way back to where we had left the rest of the company, but the street was deserted. I went up and down the street yelling, "A Co. assemble," until I had collected a sizable group, which I guided back to Bn HQ. Some of the guys must have stayed behind in the basements for the night, though, as our group didn't seem as large as before.

Arriving at HQ, I went in and reported to Capt. Svarstad that the men were here. He was still talking to Col. Hansen so he told me to have them wait. Everyone was tired, cold, and hungry, as we hadn't eaten all day, and some men didn't have any weapons, so we expected to be sent into battalion reserve where we could eat, rest, and replace lost equipment. Therefore, it was a tremendous disappointment when, after about an hour's wait, Capt. Svarstad came out and said he had orders to return to the same positions we left when we went on the roadblock, and no rations or extra weapons were available.

As platoon guide, I now found myself in command of what was left of the 1st Platoon, as Lt. Szymanski, platoon leader, and Sgt. Howard Anderson, platoon sergeant, were both missing. The next day, Supply brought us some K-rations and some equipment, but not everything. Then, Sgt. Szymanski returned. They had both gotten in with different outfits when A Co. was scattered by the tank attack. Every day a few more men came straggling in, so we hadn't lost as many men as we feared.

The story was that at the same time that our roadblock was attacked by tanks, the Germans had attacked and taken over our main line, including some heavy

---

[2] The Republic P-47 Thunderbolt was an American plane during World War II.

[3] The Me-109 was a German plane during World War II.

machine guns, which they turned on us. Later, the battalion counterattacked and regained their positions. Meanwhile, A Co. was scattered and wandered around in no-man's-land all day.

Now we were under incessant artillery fire again, but something new had been added. The Germans had brought up some railroad guns, which were huge coastal artillery cannons mounted on railroad flatcars. Their shells sounded like locomotives roaring through the air, and when they hit the ground [it] would shake for blocks around.

It was about this time that I saw my first V-1 or "buzz bomb." I was outside on guard one night when I heard the sound of a sputtering motor above and saw flames shooting out behind. The only thing I could think of was a disabled bomber trying to make it back. The next day we got a briefing on Hitler's new secret weapon. Another night, looking far off on the eastern horizon, I saw a streak of flame shooting high up into the sky. That must have been the launching of a V-2 rocket.

After a few more days online, the Bn was placed in ready reserve on Oct. 24, staying in buildings a few blocks behind the front. We could still hear and feel the artillery shelling around us, but at least we didn't have to man the foxholes.

Finally, after a few days in reserve, we left Würselen and headed back to Belgium. The casualty count was: two officers killed and five wounded; 26 enlisted men killed and 40 wounded, and four missing. 105 POWs were taken.

For nine straight days and nights we had endured the greatest concentration of firepower directed against American troops since D-Day in Normandy.[4] Compared with Würselen, Elbeuf and the Canal Drive seem like picnics.

Patrolling the Ardennes

From Nov. 1 to the 25th the Bn was stationed in the vicinity of Henri-Chapelle near Liège, Belgium. Due to the miserably cold, rainy, windy weather the men were quartered in farmhouses and barns in the area, most of them sleeping in the hayloft and eating their meals among the cows and pigs below. A training program was set up and conditioning hikes taken when the rain wasn't too hard. The main entertainment was watching the V-1 buzz bombs fly overhead on their way to Antwerp and London. Often, they would come in formations, and some of them would suddenly dive down and exploded due to the faulty guidance systems. Being up on a hill, we could see the whole area for miles around getting peppered with them.

On Nov. 25, the Bn was given the mission of a security force to protect the First Army rear area against enemy airborne attack and sabotage, and to keep the main roads and supply lines to the front open. Bn headquarters was established at

---

[4] While this statement is more personal opinion than historical fact, it does reflect the harsh intensity of that nine-day period of time and the difficulty of the battle.

Tilff with Companies B and C conducting patrols in that area. Co. D patrolled the highways between Liège and Eupen, while Co. A was assigned all of the rest of the area south to Luxembourg. Co. A's headquarters and Weapons Platoon was at St. Hubert, the 1st Platoon at Marche, the 2nd Platoon at Libin and the 3rd Platoon at Arlon. Jeep patrols were on the roads 24 hours a day in shifts and included the towns of La Roche, Marche, Rochefort, St. Hubert, Liblin, Dinant, Bastogne and Arlon.

CHAPTER TWENTY-THREE

John Petterson

John Petterson was one of the several hundred members of the 99th Infantry Battalion (Separate) that were Norwegian citizens. When the war broke out in Norway, Petterson was at sea after having delivered a shipment of oil to Yokohama, Japan from San Pedro, California. He was literally on the other side of the world. He made his way to New York and signed up for the U.S. Army.

After a three-year wait as an alien resident with no ability to be called up, his enlistment came through and Petterson joined up with the 99th Battalion at Camp Hale, Colorado for training on skis in the mountains. He was a rifleman and sharpshooter in the 99th's Company A and received a Bronze Star as well as other recognitions for his valiant service during the 99th's action in Europe.

In the story included below, Petterson recounts a harrowing scene in France as the 99th fights with the Nazis in foxholes. While he doesn't share the name of the specific battle, his account matches the hectic and confused scene that many in the 99th experienced at the battle of Würselen—the scene of an Allied pincer move to close off the Nazis at Aachen, Germany and the vigorous attempts by the Nazis to keep from being encircled.

In the time that the 99th Battalion spent in Norway at the end of the war, Petterson was able to reconnect with his fiancée, Astrid, and in June 1945, during an eight-day leave, they were married. He and his wife lived in the United States after the war before returning to Norway in the 1950s.

Petterson was the last member of the 99th living in Norway and was often recognized for his and the 99th's role in the war. He participated in a re-creation of the Victory Parade in Oslo and ceremonial visits to other key sites in 2010—65 years after the original. Through these events, Petterson met with Norwegian royalty and was received at the highest levels. He passed away in 2018 at the age of 101.

No-Man's-Land

It was "one crazy military order," you know! Completely without any sense. However, it is war, and in a war, you obey orders, period. Up to a point at least.

99th veteran John Petterson receives a plaque from Hedda Bergo, a young member of the Norwegian 99th reenactment group, at the 4th of July celebration hosted at the Western Emigration Museum at Sletta, Norway in 2014. FRONT: Vidar Arnesen, John Pettersen, Hedda Bergo, and Olaf Eidevik. BACK: John Strømseng, Ove Bergo, and Frank Nordstrøm. (Courtesy of the 99th Educational Foundation)

I didn't know where we were, but it was somewhere on the border between France and Germany. Only the officers knew where we were. That's how it was in the Army. The year was 1944—it's war. Part of the 99th Battalion was positioned close to some empty houses. The enemy, the Germans, were nearby. Aware of this fact the soldiers were hiding down in their "foxholes" waiting for the daylight, the battles, the shooting. It had been like this since the landing at Normandy.

As soldiers we were used to obey[ing] orders, to carry out dangerous missions, orders we accepted without protest. That night my company was ordered to leave our foxholes, moved down from our position on the heights, and out on an open plain. In fact, we got this order to move out onto no-man's-land and dig ourselves new foxholes. Behind us was the rest of our battalion, and in front of us probably the Germans. For some unknown reason we were positioned on the open plain waiting for the daylight. Waiting for the Germans to start shooting at us. Were we a target to provoke the enemy to give away their whereabouts?

The company established new positions in the shelter of darkness. Not a whisper between the soldiers. Later some were trying to sleep, but most of them were fighting with their feelings, because I think most of us felt uneasy in this position.

At dawn, the Germans started shooting with all their tanks and weapons, point-blank into our foxholes. I did not hear any order about retreat. Anyway, we jumped out of our foxholes and ran for our lives. Bewildered, we ran away. Everyone had to save his own life. In spite of all the military rules, all the training on retreating in an orderly manner, we just fled. The Germans directed the firing in front of us, and I shouted that we should not run into their firing. The company was split, but many of us managed, somehow, to get back to our former positions. Captain Svarstad was missing—so was half of the company.

The company had been through an extremely dangerous situation, and we were now without a dynamic leader as well. This fact resulted in [us just diving] into our old foxholes and [we] tried to get some sleep, but the craziness was to continue.

Here I let war be war, and I fell asleep until suddenly I awoke with a start—possibly because of a shell explosion nearby, which [today I believe I know] what happened. "It was night again," and bewildered I realized that I was all alone. The other foxholes were empty. Shocked, I let my thoughts fly. Did all the others run away? Are the Germans nearby? I dared not stay in my foxhole. After walking around for a while, I heard voices. I hardly dared to breathe. I didn't know whether it was friend or enemy, so I advanced carefully close to the voices. Luckily, [I got close] enough [to know] it was my own friends [from] Company A. They were just a group of soldiers standing there—something they shouldn't do. I had no proper answer as to what happened and the reason they had left their foxholes.

At this very moment I was fed up. I had enough of war, shooting, Germans, and missing command lines. Together with a colleague, we marched to one of the empty houses. In full battle uniform we walked into the house, which was empty, and we invaded the bedroom upstairs. There with the rifle [under my] armpit, we occupied the "double marriage" bed. That was the best sleeping night I got during the whole war.

Under the evaluation afterwards, this incident, where my company was ordered out into "No-Man's-Land," was never discussed. In fact, it was not even mentioned. Not so strange. It was indeed "one crazy military order."

CHAPTER TWENTY-FOUR

Robert G. Turner

*Lieutenant Colonel Robert Turner was brought in to lead the 99th Infantry Battalion
(Separate) on June 16, 1943. Until that point, Harold D. Hansen had been leading
the 99th as a major who had recently been promoted from captain. Turner joined the
99th at Camp Hale, Colorado and led the group for over a year through the time in
England and to continental Europe.*

*Turner was injured at the battle in Elbeuf in August 1944. After Turner's injury,
Harold D. Hansen was placed back into the leadership role that he had prior to
Turner's tenure. Hansen had been the original leader of the 99th, having joined as a
captain and promoted to major. Upon Hansen's return to leadership, he was promoted
to lieutenant colonel.*

*As a senior officer, Turner's letter provides a view into the perspectives of a key battle
from a leader's point of view. It was written to Yngvar Stensby in response to a question
that Yngvar had asked at a 99th reunion that they had attended together.*

*Turner was a respected leader and his letter makes it clear the value that he placed
on the heroic efforts of the members of the 99th.*

Elbeuf

January 15, 1986

Dear Yngvar:

Thanks for your most interesting letter of Jan. 10. I want to congratulate you
on being selected to the Historical Committee of the 99th. You have always
shown keen interest in the subjects. Your literary ability should help you on
such a project.

And again, I want to particularly congratulate you on the beautiful poem you
wrote called "Legacy," for the 40th Reunion, and for the men of the 99th who

lost their lives in action. I have been sent the laminated picture of the 99th Battalion Monument[1] displaying your tribute to those men, which, of course, I shall treasure.

As for the question of whose sector we were in at Elbeuf, on the evening of August 24, Col. Sidney R. Hinds, commander of the 41st Armored Infantry, my immediate commander, gave me orders that the 99th Bn would attack Elbeuf the following day. He felt that it was an appropriate assignment for our battalion since it was its first combat assignment; and that resistance that could be encountered in Elbeuf would be somewhat disorganized. He said that Canadian Army troops would be attacking on our left; and that

Lt. Col. Robert G. Turner took command of the battalion from Major Hansen on June 6, 1943, at Camp Hale. He led the battalion until he was wounded at Elbeuf, France, on August 26, 1944, in the unit's first battle. Hansen resumed command and led the 99th until it was deactivated in November 1945. Here Turner is seen serving on the General Staff of General Eisenhower's U.S. Army Command in Europe after his recovery, at the end of the war. (Courtesy of the 99th Educational Foundation)

we might come into contact with them. (Such contact was not reported to me, and I do not believe we had any contact with Canadians <u>during</u> our attack.)

I would say that certainly the boundary between the Canadian Army and our First Army was changed while we were in Elbeuf. As you know, during the rapid movement of American and Allied troops toward the Seine, there was little need for precise boundaries, even though perhaps at very high headquarters, the boundaries would be neatly drawn up on the map.

As for armored support, we had a tank destroyer company attached to us from the time we jumped off; but that couldn't follow us into Elbeuf; because the bridge over the railroad cut was blocked; and the railroad cut, itself, had such steep sides that armored vehicles could not cross.

To go back to the start of the attack, I will describe to you my recollections and fleeting impressions, even though my recollections may be contrary to the facts.

As I remember, I assigned A and B Cos. to the attack echelon, A Co. on the right, B Co. on the left, and C Co. in reserve, each with appropriate sections of Co. D. Since it was our first combat action, I wished to accompany the attack echelon; so,

---

[1] This is likely in reference to the monument at Malmedy, Belgium for the 99th's successful efforts to defend the city during the Battle of the Bulge.

I directed Major Hansen to take charge of the headquarters and to advance in the second echelon.

The attack echelon came under no artillery fire until we were within the town of Elbeuf; however, I learned that the second echelon did come under artillery fire. When the attack echelon reached the town of Elbeuf, the part that I was with dropped down the steep bank of the railroad cut, and came to the railroad station where a deputation of Free French and a collection of French civilians wanted to congratulate us, even breaking out bottles of wine. Fortunately, I don't think any of our men were tempted, and brushed by the French, moving into the city. Little resistance was encountered at first; but fire increased in severity as we approached the main highway, which ran transversally through the town. Some artillery fire was falling in the area where I was; but most of it exploded harmlessly on the tops of buildings.

I recalled as I moved toward the main road, I saw rifle fire coming from a building across the highway, diagonally to my left. Just then, a jeep from headquarters rolled up with machine gun mounted; so I directed them to silence the rifle fire. The jeep drove forward—then suddenly came under intense machine-gun fire, wounding one man in the leg. The jeep backed up rapidly, I jumped on and hitch-hiked for about a block.

Later I moved forward on a street going diagonally to my right where I observed a German tank. The tank swung its turret to sweep the street with machine-gun fire, so I jumped back inside a doorway. Just after the tanks swept the street with machine-gun fire, I looked out just in time to see an explosive hit the tank turret. I thought it was mortar fire; but I realized later it was a bazooka. Two Germans immediately emerged from the turret. I'm sure they didn't get very far.

At another point, I came to the town cathedral where I encountered several men of the 99th. They said they couldn't get into the cathedral and asked me if they should break the door down. I looked at these massive studded doors and told them I didn't see any point in breaking down the doors. Later I lived to regret my decision; because it was from the belltower of the cathedral that a German observer brought down artillery on our command post the next day. During the 25th reunion, I talked with at least one of the men with whom I was talking at the cathedral. Later on the 26th, our men illuminated the observer, I was told.

At the same time I was watching the German tank on the main highway, Major Hansen ran up to me carrying an M1 rifle. He informed me that he had set up the command post in a schoolhouse. Then said he would like to go forward to see what was going on. Moving through the buildings in front of us he went forward. About 20 minutes later, he returned to tell me he had joined in the firefight facing the main highway. When that skirmish was over, he returned.

When I returned to the command post, I found the commander of the tank destroyers waiting for me. He reported that his tank destroyers had finally cleared enough wreckage from the bridge so that his vehicles could get through; and that his tank destroyers were now deployed in the town.

I heard at this time, that the driver of my jeep, Francis Kampstad, reached the bridge over the railroad cut; and finding it blocked with wrecked vehicles, proceeded to winch the wrecked vehicles out of the way, although the bridge was then under heavy shellfire. I never verified that story; but did send a letter to Col. Hansen from the hospital in England. I felt that if the story was true, that Kampstad should have received recognition for his actions. I heard nothing further; perhaps Col. Hansen did not receive my letter.

As dusk was approaching on the 25th [of August], I received orders from division headquarters to continue the attack on the Seine River. I felt that the battalion was too disorganized to continue the attack then; and I feared disastrous results if we ended up attacking in the dark. So, I got the orders changed to resume the attack the following morning.

When the battalion attacked the following morning, they reached the river, quickly bringing in a considerable number of prisoners.

As I awaited news of the morning attack at the CP, I was sitting against a folding table, looking toward some 40 or 50 prisoners huddled in the corner of the schoolyard. I saw a flash of light as a shell struck a tree limb near the prisoners. In my experience, I thought the shell was a dud, instead of a "ranging round."[2] A few moments later a shell struck near the front door with devastating effect, killing several, and wounding several men. Lt. Allen Lindholm and I were among those wounded. Allen Lindholm died in the hospital. Somehow, I survived. George Hunsby accurately described the situation at the hospital in the booklet he wrote in 1973, entitled, "Reflections."[3]

With reference to the difficulties encountered in getting armored support into Elbeuf, I presume there were other means of access than the bridge over the railroad cut; some of these routes were probably located elsewhere along our front. Several French Resistance fighters started in the attack with me for the purpose of providing me with that type of information; but they all vanished somewhere as we moved forward.

Again, I want to emphasize that what I say is based upon recollections of more than 40 years ago; and may well fail to fit the facts in every case.

Perhaps this letter will be of some help to you; but in any case, I wish you the best of luck in developing historical facts about the 99th Infantry Battalion.

Sincerely,
R. G. "Bob" Turner

---

[2] An artillery shell used to estimate where the following shots should fall.

[3] Hunsby's writing is included in this book in a separate chapter.

CHAPTER TWENTY-FIVE

H. Anderson, Roland Asleson, Harold K. Hanson, Ray Helle, Morton Tuftedal and Owen Voxland

A group of six members of the 99th Infantry Battalion (Separate) combined to write a narrative of the activities of the battalion in Malmedy as part of the Battle of the Bulge. Each of these members is well known due to their involvement in the 99th's association and the efforts to tell the story. In fact, this group comprised the 99th Battalion's historian committee.

Roland Asleson received the Bronze Star and the Combat Infantry Badge for his service in action. Roland was born in 1917 in Ulen, Minnesota where he grew up and went to high school. After the war, Roland worked for the post office for 25 years before retiring in 1977. He died in 2003 at the age of 85.

Harold K. Hanson was a long-term leader of the 99th's association. He had a long history of supporting the efforts to capture, share, and engage with the 99th community. His writings are included elsewhere in this book and his legacy lives on.

Ray Helle was a lieutenant with A and B Companies of the 99th Infantry Battalion (Separate) and played pivotal roles throughout the 99th's campaigns, including a commanding role during the action in Malmedy as part of the Battle of the Bulge. Helle started the 99th Battalion's newsletter and organized it until his health started failing in 1999. In addition to the newsletter, Helle would create illustrations for the 99th's reunions. Helle was born in May 1917 in Brooklyn, New York to Norwegian immigrant parents. He died in September 1999 and is buried at Bay Pines, Florida.

Morton Tuftedal was a significant contributor to the historical archives of the 99th Battalion as well. He created a detailed set of six photo albums of the 99th based on his photography during World War II and, later in life, donated many artifacts that are now housed at the 99th's exhibit at the Vesterheim Museum in Decorah, Iowa. After the war, he served for 40 years as an auxiliary police officer, rangemaster and firearms instructor. Morton was born in Norway in 1923 and died in 2010 at the age of 86. He received a Purple Heart for injuries sustained on September 20, 1944 and remained with the 99th through to the end of the war.

Morten A. Tuftedal noted that members of Company A bivouacked the tank unit when Allied fuel supplies slowed down the advance in Belgium. He recorded the event in his scrapbook. Here his comrades are "Pilow, Odd Stark, Harold Viken, Sverre O. Satre, Magnus Odegard, Red Nelsen, E. Woodstad, and Magnus Hansen," as they perched on a light tank. The 99th had trained with tanks in Normandy and had been attached to the 2nd Armored Division since August 1944. (Courtesy of the 99th Educational Foundation)

Owen Voxland was with the 99th Battalion from Camp Hale through the end of the war and received the Combat Infantry Badge in 1944. He was born in Kenyon, Minnesota in 1919 and passed away in 1999 at the age of 79. His daughter, Jane Voxland, has been active in sharing the story of the 99th Infantry Battalion including presentations to community groups.

There are a number of H. Andersons in the 99th Battalion, so the specific individual connected to this writing is unknown. As with the others, their contributions to the 99th are appreciated.

Battle of the Bulge

Our battalion was organized by presidential proclamation signed by President Franklin D. Roosevelt in April 1942. A "confidential" authorization from Headquarters—Army Ground Forces was issued by Lt. General McNair to the Commanding General—Second Army on July 10, 1942. "Personnel must be Norwegian nationals (aliens or aliens with first papers) or United States citizen of

Norwegian extraction who can read and speak Norwegian." Authorized strength was 931 enlisted men and 70 officers.

When the "Battle of the Bulge" started the 99th Battalion was spread out from Tilff, Belgium in the north to 3 miles NW of Bastogne. Our mission was to patrol the area looking for enemy paratroopers who may jump behind our lines.

Our first indication of enemy infiltration was the night of December 16 when the third squad, 2nd Platoon of A Co. captured two paratroopers as they landed NW of Bastogne in American uniforms with American equipment and weapons. We turned them over to the MPs who stated they would be processed as spies.

On December 17 the 99th was ordered to Malmedy to assist about 80 men of the 291st Engineers who elected to hold the town. They had mined the bridges, [railroad] trestles, and trees alongside the road leading out of town. They would blow the trees over the road if the Germans tried to go through Malmedy. The only 99th unit not on patrol was one platoon of B Co. Our colonel's orders were, "Pack light, don't even bring a razor. We are leaving right now." Which we did. The chateau that housed B Co. was flattened by a "buzz bomb" as they left the area.

The convoy to Malmedy consisted of BN, HQ, B Co. HQ, and Lt. Trosvig's platoon. MPs led the way with their lights flashing trying to clear the road of the hundreds of trucks trying to make their way to the rear. The men on those trucks had been outnumbered by seasoned troops and had taken a terrific beating. They all had the same expression—dazed, bewildered, and exhausted.

How the rest of the Bn. made it to Malmedy is a mystery to me. They had to find their own way with Germans all over the place. Co. A had to race to get around in front of a German column which was driving between them and Malmedy. The rest of the battalion made their way, one way or the other. Co. B moved right into position as they arrived in Malmedy since Col. Hansen knew exactly where he wanted them. They were at the end of a road leading out of town not far from the spot where the Germans massacred 80-plus prisoners. They dug in and set up their roadblock. We could hear German armor all night and they seemed to be circling our roadblock and certainly had our attention all night.

The next morning [Dec. 18, 1944] two Germans on a motorcycle with a sidecar stopped to talk to a woman right in front of the spot where the platoon was dug in. The woman pointed to our position and everyone opened up, killing all three instantly.

The next day [Dec. 19, 1944] three Germans in a captured jeep, with two American prisoners sitting on the hood, attempted to drive through our roadblock. The Germans on the hood spotted the men dug in alongside the road, [and jumped off the hood and began] shouting, "shoot them, they're Krauts." We opened fire, killing one and wounding two. They were identified as members of the 1st SS Division.

At this point I had no idea where the rest of B Co. or the battalion was located. We could only sit tight and listen to the constant drone of German armor moving somewhere in front of us. I managed to find a regimental HQ in town where I could go in and check the situation map. It puzzles me how I could walk in and out without being challenged. I was able to keep track of what the Germans were doing and see if they were headed in our direction.

The next day [Dec. 20, 1944] six men from the 3rd Squad, 2nd Platoon of A Co. went on patrol to locate enemy positions. We ambushed three Germans and after a close-quarter fight killed one and took two prisoners. One 99er was wounded by a knife cut in the hand. One of the prisoners was an officer from the 1st SS Division. We had trouble getting back through our lines since the 291st Engineers were not told about our patrol. After being questioned by an officer from the 291st and alerting him to a larger number of tanks and other vehicles moving toward the [railroad] embankment he had one of his men take us to the CP.

During the same period of time Lt. Trosvig's platoon from B Co. changed places with a company from the 120th Regiment and their new location turned out to be the remaining portion of B Co. that had previously separated from them. They were dug in on a [railroad] trestle which made an excellent defensive position. The front line was well armed with .30- and .50-caliber machine guns and mortars.

1st Lt. Helle, ex. officer, Co. B found a room with a window on the second floor of the CP and moved up there since he was assured it had a good view of the whole defensive line. He had a look at the situation map before changing places and knew a German column was headed for the underpass of the railroad trestle, so they waited.

In the meantime, a classic textbook battle was looming. The Germans, led by Col. Skorzeny, were seasoned handpicked veterans of the 1st SS Division. He went into the Bulge with 4,000 men. How many he had left at this time I do not know but I am sure he outnumbered B Co. They went into battle with the advantage of knowing where and when the main strike would be. On the American side was a reinforced company of the 99th Bn. They also were seasoned troops with an advantage of a good defensive position. Who would win? Only time would tell, and it became a waiting game.

Then it happened. Sgt. W. Smith, B Co., who was on our outpost, called in stating an American Lt., in a jeep, followed by an M4 tank was coasting down the hill and they were about to hit a mine. Before he got an answer, the jeep hit the mine. Sgt. Smith called again stating the Lt. was calling for a medic in German and that he was returning to our lines.

The moment the jeep hit the mine our mortar platoon filled the air with flares. Looking out the CP window I could see a large number of Germans headed for the overpass. They were running toward the [railroad] embankment screaming, "surrender or die." The 99th opened fire with all available weapons and with deadly accuracy, halting the German surge just short of the [railroad] trestle/embankment. The Germans kept trying with help from a tank who sprayed machine-gun fire all along the [railroad] trestle/embankment, plus trying to set up machine guns at the base of the [railroad] embankment. The stubborn defense bought enough time to enable the artillery to get into action.

The artillery required map coordinates of the area to be hit. This was new to Lt. Helle and Trosvig and required time to figure out what was going on. With the required information plus just finding out that the 99th was taking part in another first, the information was given to the artillery unit. The new information was that [there was] a new type of shell being used for the first time. It was called "Pozit" and used a proximity fuse. The new shells explode before [they] hit the ground, spraying everything below with shrapnel. This destroyed the Germans' capability to finish the assault and they withdrew, leaving many dead and casualties behind.

What decided the outcome of this battle? We have to say it was time. About 30 or 40 seconds' worth, plus the "Pozit" shell. The prompt and efficient way the defense sprung into action made the difference, also the fact that the 99th had no intentions of letting the Germans push them out of their foxholes; even though earlier German intelligence reported them as "old men," not an inch was lost. Though Skorzeny and Peiper had more men and equipment they were not good enough.

At dawn the next morning the 3rd Squad, 2nd Platoon of A Co. was sent out on patrol, out past the paper mill and over to the hills on the left since movement was spotted in both areas. Except for several children who pointed to some houses nearby, everything appeared in order until we saw some bodies lying in front of one of the houses. There were nine American medics with their hands tied behind their backs with wire. Several were shot through the forehead with additional rounds in the belly. Due to possible booby traps we did not move anything except to record their names, etc., and turn this information in for Graves Registration with a sketch of the area. We would hear vehicles moving in the distance but could not see anything because of the terrain, trees, unlevel ground, etc.

During this period of time Malmedy was bombed three different days by American bombers, destroying the city and inflicting many casualties. More snow was falling and it got even colder, making life more uncomfortable for the men who had been living in foxholes for more than two weeks.

The next several days were spent on patrols and upgrading various sections of our line of defense. Many wounded Germans came into our lines to surrender since they needed treatment and/or could no longer tolerate the cold.

Christmas was just another day and no sign of being relieved anytime soon. We would get our Christmas dinner later. Many patrols were out to be sure a counterattack was not being organized.

On December 27 at 1600 hours C Co. sent a commando raid to the town of Hedamont. American artillery concentrated their fire on the town prior to the surprise attack. Opposing units and their positions were identified. One prisoner taken and some 30 Germans killed without one injury in C Co.

On December 29 B Co. raided the town of Otaimont with fixed bayonets, but the enemy was no longer there, but close enough to lay down a heavy concentration of machine-gun and artillery fire to harass the raiders. B Co. was fortunate to come out with extremely light casualties even though their escape routes were zeroed in.

During the period of January 1 through 6, while still on the front line of defense on the outskirts of Malmedy, the battalion was doing extensive patrolling. Enemy artillery and rocket fire was fairly heavy but there were few injuries. During the night the enemy dressed in white camouflage suits and raided forward positions but without success even though they had skis. Our winter equipment did not follow us. However, many of our men were able to acquire white material for makeshift camouflage.

On the evening of January 6 the battalion moved to the vicinity of Stavelot after our positions around Malmedy were taken over by the 30th Division. Our new position was in a pine wooded area and our thin line was in shouting distance of the German defenses. Our patrols were out all the time and had frequent clashes with the enemy.

The snow was deep and the nights bitter cold. Many of the enemy were well prepared with white camouflage and skis. They had direct artillery support for their positions. Our first offensive action was in an area called Chevehosse, on January 10.[1] The second platoon of A Co., with much needed reinforcement, attacked the same sector, taking many prisoners who provided valuable information. They had many outposts and were well fortified to prevent patrols from infiltrating across the bridge to Thieux. Through constant artillery and mortar fire from the fanatical Germans, we continued to advance, driving them from their foxholes with a steady firing of grenades, rifles, machine guns, and mortars to be killed or taken prisoners and finally knocked out their command post.

Later that day the 119th Infantry Regiment of the 30th Division attacked from the vicinity of Malmedy on our left flank to help stabilize the area. Our heavy weapons company, D Co., helped their advance by firing .50-caliber machine guns and 81mm mortars at the enemy. The Germans knew the terrain we were in and shelled our positions with great accuracy, and because the area was so heavily wooded the tree burst from mortar and artillery fire was very devastating, causing many casualties.

On January 15 the 517th Parachute Regiment attacked up along our right flank. Therefore, with the 517th on our right flank and the 119th on our left flank they

---

[1] It is unclear what location is being referenced. Chevehosse is not located on any modern maps.

took over the area that the 99th had been defending. Though we pulled back we supported the attacking units with 81mm mortars and .50-caliber machine-gun fire from our heavy weapons company, D Co. The next several days the 99th put out many patrols looking for bypassed enemy units and men missing from the 99th Battalion.

After 31 days of continuous fighting, living in snow-covered foxholes at sub-zero temperatures, and being under observation and unrelenting artillery fire from the enemy, the tired and bearded men of the 99th Infantry Battalion (Sep.) were formally relieved from their front-line positions on January 18.

Commanders, Awards and Locations

The below information is collected from George Hunsby's writings.

Commanding Personnel of the 99th

1. Morning reports of HQ 99th Inf. Bn (Sep.) redesignated HQ & HQ Co., 99th Inf. Bn 474th Inf. Regt. From August 15, 1942 thru November 2, 1945 show the following commanding officers and movement of unit as follows:

August 15–20, 1942	1st Lt. Waskelo
August 20–21, 1942	Capt. Leer or (Lear)
August 21, 1942–January 16, 1943	Capt. Hansen, Harold D. 0-23 468 (appointed major October 24, 1942)
January 16–23, 1943	Major Shirley
January 23–June 16, 1943	Major Hansen, Harold D. 0-23 468
16 June 16–August 29, 1944	Lt. Col. Turner, Robert G. 0-16 809
August 29, 1944–November 1, 1945	Major Hansen, Harold D. 0-23 468 (promoted to lieutenant colonel November 12, 1944)

The Awards Won by the 99th Battalion (Sep.)

The 99th Inf. Bn (Sep.) was awarded battle participation in the following campaigns during the dates shown. These campaigns have been announced in theater orders, and later confirmed in Department of the Army General Orders:

Normandy Campaign from 22 June 1944 to 24 July 1944—War Department General Orders 102/45

Northern France Campaign from 25 July 1944 to 14 September 1944—War Department General Orders 103/45

Rhineland Campaign from 15 September 1944 to 16 December 1944—War Department General Orders 118/45

Ardennes–Alsace Campaign from 17 December 1944 to 18 January 1945—Department of the Army General Orders 63/48

474th Inf. Regt. (Parent Organization):

Central Europe Campaign from 4 April 1945 to 11 May 1945—War Department General Orders 116/45

The 99th United States Infantry Battalion was cited twice in the Daily Orders of the Belgian Army and granted the Fourragère in 1940.

Royal Decree Nr. 1904, dated August 31, 2017

The 30th United States Infantry Division and its attached units were transferred from the Vth Corps to the XIXth Corps for the period from January 17 to 21, 1945 and then to the XVIII Airborne Corps from January 22 to 25, 1945. During the period while operating with these corps, they successfully defended the Northern shoulder of the German penetration in the Ardennes in the vicinity of MALMÉDY, STAVELOT, LA GLEISE, STOUMONT, TROIS PONTS, Belgium. The division and its attached units repelled repeated heavy enemy attacks and prevented continuation of the breakthrough in the direction of SPA and LIÈGE, the capture of which would have meant the loss of vital supply installations. During the latter part of this period, the division and its attached units attacked and drove the enemy from all Belgian territory within its zone.

(Decree of the Prince Regent Nr. 1393, dated November 20, 1945)

On September 2, 1944, at 09.30, reconnaissance elements of the 2nd Armored Division crossed the Belgian border near RUME. They were the first American troops to enter Belgium and marked the beginning of the deliverance of this country. The division fought violently and turned the enemy at the ALBERT canal, liberating the towns of TOURNAI, WAVRE, TIRLEMONT, SAINT-TROND and HASSELT.

(Decree of the Prince Regent Nr 3864, dated 28 April 1947)

Brussels, 26 September 2017.
The 2nd Armored Division, XIX Corps with attached units was awarded the Belgian Croix de Guerre. The 99th Inf. Bn (Sep.) is listed in the Department of the Army General Orders as an attached unit.

BELGIAN CROIX DE GUERRE, is awarded under Decree No. 514, 22 May 1945, as amended by Decree No. 3864 28 April 1947, by Charles, Prince of Belgium, Regent of the Kingdom, with the following citation:

> On 2 September 1944, at 0930, its reconnaissance elements crossed the Belgian border near Rume. These were the first American troops to enter Belgium and this marked the beginning of the liberation of the country. The Division fought violently and threw back the enemy on the Albert Canal. This Division liberated the towns of Tournai, Wavre, Tirlemount and Hasselt.

The 30th Infantry Division (XIX Corps) with attached units was awarded the Belgian Croix de Guerre. The 99th Inf. Bn (Sep.) is listed in the Department of the Army General Orders as an attached unit.

BELGIAN CROIX DE GUERRE, awarded under Decree No. 1393, 20 November 1945, by Charles, Prince of Belgium, Regent of the Kingdom, with the following citation:

> The 30th Infantry Division of the United States and its attached units were transferred from V to XIX Corps during the period from 17 to 21 Dec. 1944, and then to the XVIII Airborne Corps from 22 to 25 January 1945. During the period in which they operated in these corps, they defended successfully the north flank of the German penetration into the Ardennes, in the surroundings of Malmedy, Stavelot, LaCleize, Stoumont, and Trois-Ponts in Belgium. The division and its attached units pushed back the violent and repeated attacks of the enemy and prevented the continuation of the breakthrough in the direction of Spa and Liège, the conquering of which would have meant the loss of important supply installations. During the last part of this period, the division and its attached units attacked and chased the enemy from the whole Belgian territory in its zone.

Casualties Suffered by the 99th

Total time in combat: 101 days.
Killed by enemy action: 52 men.

Wounded by enemy action: 207 men.

Missing in action: six men reported, all later accounted for.

Individual Medals Won by Men of 99th

Silver Stars: 15

Bronze Stars: 20

Purple Hearts: 305

Good Conducts: 763

Combat Infantry Badges: 814

Bibliography

Andersen, Arlow W. *The Norwegian-Americans*. United States: Twayne Publishers, 1975.

Barbier, Mary. *D-Day Deception: Operation Fortitude and the Normandy Invasion*. Stackpole Military History Series. Mechanicsburg, PA: Stackpole Books, 2009.

Baumer, Robert W. *Aachen: The U.S. Army's Battle for Charlemagne's City in World War II*. Mechanicsburg, PA: Stackpole Books, 2015.

Beito, Gretchen, and Mildred Furuseth. *Furuseth in the 99th Infantry Battalion (Sep)*. Gonvick, MN: Richards Publishing Co., Inc., 2020.

Beevor, Anthony. *Ardennes 1944: The Battle of the Bulge*. New York, NY: Penguin Books, 2005.

Bergen, Howard R. *The History of the 99th Infantry Battalion (Separate)*. Oslo: Emil Moestue, 1946.

Bergstrom, Christer. *The Ardennes, 1944–1945: Hitler's Winter Offensive*. Havertown, PA: Casemate / Vaktel Forlag, 2015.

Bradley, Omar Nelson and Herman Finkelstein Collection (Library of Congress). *A Soldier's Story*. 1st ed. New York: Holt, 1951.

Cole, Hugh Marshall. *The Ardennes: Battle of the Bulge*. United States Center of Military History, U.S. Army, 1994.

Cole, Wayne S. *Norway and the United States, 1905–1955: Two Democracies in Peace and War*. 1st ed. Ames: Iowa State University Press, 1989.

Edsel, Robert M., and Bret Witter. *The Monuments Men: Allied Heroes, Nazi Thieves, and the Greatest Treasure Hunt in History*. New York: Back Bay Books/Little, Brown and Company, 2013.

Giles, Janice Holt, and United States Army Corps of Engineers. *The Damned Engineers*. 2nd ed. Studies in Military Engineering, No. 1. Washington, D.C.: Historical Division, Office of Administrative Services, Office of the Chief of Engineers, 1985.

Heimark, Bruce H. *The OSS Norwegian Special Operations Group in World War II*. Westport, CT: Praeger, 1994.

Hesketh, Roger. *Fortitude: The D-Day Deception Campaign*. United Kingdom: Overlook Press, 2002.

Hewitt, Robert L. *Work Horse of the Western Front: The Story of the 30th Infantry Division*. United States: Lucknow Books, 2015.

Kelly, John W. *Company "D" United States Army*. Oslo: Kirstes Boktrykkeri, 1945.

Kenney, Dave. *Minnesota Goes to War: The Home Front during World War II*. St. Paul: Minnesota Historical Society Press, 2005.

Lindbæk, Lise. *Norway's New Saga of the Sea: The Story of Her Merchant Marine in World War II*. 1st ed. An Exposition-Banner Book. New York: Exposition Press, 1969.

Lovoll, Odd S. *Two Homelands: A Historian Considers His Life and Work*. St. Paul, MN: Minnesota Historical Society Press 2018.

Nyquist, Gerd. *The 99th Battalion*. First U.S. ed. Reading, PA: Aperture Press, 2014.

Pallud, Jean-Paul, and David Parker. *Ardennes 1944: Peiper & Skorzeny*. Oxford: Osprey Publishing, 2013.

Parker, Danny S. *Fatal Crossroads: The Untold Story of the Malmedy Massacre at the Battle of the Bulge.* United States: Hachette Books, 2011.

Pergrin, David. *Engineering the Victory, The Battle of the Bulge: A History.* Atglen, PA: Schiffer Military/Aviation History, 1996.

Pergrin, David E., and Eric Hammel. *First Across the Rhine: The 291st Engineer Combat Battalion in France, Belgium and Germany.* New York: Macmillan Publishing Company, 1989.

Pisani, Robert Antoni. *The Canal Drive: The 99th Infantry Battalion and the Liberation of Belgian Limburg, September 1944.* United States: Antoni Pisani Publishing, 2012.

Plank, Harold F. *Memoirs of World War II: The Story of a Tioga County Soldier.* Cincinnati, OH: Revivalist Press, 2002.

Schadewitz, Michael. *The Meuse First and then Antwerp: Some Aspects of Hitler's Offensive in the Ardennes.* Canada: J.J. Fedorowicz, 1999.

Scharf, Erich. *Remembrance of My Service in World War II.* Santa Fe, NM: E & C Book Publishers, 1999.

Skard, Sigmund. *The United States in Norwegian History.* Contributions in American Studies, no. 26. Westport, CT: Greenwood Press, 1976.

Urnes Beito, Gretchen. *Furuseth in the 99th Infantry Battalion (SEP).* N.p.: Richards Publishing Company Incorporated, 2020.

Walthall, Melvin C. *We Can't All Be Heroes: A History of the Separate Infantry Regiments in World War II.* 1st ed. Hicksville, NY: Exposition Press, 1975.

Wells, Red, and Sharon Wells Wagner. *Red Wells: An American Soldier in World War II and the 99th Infantry Battalion (Separate), the Viking Battalion: A Life Story.* Charleston, SC: BookSurge Pub., 2006.

Whiting, Charles. *Bloody Aachen.* London: Leo Cooper, 1976.

Wijers, Hans. *Battle of the Bulge, Vol. 2: Hell at Bütgenbach/Seize the Bridges.* Mechanicsburg, PA: Stackpole Books, 2010.

Witte, David R. *World War II at Camp Hale: Blazing a New Trail in the Rockies.* Charleston, SC: The History Press, 2015.

Zaloga, Steven. *Battle of the Bulge 1944 (1): St. Vith and the Northern Shoulder.* Oxford: Osprey Publishing, 2013.

Index